Parchment, Printing, and Hypermedia

NEW DIRECTIONS IN WORLD POLITICS
John Gerard Ruggie, General Editor

D0905557

Parchment, Printing, and Hypermedia

Communication in World Order Transformation

Ronald J. Deibert

COLUMBIA UNIVERSITY PRESS   NEW YORK

Columbia University Press

Publishers Since 1893

New York, Chichester, West Sussex

Copyright © 1997 Columbia University Press

Photo Credits:

Figure 3, page 172, courtesy of Aerial Images, Inc.

Figure 5, page 190, courtesy of Visual Artists and Galleries Association, Inc.

Library of Congress Cataloging-in-Publication Data

Deibert, Ronald J.

Parchment, printing, and hypermedia : communication in world order transformation

Ronald J. Deibert

p. cm — (New directions in world politics)

Includes bibliographical references and index

ISBN: 0-231-10712-9 (cl: alk. paper)

     0-231-10713-7 (pbk.)

1. Communication — Technological innovations — History.

2. Civilization — History.

3. Communication and culture — History.

P96.T42 D45   1998 302.2 — 21 97-015336

∞   CIP

Casebound editions of Columbia University Press books are printed on permanent and durable acid-free paper.

Printed in the United States of America

c 10 9 8 7 6 5 4 3 2 1

p 10 9 8 7 6 5 4 3 2 1

NEW DIRECTIONS IN WORLD POLITICS

John Gerard Ruggie, General Editor

John Gerard Ruggie, editor, *Multilateralism Matters: The Theory and Praxis of an Institutional Form* 1993

Barry Buzan, Charles Jones, and Richard Little, *The Logic of Anarchy: Neorealism to Structural Realism* 1993

Ronnie D. Lipschutz and Ken Conca, editors, *The State and Social Power in Global Environmental Politics* 1993

David A. Baldwin, editor, *Neorealism and Neoliberalism: The Contemporary Debate* 1993

Karen Litfin, *Ozone Discourses: Science and Politics in Global Environmental Co-operation* 1994

Ronnie D. Lipschutz, editor, *On Security* 1995

Peter J. Katzenstein, editor, *The Culture of National Security: Norms and Identity in World Politics* 1966

Edward D. Mansfield and Helen V. Milner, editors, *The Political Economy of Regionalism* 1997

Robert Latham, *Modernity, Security, and the Making of Postwar International Order* 1997

Contents

Preface

The main contention of this book is that the landscape of world politics is undergoing rapid and fundamental transformations related to the advent of digital-electronic telecommunications — what I call the hypermedia environment — and that the most useful way to fathom these transformations is through the lens of "medium theory." Admittedly, the picture that emerges through this lens will be discomforting to many: postmodern world order is a place inhabited by de-territorialized communities, fragmented identities, transnational corporations, and cyberspatial flows of finance. It is a world in which brokers, cultists, and khalifs are as much in prominent relief as Canadians, Poles, and Kuwaitis. It is, paradoxically, a world made up of plural worlds, multiple realities and irrealities — digital artifacts stitched together in a web of spectacles, cineplexes, and Segas. Not a single "global village," and even less a system of territorially-distinct nation-states, postmodern world order is, rather, a pastiche of multiple and overlapping authorities — a quasi-feudal, "multicentric" system.

"Medium theory" was first articulated by Harold Innis and then brought to a much wider audience by Marshall McLuhan, both of whom were Canadian scholars who taught at the University of Toronto, where I now have the good fortune to teach. The central proposition of medium theory is that changing modes of communication have effects on the trajectory of social evolution and the values and beliefs of societies. Medium theory traces these effects to the unique properties of different modes of communication — to the way information is stored, transmitted, and distributed through different media at different times in history. It focuses on the material properties of communications environments rather than on the content of the message being conveyed, hence McLuhan's well-worn quip: "the medium is the message."

In the pages that follow, I reformulate medium theory, embedding it in what I call an "ecological holist" framework designed to "get back to the roots" of this approach. At the heart of these modifications are the drawing out of the "media as environments" metaphor alluded to above, and the use of an evolutionary analogy to describe the processes by which social forces and ideas at the margins of society are brought into the center by the unintended consequences of technological change. Contingency figures prominently in my analysis, with the central mechanism of change being a kind of chance "fitness" between social forces and ideas on the one hand, and communications environment on the other. With this revised medium theory as my analytical lens, I retrace previous changes in modes of communication for their effects on world order transformation: the parchment codex and the rise of the Roman Catholic Church in the Middle Ages; the development of the printing press and the medieval-to-modern transformation of political authority; and the emergence of the hypermedia environment and contemporary changes of world order. Hence, while I do believe that we are living in "postmodern" times, not least of which because I believe "postmodernism" as a *mentalité* will flourish and thrive in the hypermedia environment, the theoretical tools that inform my book are anchored in a historical-materialist perspective. Mumford, Innis, and Braudel, as opposed to Derrida, Foucault, or Lyotard, form the main inspirational backdrop for the analysis that follows.

There were many people who contributed in one way or another to the construction of this study. First, I owe an enormous debt of gratitude to my friend and personal advisor, Mark Zacher. Mark has helped me along every step of this study. It was Mark who first suggested that I look into doing research in an area that I enjoy as a hobby. After concluding that there were no subfields related to eating pizza, Mark said that I should exploit my penchant for watching TV by researching communications. Since then, Mark has been an unwavering supporter and a diligent critic. His integrity and enthusiasm for the discipline are a constant source of inspiration.

I would also like to thank the many people who have read various versions and pieces of the text through its many different lives, including Darcy

Cutler, James Der Derian, Dan Deudney, David Elkins, Paul Heyer, Rod Hall, Kal Holsti, Robert Jackson, Tsuyoshi Kawasaki, Paul Marantz, Richard Matthew, Richard Price, James Rosenau, Hendrick Spruyt, William Stanbury, and Steve Weber. I am very grateful to the Institute of International Relations at the University of British Columbia, and especially its Director, Brian Job, for help in numerous ways. My colleagues at the University of Toronto, particularly Thomas Homer-Dixon, Franklyn Griffiths, Bob Matthews, Lou Pauly, Janice Stein, and David Welch, have made for a very dynamic IR environment — I look forward to many years of continued exchanges with them. Kate Wittenberg, Leslie Bialler, and the rest of the staff at Columbia University Press were very helpful, patient, and humorous — I enjoyed working with them enormously. I would like to thank and acknowledge the financial support for this project provided by the Social Sciences and Humanities Research Council of Canada and the Canadian Department of National Defence/Military and Strategic Studies Program. Special thanks are reserved for my very good friend and colleague Neal Roese, who has read the entire manuscript and provided valuable doses of critical skepticism at crucial junctures. Finally, and most important, I would like to thank my wife and best friend Anna. It is to her, and to my children Emily, Rosalind, and Ethan, that I dedicate this book.

Ronald J. Deibert
May 1997

Parchment, Printing, and Hypermedia

Introduction

There is a sense among a growing number of observers of the world today that the present era is one in which fundamental transformation is occurring. Among International Relations theorists,[1] for example, John Ruggie has argued that we are witnessing "a shift not in the play of power politics but of the stage on which that play is performed."[2] Similarly, James Rosenau contends that the present era constitutes a historical breakpoint leading to a "postinternational politics"[3] while Mark Zacher has traced the "decaying pillars of the Westphalian temple."[4] This belief in epochal change is mirrored outside of the mainstream of International Relations theory in, for example, pronouncements of a coming "information age,"[5] "postindustrialism,"[6] "postfordism,"[7] or, more generally, "postmodernism."[8] While these analyses differ widely in terms of their respective foci and theoretical concerns, there is at least one common thread running through each of them: the recognition that current transformations are deeply intertwined with developments in communication technologies—popularly known as the "information revolution."

Communication is vital to social cohesion. The ability to communicate complex symbols and ideas is generally considered to be one of the distinguishing characteristics of the human species. Yet in the International Relations field little or no attention has been given to the wider implications of large-scale shifts in the means through which humans communicate. In part, this can be attributed to the discipline's conservative tendencies; as

Ruggie points out, International Relations theorists are not "very good . . . at studying the possibility of fundamental discontinuity in the international system."[9] With studies of transformation in general being rare, it should come as no surprise that few focus on the implications of changing communication technologies. Those that do attempt to account for change in the international system typically focus on modes of either production or destruction as the most important variables.[10] When considered at all, communication technologies are typically viewed through the prism of, or are reduced to, these other factors. Even in analyses that point to the independent role of "ideas" or "knowledge" in shaping various aspects of world politics, little corresponding attention is given to the specific form in which ideas and knowledge are stored, transmitted, and distributed.[11] For a discipline concerned arguably more so than others with the "Big Picture," this silence is remarkable and contrasts sharply with what is found outside of the International Relations field, where popular accounts and speculations proliferate. It is also remarkable when we look to the past, where even a quick glance suggests that important historical junctures coincide with major changes in communication technologies. To take just a few examples:

- the so-called "Great Leap Forward" some 35,000 years ago—the evolutionary juncture at which modern peoples displaced Neanderthals—coincides with physiological changes in the vocal tract that permitted the spoken word;
- the invention of writing coincides with the development of the first civilization in the form of the city-states of ancient Sumeria;
- the development of the alphabet and the spread of literacy *ca* 700 B.C. in ancient Greece coincides with the onset of the Greek enlightenment;
- the development of movable type and the spread of printing in western Europe coincides with the Renaissance and early Modernity.

My main argument here is that these coincidences are no coincidences at all; that changes in modes of communication—the various media by which information is stored and exchanged—have significant implications for the evolution and character of society and politics at a world level. In making this argument, I will be retrieving a theoretical position that, while largely absent from International Relations literature, nevertheless has a long intellectual lineage—this is "the history of communications as an aspect of the general history of civilizations."[12] While its major proponents are associated with twentieth-century scholarship, the themes that are raised can be traced as far back as Rousseau, Locke, and even Plato. Its nuances and metatheoretical orientation harken back to a late nineteenth-early twentieth century tradition of scholarship grounded in cultural materialist thinking, associated with thinkers such as Gordon Childe, Lewis Mumford, and Edward Tylor. However, it is the Canadian economic historian Harold Adam Innis who is generally recognized as the first to have articulated and applied the theory. The core of this "medium theory" approach is aptly summarized by Paul Heyer:

> Loosely stated it refers to the belief that the transformation of basic information into knowledge is not a disembodied process. It is powerfully influenced by the manner of its material expression. In other words, the medium is never neutral. How we organize and transmit our perceptions and knowledge about the world strongly affects the nature of those perceptions and the way we come to know the world.[13]

My objective is to develop a theoretical and analytical framework, derived and modified from the tradition of scholarship alluded to above, and apply it to the question of world order transformation. As will be made clear throughout this study, my purpose in doing so is not to assert that communication technologies offer a "master key" to the unlocking of human history, nor is it even to argue for the priority of the mode of communication over other forces of change. Rather, it is to construct a *lens* through which we can interpret the relationship between large-scale changes in modes of communication and world order transformation—a *problematique* that should be of central importance to International Relations theorists today, yet is not. Doing so, I believe, can then provide some insights into the character of an emerging *postmodern* world order as well.

In the remainder of this chapter I will provide a general introduction to the theoretical backdrop and central focus of the study: the role of communication technologies in world order transformation. Because this level of analysis is unusual in comparison to the majority of International Relations theorizing, a significant portion of the introduction will be spent situating this study as a contribution to what Charles Tilly refers to as "world-orical" research.[14] As will be shown below, this study "problematizes" the taken-for-granted foundations and structures that are typically "assumed away" by most theorists. It requires, then, a "desensitization" exercise, one that strips away those presuppositions to provide an orientation for the analysis to follow. Chapter 1 will then provide a more detailed overview of the theoretical perspective that informs this study.

Theorizing the Communications Revolution

That we are currently living through a revolutionary change in technologies of communication is beyond dispute. The signs and evidence of this change are no more apparent than in the technology I use to write these words. With the touch of a few buttons, I could send this entire study within seconds to any one of millions of people around the planet. With a few coding alterations, I could "post" it to my World Wide Web page on the Internet making it immediately accessible to millions of anonymous people many of whom might live thousands of miles apart from each other and from me. If I so desired, I could "enter" the Library of Congress in the United States—without ever leaving my chair in Toronto, Canada—and access whatever it currently has stored in digital-electronic format, which is growing exponentially. Anecdotes and illustrations similar to those above are plentiful and well-known. But how do we understand—amidst the maelstrom of changes occurring around us—the wider implications of these developments? How can we assess where we are heading? How do we do so without being swept up in the hype? In other words, where can we find a proper framework or guide that will give us some perspective on the relationship between these changes and society and politics at a world level?

Those groping for answers to these questions would be hard pressed to find many preliminary leads within the International Relations literature. There is no tradition of International Relations scholarship that takes communications *per se* as its central focus. The one scholar who is an exception to this generalization—Karl Deutsch—wrote most of his studies prior to the recent developments surrounding the so-called "information revolution."[15] Moreover, as his work focused on measurable *flows* of communications across borders largely without regard to the different media employed, it is of limited use to those interested in changing communication *technologies*.

More recently, of course, there have been a growing number of studies that allude to "information technologies" or the "media," but many of them subsume communications under a theoretical perspective that privileges other independent variables, such as the capitalist mode of production by Marxists and neo-Marxists, or weapons technologies by security materialists.[16] The few exceptions in which communication technologies do play an important role include James Rosenau's *Turbulence in World Politics*,[17] some recent and thought-provoking postmodern and poststructuralist works,[18] which have attempted to tap into the new sensibilities of cyberspace, and an edited book on the "political economy" of communications.[19] Some military analysts have also begun to focus on the "revolution" in military-strategic affairs unleashed by new communication and information technologies.[20] These few forays are an important sign that at least some attention is beginning to be paid to communication technologies in the International Relations field. However, the issue-area as a whole remains seriously underdeveloped. While sharing some significant commonalities with each of these various analyses, both the theoretical perspective and scope of this study make it a substantially different and, as I hope to demonstrate, significantly novel contribution. More will be said about the dearth of scholarship in the International Relations/communication technologies nexus in chapter 1.

Outside of the International Relations field there is, of course, plenty of often insightful and entertaining popular speculation about the impact of new communication technologies on society, culture, and politics. Such literature, is of course not written in a social science mode and thus tends to be more journalistic or sensational than systematic. Here, the problem is not so much a dearth of scholarship as it is a surfeit of hyperbole. One finds the opinions of Luddites and optimists that seem to accompany every technological innovation of the last two centuries, only now they are magnified a thousandfold by the reproductive and distributive capacities of the communication technology itself![21] Corralling this virtual stampede of publications is surely one of the more challenging tasks in writing a study such as this one. For example, James Beniger has listed with exasperation no less than seventy-five books written between 1950 and 1984 dedicated to major societal transformations associated with new communication technologies.[22] Depending on the author, we are now in the midst of, or are or transforming into, "posthistoric man," "postcapitalist society," the "end of ideology," the "computer revolution," the "postcivilized era," the "age of discontinuity," the "technetronic era," a "republic of technology," a "wired society," and, of course, "the third wave."[23] In this headlong rush to grasp the implications of a seemingly endless chain of improvements in the speed and scope of communications, hype about "what's in store" for us in the misty future—*what we will be able to do*—often displaces informed analyses of what is going on here and now.[24] Depending on the moral proclivities of the author, the result is typically an invocation of either optimism or despair that can make for entertaining reading, but poor analysis of contemporary trends in world politics.

One tradition of scholarship that does take as its central focus the impact of changing communication technology on society and politics falls under the rubric "medium theory."[25] This approach is associated with (but by no means exclusive or original to) Marshall McLuhan, arguably the most cited, but least understood, theorist of the "information age."[26] At the heart of medium theory is the argument that changes in modes of communication—such as the shift from primitive orality to writing or the shift from print to electronic communications—have an important effect on the trajectory of social evolution and the values and beliefs of societies. Medium theory traces these effects to the properties of the medium itself regardless of the content or the message being transmitted. In other words, different modes of communication, it is argued, have a certain "logic" or "nature," not in any determinist sense, but only in the sense of making certain types of communication easier or more difficult.[27] As communication is such a vital part of human existence, a change in the mode of communication will have substantial effects on factors such as the distribution of power within society, the nature and character of individual and social cognition, and the values and beliefs that animate a particular population.

Medium theory has received less attention than one might expect given recent developments in communication technology—a neglect that is probably at least indirectly related to the way it was introduced to a wider audience by its two main practitioners: Harold Adam Innis (the "father" of medium theory) and Marshall McLuhan ("the oracle of the electronic age").[28] Both theorists had a notoriously dense and complex writing style—a limitation that both invited misinterpretation and discouraged further investigation. Innis's writings seem rushed—as if they were working drafts for a larger project that was never completed before his relatively early death. McLuhan, on the other hand, practiced a self-conscious "mosaic" style of writing that consisted mostly of bulletlike aphoristic probes designed to challenge the reader. However, one person's "probe" is another's "gross generalization." While achieving widespread popular notoriety, McLuhan's work was received less kindly in academic circles—a reflection perhaps not so much of the poverty of McLuhan's analysis as of the envy that seems to arise within academia when a scholar achieves widespread fame. Whatever the root cause, by the time of McLuhan's death in 1980 the substance of medium theory had been reduced to a few well-worn clichés, like the "global village" or "the medium is the message." To this day most remain unaware of the theoretical grounds that underlie such claims.

In chapter 1, I provide a substantial elaboration and modification of medium theory designed to resurrect the core propositions of this approach while shedding those elements that have come to be seen through criticism and the passage of time as misguided, overstated, or merely tangential. The majority of these elaborations and modifications are attempts to "get back to the roots" of this approach, so to speak—to unearth what I see as the cultural materialist or social anthropological grounds out of which medium theory developed. In doing so, I am linking the basic postulates of medium theory to a much deeper tradition of scholarship that includes figures such as Gordon Childe, Lewis Mumford, and the French *Annales* school of medieval historians, associated with Fernand Braudel, Marc Bloch, and more recently Georges Duby and Jacques Le Goff. Embedding medium theory in this deeper tradition of scholarship enables me to articulate a more holistic view of the role of communication technology in social change, one that is able to confront and overcome the most basic perceived fault in medium theory: technological determinism. It also enables me to situate medium theory more clearly within the International Relations field. As I will point out in chapter 1, what I call the "ecological holist" position that underlies my version of medium theory aligns me closest to the work of historicists in the field, such as John Ruggie, Robert Cox, and Daniel Deudney. It also bears a close resemblance to the social constructivist approaches developed by Alexander Wendt, Friedrich Kratochwil, and Nicholas Onuf. And it diverges fundamentally from the more ahistorical, rationalist approaches associated with mainstream neorealist and neoliberal theories. Indeed, what I believe to be one of the more important contributions of this study is the argument that the elements of international politics which mainstream rationalist approaches presuppose to be "natural," "essential," and "unchanging" are, in fact, the products of historical contingencies and thus subject to change over time.

The Study of World Order Transformation

Fundamental changes, such as those being pursued here in communications, by definition resonate throughout the whole of society leaving virtually nothing untouched. Presented with this overwhelming scope of change, the analyst concerned with explaining specific relations must narrow the focus considerably. While medium theory has been applied in the past to a wide range of issue-areas at a variety of levels of analysis, my focus in this study is on the relationship between changes in modes of communication and *world order* transformation. It is important, then, to specify clearly what is entailed by this analytical focus.

When most people think of "international relations" they tend to think of the relations between states or nations, be it in the form of war, trade, or diplomacy. Indeed, the majority of scholarship in the International Relations field focuses on these very same types of questions—that is, on the *interactions* between political units whose existence is more or less considered unproblematic. Theories of international relations generally assume a basic structure—they take for granted the division of political authority into territorially distinct sovereign states and they theorize about the relations between those states. As Robert Cox has pointed out, this level of analysis is appropriate under conditions of "apparent stability or fixity in power relations," when the basic structure of the system can be taken for granted.[29] However, when fundamental change is thought to be occurring in the very parameters in which such interaction takes place, a deeper level of analysis is required, one that problematizes what is normally assumed away.

This deeper level of analysis focuses on the structure of political authority at a world level, or what is generally referred to as "world order."[30] Since this level of analysis occupies a crucial place in this study, it may be useful to unpack "world order" and more carefully delineate what is meant by the term. First, world order does not necessarily have to correspond to the planet as a whole; in other words, we can think of world order on a number of different levels, from fairly self-contained regional groupings to the globe itself. Second, world order, in its standard formulation, typically refers to the structure of political authority or system of rule found in a specific world at a particular time in history.[31] In general terms, it refers to the "basis on which the human species is socially individuated and individuals in turn bound together into collectivities."[32] It does not focus on the ongoing, day-to-day relations between these units, nor even whether these day-to-day relations form some discernible recurring pattern—say, the predisposition toward bandwagoning under a particular distribution of power.[33] Rather, it focuses attention on the nature and spatial organization of the units themselves— from the ideas, values, and principles that sustain and underpin this organization to the institutional and functional embodiments of the actual units of political authority.

"Political authority" is perhaps best defined more precisely as the "right to set the rules of the game."[34] Although it is one of the most basic and important notions in politics, it is also one of the most intractable and confusing. For example, although most people locate authority today in sovereign-territorial states, not all systems of rule have been territorially based and/or mutually-exclusive. John Ruggie, for example, has pointed to medieval feudalism as a system of rule characterized by multiple and overlapping layers of political authority (of which more will be said below).[35] Also often confused are the notions of political authority and state "control" or "autonomy."[36] When observers point to flows of commerce or communications across state borders and see in them the "end of the sovereignty" or a loss of authority, what they are often pointing to is, in fact, a loss of state control. While there may be some sort of a *relationship* between such a loss and the recasting of political authority over time, as Janice Thomson notes, the two concepts should be carefully distinguished.[37] It is the specific form in which political authority is manifested at different times and in different contexts that is the proper focus of world order studies, and not the ability (or lack thereof) to control flows or act autonomously.

One way to help conceptualize the study of world order is by way of an architectural analogy. Different buildings employ a variety of principles and styles upon which space is ordered and rooms arranged and divided. Buildings also serve particular functions: stairwells or exits are placed in strategic locations while hallways may be designed to accommodate large flows of foot traffic, or conversely, to facilitate privacy and exclusion. An architectural analyst studying the spatial order of a particular building will not concern him or herself with the conversations or relations of the people occupying the building, but will focus instead on the building itself, perhaps beginning with the social nuances and cultural styles that inform the design, moving next to the general architectural principles that undergird the structure as a whole, and finally outlining in careful terms the division of space within the building—the number and arrangement of rooms and floors. Similarly, in an analysis of the architecture of *world order*, the concern is not so much with the relations between "units" of political authority as it is with the constitution of the "units" themselves. Here, the focus is on the social nuances and cultural styles that give meaning to order, to the principles and rules that constitute and legitimate political authorities, and finally to the nature and character of the institutions that structure and differentiate the practice of political, economic, and social organization. The study of world order is thus above all the study of the organization of political space—the architecture of political authority—at a world level.

While "political" authority is the prime focus, it is important to emphasize that a variety of factors will influence the nature or character of a particular world order, including the organization and production of subsistence, the provision of physical security, and the supply of spiritual, religious, or other metaphysical yearnings. Consequently, studies of world order should be wide-ranging and sociological in their scope, willing to track a deep current of forces that might not otherwise be associated with a narrow definition of "politics" *per se*. It is also important that studies or world order not conflate what are essentially theoretical categories with the substance of the world order in question. In other words, we should not presuppose the "modern" distinction maintained between "politics," "economics," and "religion" in the composition of past or future world orders. For those living at the time these categories may be inextricably linked—in fact, the very distinction might have little or no conceptual currency in the language of the day. This heuristic focus on world order as the "structure of political authority" may even come to be seen in the passage of time as parochial and typically "modern," but it has not yet exhausted its intellectual "cash-value."[38]

By these terms, world order is an example of what is called the *longue durée* by the *Annales* school of historians. As Ruggie points out, the *longue durée* does not refer simply to a long period of time: "It depicts the lives of large-scale historical structures, as opposed to day-to-day events, structures which may shape those events for extended periods of time."[39] These historical structures become so much a part of the enduring practices of people that they "come by them to be regarded as fixed attributes of human nature and social intercourse."[40] Of course, they are not. We know as much because not all systems of rule throughout the course of human history have assumed the same form. In other words, there have been "breaking points" between past world orders where the architecture of political authority has undergone transformation. Whether the current period can be defined as one of those breaking points is a question that is beginning to occupy a considerable amount of scholarly attention in the field. It is for this reason that theorists have increasingly looked back to the origins of the sovereign state-system—to the medieval-to-modern transformation of political authority—and have begun to "problematize" modern world order itself.

Similarly, my research strategy in this study has been to go back and explore the transformation that ushered in the sovereign states system in an attempt to draw lessons and apply them to contemporary changes. Like today, the medieval-to-modern transformation of political authority coincided with a major shift in the way people communicated, with the invention of the printing press by Gutenberg. Using medium theory as a guide, in part 1 of this study I examine the way this change in the mode of communication played a part in the transformation of political authority. Then, using the same theoretical and analytical lens, I turn in part 2 to the contemporary era, and examine the relationship between new digital-electronic-telecommunications—what I refer to as the *hypermedia* environment—and the modern to postmodern transformation of political authority.

In its focus on communication technologies, the scope of this study is necessarily limited in important ways—particularly in part 1, which focuses on the medieval-to-modern transformation. My primary goal is to develop a *lens* through which to interpret changing communication technologies and world order transformation. Those searching for a more comprehensive or general treatsment of the rise of the state or a history of the Middle Ages would be well advised to look elsewhere. That said, I do believe that this study can provide an important guide to where we are headed today. Communication technologies are unique insofar as they are implicated in all spheres of human interaction—from production to security to knowledge and culture. As a consequence, changes in communication technologies both influence, and provide a window on, changes in other spheres of life. In focusing on changing modes of communication, then, we may be able to gain insight into the nature and direction of world order transformation as a whole. In setting the stage for the analysis to follow, the remainder of this chapter provides a general description of the medieval and the modern world orders.

The Architecture of the Medieval and Modern World Orders

Generalizing about the architecture of the medieval world order is an inherently dangerous enterprise. Gone are the days when the "Middle Ages" were viewed in static, sterile terms. The trend in medieval studies today is toward an affirmation of cultural diversity and idiosyncrasy, a view of life from the "bottom up," so to speak.[41] Structural features invariably tend to mask this rich complexity and diversity of medieval life, so there is always a risk of running roughshod over a thicket of contradictory nuances between different eras and regions that might diverge from the more general pattern. However, the study of structures by definition necessitates a degree of generalization in order to "give expression to phenomena deeper than everyday reality and to capture movement of a slower tempo."[42] At the risk of necessarily sidestepping important contextual details and "numberless tiny areas,"[43] some broad generalizations about the form of world order during the High to late Middle Ages (a period running roughly from the eleventh to the fifteenth centuries) can be made that would probably find agreement among most medievalists.[44]

Despite the existence of competing and overlapping local and regional sentiments, it is safe to say that all of western Europe at this time defined itself as part of a single spiritual community. "Almost all medieval men moved contradictorily between two sets of horizons," notes Le Goff, "the limited horizons of the clearing in which they lived, and the distant horizons of the whole of Christendom."[45] In cosmological terms this spiritual community was ordered hierarchically, "a Great Chain of Being" with Christ poised at the top of the apex, followed by the Church, and by extension its visible head, the Pontiff, who acted as an intermediary between God and temporal life.[46] It was a society deeply imbued with religion from top to bottom, one in which the "destinies of man and the universe" were perceived within boundaries "traced by a Westernized Christian theology and eschatology. . . ."[47] All past and present believers were linked together seamlessly in a great *corpus mysticum*.[48]

Although the unity of Christendom provided a broad sense of common identity, especially in relation to the non-Christian world, it never crystallized into a single political structure, in part because "the actual social structure of power, the difficulties of travel and communication, the confused pattern of local and regional differences prevented any such expression."[49]

Late medieval political rule was characterized by multiple and overlapping layers of authority, resting primarily on hierarchical and personalized feudal relations, with often competing jurisdictions among various social and cultural cells. In Perry Anderson's words, it was "a jungle of particularist dependencies."[50] In most cases, vertical and horizontal powers were entangled within the same nonexclusive territorial spheres, making it difficult to determine to which of the many lords, churches, towns or princes people were subordinate.[51] The vestiges of Roman Imperial authority, the interweaving papal-monastic networks, the fluid hereditary kingdoms, free cities, Germanic settlements, and scattered dukedoms, all co-existed together in a political space determined not so much by territorial boundaries, as by the sacred tributaries of the Christian commonwealth and the personal linkages of the feudal system of rule. As Hendrick Spruyt put it, "the church, Holy Roman Empire, and feudalism" were all based on "nonterritorial logics of organization."[52]

In the medieval world order, there were no sharp demarcations between "inside" and "outside," or between "private" and "public" realms, as each blended seamlessly into the other in a patchwork of personalized jurisdictions. The modern notion of dividing political space into mutually exclusive sovereign political entities would have been considered by philosophers of the time as a "repulsive anarchy, a contradiction to their basic assumption of a hierarchically ordered universe—almost a blasphemy."[53] If there was any clear dividing line that cut through society it was a trifunctional one, as Duby has explained, among those who prayed, those who fought, and those who labored.[54] Although in formal terms the late medieval period was anarchic (lacking a supreme political authority), it was one in which the constituent units considered themselves to be "municipal embodiments of a universal community."[55] This sense of inclusive rights and overlapping jurisdictions provided the distinctive characteristics of the architecture of medieval world order. As Ruggie aptly describes it, the medieval world order "represented a heteronomous organization of territorial rights and claims—of political space."[56]

The transformation from this medieval heteronomous structure to the modern world of territorially distinct, mutually exclusive sovereign nation-states was a slow process encompassing changes that span centuries. Although theorists traditionally date the modern states system to the Peace of Westphalia in 1648, there is no one single year that signals its emergence, making the assigning of a time-line somewhat arbitrary.[57] For years elements of what might be considered "medieval" coexisted with what are now considered benchmarks of the "modern."[58] Furthermore, within this transformation no single overarching variable stands apart as a primary driving force; instead the origins of the modern world order lay in what Michael Mann calls "a gigantic series of coincidences."[59] Drawing from the *Annales* school, Ruggie's recent essay on the medieval to modern transformation provides a compelling overview of some of these multifaceted "coincidences," beginning with base material changes in ecodemographics and the environment, moving upward to military and productive technologies, to explorations and travels, to shifts in strategic and commercial relations, and resting finally on important changes in *mentalites collectives*. Assigning weight to different variables within this complex may be somewhat futile if not misguided given the interwoven series of contingencies involved. At best what we might conclude from the medieval-to-modern transformation is that "when the creation of a new mental attitude falls together with extensive material and economic changes, something significant happens."[60] The result, over a period of centuries, was the emergence of the modern world order: territorially distinct, mutually exclusive, sovereign nation-states.

The key feature of the modern world order is implicit in the definition above—the parcelization and segmentation of all economic, social, and cultural activity into mutually exclusive, functionally similar political entities, or territorial "bundles."[61] Displacing the nonterritorial logics of organization that had characterized the feudal system of rule, political authority gradually coalesced into administrative control over fixed territorial spaces.[62] At a more specific level, the transformation entailed the creation of centralized state bureaucracies that ruled these territorial spaces from a single center. As part of this "centering" process, the medieval Christian Commonwealth was atomized into discrete community identifications centered first on the person of the monarch, and later on national-linguistic ties, or the "nation." At its foundation, however, the division of political authority into territorially distinct, sovereign nation-states defined the architecture of modern world order in Europe.

This mode of organizing political space spread gradually, by imitation and force; by the twentieth century, it would encompass the entire planet, and it was strongly reaffirmed following decolonization in the mid-1950s.[63] Today it stands as the dominant "paradigm" of world order at a global level.[64] The institutional depth of this paradigm is strong, as evidenced by the wide range of social, political, and economic activities that reinforce it daily. At the most basic level, the overwhelming majority of people around the world vote in a single state, carry passports of a single state, and consider themselves to be citizens and thus subject to the government and laws of a particular sovereign state.[65] Breaches of sovereign territorial boundaries are still strongly condemned, as revealed by the international community's reaction to the Iraqi invasion of Kuwait.[66] And the majority of independence movements around the world still overwhelmingly define their political goals in terms of sovereign aspirations. It was with these many interlocking ideas and social practices in mind that Stephen Krasner concluded that "The breadth of the state in terms of its links with other social entities, and the depth of the state reflected in the very concept of citizenship as a basic source of individual identity, make it very hard to dislodge."[67]

However, as pointed out in the opening pages of this introduction, a number of scholars are now beginning to question the continued viability of this mode of organizing political space. For many, there is a sense of profound transformation at work in world politics today—transformations that some believe are on an epochal scale, reaching beyond just the end of the Cold War into the very organization of politics and community itself. Everything from environmental to economic and military changes are increasingly seen as presenting fundamental challenges to the architecture of modern world order.[68] For others, however, such changes signal nothing new of significance, and the sovereign state system remains the fundamental basis of world order.[69] It is in the hope of contributing in a constructive way to this debate that this study is put forth. As will be revealed in the pages to follow, the conclusions reached strongly suggest that many of those interlocking elements that have traditionally provided the "institutional depth" for the modern world order paradigm are being rapidly dismantled. The architecture of political authority is undergoing profound transformation. While it is far too early to provide a clear outline of that emerging world order, the trends unearthed point *away* from single mass identities, linear political boundaries, and exclusive jurisdictions centered on territorial spaces, and *toward* multiple identities and nonterritorial communities, overlapping boundaries, and nonexclusive jurisdictions. Whether these developments continue in this direction or not depends on a variety of contingent factors in the future. But certainly changes in communication technologies occurring today suggest they will.

1 Medium Theory, Ecological Holism, and the Study of World Order Transformation

The poverty of the many existing, mostly speculative analyses of the "information revolution" reveals the inherent difficulties of assessing sweeping changes as they unfold. Without the confidence of hindsight, and with no God's-eye vantage point, theory becomes an essential, though necessarily context-bound, tool by which to bring order to the apparent chaos that floods from abrupt ruptures in social and political institutions. Given the lack of attention International Relations scholarship traditionally devotes to communications, my first steps in this direction must be across disciplinary boundaries—a potentially dangerous expedition, though one that also offers the prospect of shaking loose dogmatic assumptions riveted in place by prolonged and artificial disciplinary closure.[1]

At the same time, it is important to recognize that approaches lifted from other fields are likely to suffer their own peculiar deficiencies. We should be careful to avoid cross-disciplinary hero-worship for its own sake. At the very least, it is unlikely that any theory devised within a particular discursive field with its own set of problems can be transplanted wholesale to another without significant modification. To accommodate my own specific *problematique*, the rudimentary insights of Innis, McLuhan, and other medium theorists will be embedded in an evolutionary approach called "ecological holism." Although the label is new, the approach itself actually synthesizes and expounds what is already implicit in the work of many medium theorists—that is, an open-ended, nonreductionist, thoroughly historicist view of human existence that emphasizes contingency over continuity both in terms of the trajectory of social evolution and the nature and character of human beings. As will be made clear below, while this approach differs in significant ways from mainstream International Relations theorizing, it does find resonance in the work of at least one prominent theorist—namely, John Ruggie—and has important commonalities with others as well.

In this chapter, I begin with an overview of the extant literature on communications within the International Relations field. As will be revealed below, there is a dearth of scholarship that takes communications as its central focus. Moreover, what little exists is either flawed in significant ways, or is improperly designed for my central task: an examination of the relationship between changes in communication *technologies* and social and political change at a world-order level. I then outline the central tenets of medium theory, and offer a profile of some of the main contributors to this approach, including the issues to which they have applied their insights. Using the various criticisms of medium theory as a backdrop, I then put forward a substantial elaboration and modification of medium theory, tailoring it to the specific concerns of the study, and situating it more clearly within the International Relations field. The analytical scheme used to organize the research in the ensuing chapters will emerge from the modifications made to medium theory.

International Relations Theory and Communications

There is no distinct "school" or "paradigm" of communications within the field of International Relations. In fact, there are few International Relations theorists of communication at all (the one important exception being Karl Deutsch). Individual theorists may allude to communication or information in their studies, but rare are the cases where an overtly communications approach is adopted. Although the communications/International Relations nexus remains underdeveloped, some distinct themes or issue-areas can be identified where the interaction between the two is given more than passing notice.

To the limited extent International Relations theorists have dealt with communications explicitly, the focus has primarily been on *content* to the exclusion of technology—the inverse of the theoretical perspective to be employed here. For example, considerable work has been done on propaganda as an instrument of foreign policy, noting the way a state will manipulate messages to garner international support or undermine foes.[2] Other studies working in the content vein have focused on media representations, or the "framing" of international events, and the way these representations may influence domestic opinion and thus foreign policy outcomes.[3] These particular approaches were common during and after the Vietnam War, when the novelty of "the first televised war" captured the attention of many scholars.[4] An important subset of this approach includes the many studies that examine the relationship between content and *situation*. In this group we would find studies on communication during crises;[5] intercultural communications;[6] communications in negotiations and bargaining;[7] and wartime and/or diplomatic communications.[8]

A further subset of the content-based approaches includes those that deal with *control*. Work in this area typically examines the way ownership of media creates an ideological bias that circumscribes and shapes debate to further the interests of capital or the state.[9] For example, the Gramscian school of International Relations theory emphasizes the relationship between control over media and cultural hegemony by transnational elites.[10] Another common focus of control-based approaches is on how flows of information deepen and solidify structures of dependency between the information-rich North and the information-poor South.[11] Policy proposals designed to rectify this imbalance, such as that for a New World Information Order, were a direct outgrowth of the conclusions reached by these theorists.[12] Control-based studies thus tend to emphasize the way communication flows threaten "cultural sovereignty" or state autonomy while extending cultural imperialism.[13] Although the focus of these analyses is on control of the medium, the intent is to show how such control determines *content*, which is the ultimate concern. From this perspective, new communication technologies are important insofar as they enhance the efficiency and scope of such control, and hence the potential penetration of hegemonic ideologies. But they are ultimately seen as subsidiary variables within an overarching global-capitalist mode of production, rather than as transformative in their own right.

Not all of the work on communications by International Relations theorists deals exclusively with content; the pioneering work by Karl Deutsch on communications *flows* is an important exception.[14] Deutsch, who is probably the figure most identifiable with the communications/International Relations nexus, constructed a formidable and innovative body of work unique for the central role he assigned to communicative interaction in the explanation of political behavior. When opening any of Deutsch's many works, the reader cannot help but be struck by a sharp contrast: while Deutsch crafts elegant historical interpretations, rich in detail, as backdrops for his analysis, when his attention turns to explanation, however, an overarching, almost obsessive compulsion for statistical rigor predominates. His concern for the quantitative is so strong that Deutsch's formal analysis of communication is thus restricted to the one part of the communication process that can be measured: flow. For Deutsch, communication flows determine the level of national and international integration. Concentrated clusters of communication patterns—measured in terms of the density and flow of postal or telephone exchanges, for example—distinguish separate communities. The unevenness of this distribution helps explain why nationalism is so prevalent in world politics. The flip side of this equation—and the explanation for integration, according to Deutsch—is that the density of the flow determines the scope of the community. As flows increase, parochialism dissolves.

Deutsch's work is perhaps best situated as one important part of the modernization genre of scholarship that flourished among political scientists, development theorists, and sociologists between 1950 and 1980.[15] These theorists acknowledged that the properties of media were important, but only along one narrow dimension: the extent to which they enhanced the flow or efficiency of communications. Such flows were seen as the tools by which local identities might be dissolved and then displaced by a more solidified, national identity as part of a more general state-building project. Hence, increased literacy among a population was seen as a key to general political development, as was the creation and maintenance of a centralized "mass media" system. In focusing on the potential development of a pluralistic security community in Europe and elsewhere, Deutsch and his colleagues were simply extending this modernization paradigm beyond national borders.

The main problem with Deutsch's analysis is that it adopted a naive view of the assimilative tendencies of increased communication. Extrapolating from Deutsch's hypotheses, one would expect a single community of humanity as communication becomes more dense, from tribes to nations to regions to supranations. Yet the opposite is as often the case. Increased communication flow does not, by necessity, lead to common identities.[16] Flow by itself tells us little about the nature of the interaction. In other words, increased intercultural communication can easily lead to hostile backlashes rather than to seductive integration. Although students of Deutsch continued his approach into the 1970s and beyond, the utility of a purely quantitative analysis of communication flows is limited.[17]

As in the field of communications proper, the overwhelming majority of studies on international relations and communications focus on some aspect of message content. In these studies, the specific message being transmitted is thought to be the important variable; changes in the medium through which the message is imparted are abstracted from the analysis. Those that do not deal exclusively with *content* focus instead on communications *flows*, as exemplified in the work of Karl Deutsch. In both of these cases, the medium itself is viewed as neutral and invisible. Changes in the technology of communication are also ignored.

Medium Theory

Medium theory flips this abstraction, so to speak, focusing exclusively on the intrinsic properties of the medium itself. Most important from this perspective is the way large-scale changes in modes of communication shape and constrain behavior and thought independent of message content, and in doing so help to restructure social and political institutions. According to this perspective, media are not simply neutral channels for conveying information between two or more environments, but are rather environments in and of themselves.[18] To put it simply, medium theory holds that communication "is a sphere where the *technology* involved may have an immense significance for the society in which it occurs, and perhaps radically affect the concurrent forms of social and economic organization."[19] Unlike content-based analyses of communications, medium theory is necessarily *historical* in its approach, contrasting different media environments across time, and tracing changes in the technology of communication for their effects on the evolution of social and political order.[20]

Although medium theory is associated primarily with twentieth-century scholarship, many of its core propositions can be unearthed in classic texts dating back to ancient Greece. In the *Phaedrus* and the *Seventh Letter*, Plato has Socrates raise strong objections to the newly emerging written form, arguing that it destroys memory and weakens the mind, even though, ironi-

cally, Plato's own analytic epistemology was strongly conditioned by the effects of writing on mental processes, as Eric Havelock, Walter Ong, and
Ernst Gellner have argued.[21] Moral injunctions against the expression of
ideas in specific media can be found in the Old Testament, where the Second Commandment prohibits the iconographic depiction of God.[22] In the
Essay on the Origin of Languages, Rousseau takes up a common theme in
medium theory—the transition from primitive orality to writing—arguing
that writing transforms the meaning of words and diminishes their vitality
by suppressing dialects: "The more a people learn to read, the more are its
dialects obliterated."[23] What each of these perspectives shares is the central
proposition of medium theory: that the medium of communication—far
from being an empty vessel or transparent channel—has a significant influence on the nature and content of human communication.

Probably the most famous (or infamous, depending on specific viewpoints) practitioner of medium theory is Marshall McLuhan, as one of his
well-known aphorisms, "the medium is the message" attests. In a series of
highly publicized books written during the 1960s, McLuhan brought attention to the central principles of medium theory, mostly through his idiosyncratic style of writing, which was peppered with one-line aphorisms and gross
generalizations that became catch-phrases of the decade.[24] As Lapham notes,
"Seldom in living memory had so obscure a scholar descended so abruptly
from so remote a garret into the center ring of celebrity circus."[25] Indeed,
few scholars can rival McLuhan for achieving such popular notoriety—a
rise McLuhan himself seemed to relish as proof of his own proclamations.
Appearing in Woody Allen films and popular television shows, and professing
to speak in the disconnected, pastiche mode of the "electronic age," Mc-
Luhan saw his role in therapeutic terms: he was to be the oracle of a new
world on the verge of being born. Not surprisingly, the self-imposed transformation from bookish literary professor to postmodern electronic guru
alienated many still ensconced in the tombs of *typographica*. In an ironic
twist of his theorizing, McLuhan's meteoric rise may have had the unfortunate consequence of obscuring the message beneath the messenger.

Clothed in the "mosaic" form of argumentation McLuhan preferred
("mosaic" in contrast to the linear-style of reasoning which McLuhan believed to be a product of the Age of Typography), McLuhan's message took
as its starting point some of the more basic themes of medium theory, re-
weaving them into electronic age prophecy. Like other medium theorists,
McLuhan believed that changes in modes of communication have impor-

tant consequences for society—that there are deep, qualitative differences between one communications mode and another, differences that are in turn reflected in the nature of the communications epoch. For McLuhan, history can be divided into four such communications epochs, each of which corresponds to the dominant mode of communication of the time: oral, writing, printing, and electronic. McLuhan's unique contribution was the argument that in each of these communications epochs, different media act as *extensions* of the human senses with consequences for both cognition and social organization. For example, "oral societies" live primarily in an "ear culture," while writing, and to a greater extent print, makes the sense of sight dominant. Following McLuhan's sensory classification, the electronic revolution returns us to the world of primitive orality, to village-like encounters, but now on a global scale: hence, "the global village."[26]

One of the more popular, but confusing aspects of McLuhan's analysis is his binary distinction between "hot" and "cool" media.[27] "Hot" media extend a single sense in high definition; "cool" media are low in definition, requiring audience participation. For McLuhan, examples of the former include print, radio, and film, while examples of the latter would include colloquial speech, telephone, and television.[28] Though clearly the distinction is debatable (by most accounts, print is a less passive medium than television in terms of audience participation) like many of McLuhan's "probes" it had the unfortunate consequence of directing debate about medium theory away from its core propositions to McLuhan's more spectacular but incidental contributions. "McLuhanesque" slogans—such as "the electric light is pure information" or "electric circuitry is Orientalizing the West"—became so associated with medium theory that by the time of McLuhan's death in 1980 few outside of the communications field were aware of the approach.[29]

Although he was clearly the most famous, McLuhan was merely one among a number of other scholars working along medium theory lines in the 1950s and 1960s. The interaction among these theorists was strong. Many of them met regularly at the University of Toronto—constituting an informal group now referred to as the "Toronto School of Communications."[30] Generally considered the founder of this "school" was the Canadian economic historian Harold Adam Innis.[31] Innis had established himself as an expert on trade in Canadian staple resources before turning to the history of communications.[32] McLuhan's analysis was significantly influenced by Innis's approach—so much so, in fact, that McLuhan had once described his own work as merely a "footnote" to Innis's scholarship. Although both shared a notoriously dense and complex writing style, Innis's work was more conventional in academic terms. Furthermore, Innis and McLuhan operated at different levels of analysis.[33] While McLuhan directed most of his concerns to the effect of media on sensory organization and thought, Innis concentrated primarily on large-scale social organization and culture, or, to cite one of Innis's more famous titles, on *Empire and Communications*.[34] Heyer outlines the central themes in Innis's medium theory:

> History is perceived as a series of epochs separated by discontinuity. Each is distinguished by dominant forms of media that absorb, record, and transform information into systems of knowledge consonant with the institutional power structure appropriate to the society in question. The interaction between media form and social reality creates various biases, which strongly affect the society's cultural orientation and values.[35]

Two prominent aspects of Innis's work are his views on space/time biases of different modes of communication, and on monopolies of knowledge. Innis argued that different media often exhibit an inherent bias toward either time or space, and that these biases are reflected in the character of civilizations. Durable media that are difficult to transport—such as stone, clay, or parchment—have a time-bias; these societies tend to be tradition-oriented, giving emphasis to custom and continuity over change, and with a strong attachment to the sacred. Furthermore, time-biased civilizations often lead to hierarchical social orders with elite groups, such as Egyptian high priests or the medieval Catholic clergy. Space-biased media, such as papyrus or paper, are lighter and more portable and tend to support expansionist empires characterized by large administrative apparatuses and secular institutions. Using a form of dialectical analysis, Innis argued that both types of civilizations have a tendency over time to ossify into rigid and unresponsive regimes. A reaction occurs at the fringes of society, where marginalized groups take advantage of new technologies of communication, which in turn results in the ascendancy of a new order.

Clearly, Innis was very much a part of the early-twentieth-century tradition of *civilizational* analysis, associated with Oswald Spengler, Arnold Toynbee, and Pitrim Sorokin.[36] As with these theorists, Innis's work has been criticized for a kind of cyclical determinism, whereby history is viewed as having a master logic that manifests itself in the unending rise and fall of civilizations. Certainly one could take a "strong" reading of, for example, his space/time bias categories and see in them a kind of reductionism at work. However, a more generous reading of Innis's work would highlight his emphasis on social and historical context, on the way different media have *potentialities* for control according to the way they are employed in different circumstances. For Innis, the emphasis is on the interaction between this social context and medium form, rather than on the mode of communication in abstraction: "A medium of communication has an important influence on the dissemination of knowledge over space and over time and it becomes necessary to study its characteristics in order to appraise its influence *in its cultural setting*."[37] From this reading, Innis's space/time biases are seen more as shorthand designates for the constraints imposed on certain types of communications by particular media, rather than programmatic statements on the nature of communications itself. Above all, Innis was concerned with understanding civilizational transformation through the lens of changing medium technology—a hitherto novel focus that required significant conceptual innovation to alert readers that communication media are not mere empty vessels.

As noted in my introduction, medium theory did not generate a widespread academic following initially, possibly as a result of its introduction by Innis and McLuhan. Innis's relatively early death foreclosed the possibility of his completing the more comprehensive project suggested by his two preliminary works, *Empire and Communications* and *The Bias of Communications*. As a consequence, he is known mostly through second-hand interpretations. In the case of McLuhan, his idiosyncratic style probably did more to obscure the theoretical basis of his work. Quite intentionally, McLuhan chose to ignore the social science conventions of the day and suffered a predictably dismissive response from academia. However, his "mosaic" style of writing may be more resonant with contemporary postmodern audiences as evidenced by the McLuhanesque renaissance that appears to be gaining momentum.[38]

Nonetheless, medium theory has proved to be a useful tool for a wide variety of scholars working in different issue-areas, many of whom offer a more conventional academic style of analysis than either of the two. A contemporary of Innis and McLuhan and a member of the informal "Toronto School," classicist Eric Havelock has studied the transition to alphabetic literacy in ancient Greece, analyzing its impact on classical epistemology.[39]

In a similar vein, social anthropologists Jack Goody and Ian Watt have studied the transition from primitive orality to writing for its impact on both cognition and social organization, as has Walter Ong from a more general perspective.[40] Historian Elizabeth Eisenstein has undertaken an extensively documented analysis of the cultural and scientific changes associated with the shift from script to print in medieval Europe.[41] And though less often associated with the formal approach, many of the central propositions of medium theory can be found in the work of cultural anthropologists like Lewis Mumford and Ernst Gellner, who emphasize the role of technology in social change.[42] While most of these theorists touch on large-scale historical changes associated with innovations in communication media, none have focused exclusively on the issue with which I am concerned here: world order transformation. The next section provides an overview of the modifications and elaborations that I make to medium theory in order to accommodate it to this *problematique*.

Theory and Epistemology

As alluded to above, no theory is without its warts, and medium theory is certainly not exempt. In order to accommodate this particular approach to my own set of questions, some retooling will be necessary if only to overcome some of the more confusing aspects of McLuhan and Innis's notoriously difficult styles. The elaborations and revisions to medium theory that follow can be grouped into two categories, both of them having to do with the question of causality. The first is with respect to the relative emphasis placed on communication technologies as independent variables; the second has to do with clearly articulating the exact nature of the effects that arise from a change in the mode of communication. I will consider each of these in turn.

Toward a Nonreductionist Medium Theory

A recurring criticism of medium theory is that it tends toward a form of monocausal reductionism and technological determinism. Certainly McLuhan bears the brunt of this criticism, though other medium theorists are not immune. Not unusual would be Carey's harsh indictment of McLuhan for a thorough "technological determinism" that closed down new ap-

proaches to communication technology, and left us with only "a soggy conclusion rather than with detailed scholarship."[43] Book reviews of medium
theorists are particularly repetitious, so much so that one gets the impression
that reprimanding medium theory on this score is a formulaic device. Thus
Havelock's work on the Greek enlightenment is castigated for "clinging . . .
to a simplistic reductionism" that "seems to want to make alphabetic literacy
the *sole* cause of the change . . ."[44] In Eisenstein, one reviewer detects "a
certain reductionist streak" and "a tendency to overestimate printing as
against other forces of change."[45]

Indeed, a cursory glance at McLuhan's work in particular might offer
substantiation for these criticisms, especially given his penchant for poetic
hyperbole—a style of writing that does not lend itself well to caveat. Super-
ficial illustrations of technological determinism are not hard to find in books
conceived as aphoristic "probes" rather than scientific treatises. In fact, Mc-
Luhan's work is constituted by them. In describing his project, McLuhan
once admitted that "I don't explain—I explore"—a revealing quote that begs
the question of the grounds on which such analysis should be held accountable.[46] While a strong argument could be made that a charge of technological determinism is probably beside the point of much of McLuhan's work,
the charge itself should be taken seriously in any analysis, such as this one,
that attempts something more conventional than bullet-like, aphoristic
probes.

Figure 1 offers a picture of the technological determinist/monocausal
reductionist model of change. Though no one particular medium theorist
can be said to subscribe fully to such a simplistic model of change, some
employ language or semantic inflections that are at times consistent with
such a picture of the interplay between technology and society. Eisenstein's
use of the word "agent" to describe an inanimate technology—the printing
press—is a case in point.[47] Moreover, this base/superstructure model is a
familiar one across a variety of theoretical perspectives (orthodox Marxism
being the prime example) where single overarching "master" variables are
held as determinant.[48] When critics of medium theorists reprimand them
for technological determinism they are implicitly invoking this flawed picture of causality. Any attempt at revising medium theory should confront
the many interrelated pitfalls inherent in such a simplistic model of change.

The most serious flaw in this model is that it tends to view the introduction of a new technology of communication as an autonomous force with
certain definite and predictable results irrespective of the social and histor-

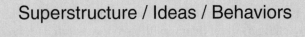

FIGURE 1. The technological determinist/mono-causal reductionist model of change

ical context in which it is introduced. Specific social phenomena are seen as invariably tied to a specific technology, as if the technology itself had the power to generate behaviors and ideas *de novo*. Thus, technological determinists tend to put forward such reductionist claims as "the printing press created individuality" or "the Reformation is the child of the printing press"—claims that clearly fall apart upon closer investigations that reveal the multiplicity of factors in their development. By attributing "generative" causal powers to the mode of communication, the technological determinist model tends to slight the extent to which the technology itself emerges out of a particular context and is itself influenced by social, cultural, and historical forces. This relative neglect of contextual factors is especially misleading not only because it tends to privilege the technology over other factors, but also because it produces faulty projections for the introduction of a similar technology in different cultures and contexts. Furthermore, the picture of causality employed sets up a strong binary opposition between the "material" and the "ideal," with social forces and ideas placed in a subordinate, derivative position to the material instrument of technology. And because social consequences are seen as arising out of, or generated by, the technology itself in this way, the technological determinist model portrays historical change as a radical disjuncture, with the technology as the hinge — a view of epochal change now widely discredited among historians.[49]

To avoid these pitfalls, we must underscore the "social embeddedness" of technology. We must place greater emphasis on the historical and social context in which technologies are introduced, an insight most forcefully made by social constructivists of technology.[50] These theorists trace the way social needs develop toward which certain innovations are applied. The most comprehensive of them show how social forces in conjunction with available material resources and technical knowledge mold the construction and invention of new technologies. In doing so, they dispel the illusion maintained by the technological determinist that technologies enter society and generate specific social forces and/or ideas *de novo*. As I will show in chapters 2 and 5, the emergences of printing and hypermedia respectively were not sudden, "out-of-nowhere" developments. In both cases, social needs drove technological innovation. The creation of new technologies was, in turn, dependent on the existing stock of scientific knowledge (broadly understood) as well as the available material resources. Technologies are always, in this sense, socially constructed.

But despite its strengths as a corrective to the technological determinist model, the social constructivist position has a tendency to fall into the opposite trap and slight, if not ignore altogether, any independent effects attributable to the technology itself *once introduced*. It is important to remember that although social forces may give direction to technological innovation, they are not completely determinant; once introduced a technology becomes part of the material landscape in which human agents and social groups interact, having many *unforeseen effects*. These are the effects the medium theorist is most concerned with. As I will show in part 1 of this study, one of the more enthusiastic early supporters of printing technology—one of the main social groups responsible for its rapid spread—was the Roman Catholic Church. But the same bishops and monks who actively encouraged the establishment of local printing houses never anticipated the way heresies, like the Protestant Reformation, would thrive with the widespread availability of this new technology. The full effects of printing went unforeseen by the very actors who encouraged and shaped its early development. So, while social constructivists of technology underscore the way social forces shape technological innovation, they tend to overlook the possibility that technological innovation, in turn, could have an impact on society itself. But if technological determinists give a misleading portrayal of these unforeseen effects and social constructivists slight them altogether, where does that leave us?

The way I suggest we articulate this process is by reflecting on and amplifying one of the more prominent metaphors in medium theory—*media as environments*—and by the use of a Darwinist evolutionary analogy to describe the processes by which marginal forces on the borders of society are brought into the center by the unintended consequences of technological innovation.[51]

In classical Darwinian theories of evolution, environmental changes strongly condition the differential survival and reproduction of species.[52] Although species are vitally dependent on their environment, the environment itself cannot be said to engage in the selection process by acting on species; rather, innovations and genetic mutations produce a variety of physical characteristics which, in turn, are selected blindly according to their "fitness" or match with the environment. Not to be confused with nineteenth-century "Social Darwinist" views of progressive development,[53] evolution from this perspective assumes no inherent direction or purpose but is a contingent, open-ended historical process.

Similarly, a change in the mode of communication (environment) will "favor" certain social forces and ideas (species) by means of a functional bias toward some and not others, just as natural environments determine which species prosper by "selecting" for certain physical characteristics. In other words, the properties of a communications environment—the unique ways in which information can be stored, transmitted, and distributed in that environment—"favor" the interests of some social forces and ideas over others. These social forces and ideas flourish or thrive, while others are placed at a significant disadvantage and tend to wither over time. Unlike both the technological determinist and social constructivist positions, unintended consequences loom large from this perspective. We would anticipate, in other words, that some social forces and ideas that were marginalized in one communications environment may resonate strongly once that environment changes. Likewise, those actors and groups that initially gave support to, and drove the early development of, a new technology of communication may find themselves at a disadvantage once the full characteristics of the new communications environment take root.

This Darwinist evolutionary analogy is particularly useful because it moves away from the technological determinist view of technologies "generating" specific social forces and ideas. It affirms that the genesis of social forces and ideas ultimately reflects a multiplicity of factors that cannot be reduced to a single overarching "master" variable. Instead, it focuses on the existing stock of social forces and ideas, asking which will likely flourish or wither depending on their "fitness" or match with the new communications environment. It "flips" the picture of causality, so to speak. From this perspective, a new mode of communication is not an "agent" but rather a passive, structural feature of the technological landscape in which human beings interact. It imposes certain constraints or limitations on the nature and type of possible human communications, while facilitating other types, but it does not impose thought or behavior in any crude one-to-one fashion. It is an environment. And like natural environments, when it changes some species will be favored while others will be disadvantaged, *not* because of an active intervention on the part of the environment itself, but rather because the functional properties of the environment either reinforce or constrain the characteristics and interests of the species within it. The perspective is historically *contingent*, insofar as the type of effects that ensue from a change in the communications environment depend entirely on the extant social groups, institutions, and ideas of the time in question.

To extend the analogy, there are two quite distinct "species" upon which the selection process bears in a changing communications environment, which brings me to my second modification to medium theory.

Two effects: Distributional Changes and Changes to Social Epistemology

When a communications environment undergoes fundamental transformation, two different types of effects can be discerned. Consider the following quote by Goody:

> Systems of communication are clearly related to what man can make of his world both internally in terms of thought and externally in terms of his social and cultural organization. So changes in the means of communication are linked in direct as well as indirect ways to changes in the patterns of human interaction.[54]

Goody is alluding to the dual effects of any change in communication technologies. I call these two effects *distributional changes* and *changes to social epistemology* respectively.

On the one hand, a change in the communications environment has specific tangible, *distributional* effects on the social and political infrastructure. In Innis's formulation, "Inventions in communication compel realignments in the monopoly or the oligopoly of knowledge."[55] This effect depends on two assumptions alluded to above: first is the most basic proposition of medium theory, that specific communications environments have a certain "logic" or "nature" not in any determinist sense, but only in the sense of "making human communications of certain types easier or more difficult."[56] The second assumption is that society is made up of discernible social forces that, while not necessarily "rational" in the *Homo economicus*, utility-maximizing sense of the term, are nonetheless motivated by certain historically and culturally varied interests and goals. By "social forces," I mean actual social groups, actors, and various forms of social organization—all normative or goal-driven social behaviors. The methodological task becomes clear when the two assumptions are married: identifying those social forces whose interests, goals, and logics of organization are likely to "fit" with the new communications environment, and those whose do not. Typically, those social forces whose interests, goals, or logics "fit" the new communications environment do not just survive in the same form as before. They are empowered by the new means of communication at their disposal. They find a "niche" and flourish, and, as a result, become a more prominent feature of the world political landscape. Likewise, social forces that may have thrived in one communications environment may find themselves at a significant disadvantage once that environment changes.

But the question naturally arises: Why cannot social forces merely adapt or control technologies to their own ends? One obvious reason is that the properties of a communications environment might be at such fundamental odds to the core interests, or *raison d'être*, of particular social actors or groups that they have no choice but to resist vigorously (often with little success) the further spread of that environment. But part of the reason also relates to the relative inflexibility of social forces. Because social forces acquire a certain "path-dependency" or institutional inertia based on the shared habits of thought and action of the multitudes of individuals that comprise them, they cannot easily adapt to new circumstances. Their institutional incumbency, as Gould calls it, "reinforces the stability of the pathway once the little quirks of early flexibility push a sequence into a firm channel."[57] Likewise Spruyt notes how "transaction costs, set belief systems, and standard operating procedures mitigate against frequent overhaul" of social forces and institutions.[58]

Human beings tend to be creatures of habit, and social forces comprise many habitual individuals all of whom have limited lifespans and thus relatively short time-horizons. The consequences of today's short-term choices—such as promoting the development of a new technology that will make specific tasks simpler or more efficient (cheaply reproducing bibles, for example)—are not usually understood in terms of their long-term implications or unintended consequences. As I will outline in later chapters, this certainly describes the predicament of the Roman Catholic Church vis-à-vis the printing press. These distributional changes—changes, that is, in the relative power of social forces—are perhaps the most direct consequence of a change in the mode of communication.

On the other hand, to return to Goody's remarks above, a change in the communications environment affects not just social organization, but also the "internal" world of ideas and ways of thinking.[59] Communication environments, in other words, also select ideas, social constructs and modes of cognition. To take but one specific example often cited by medium theorists, the introduction of writing encourages abstract thought because words and ideas can be manipulated and compared to a greater extent than they can in oral societies.[60] Here we are concerned with the way communication technologies influence what Ruggie labels a transformation in *social epistemology*.[61] Social epistemology refers broadly to the web-of-beliefs into which a people are acculturated and through which they perceive the world around them.[62] It encompasses an interwoven set of historically contingent intersubjective mental characteristics, ranging from spatial or temporal cognitive biases, to shared symbolic forms, to various group identities, or to "imagined communities," which are unique to a specific historical context, and differentiate one epoch from another.[63] Among French social theorists and medievalists it is referred to as *mentalités collectives*—the shared mental predispositions of a population in time—and it plays a crucial role in their interpretation of cultures.[64]

In highlighting changes to social epistemology, medium theory has a close affinity to sociology of knowledge or social constructivist approaches.[65] At its most basic, what these perspectives share is the belief that a wide range of social, economic, and political factors shape the genesis and structure of human thought and behavior, and thus the contours of social epistemology. Medium theory adds a materialist dimension to these perspectives by focusing on changes in communication technology. A common example of an argument linking technological innovation and social cognition in this way is Lewis Mumford's treatment of the impact of the clock on Western society in *Technics and Civilization*.[66] Prior to the clock, the measure of time was determined organically, that is, by the sun and the seasons; beginning in the fourteenth century, the measure of time was reoriented by the clock with important social ramifications. The clock "dissociated time from human events and helped create the belief in an independent world of mathematically measurable sequences . . ."[67] As Mumford goes on to explain:

> When one thinks of the day as an abstract space of time, one does not go to bed with the chickens on a winter's night: one invents wicks, chimneys, lamps, gaslights, electric lamps, so as to use all the hours belonging to the day. When one thinks of time, not as a sequence of experiences, but as a collection of hours, minutes, and seconds, the habits of adding time and saving time come into existence. Time took on the character of an enclosed space: it could be divided, it could be filled up, it could even be expanded by the invention of labor-saving instruments. . . . Abstract time became the new medium of existence. [68]

Mumford's social construction of time nicely illustrates the type of interpretive approach that should be employed when attention turns to the effects of the mode of communication on social epistemology. Effectively exploring the link between communication technology and social epistemology moves us considerably into the realm of semiotics and the study of symbolic forms. This move necessitates a much richer type of interpretive analysis than the methodological strictures of more positivist-oriented theorizing allows: thick, as opposed to thin, description in Clifford Geertz's formulation.[69] We must be able to tap into and unearth the constitutive social norms of a period, the unconscious boundaries and biases that frame experience, the symbolic forms that give meaning to behavior for a people.[70] These social norms and symbolic forms are crucial because they provide what might be called "the metaphysical underpinnings" of the constitutive features of world order. If only by unconscious biases and orientations common to a people, "social epistemology" is implicated in the architecture of world order. Medium theory, as used here, does not argue that the mode of communication *generates* these symbolic forms and cognitive biases; rather, it argues that changes in the mode of communication will "favor" or allow for the selection among the extant symbolic forms and biases of a society, thus giving rise to a new social epistemology—rethreading the webs of significance, in other words.

It is important to emphasize that the "fitness" between elements of social epistemology and a new communications environment is largely an *intergenerational* as opposed to an *intrapsychic* process. In other words, it does not mean that each individual person will suddenly abandon long-held metaphysical presuppositions and cognitive biases as a result of their exposure to a new communications environment. New technologies of communication do not carry within them mysterious magical properties that overpower those with whom they come in contact. Nor do they come equipped with their own special social epistemology. "Individualism" as a symbolic form is not invariably tied to the printing press (although, as I hope to demonstrate below, the former flourished in the environment of the latter). Rather, it means that in a particular communications environment, particular elements of social epistemology will have a better chance of finding a "niche" and thus surviving and flourishing over time. In other words, an increasing portion of those acculturated into a new communications environment will come to see a particular symbolic form or social construct as more "natural" and "reasonable"—more consistent with their overall communications experience—and it is through this intergenerational "selection" process that it will flourish over time.

Treating changes to social epistemology in this way—that is, as a kind of "selection" process in which specific ideas, symbols, values, and beliefs flourish or wither depending on a chance "fitness" with the communications environment—bears a close resemblance to an approach developed by biologist Richard Dawkins, and taken up by others, called "memetics."[71] Dawkins and other practitioners of memetics believe that the basic principles of "descent with modification" that Darwin outlined apply not just to "genes" but to the processes of cultural evolution as well—to the relative survival of different cultural units that Dawkins called "memes":

Examples of memes are tunes, ideas, catch-phrases, clothes, fashions, ways of making pots or building arches. Just as genes propogate themselves in the gene pool by leaping from body to body via sperm or eggs, so memes propogate themselves in the meme pool by leaping from brain to brain via a process which, in the broad sense, can be called imitation. If a scientist hears, or reads about, a good idea, he passes it on to his colleagues and students. He mentions it in his articles and his lectures. If the idea catches on, it can be said to propogate itself, spreading from brain to brain.[72]

Although Dawkins and other practitioners of "memetics" have not, as far as I know, conceived of a selection mechanism that includes changing modes of communication, there is an obvious compatibility in the approaches. And Dawkins's lengthy list of typical "memes" (tunes, ideas, catchphrases, etc) brings up an important analytical point: the ideas, values, beliefs, symbolic forms, and social constructs that comprise the social epistemology of a time would obviously blanket a wide spectrum of diverse traits. Tracking down every single one of those that flourish and wither with a change in the mode of communication would surely be a formidable task. So for analytical purposes I have broken them down into a manageable (though not necessarily exhaustive) set. In the chapters to follow that focus on changes to social epistemology (4 and 7), I examine three specific elements: *individual identities*, *spatial biases*, and *imagined communities*. As I hope to demonstrate, changes in all three of these elements (the way "the self" is conceived, the way space is ordered, and the way group identities are imagined), are crucial in providing what might be called the "metaphysical underpinnings" of world order. As I also hope to show, changes in modes of communication have an important impact on their evolution.

In sum, changes in modes of communication have an important effect on the nature and character of society and politics. These effects vary in terms of the social and historical context in which the technology is developed. New technologies of communication do not *generate* specific social forces and/or ideas, as technological determinists would have it. Rather, they *facilitate* and *constrain* the extant social forces and ideas of a society. The hypothesized process can be likened to the interaction between species and a changing natural environment. New media environments favor certain social forces and ideas by means of a functional bias toward some and not others, much the same as natural environments determine which species prosper by "selecting" for certain physical characteristics. In other words, social forces and ideas survive differentially according to their "fitness" or match with the new media environment—a process that is both open-ended and contingent.

There are two conceptually distinct ways in which these effects operate: distributional changes and changes to social epistemology. Distributional

changes refer to changes in the relative power of social forces, while changes
to social epistemology refer to changes among elements of the prevailing
mentalités collectives. These two conceptually distinct effects will in turn
provide the basis for the analytical scheme to be employed in the chapters
to follow. The study is divided into two parts, both of which are comprised
of three chapters:

- the first chapter in each part provides a historical and descriptive
  overview of the development of a new communications
  environment—printing in part 1 and hypermedia in part 2
  (chapters 2 and 5);
- the second chapter examines the distributional changes that result
  from the change in the mode of communication (chapters 3 and
  6);
- the third chapter examines the changes to social epistemology that
  result from the change in the mode of communication (chapters 4
  and 7).

Ecological Holism and Medium Theory

Having made these substantial modifications and elaborations to medium
theory, I am now in a better position to articulate more clearly the metatheoretical assumptions on which this study rests. The nonreductive, evolutionary medium theory approach outlined above must, by necessity, encompass a much wider perspective on the dynamics of human/technological
interaction than the simple monocausal picture portrayed in figure 1. Figure
2 depicts what I call an "ecological holist" picture of human existence. This
figure essentially unearths and clearly articulates the cultural materialist underpinning that is at least implicit in the writings of Innis, and perhaps most
explicit in the work of those medium theorists with a social anthropological
background like Goody, Mumford, and Gellner. It is significantly influenced
by the work of the French *Annales* school of historians, represented by Braudel, Duby, and Le Goff. Each ring in the figure refers to a conceptually
distinct component of human existence, none of which are reducible to the
others. The lines separating each component are not rigid, but blend into
one another at the margins.

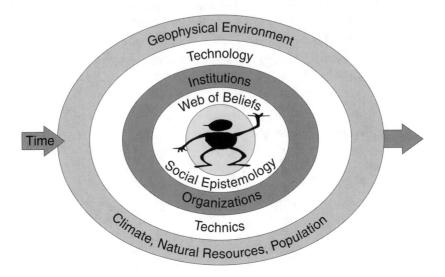

FIGURE 2. Ecological Holism

At the center are the basic inherited *neurophysiological adaptations and traits* shared by the species as a whole. Not to be confused with crude classical realist speculations on a fixed and determining "human nature," nor with the neoclassical "rational" actor assumptions,[73] these dispositions are confined to certain morphological or neurological properties shared by the species as a whole. The mere fact that they are so general as to be able to accommodate the vast diversity of cultures that have existed throughout history means that they will have little bearing on our analysis.[74]

The first ring refers to the *web-of-beliefs*, or what I referred to earlier as "social epistemology." To reiterate, it includes a historically contingent web of intersubjective values, beliefs, cognitive biases, and symbolic and linguistic forms into which a people are acculturated. This web-of-beliefs is not species-wide, but variable from culture to culture or epoch to epoch. It forms the broad epistemic lens through which a people interpret and act on the world around them. The web-of-beliefs blends into the next ring, which is composed of formal and informal *institutions*, ranging from states and corporations and organizations on the formal side to habits of actions and general modes of organizing human interaction and subsistence on the informal side.[75] Situated between the material environment and institutions is *technology*. In its narrow sense, technology refers to applied knowledge, but here the term is used in its more common sense to encompass both practical or applied knowledge (formally, technology) as well as the material instruments or artifacts of technology (formally, technics), such as the printing press.[76] As a material artifact, technology is constrained by the available resources of a time and place; but as a tool it is always conditioned by and emerges out of existing social institutions, knowledge, and skills—what we earlier referred to as the "social embeddedness" of technology. In ontological terms, technology should not be seen as merely an appendage *to* human society, but a deeply intertwined constitutive feature *of* human society. In Mazlish's words:

> The evidence now seems strong that humans evolved from the other animals through a continuous interaction of tool, physical, and mental-emotional changes. The old view—that humans arrived on the evolutionary scene fully formed and then proceeded to discover tools and the new ways of life that they made possible—no longer appears acceptable.[77]

The last ring refers to the material or *geophysical environment*, including demographics, disease, climate, and natural resources, all of which have a loose constraining effect on the broad trajectory and character of social evolution.[78] For millennia theorists have speculated on the impact of these broad material factors on the nature of human societies, and there is a strong tradition of "natural" theorizing reaching back to the ancient Greeks.[79] For the time-frame of most analyses, however, these basic material factors can be assumed away as relatively insignificant. But in studies that focus on the *longue durée*, they take on more importance.[80]

Although the figure may give the appearance of stasis, it is important to emphasize that ecological holism is fundamentally *historicist* in outlook, meaning that human existence is seen as a continuously evolving interplay between environmental and technological conditions, formal and informal institutions and practices, and intersubjective values and beliefs. From this perspective, "rationalities," identities, nations, and states—though potentially stable in their basic contours over relatively long periods of time—are nonetheless products of historical contingencies and thus subject to change as nature and society evolves.[81]

It is also important to be clear that change from this perspective is not the unfolding of predetermined patterns, or teleological processes, but rather "the grand aggregation and multiplication of the actions of individuals and groups in concrete historical circumstances as these individuals are responding to a multiplicity of biological, psychological and social needs."[82] Thus chance or contingency play an important part in the nature and direction of social evolution. From an ecological holist perspective, conceptual, technological, economic, or other changes in human patterns of interaction can alter the human developmental path in unexpected ways that defy more linear notions of change. In this respect, ecological holism runs contrary to those theories that argue for the existence of recurring "long-cycles" or progressive "stages of development" through which all societies are assumed to pass.[83] It is informed by a "Darwinist" view of history—that is, one that sees no unfolding logic to history, but only "descent with modification."[84]

Of course, fundamental change in the basic structures of human society is not continuous but episodic given the relative stability and endurance of human institutions, ideas, and habits. In Gaddis's words, "conditions can persist for years with so little alteration that people come to accept them as permanent."[85] In the past, there was a tendency among some social theorists to look for a single "master" variable that could be seen as driving all episodes of fundamental change, whether it be the mode of production or technologies of destruction. But according to the ecological holist perspective advanced here, the specific source of fundamental change at any one time in human history cannot be stated on a priori grounds, and typically reflects a multiplicity of factors—both material and ideal—that happen to converge in the form of a sudden transformation in human patterns of interaction.[86]

Medium theory can be seen as a subsidiary approach embedded in an ecological holist perspective, isolating those changes that are encouraged and facilitated by a change in the mode of communication. This focus should not be taken as an assertion of the fundamental primacy of communications over other spheres of human existence, but merely a heuristic division of scholarly labor. Technological changes in communications media are one among many other important innovations that produce novelty in social interaction. Yet because communication—like production and security—is so vital to human existence, these changes will likely have far-reaching implications. Thus while in this study I am focusing on the relationship between changing modes of communication and world order transformation, the focus itself should not be equated with a kind of "master narrative" to history centered on communications.

Ecological Holism, Medium Theory, and International Relations Theory

It should be clear from the overview that the tenor of medium theory is clearly aligned with the "historical sociology" side of the International Relations field, as opposed to the more ahistorical approaches Robert Keohane identifies as "rationalist."[87] Robert Cox points out that rationalist approaches, which he calls "problem-solving," are suitable to "periods of apparent stability or fixity in power relations."[88] Surprisingly, these approaches represent the majority of the field today, even though we appear to be in an era of fundamental transformation. As Gellner remarks: "The great paradox of our age is that although it is undergoing social and intellectual change of totally unprecedented speed and depth, its thought has become, in the main, unhistorical or ahistorical."[89]

The two dominant approaches in the field today—neorealism and neoliberalism—are ahistorical not because they are unable to amass "historical" details in support of their claims, but rather because they seek essentially to escape history by grounding their theories in fundamental presuppositions—be it the anarchic structure or the desire to maximize utilities—which are posited as universal (i.e., timeless, contextless) foundations.[90] In Adler's terminology, they are both examples of what he calls theories of "being"—"a prevalent notion that sees everything in nature and society as static and mechanistic, including change."[91] For neorealists especially, the main components of the international system are treated as if "suspended in space"—"time has little to do with them, and movement and change are linear. . . ."[92] Even those cyclical theorists like Robert Gilpin who appear to give a more dynamic treatment to the international system by allowing for differential growth still present change as merely the rearrangement of rationally motivated "units" under the universal constant of a constraining anarchic order.[93] Likewise, neoliberalism offers what Wendt calls a "behavioral conception of both process and institutions: they change behavior but not identities and interests."[94] For all their apparent differences over the question of relative versus absolute gains, neoliberals and neorealists are alike in assuming the natural order of world politics to be one of unitary rational actors in an anarchic setting.[95]

The alternative to theories of being, according to Adler, are theories of "becoming"—those that see human existence "as a permanent process of change and evolution, even that which appears to be static"—a category that obviously includes ecological holism.[96] There are few examples of the type of full-blown historicism characteristic of theories of "becoming" in the International Relations field, although that is changing. Increasingly, a number of scholars see their work as falling outside of either the neorealist or neoliberal camps, and what might be termed a "historicist" school of International Relations theorists can be identified in the field.[97] The common denominator of this school is a shared view of human institutions and practices (including states, nations, identities, and interests) as products of historical contingencies and thus subject to change over time. Historicists see politics not as a cyclical, recurring phenomenon (as neorealists clearly do) but rather as an open-ended process.

Historicists can be differentiated in terms of the relative weight they place on the "material" versus the "ideal" as explanatory variables—a distinction that harkens back to Marx and Hegel respectively. For example, Robert Cox's "historical structures" approach, which explicitly articulates an open-ended evolutionary theory that takes into account material environments, institutions, and intersubjective values and beliefs, ultimately falls toward the "material" end of the spectrum because of the overriding importance attached to the mode of production as a determinant variable.[98] Likewise, Daniel Deudney's ongoing reconstruction of materialist geopolitical theories—which explores the relationship among broad environmental conditions, changing technologies of destruction, and world order formation—also falls toward the "material" end because of the weight given to military technologies.[99] Toward the "ideas" end of the spectrum fall the social constructivist theories of Wendt, Kratochwil, and others, which focus on the historical malleability of interests, identities, and institutions.[100] These approaches tend to concentrate purely on the interaction between social epistemology and institutions to the exclusion of environmental or technological factors. They lack the "grounding" of the more materially encompassing theories outlined above, and tend to downplay or ignore material factors as causally significant variables in politics.

As shown in Figure 2, ecological holism can be seen as an attempt to overcome this binary opposition between "material" factors and "ideas," which are seen not in either/or terms, but as part of a single whole. Ecological holism takes as its starting point the basic materialist position that human beings, like all other organisms, are vitally dependent on, and thus influenced by, the environment around them. However, it recognizes that because human beings have the unique ability to communicate complex symbols and ideas, they do not approach their environment on the basis of pure instinct (as other organisms do) nor as a linguistically naked "given," but rather through a complex web-of-beliefs, symbolic forms, and social constructs into which they are acculturated and through which they perceive the world around them. As Luke describes:

> The ways in which people apprehend their environment is (pre)formulated by the statements about ideas, "reality," objects, facts, relations, and so forth that organize a particular field of reference. The human subject in any given historical era apprehends her or his world, the self, and the relations between self and others on the basis of historical discursive practices that name, locate, and organize concrete and abstract knowledge and experience.[101]

There are few examples of ecological holism in the field today, though Ruggie's work on historical transformation is a clear exception. In "Territoriality and Beyond," Ruggie states the ecological holist position that "material environments, strategic behavior, and social epistemology" are "irreducible to one another."[102] Other examples that are perhaps less explicitly illustrative include the work of Ernst Haas and Emanuel Adler, who share the view that "politics is a historical process that changes with physical changes and the evolution of meanings."[103] In their empirical work, both Haas and Adler have focused on a more narrow time-frame in which "physical changes" can be treated as a "given" for the purposes of analysis. Thus Adler's work on "epistemic communities" bears a strong resemblance to the social constructivism of Wendt and Kratochwil—the major difference being the latter are not explicit about the extent to which material, geophysical factors are part of their ontology.[104] Of course, the differences between ecological holism and social constructivism are minimal compared to their similarities, especially in contrast to mainstream rationalist approaches, which treat interests and identities as relatively fixed. However, ecological holism provides a more comprehensive picture of human existence, one that is vital for an examination of the type of large-scale historical changes undertaken here.

On Methodology

Obviously, the version of medium theory I have put forward is incompatible with a positivist methodology. Most important, the emphasis on historicity and radical contingency in social evolution clashes with the idea of laws standing apart from history, and thus, by extension, the use of the deductive-nomological or covering-law model of inquiry. But the covering-law model is not the only available methodology for the type of analysis in which I am engaged in this study. In recent years, theorists have begun to explore the use of *historical narrative* as a mode of explanation.[105] This mode seeks to link occurrences along a temporal dimension, tracing the variables and contingencies that were important in taking the evolutionary path down one road as opposed to another. Of course, narrative explanations are not confined to human personalities or what has often been called disparagingly the "history of events." As Donald Polkinghorne put it, "the narrative scheme organizes the individual events it addresses using a framework of human purposes and desires, including the limits and opportunities posed by the physical, cultural, and personal environments."[106] Nor do historical narratives preclude clear analytical schemes or logical protocols to increase the verisimilitude of their accounts. The use of counterfactuals is crucial to this mode of explanation, as are structured, focused comparisons.[107] So in the pages to follow, my arguments establishing the importance of changing modes of communication will rely not just on as much empirical evidence as can be gleaned from primary and secondary sources, but on logical arguments as well, pointing to "what might have been" had there been no change in the communications environment at all. Most important, though, in looking to the past in a structured, focused way, I have also constructed an analytical lens through which to interpret changes that are occurring today. In the long run, it is the relative utility of the latter that will ultimately prove to be the most important measure of this study.

Part 1

Printing and the Medieval to Modern
World Order Transformation

2 From the Parchment Codex to the Printing Press: The Sacred Word and the Rise and Fall of Medieval Theocracy

In 1212, Pope Innocent III—without a military force of his own—orchestrated a great coalition of western European princes designed to oust Otto IV of Brunswick as King of Germany and halt his bid for hegemony over Italy by installing Frederick II (Innocent's ward) in his place. Carrying out the Pope's bidding was Philip Augustus of France, who soundly defeated Otto's forces at the battle of Boivines in 1214. During the same period, Innocent became embroiled in a lengthy dispute with King John of England over the election of Stephen Langton, Innocent's appointment to the see of Canterbury. Although King John was initially hostile and recalcitrant, Innocent suspended church services throughout England and, turning again to Philip Augustus for help, threatened the invasion of England. Bowed under the awesome putative power of the Papacy, John not only conceded to the appointment of Langton as archbishop, but also recognized Innocent as his own feudal overlord.[1] The controversy resembled another instance 150 years earlier when a dispute between Pope Gregory VII and German King Henry IV over ecclesiastical appointments resulted in a Papal Bull of excommunication, which effectively freed Henry's subjects from their oath of fealty to him. The King's support rapidly diminished, and the once-powerful Henry was forced to seek absolution from Gregory—a humiliating defeat borne not of superior military force, but overwhelming moral authority.[2] The suasive power of successive popes in this respect is perhaps best evidenced by the ongoing series of military crusades called for by the Church against other civilizations, which were then undertaken willingly by princes, knights, and commoners.[3]

These illustrations all exemplify the power of the Roman Catholic Church over, and penetration into, secular authority during its zenith in the High Middle Ages. From the perspective of much of mainstream International Relations theorizing it is truly a remarkable anomaly that with no private army of its own, and initially no great material wealth, the small bishopric of Rome could eventually develop into "the most powerful feudal court in Europe, receiving oaths of allegiance from princes and kings, exacting taxes and interfering in affairs of state throughout Christendom. . . ."[4] The Church was the one institution that straddled all of the competing, cross-cutting jurisdictions of medieval political authority, and though its effectiveness and dominance were more than once undermined by secular power or incompetent rule, from the eleventh to the thirteenth centuries it came close to unifying western Europe under a centralized "papal monarchy." What explains the Church's predominance? According to Curran, its power cannot be understood without reference to "its early dominance over institutional processes of ideological production that created and maintained support for its exercise of power."[5] To understand the papacy, then, we must also understand the mode of communication.

In this chapter, I provide a historical narrative of developments in communication technologies leading up to the development of the printing press in western Europe. The bulk of the chapter will be devoted to an examination of the way the Church's hegemony over the medieval world order was supported by the communications environment of the time. This examination will then set the stage for an overview of the development of printing and the change in that communications environment. The printing press did not arrive on the European scene like a flash in the dark, but was the product of slow, converging social pressures for more efficient communications. It represented a much wider ferment in western European society as a whole, partially in response to the spiritual decline and growing secularism of the Roman Catholic Church. The purpose of this chapter, then, is to situate the change in the mode of communication in its historical context—to underscore what I earlier called the "social embeddedness" of technological innovation. The consequences for world order transformation of this change in the communications environment will then be taken up in the ensuing two chapters.

The Sanctity of the Written Word

Language and communication are such integral components of human life that it is difficult to imagine a time without the abstract symbols regularly employed by humans to convey meaning. Yet if we look back 35,000 years to the evolutionary juncture when modern humans displaced Neanderthals, and assume that human beings have been able to communicate the spoken word in some capacity since then, we must then move forward to nearly 32,000 years to find the point at which a crude form of writing was first invented.[6] Thus for most of its time on Earth the modern human species was characterized by primitive orality. Of course, human beings had been drawing pictures and scratching marks as memory aids for millennia prior to the invention of writing, but these pictographs and markings cannot be included as examples of true written scripts, which do "not consist of mere pictures, of representations of things, but [are] representation[s] of an *utterance*, of words that someone says or is imagined to say."[7] Most scripts have their origins in and probably evolved out of such graphic arts. They certainly depend on the same physical attributes: that is, the ability to manipulate tools with an opposable thumb and coordinated by the eye, ear, and brain.[8] The difference lies in the degree to which the graphic system of writing "succeeds in duplicating the linguistic one, that is, in the extent, first, of word-to-sign (semantic) correspondence and, secondly, of phonetic correspondence."[9]

The first such written system that we know of was developed among the Sumerians in Mesopotamia beginning around 3500 B.C. Archaeological evidence suggests this writing system evolved out of the use of clay tokens, which were used to record payments and inventories of grain following the shift to agricultural production at the beginning of the Neolithic period.[10] As society grew more complex and came more to depend on the clay tokens for facilitating transactions, the tokens themselves were dispensed with in favor of two-dimensional symbols that corresponded to the three-dimensional shapes of the tokens. This first undeciphered pictorial system from the city of Uruk IV is thought to have evolved gradually into the cuneiform (wedge-shaped) orthography used to write down the language of the Sumerians around 3100 B.C.—the earliest known system of writing.

There is a temptation in tracing the impetus for the development of writing to reduce it solely to the functional imperatives of economics or urbanization, but it is important to bear in mind that the reproduction of writing—whatever its ultimate origins—has always been closely associated with a spiritual elite. Social anthropologists and historians have usually attributed this association to the fragility of texts or tablets, which seem to favor the privileging of a class of clerics who are charged with the preservation of sacred norms and rules.[11] An even more compelling explanation probably lies in the point of view of those who first developed writing—a capability that "could not be credited to mere mortals."[12] It is not surprising, then, that most early civilizations acquainted with writing shrouded their origins in myths and legends, such as the Egyptian god Thoth—the creator of writing.[13] Nor is it surprising that those charged with reproducing and interpreting the word should be revered. According to Gellner, "the mysterious power of writing in recording, transmitting, and freezing affirmations and commands soon endows it with an awe-inspiring prestige, and causes it to be fused with the authority of ritual specialists."[14] The priest or cleric, as custodian of the sacred text, is a mediator with the forces or Deity "beyond" and thus achieves an empowerment associated with the skill required to interpret the word— a general pattern found especially among religions of the Book, such as Islam, Judaism, and Christianity.[15]

Looking back from the perspective of our own time, when the word has been dissolved into an electronic code and copies are cheap and plentiful, it is difficult to appreciate fully the way the text itself could have value beyond the words it contains. Yet it is important that we approach the manuscript culture of medieval Europe from this perspective of the distant origins of the sacred word for it helps to shed light on the privileged status of the medieval clergy. Similar to the position of ancient scribes in other cultures, medieval Church clerics were the guardians of the word, and the "Word was God." As a religion of the Book, the Roman Catholic Church carried over many of the same general attributes found in other such religions, including the veneration of the word and the reverence of those charged with its reproduction. One important pillar of Church authority, then, was the privileged position enjoyed by the literate clergy as guardians of the text in a largely illiterate society. As Anderson puts it, "The astonishing power of the papacy in its noonday is only comprehensible in terms of a trans-European Latin-writing clerisy, *and* a conception of the world, shared by virtually everyone, that the bilingual intelligentsia, by mediating between vernacular and Latin, mediated between earth and heaven."[16]

Consider, for example, the status of language during the early to High Middle Ages. At this time language and words were not generally conceived of as arbitrary and thus interchangeable signs (as they are today), but rather channels to ontological truth—emanations of reality rather than representations of it.[17] The spoken and the written word were considered to be continuous with nature, a belief reflected in the view that the meanings of words were tied to the things signified. This "Adamic" view of language sought knowledge through finding the divinely ordained, natural homology between words and things that was set down following Creation by Adam.[18] Michel Foucault describes how according to the Adamic view:

> There is no difference between the visible marks that God has stamped upon the surface of the earth, so that we may know its inner secrets, and the legible words that the Scriptures . . . have set down in the books preserved for us by tradition. The relation of these texts is of the same nature as the relation to things: in both cases there are signs that must be discovered.[19]

Accordingly, texts were considered sacred fonts of wisdom from a pure past and an Other World—a belief that often manifested itself in worship of the medium itself, to which was attributed metaphysical, quasi-magical powers. Marc Drogin explains:

> Since God or the gods invented the alphabet—everyone believed it to be divine inspiration—the letters were holy. Since it was letters that formed words, the words were equally holy. In a time when what was holy was born of the miraculous and when the fine line between miracle and magic was difficult to discern, the three terms could be easily interchanged. Letters and words were miraculous in origin and therefore were the stuff of magic.[20]

Drogin notes how it was not uncommon to find the mingling of words or texts in medicinal instructions, such as the herbal mixture called the holy salve in which the person preparing the mix is directed to write in it with a spoon: "Matthew, Mark, Luke, and John."[21] An eleventh-century manuscript advises patients prone to fever to wear strips of parchment around their necks on which is to be written "In the name of Our Lord, who was crucified under Pilate, FLEE YE FEVERS."[22] The mysterious powers attributed to the text help to explain the crusaders' odd practice of wearing a parchment scroll beneath their coats of mail, or having prayers and odd letter combinations inscribed on their weapons. Rituals such as these make sense only if the person performing them is acculturated into the belief that the word or text has a connection to the Divine. The exceptions to this rule are equally instructive for in the very defiance of the sanctity of the word, they reveal the scope and depth of the norm. For example, in 1022 a group of heretics were burned in Orleans for referring to the clergy's knowledge as human fabrications "written on the skins of animals," as opposed to what the heretics believed was the "law written in the inner man by the Holy Spirit."[23]

Although the Roman Catholic Church's sharing of this general tendency found among other religions of the Book does offer some insight into the power and status of the medieval clergy, it does not explain how the Church arrived at this position from its "obscure beginnings as a small persecuted community in the capital of the Roman Empire,"[24] nor how the Church's fortunes were related to a specific technology of communication. For a comprehensive explanation along these lines, we must trace the vagaries of the mode of the communication following the collapse of the Roman Empire in the fifth century. As will be shown below, the Church's rise to prominence was contingent on a combination of fortuitous circumstances in which we could include the peculiarities of the mode of communication. A variety of other historical contingencies not so fortuitous from the Church's perspective then contributed to its demise.

The Rise and Fall of Medieval Theocracy

The internal disintegration of the Roman Empire in the fourth and fifth centuries, compounded by successive waves of "barbarian" invasions, left much of western Europe outside the bounds of Roman administration.[25] In its heyday, the Roman Empire governed itself through the administration of a literate bureaucracy among whom communications rested significantly on light-weight papyrus rolls, easily transportable on a highly efficient network of roads.[26] With the Empire's demise, much of western Europe returned to a state of primitive orality and personalized forms of rule characteristic of the Germanic invaders.[27] In the city of Rome, the collapse of Imperial authority created a void into which the only plausible alternative was the bishopric of the Catholic Church, an alternative that was facilitated by the work of successive Christian emperors, who endowed the Church with special privileges and helped to outlaw paganism. Though many popes were weak and ineffectual through this period, the first who seemed to have perceived the opportunity for the bishopric of Rome was Pope Leo I (r. 440-461; also known as St. Leo the Great). By negotiating with the invading Huns and Vandals for the safety of the city of Rome, and by asserting the so-called Petrine Doctrine (which sought to link the Roman see directly to St. Peter) Leo vastly increased the prestige of the papacy throughout western Christendom. As Cantor explains, "half-consciously the pope worked to make the Roman episcopate the successor to the Roman state in the West."[28]

Leo's prominent ideological work was complemented by the growth of a literate monastic network that gradually spread through western Europe. Throughout the period of Imperial disintegration, many aristocrats converted to Christianity, carrying over to the Church their literary education and respect for the preservation of the written word characteristic of late antiquity.[29] To be sure, while the Church would soon count among its ranks nearly all literate individuals in Europe, literacy as a whole was limited to a small group. The norm for western Europeans, for whom much of life was violent and chaotic, was the spoken word.[30] Even many Church priests were confined to the bounds of primitive orality, unable to comprehend the Latin phrases they regularly parroted for their parishioners. But the veneration and preservation of the word that was carried over by former Roman aristocrats gradually became fused with the practices of monasticism, making the Church an island of literacy in an otherwise oral culture. In Cantor's words:

> The Latin church was preserved from extinction, and European civilization with it, by the two ecclesiastical institutions that alone had the strength and efficiency to withstand the impress of surrounding barbarism: the regular clergy (that is, the monks) and the papacy.[31]

The molding of Christian monasticism around the preservation and veneration of the written word was first given doctrinal formulation in the works of St. Benedict and Cassiodorus in the early Middle Ages, where the idea of the monasticist scriptorium was outlined and book copying was portrayed as a sacred act.[32] Doctrines flowing from these two figures instilled the close connection between the ability to read and the religious life of the monk, as well as the cultural and spiritual importance of the conservation and transmission of the written word. "This meant that the monastery needed to have the means—a library, a school, a scriptorium—that quite naturally made it an exclusive and culturally privileged place."[33] One reason why the monasteries thrived in the early Middle Ages was precisely this exclusion from the disorder of life outside. Ironically, their self-imposed isolation also acted as a magnet for those drawn to learning, for "the Benedictine monastery alone, during the early Middle Ages, had the continuity, the dedication, the library, and the substantial supply of teachers to serve as an effective educational institution."[34]

Another reason why the monastic network thrived in the early Middle Ages relates to a choice of media in the early history of the Catholic Church. The Roman Empire had developed a relatively efficient postal system and bureaucracy based mostly on the use of the light-weight, but fragile, papyrus rolls.[35] Archaeological evidence of the earliest Christian Bible codices from Egypt reveal that the Christian community was nearly alone in favoring parchment over the papyrus roll.[36] Early Church fathers and missionaries preferred the parchment codex because it was both more suitable for easy reference than the cumbersome scroll and it was more durable under poor traveling conditions—an especially important feature for traveling preachers. Some historians believe that Christians remained wedded to the parchment codex because they were a persecuted sect without access to the papyrus leaves used by official Rome.[37] In any event, parchment, rather than papyrus, was the medium of choice for the Christian religion, and it remained so into the Middle Ages as a result of both institutional inertia and functional complementarity. If only out of the sheer force of habit, in other words, the Christian community formed an institutional bond with parchment—a fortuitous choice as circumstances would later reveal.

According to medium theory, communications environments have distributional consequences insofar as they empower specific social forces; the relationship between parchment and monasticism is a clear illustration in this respect. As Innis notes, "Parchment as a medium was *suited* to the spread of monasticism from Egypt throughout western Europe."[38] Parchment, or *membranae*, was manufactured from the hides of animals, a variation on leather making.[39] Unlike papyrus, which was grown almost exclusively in the Egyptian Nile delta region, parchment was especially suited to the decentralized agrarian-rural monastic network that spread through western Europe after the collapse of the Roman Empire. Individual monasteries could remain self-sufficient, manufacturing parchment from the skins of their own livestock or those from the surrounding farms. Sheep, cows, goats, rabbits, and squirrels all provided the skins for various qualities of parchment. Goose quills were used for pens, while ink was supplied out of a combination of gall nuts, organic salts of iron, and lampblack. All of these materials were in abundance in the woods and valleys of western Europe in the early Middle Ages.[40] Furthering the papal-monastic interests was the near-total disappearance of papyrus from western Europe at this time. The pre-fifth-century Roman Empire was able to sustain the importation and production of papyrus rolls by its links to the eastern Mediterranean and beyond. Following the collapse of the Empire and the accompanying rise of Islam in Egypt and elsewhere, however, papyrus exports to the West significantly diminished, leaving parchment the sole remaining medium of written communications.[41] Parchment—in a sense by default—became the dominant medium of written communications. Coincidentally, it was also the medium produced by Roman Catholic monastic orders.

We can see, then, how the mode of communication "favored" the interests of the Roman Catholic Church. Parchment and the papal-monastic network formed a symbiotic relationship in the communications environment of the early Middle Ages: monasteries were largely self-contained islands of literacy and centers of knowledge reproduction in an oral-agrarian environment. Parchment was the medium of choice of the early Church fathers. It was sustained as such through institutional inertia and functional compatibility with missionary/monastic life. It was produced from materials that were in abundance in western Europe, and it had no serious rival. Secular literacy had virtually disappeared in most of western Europe leaving the clergy as the sole custodians and suppliers of written information. From these converging circumstances surrounding the communications environment of the time, then, the Roman Catholic papal-monastic network began to flourish and spread throughout Western Europe. Its monopoly over the reproduction of written information was to have significant consequences for the prevailing cosmology of the medieval world order.

Structural Characteristics of the Church's Hegemony in the High Middle Ages

Given the Church's early monopoly over written communications, it is no surprise that knowledge reproduction was distorted—"pagan writing was neglected and Christian writing emphasized."[42] Cantor points out that Benedictine monasteries took a functional, Augustinian approach to copying classical texts, using them in a secondary derivative sense, and passing over those that contradicted the Gospels or had little relevance to Christian doctrine.[43] Likewise, Miccoli notes how monks were instilled into a ritual that emphasized "a deep assimilation of God's word through a constant and repeated rereading of Scripture (*meditatio* and *rumunatio*)."[44] In principle, ancient pagan works had no autonomy in the official Church cosmology, but were tolerated for instrumental reasons—that is, "as they contributed to the linguistic and literary formation of the monks."[45] Of course, it was precisely because of the toleration of pagan authors—even in a subordinate sense—that many important classical works were transmitted. Ironically, other classical works were passed on to posterity quite by accident: when parchment was in short supply, monks would often re-copy the Gospels over pagan works, and it is through this recopying process that many ancient texts were rediscovered.[46] But the fact remains that "between the sixth century and the middle of the eighth century, virtually all classical texts ceased to be copied."[47] As suggested above, this selective reproduction was not so much a matter of deliberate censorship as it was a combination of indifference and priority. At the very least, it was a product of the heavy demand placed on scribes to copy the scriptures alone. Important in this respect is the relatively expensive and laborious manuscript copying process, which may have been a seasonal activity in parts of Europe.[48] Nonetheless, the monastic reproduction process was clearly biased toward the Holy Word, and as a result it both reaffirmed and reinforced a reading of history that emphasized the destiny of the Church in that historical process, to the exclusion of other possible interpretations. In Miccoli's words:

> when monasticism reduced all other reality to its own image and its own religious and cultural schemata in the aim of bending them to an explanation and exaltation of the choice and the experience of monastic life, it discovered the subterranean ideological, political, and

social roots of its own origins that provided further support to its affirmation in history.[49]

While it would most certainly be wrong to portray the Church as a quasi-
totalitarian organization—a medieval "Big Brother"—the monopoly over the
written word did confer special advantages. At the very least, the guarding
and sifting of organized knowledge kept a loose discursive boundary on cosmological speculation, especially in the early Middle Ages. We must not
forget in this respect that monasteries were, for most of the Middle Ages, the
sole educational outlet instructing, "at a conservative estimate 90 percent of
the literate men between 600 and 1100 . . ."[50] Duby makes the important
point that no distinction was made between culture and propaganda during
the Middle Ages since "to educate was to convert."[51] Those who did not get
formal education attended mass. Curran asserts that the "proportion of the
adult population in Europe regularly attending mass during the central Middle Ages was almost certainly higher than the proportion of adults in contemporary Europe regularly reading a newspaper."[52] And the papal curia
exercised a tight control over the content of the mass through set liturgies,
reinforcing a macro-micro coordination of Church doctrine throughout
western Europe.[53]

This hegemony over cultural and ideological production was buttressed
by the maintenance of huge Papal archives which provided important political and legal leverage; forgeries, like the infamous Donation of Constantine, were used by the Papacy to provide legitimacy to assertions of Church
authority over, and independence from, secular rule.[54] This particular document first emerged during the eighth century, and was used throughout
the Middle Ages as evidence of a supposed grant from the Roman Emperor
Constantine to Pope Sylvester I conceding supreme authority to the Pope
over Italy and the rest of the western Church.[55] The Donation of Constantine
was hardly an exception: forgeries were prominent ways of establishing privileges, especially monastic charters. For example, following the Norman
Conquest of England forgeries among the local Black monks rose dramatically.[56] In addition, the Church's monopoly over the reproduction of legal
documents provided an important tangible base to which justifications of its
place in the social and political hierarchy could be referred. In the communications environment of the Middle Ages, few if any other groups had
access to such a formal resource.

The Church's influence over ideology did not rest with matters purely cosmological. Because the aristocracy throughout much of the Middle Ages were generally illiterate, they depended on the interposition of clergy to help carry out various administrative functions. This comfortable interlocutor position meant that the Church was able to intervene, if only indirectly, in secular, as well as ecclesiastical, matters. As Bloch points out, "the princes were obliged to rely on the clerical element among their servants for services that the rest of their entourage would have been incapable of rendering."[57] Thus William of Normandy turned to the monks after his conquest of England "to organize a wiser and more prudent administration of the crown's holdings."[58] More so than other members of society, church clerics and monks had a reputation for "an introspective wisdom and a power of analysis, a capacity for detached realism" that made them attractive for secular administrative functions—a capacity related, no doubt, to their ability to read and write.[59] By the twelfth century it was not uncommon to find Benedictine monks employed as royal chancellors, state advisers, and chief ministers for secular rulers—a considerable shift from their origins as members of self-contained, isolated islands of literacy in the ninth century.[60] Of course, intervention along these lines had important political consequences. According to Marc Bloch:

> It is important to realize that the decisions of the powerful of this world were sometimes suggested and always expressed by men who, whatever their national or class allegiances, none the less belonged by their whole training to a society by nature universalist and founded on spiritual things. Beyond question they helped to maintain, above the confusion of petty local strife, a concern for certain wider issues. When required . . . to give written form to acts of policy, they felt impelled to justify them officially by reasons drawn from their own moral code.[61]

Gradually, the Church came to rely more and more on written administration and formal documentation to underpin its authority. By the mid-twelfth century, under Alexander III, the administrative and judicial activity of the papal curia expanded and became more specialized—a reflection of the way the written word permeated all Church activity.[62] Correspondences issued from Rome increased dramatically during this period. Church doctrines—formulated at the official Lateran Councils—were issued in formal

proclamations, such as the *Decretum*, and accepted authoritatively throughout much of western Christendom.[63]

While written communications were the backbone of the papal-monastic
information network, the Church disseminated its message to the local populations through a medieval multimedia experience designed to accommodate mass illiteracy. As Le Goff points out:

> Latin Christianity made an important choice in the Carolingian ep-
> och. It chose images, rejecting the nonfigurative art of the Jews and
> the Moslems and the iconoclasm of Greek Byzantine Christianity and
> firmly establishing medieval Christian anthropomorphism.[64]

The Church consciously employed the image to convey the Christian
message to the illiterate masses in a way that was deeply symbolic. Probably
the best-known medieval dictum on art is Gregory the Great's pronounce-
ment that pictures are the "books of the illiterate."[65] This was a time prior
to the emergence of imitation and perspective characteristic of "realism" —
a time in which the didactic and ideological purposes of forms in paintings
and sculptures far outweighed in significance their aesthetic value. Visual
art "was not so much an expression of the visible world, as of the spoken
word in a still predominantly oral society."[66] The images reproduced in out-
wardly visible signs the social and cosmological hierarchy of the times.[67] For
example, colors had a symbolic content as part of a hierarchical value system
in which red and blue were marks of power and status, while yellow was the
color of evil and deceit.[68] Though imagery was found on the margins of
manuscripts, most of the population encountered them on the walls and
stained glass of local cathedrals, which invariably featured the macabre tor-
tures of hell alongside the visual narratives of Christ's teachings. The cathedrals themselves, in their very form, were significant in a symbolic sense as
well: "the construction of churches towering over their pastoral flock sym-
bolized the looming presence of God over all aspects of life."[69] This multimedia experience did a great deal to shape the character of the medieval
mentalité, which did not share the cognitive boundaries so characteristic of
modernity between the "real" and the "imaginary," or the "natural" and the
"metaphysical."[70]

Although my theoretical lens has been focused on the constraints imposed and the opportunities created by the communications environment,

other factors were responsible for the Church's rise to hegemony. Most important in this respect is the appeal of the message regardless of the medium: we should not lose sight of the fact that Christianity offered a coherent and compelling narrative of justice that both explained the disorder of the times and offered a promise of salvation in an Other World.[71] This coherent moral vision strongly resonated in the chaotic environment of the early Middle Ages in Europe, where disorder and brutality were the norm for most people. The Church was also particularly adept at tailoring its message to suit the vagaries of local communities, especially in the early Middle Ages when myths and rituals of pagan sects were made compatible with the teachings of Christ. Under the astute stewardship of Pope Gregory I (the Great), the Church purposefully assumed a quasi-magical hue to conform to the pagan rituals of the Germanic and Frankish peoples.[72] As Curran points out, "the whole paraphernalia of ecclesiastical sorcery and ritual was of crucial importance in mediating an ecclesiastical construction of reality that underpinned papal hegemony."[73] Each regular routine of daily life was informed by elaborate and mystical church rituals, such as baptism, confirmation, marriage, and burial. The Church actively encouraged the veneration of saints with miracle powers—a superstition strongly reminiscent of the pagan worship of various natural gods.[74] And each of these adaptations was a mixture of "cosmic-universal and the mundane-particular" so that "however vast Christendom might be, and was sensed to be, it manifested itself *variously* to particular Swabian or Andalusian communities as replications of themselves."[75]

While it is true that a coherent and persuasive message, coupled with astute leadership, helped contribute to the Church's success, it was the hospitable communications environment that was critical in underpinning the papal-monastic network as "the dominant institution in Europe's information system."[76] The early choice of the Church fathers to adopt parchment turned out to be a fortuitous one that favored the spread of the papal-monastic network throughout western Europe. The absence of widespread literacy, the decline of papyrus as an alternative medium of written communications, plus a material environment whose properties favored the production of parchment, were all significant elements in the success of the early Church. Its monopoly over written documentation would, in turn, provide an important source of leverage over secular rulers both in terms of justifying the Church's place in medieval cosmology, and, more concretely, in terms of supplying administrative personnel for secular rulers. Once the communications environment changed, however, the Church was placed at a severe disadvantage.

Counter-Hegemonic Forces and the Decline of the Church

No sooner had the Church reached its pinnacle of power in the High Middle Ages than counter-hegemonic forces began to surface that would eventually undermine its authority.[77] Many of these forces emerged precisely in reaction to the Church's monopoly over written information. By the thirteenth and fourteenth centuries, the papacy had become so permeated with and dependent on the written word that its institutions grew more legalistic and bureaucratic, with the papal curia evolving into a complex, top-heavy, administrative organ. Throughout the High Middle Ages, successive popes and Church prelates were likely to be just as informed by canon law and practical affairs as they were in spiritual matters.[78] Such a formalist-legalist infrastructure had the unfortunate consequence of gradually distancing many of the Church administrators from the spirit of popular devotion that had helped make Christianity a success in the first place. As Cantor relates:

> The lawyer-popes of the twelfth and thirteenth centuries were far more successful in fulfilling the administrative than the spiritual responsibilities of their office. Their juristic education and bureaucratic experience did not tell them how to cope with the emotional religiosity and heretical inclinations of the urban communities.[79]

Underscoring the pervasiveness of the written word, Barraclough notes that the "papal curia had the atmosphere of a law-court or business-office."[80] Within the Church many lower-level clergy grew skeptical of the formal ecclesiastical hierarchy, believing that Rome had less and less affinity to the teachings of the Gospels or the standards of apostolic poverty.[81] The most apparent sign of this smoldering dissatisfaction was the sudden ignition of popular heresies in various periods and regions. Many of these heresies defined themselves in fundamentalist, back-to-basics terms, hostile to the abstract, legalistic machinery that now characterized the Roman Catholic Church.[82] Beginning in the eleventh century, hermit-saints preaching ascetic tendencies and withdrawal from the spiritual degradation of worldly life made their appearance.[83] These heretical movements were the first in a series of popular challenges to Church hegemony on spiritual matters that, over the next few centuries, would eventually culminate in the Protestant Reformation—a topic that will be taken up again in the following chapter.

A second area where the transnational authority of the Roman Catholic Church was being challenged was in the sphere of knowledge reproduction. As outlined above, from the fall of Rome to the twelfth century the papal-monastic network maintained a near-total monopoly on the reproduction of the written word. From the end of the twelfth century onward, however, a profound social transformation took place.[84] Gradually, secular literacy began to rise among the urban populations, and in particular among secular administrators—a slow shift that signals the first signs of a changing communications environment. The increasing reliance on the scribe and the written word that accompanied rising secular literacy placed strains on the functional capacity of the monastic network to meet the demands of a growing literate populace. Centers of knowledge reproduction, many of which were not contained within the formal Church hierarchy, arose to service this increased demand. For example, one area in society where the demand was high and where an alternative book trade developed was within the newly founded universities.[85] A new reading public was generated by the estabishment of universities that, while still chiefly clerical, was not formally attached to a religious organization but to the corporate university community. Professors and students needed texts for their courses, and libraries were established within universities to meet the demand for manuscripts. Professional craftsmen, organized as Guilds of Scriveners or Stationers, were then hired by the university to reproduce scholarly texts.[86] The establishment of these universities represented a growing "secularization" of learning and education that further undermined the monopoly of knowledge maintained by the monastic orders up to the High Middle Ages.

In other areas of society too, new reading publics emerged that yearned for secular literature. For example, an urban literate bourgeois class was first appearing alongside the nobility and the clergy. As Thomas describes, "Lawyers, lay advisers at Court, state officials, and, later on, rich merchants and town citizens—all needed books, not only in their own subjects like law, politics or science, but also works of literature, edifying moral treatises, romances and translations."[87] Works in the vernacular began to appear as growing exceptions to the Latin norm and as reflections of the gradually rising strength of local, secular identities and communities. Yet a further erosion of the monastic monopoly was the rise of government bureaucracies requiring secular, literate administrators who were increasingly siphoned off from the universities. This change was reflected in the supercession of law over theology as the specialization of choice for most students.[88] Even within largely illiterate circles social relations were gradually succumbing to the written word: by the thirteenth century, property transactions between peasants were being recorded by charter rather than the oath.[89]

These converging pressures naturally focused attention on ways of "improving the supply of manuscripts to meet the rising level of demand."[90] Traditional monastic techniques were insufficient to service the increasing dependence of all spheres of society and economics on the written word. As a result of these rising pressures, manuscript reproduction (which now occurred increasingly outside of the papal-monastic network) grew more specialized and complex. Separate workshops sprouted to deal with various components of the reproduction process, with copyists in one shop, rubricators in another, and illuminators in yet another.[91] Another improvement was the advent of paper as an alternative material to parchment. Paper first made its appearance in western Europe in the twelfth century; it was imported into Italy by Arab merchants, who themselves had acquired it from China in the eighth century.[92] Paper production techniques were also acquired by the Christian West following the reconquest of Spain from the Muslims, who had been using paper regularly since at least the tenth century.[93] Unlike parchment, which was expensive to produce, heavy in form, and generally difficult with which to work, paper was cheap and light-weight. By the late fourteenth century, paper was being offered for sale in Europe for about one-sixth the price of parchment.[94] But despite its apparent superiority, paper was initially slow to spread throughout Europe. Resistance was probably due to a combination of its relative fragility, craftsmen's inertia, and religious bigotry. The Abbot of Cluny, Peter the Venerable, was probably not alone in having a contempt for paper because of its association with the "infidel" Jews and Arabs.[95] Once the social demand for cheaper books intensified, however, paper spread rather quickly and the resistance gradually evaporated.[96] According to Febvre and Martin:

> the demand for paper was felt in many new fields: teaching spread, business transactions became more complex, writing multiplied and there was a growing need for paper for non-literary uses, by tradesmen,

haberdashers, grocers, chandlers. A whole new species of trades was created which depended on paper: carriers, box-makers, playing-card makers, bill-posters and related trades.[97]

The Printing Press

Of course, these very same converging social pressures for more efficient communications focused energy not only on the material on which the written word was produced, but also on the *technique* of reproduction. As Schottenloher put it, "The actual shining hour for paper, however, came only with the discovery of printing, when printing found in paper its most powerful ally."[98] An example of the widespread pressures in the fifteenth century for a method of manuscript reproduction can be found among the many multiple claims to the invention of the printing press. For instance, many Dutch believe that their countryman Laurens Janszoon Coster should be given credit for experimenting with movable wooden character types in the 1430s.[99] In France, documents from Avignon reveal that between 1444 and 1446 contracts were issued to Procopius Waldvogel to teach the art of "artificial writing."[100] Whether accurate or not, however, the most widely attributed inventor of the printing press in Europe is the Mainz goldsmith Johann Gensfleisch zur Laden, or Gutenberg. The source of this judgment is a number of cryptic documents surrounding a series of lawsuits that date to 1439 in Strasbourg. The documents reveal that Gutenberg and his creditors were involved in a legal tussle over a number of Gutenberg's inventions, one of which was a new art that involved the use of a press, some pieces (*Stucke*), some forms (*Formen*) made of lead, and things related to the action of the press (*der zu dem Trucken gehoret*).[101]

As Dudley points out, Gutenberg's invention was actually a synthesis of the punch the goldsmiths used for striking inscriptions into metal, the wine-press (which had come to Germany from the Romans), and the perfection of an ink that would adhere to metal type.[102] Although paper had come to Europe from China through the Arabs, and although the Chinese and the Koreans had been employing a similar method of printing with movable characters since the tenth century, the evidence suggests that the development of the European printing press was an autonomous development.[103]

The first printed works did not immediately change the appearance and form of medieval manuscripts; in fact, the early printers went to great lengths to produce precise imitations. So closely do some of the early printed works resemble manuscripts that they are virtually indistinguishable to the untrained eye. Febvre and Martin note that "The 42-line Bible for example was printed in a letter-type which faithfully reproduced the handwriting of the Rhenish missals."[104] Before 1500 the majority of printed works—about 70 percent—were in Latin, with about 45 percent of them being religious in content.[105] What *was* revolutionary about the new invention was the truly profound impact it had on the quantities that could be produced and distributed and the time it took to produce them.

About 20 million books were printed *before 1500* in Europe among a population at the time of about 100 million.[106] This number of books, produced in the first fifty years of printing, eclipsed the entire estimated product of the previous thousand years.[107] Febvre and Martin estimate that 150 million to 200 million were then produced in the next hundred years.[108] In relative terms, the output of printed material was not just a change in kind, but a true revolution in communications. Of course the ability to reproduce large volumes of material with such ease meant that printed works were also significantly cheaper to produce than manuscripts. For example, in 1483 the Ripoli Press charged three florins per quinterno for setting up and printing Ficino's translation of Plato's *Dialogues*. Eisenstein estimates that a scribe might have charged one florin per quintino for duplicating the same work. However, while the Ripoli Press would have printed 1,025 copies, the scribe would have turned out only one.[109]

Although the technology itself was revolutionary, what fueled the spread of the printed word, as Anderson points out, was its convergence with the early printers' commercial ethos and an available market across Europe hungry for printed material.[110] Following the initial activities in Mainz of Gutenberg and his partners, Fust and Schoeffer, printing centers were established in a number of cities throughout western Europe to exploit the new market. Menthelin printed a Bible in Strasbourg in 1459. By 1475, printing workshops had been established throughout the Rhineland, and in Paris, Lyons, and Seville.[111] By 1480, printing centers had sprouted through all of Western Europe, from Oxford and London to Krakow and Budapest, from Lubeck and Rostock to Naples and Cosenza—in all to 110 towns stretching across western Europe.[112] By 1500, the number of towns with printing centers had risen to 236.[113] By the sixteenth century, western Europe had entered a new communications environment at the center of which were cheap, mass-produced printed documents emanating from the many printing presses stretched across the land.

In this chapter, I have traced the development of communication technologies through the Middle Ages leading up to the invention of the printing press in the mid-fifteenth century. I have argued that the rise of the Church in the early Middle Ages was contingent on the communications environment of the time. Its spiritual attachment to literacy and the reproduction of the written word, its use of parchment as a medium of communication, and the specific material and ecological circumstances of western European all helped produce a hospitable environment for the Church's rise to hegemony in the Middle Ages. While the Roman Catholic Church had maintained a monopoly over written communications up to the twelfth century, from that point onward a gradual change in the communications environment began to occur, as evidenced by the growth of secular literacy and the use and reproduction of written documents outside of the formal papal-monastic network. In this respect, the invention of printing actually represents the culmination of slowly accumulating social pressures. In other words, the invention of printing was not a sudden "out-of-nowhere" development, but was an outgrowth of converging social pressures for more efficient communications. In conjunction with the broader social and economic conditions of the time, however, once printing began to spread through Western Europe, it revolutionized the communications environment with significant consequences for society and politics. In the next two chapters, I examine the ways in which the emergence of this new communications environment played a part in the transformation of the medieval world order.

3 Print and the Medieval to Modern World Order Transformation: Distributional Changes

Changes in the mode of communication have far-reaching, fundamental implications for the social and political infrastructure of an era and for the trajectory of social evolution. In chapter 1 I outlined two conceptually distinct effects that arise from a change in the mode of communication: distributional changes and changes to social epistemology. In this chapter, I concentrate only on the former.

Distributional changes are changes in the relative power of social forces as a consequence of the change in the mode of communication. Because modes of communication transmit and store information in unique ways, social forces whose interests match a communications environment will be favored while those whose interests do not will be placed at a disadvantage. Social forces survive differentially, in other words, according to their "fitness" with the new media environment—a process that is both open-ended and contingent. Thus, medium theory offers neither an explanation of the genesis of particular social forces, nor why they were animated by particular interests as opposed to others. Its purpose is to explain why those forces flourished or withered at a particular historical juncture.

Distributional changes undercut some social forces while they advance the interests of others. In this chapter, I examine the way distributional changes associated with the development of printing played a part in the medieval-to-modern world order transformation in Europe. I begin by examining the way the change in the mode of communication helped to

dissolve the architecture of political authority in the late Middle Ages. Specifically, I explore the way two social forces, the Protestant Reformation and
scientific humanism, were favored by the new media environment to the
disadvantage of the Roman Catholic Church. I then examine the way transformations in socioeconomic relations that were encouraged by the change
in the mode of communication helped to undermine the basis of feudal
social relations and pave the way for modern contractual socioeconomic
relations among an increasingly important segment of the late medieval
population: the urban bourgeoisie. This particular distributional change had
what we might call a "leveling" effect on patterns of political and economic
obligation, at least in urban areas, cutting through the entangled webs of
personal loyalties characteristic of the feudal era and opening up the possibility for common rule from a single center. Finally, I turn to the way the
change in the mode of communication favored the rise of modern state
bureaucracies and centralized political authority throughout parts of western
Europe. As many have pointed out, the converging interests of the latter two
social forces—the urban bourgeoisie and centralizing state monarchies—
were crucial in molding the architecture of modern world order in Europe.

The New Media Environment and the Dissolution of the Medieval Order

The Protestant Reformation

As outlined at the end of the previous chapter, by the fourteenth and
fifteenth centuries strong social forces were emerging with novel agendas
and interests that were pushing at the margins of the Church's hegemony
over knowledge reproduction. Some of these social forces can be characterized as reactionary movements within the Church itself. In this category, we
would include the various religious "heresies" that periodically and sponta-
neously surfaced throughout western Europe beginning in the twelfth century. Although their specific goals and ideologies varied considerably, these
heretical movements arose during the High Middle Ages mostly in reaction
to the Church hierarchy, which, as pointed out in the previous chapter, was
assuming a more legalistic and secular face distanced from the popular devotion that marked its appeal during its embryonic days as a missionary sect.[1]
The topheavy administrative organs of the Papal government appeared less

"other-worldly" and more corrupt, especially as successive popes engaged in or succumbed to power-political machinations—an image doubly reinforced by events such as the Great Schism.[2] This decline in Church popularity is reflected in the way many Christians saw the "Black Death" plague that swept through western Europe in the fourteenth century as a symbol of God's dissatisfaction with the corruption of the Church.[3]

Prior to the emergence of printing, the Church had been relatively successful in squelching and containing heresies primarily "because it always had better internal lines of communication than its challengers."[4] Those that were not stamped out by violence, or *compelle intrare*, were more than likely to be coopted by a form of special privilege or to be ignored altogether, as various heresies flickered and then faded without means of mass communication.[5] Febvre and Martin wonder "what might have happened if some of the earlier heresies (the Hussite, for example) had the power of the press at their disposal—power that Luther and Calvin used with great skill, first in the attack on Rome and then in the diffusion of their new doctrines."[6] The Inquisition, established in the thirteenth century, was a reflection of both the growing heretical elements within society and the Church's more stringent reprisals against them.[7] It remained an effective countermeasure so long as the doctrines flowing from heretical movements could be halted by taking measures against the persons upon whom the widespread transmission of such doctrines depended. With the rapid dissemination and publication afforded by printing, however, heretical movements had a much better chance of spreading their message beyond the locality in which they emerged, making it much more difficult for the Church to take effective countermeasures.

To illustrate the way technological innovations have unintended consequences, and how fathoming such consequences are difficult for those living through them, it is interesting to note that the Church was initially enthusiastic about the printing press, making thorough use of it, for example, in its anti-Turkish crusade.[8] One particular cardinal, Nicholas of Cusa, referred to the printing press as a "divine art" because of the way that the technology would enable poor priests who would otherwise be unable to afford Bibles to have access to cheaper, mass-produced versions.[9] And it is somewhat ironic that the first dated printed product from Gutenberg's workshop was an indulgence—the very emblem of Church corruption in the eyes of the Protestant Reformation.[10] In fact, the demand for printed books and liturgies among Catholic churchmen drove the initial establishment of printing presses throughout Europe in the latter half of the fifteenth century. Some of the largest monasteries, like Cluny and Citeaux at Dijon, invited printers from Germany to set up printing workshops and to teach monks the art of printing.[11] The early printers thrived on commissions from monasteries and cathedrals for Latin bibles, missals, psalters, and antiphonaries.[12] In one of the first books printed by the Brothers of the Common Life in Rostock there appeared the dedication that printing was the "handmaid of the Church."[13] Only hindsight could tell them how wrong they were.

It is well known among historians and laypersons alike that the printing press was closely intertwined with the Protestant Reformation. What is often confused is the specific causal relationship between the two, with technological determinists often attributing to the printing press the genesis of the Protestant Reformation itself.[14] However, prior to print there were many other similar outbreaks of heresies, which clearly mitigates any simplistic one-to-one connection. And certainly the outbreak of the Protestant Reformation cannot be explained without reference to the deteriorating economic and social conditions of central and northern Europe, which created an oppressive and intolerable environment for many.[15] As Luke describes, "Before Luther became a figure of public and political interest in 1517, German burghers and peasants, artisans and merchants, and many humanist academics shared a feeling of unrest and dissatisfaction with existing social, economic, and political-religious conditions, and were ready for a change towards what for them promised to be a more just and Christian society."[16] What could be said with confidence is that printing had a revolutionary effect on the extent to which one particular heresy could spread widely and rapidly with devastating consequences for the Church's containment strategies. In other words, the properties of the printing environment favored the interests of the Protestant Reformation to the disadvantage of the Papal hierarchy.

How did the Protestant Reformation "fit" the printing environment? Most revolutionary was the way that printing afforded an opportunity for one person to reach a mass audience in an unprecedentedly short period of time. In 1517, the German theologian Martin Luther publicized 95 theses in Latin criticizing a variety of Church practices, centering mostly on the rise in tithes, indulgences, and benefices. As Dudley notes: "A century earlier, the issue might have smoldered for years before breaking into flame. Even then, its effects would have been purely local, as in the case of the followers of John Huss whose revolt (1419–1436) had been confined to Bohemia."[17]

Within fifteen days Luther's theses had been translated into German, summarized, and distributed to every part of the country.[18] During Luther's life, five times as many works authored by Luther alone were published than by all the Catholic controversialists put together.[19] Martin Luther alone was responsible for 20 percent of the approximately 10,000 pamphlet editions issued from presses in German-speaking territories between 1500 and 1530.[20] Initially, the volume increased dramatically, with Luther's published output rising from 87 printings in 1518 to a high of 390 printings in 1523.[21] As Anderson put it, "In effect, Luther became the first best-selling author *so known*."[22] And of course the rise in output was not restricted to that emanating from Luther alone; from 1517–1518—the first year of the Reformation—there was a 530 percent increase in the production of pamphlets issued from German speaking presses.[23] Prior the emergence of the printing environment, heresies similar in form to the Protestant Reformation could not count on such a quick ignition rate.

There were other ways in which the printing environment matched the interests of the Protestant Reformation. Printing permitted the mass production of small, cheap pamphlets that favored the Reformer's strategic interest both in rapid dissemination of propaganda, in the form of cheap placards and posters, and the concealment of heretical printed works from authorities by both producers and consumers. Pamphlets were produced in quarto format—that is, made up of sheets folded twice to make four leaves or eight pages—and without a hard cover, and were referred to by the German term *Flugschriften*, or "flying writings."[24] Edwards describes how the pamphlets were "easily transported by itinerant peddlers, hawked on street corners and in taverns, advertised with jingles and intriguing title pages, and swiftly hidden in a pack or under clothing when the authorities made an appearance."[25] Edwards goes on to explain how the pamphlets were "ideal for circulating a subversive message right under the noses of the opponents of reform."[26] As the pamphlets did not require a large investment in either manpower or material as did large manuscripts, they were inexpensive to produce and could be turned out quickly to respond immediately to the day-to-day battles of the ongoing religious polemics.[27] Although precise estimates are difficult to determine, historian Hans-Joachim Kohler figures that the average *flugschriften* cost about as much as a hen, or a kilogram of beef—certainly not insignificant, but well within the reach of the pamphlet's intended audience, the "common man," and much less expensive than the cost of a well-crafted parchment manuscript.[28]

To reach a wider, mass audience the pamphlets and other publications were printed in the vernacular—the form itself a direct challenge to the Church hierarchy whose power rested on performing an intermediary function between the vernacular and sacred Latin scripts. As Edwards points out, printing not only helped spread Luther's message, it "embodied" it in its very form by presenting challenges to doctrine in the vernacular press.[29] Luther's explicit aim was to put a Bible in every household—an aim that was functionally complemented by the standardization and mass production afforded by movable type. One printer alone, Hans Lufft, issued 100,000 copies of the Bible within forty years between 1534 and 1574.[30] Febvre and Martin estimate that about one million German Bibles were printed before mid-century.[31] In so doing, printing helped to undermine the legitimacy of centralized knowledge reproduction by providing the means "by which each person could become his or her own theologian."[32] John Hobbes wrote disapprovingly how "every man, nay, every boy and wench that could read English thought they spoke with God Almighty, and understood what He said."[33]

Fueled by the new means of communication, the Protestant Reformation reached a level of mass support unprecedented among prior heresies in Europe during the Middle Ages. A "colossal religious propaganda war" ensued, in Anderson's words, that would soon envelop the whole of Europe.[34] At the heart of this war were the cheap, mass-produced pamphlets emanating from the many printing presses that sprouted throughout Europe in response to the market created by the religious upheaval. The pamphleteers carefully employed a combination of text and illustration to reach as wide an audience as possible. Devastating, "blasphemous" caricatures invariably featuring perverse and disfigured representations of eminent Church officials rolled off the printing press in droves—an often neglected historical detail of the sixteenth-century religious propaganda wars made possible by the printing press.[35]

But, a skeptic might ask, what about the low literacy rates in early modern Europe? How much weight should we give to the printing press when the ability to read and write was still out of reach for the vast majority of people? Although literacy was still relatively low among most of the lower classes, the spread of the printed word worked in tandem with traditional means of oral communications in what Kohler calls a "two-step" communications process.[36] Evangelical preachers spread by word of mouth polemical works freshly issued and/or smuggled in from the many printing houses that served as "nerve centers." We should not underestimate, therefore, the extent to which the illiterate could have access to the printed word through those that could read. So while the Reformation was very much an *oral* process at a mass level, it was the vast distribution of printed material that fueled the process at the crucial elite level.[37] Moreover, Protestantism deliberately inculcated in its followers the importance of literacy and Bible reading, and as a consequence literacy rates grew markedly higher over time in Protestant versus Catholic regions.[38]

While the printing environment may have favored the strategic interests of Protestantism, it worked against those of the Roman Catholic Church. Given its exploitation of the printing press, Protestantism was able to take the early offensive in the polemical struggles, with Rome often being forced to take the somewhat desperate and futile position of opposing and containing print in the name of doctrine. Anderson affirms that the reformers were "always fundamentally on the offensive, precisely because [they] knew how to make use of the expanding vernacular print-market being created by capitalism, while the Counter-Reformation defended the citadel of Latin."[39] Thus it was Rome which felt the need to formulate the *Index Librorum Prohibitorum* of banned printed material.[40] As Eisenstein notes:

> Catholic policies framed at Trent were aimed at holding these new functions in check. By rejecting vernacular versions of the Bible, by stressing lay obedience and imposing restrictions on lay reading, by developing new machinery such as the Index and Imprimatur to channel the flow of literature along narrowly prescribed lines, the post-Tridentine papacy proved to be anything but accommodating. It assumed an unyielding posture that grew ever more rigid over the course of time.[41]

The *Index*, continuously updated throughout the sixteenth century and beyond, had the ironic effect of spurring a market for the printed material contained therein by making it appear taboo, and thus even more attractive.[42] Even prior to the Protestant Reformation the Church had issued decrees forbidding the printing of books unauthorized by the Papal hierarchy. In 1515 Pope Leo X issued an edict to the Holy Roman Empire "that no license should be given for the printing of a book until it had been examined and approved by an authorized representative of the Church."[43] By restricting the publication of unauthorized printed material in this way, however, the

Church's strictures created a large black-market book trade fed by printing presses housed in non-Catholic regions.[44] It also resulted in strong pressures from Catholic printers who were placed at a severe disadvantage by not being able to enter into the newly emerging market for printed material—especially the material forbidden by the Church. For example, in 1524 the printers of Leipzig petitioned their Catholic duke that they were in danger of losing "house, home, and all their livelihood" because they were not allowed to "print or sell anything new that is made in Wittenberg or elsewhere. For that which one would gladly sell and for which there is demand," they said, referring to the Protestant literature, "they are not allowed to have or sell. But what they have in abundance," referring to Catholic literature, "is desired by no one and cannot be given away."[45] In short, the Church's strategic interests clashed with the properties of the newly emerging communications environment.

The way these religious divisions spilled over into the secular parts of the Christian Commonwealth is well-known. Their impact on the architecture of medieval world order—in particular, the transnational hegemony of the Roman Catholic Church—was devastating. Soon much of Europe was divided into competing religious territories—a chasm that initially corresponded with pro- and anti-print factions. As Anderson explains, "nothing gives a better sense of this siege mentality than François I's panicked 1535 ban on the printing of *any* books in his realm—on pain of death by hanging."[46] The Protestant Reformation ripped into the increasingly tenuous cosmological bind that held Christendom together under a single society. While it is certainly true that the roots of the Protestant Reformation reach back before the development of printing, it is unlikely that it would have been as profoundly consequential in this regard without the change in the communications environment. One need only look at the fate of previous heresies, like the Hussite, that withered without the availability of printing. Printing helped to displace "the mediating and intercessionary role of the clergy, and even of the Church itself, by providing a new channel of communication linking Christians to their God."[47] In conjunction with individualistic push of Protestant ideology, printing weakened the intermediary function that had buttressed the privileged social position assumed by the clergy. While Protestantism presented a frontal assault on the religious core of the official Church cosmology, a second discernible social force was gradually undercutting it from a more holistic perspective.

Scientific Humanism

As Anderson and others point out, the early printers represented one of the first manifestations in Europe of groups of commercial entrepreneurs dedicated to making a profit.[48] Consequently, they were primarily concerned with finding markets for their books and printed materials. Once the market for religious pamphlets became saturated, booksellers needed to find alternative outlets for their products. One particular emerging social group yearning for mass-produced printed material at the time was the scientific humanist movement. Over the course of the first century of printing, a shift occurred in the content from primarily Latin-based religious themes to scientific humanist works written in vernacular languages.[49] Like the expansion of Protestantism, the growth of scientific humanism helped to undermine the authority of the Roman Catholic Church by directly challenging the cosmology upon which its authority rested. And also like Protestant groups, social forces in favor of scientific humanism flourished in the newly emerging communications environment.

Although modernist histories of science have tended to portray the emergence of the so-called "Scientific Revolution" as a sharp historical juncture when the fetters of religious false consciousness were thrown aside for the wisdom of pure empiricism by a few path-breaking individuals, the roots of scientific humanism as a social force can actually be traced back to the late Middle Ages.[50] In Italy and in northern Europe, the growth of universities, coupled with a more hospitable urban setting, furnished the grounds for a stimulating intellectual environment characterized by intense debates surrounding the rediscovery of classical Greek and Roman texts.[51] At the same time, latent in European society was a growing dissatisfaction with the prevailing cosmology for more practical, secular reasons. The Ptolemaic, earth-centered picture of the universe, supported by official Church doctrine, no longer seemed adequate, for example, to the imperatives of ocean navigation, which was assuming a more important place as commerce and trade expanded. Nor could it be easily squared with observations of the heavens made with the aid of new technical discoveries—foremost among them the telescope—that furthered skepticism about its core assumptions.[52] Prior to printing, beliefs that contradicted the official Church cosmology could be contained with relative success through the same basic mechanisms, such as the Inquisition, that held other religious heresies in check. After printing,

however, it became much more difficult for the Church to halt the flow of
the new science, especially since scientific humanism (like Protestantism)
had a strategic interest in the widespread dissemination of knowledge and
information—an interest that overlapped with that of the new printing industry.

To understand the "fitness" between scientific humanism and the printing environment, we need to look back prior to the invention of printing:
to the establishment of universities in the High Middle Ages. As outlined
in the previous chapter, the swelling numbers of students and professors
in the High to late Middle Ages created a market for books that spurred
on the development of "in-house" university manuscript copying centers
that were not formally tied to the monastic network. This market might have
remained limited, however, were it not for the introduction of a new science—animated mostly by rediscovered Aristotelian works—that gradually
refocused intellectual energy on "observation" and critical comparison of
observations as opposed to pure reflection on traditional wisdom that characterized the predominant neoplatonism of the day.[53] Although the new
"empiricists" propagated the myth that they were "turning away" from the
dusty parchment books of the Church Fathers to "pure" examinations of the
"Book of Nature," we should cautiously avoid treating the myth, as Eisenstein
suggests, as anything more than a metaphor for the break from religious
ties.[54] In fact, the printing press significantly fueled the sudden wave of
scientific innovation that characterized the sixteenth and seventeenth centuries by facilitating the rapid dissemination and exchange of knowledge and
ideas. Contrary to myths, the new science was critically dependent on the
printed word.

While it is true that the entire printed output contained as much chaff
as wheat (early modern counterparts to the "trash" television of today) the
sheer volume of printed material that could be accessed by a single individual, or groups working cooperatively on a single project, was truly revolutionary, especially as it converged with the interests of the new scientific
curiosity. Eisenstein argues that while:

> the duplication in print of extant scribal maps and ancient geograph-
> ical treatises, even while seeming to provide evidence of "backsliding,"
> also provided a basis for unprecedented advance. . . . Before the out-
> lines of a comprehensive and uniform world picture could emerge,

incongruous images had to be duplicated in sufficient quantities to be brought into contact, compared, and contrasted.[55]

Thus it was not uncommon to find, as Febvre and Martin point out, many examples of printed material that furthered medieval, Ptolemaic theories at the same time as the new sciences.[56] But what was revolutionary was the conjunction of a new intellectual mind-set *alongside* the sudden and dramatic increase in the sheer volume of circulating works. Contradictions became more difficult to reconcile once Arabists were set alongside Galenists or Aristotelians against Ptolemaists *in a single study*.[57]

There were other ways, beyond benefiting from the sheer volume of circulating material, in which scientific humanism fit the printing environment. Consider, in this respect, how innovations new to print—such as cross-referencing and indexing—functionally matched an intellectual interest in the systematic comparison and critical evaluation of knowledge that characterized the new science.[58] The printing environment favored the *esprit de système* of the age—the desire to catalogue and organize every topic into a consistent order—by permitting the use of new devices like pagination, section breaks, running headers, title pages, index cards, standardized copies, and so forth, that would be virtually impossible (or at least very difficult) to undertake without mechanized reproduction.[59]

More subtle forms of "fitness" can be found as well. Consider the way the new sciences' stress on detached analytical, "impersonal" modes of reflection and reasoning benefited by the move away from the oral transmission of ideas, to individualized study of standardized texts.[60] Or consider the way the idea of progress and cumulation of knowledge was encouraged by the duplicative powers of printing, by the sudden increase in the volume of circulated material, and by the way cross-referencing and indexing could facilitate the "building" and synthesizing of existing theories. Multiple reprints and numbered editions made possible a process of critical feedback whereby errors and omissions in an original text could be identified and corrected in subsequent editions.[61] By contrast, manuscript deterioration was a constant problem in medieval Europe such that enormous energy was channeled into the preservation and recopying of important texts while countless others were allowed to drift into oblivion. Lack of standardization, localized chronologies, imprecise cataloguing, and oral transmissions can all be seen as further constraints on the idea of progress and the cumulation of knowledge. With printing, however, preservation became much less of a concern since multiple copies could be made at diminishing costs. And the exchange and circulation of standardized texts favored the notion of a progressive accumulation of ever more accurate ideas. Rice elaborates:

> Printing gave scholars all over Europe identical texts to work on. Referring precisely to a particular word in a particular line on a particular page, a scholar in Basel could propose an emendation which could be rapidly checked by his colleagues in Rome or Florence. From such corrections and discoveries a critical edition would emerge, to be superseded by another and yet another until something approaching a standard text had been achieved.[62]

The idea that civilization was progressing away from error through the winnowing away of false or distorted theories "fits" a communications environment where printed material (if not "knowledge" per se) was visibly and quite literally *accumulating*.[63]

Like the Reformation, the secularization of knowledge and learning that ensued worked against Rome's controlled interpretation of the order of things, gradually overturning the medieval cosmology upon which Papal authority derived its legitimacy. The new communications environment "favored" the interests of these two social forces to the disadvantage of the papal-monastic information network. As shown in the previous chapter, this network was critical in maintaining the Church's transnational hegemony over much of western Europe and thus of the ideological foundation of the medieval world order. Working in tandem with the ideas and interests of the Protestant Reformation and scientific humanism, printing helped to undercut the intermediary and privileged function of the clergy in medieval society, opening up the reproduction of knowledge to commercial, secular printers whose main concern was not the dissemination of a particular religious cosmology, but rather the accumulation of profit. As Curran attests:

> The development of a lay scribal and print culture also undermined the ideological ascendancy of the Church. The growth of commercial scriptoria and subsequently commercial printing enterprises made it more difficult for the ecclesiastical authorities, who had previously directly controlled the means of book production, to exercise effective censorship. The failure of the Church to maintain its domination over

centres of learning in the later middle ages also weakened its grip on the content of elite culture.[64]

While the Roman Catholic Church worked frantically to control the new mode of communication through censorship and patronage, it was unable to stem the tide of unforeseen consequences that were ushered in with the introduction of printing—a technology it had itself initially applauded. With the development of printing, the Church's dominant place in medieval world order collapsed. The remainder of this chapter examines the way the new mode of communication facilitated the rise of social forces that helped constitute the modern world order.

The New Media Environment and the Constitution of the Modern Order

Two social forces whose interests converged were critical in the constitution of the modern world order in Europe. One was the emergence of an *urban bourgeoisie* committed to commercial exchange, contractual socio-economic relations, and capitalist entrepreneurship. The emergence of this particular social force had what we might call a "leveling" effect on the tangled particularisms of feudal social relations, opening up the possibility of common rule from a single center. The mere possibility might have remained undeveloped were it not for the values that animated this new class of entrepreneurs, who shared a collective interest in some form of centralized rule to satisfy the need for both security and standardization. Coincidentally, their interests were met by centralizing state monarchs, who were willing to provide rationalized, bureaucratic administration of internal affairs in exchange for financing from the urban bourgeoisie to fight external wars. In this way, *centralized state bureaucracies*—a primary feature of modern world order—began to emerge from the cross-cutting, personalized forms of non-territorial rule characteristic of the feudal era.

The literature on the rise of the modern state in Europe is already well-developed, and it is not my intention here to provide another historical narrative of this process. Debates have raged among theorists over whether changes in military technologies, population growth, or some other combination were the factors ultimately responsible for the rise of the modern state.[65] My focus in this section is different from these studies. I am not concerned with explaining the roots of the urban bourgeoise and centralized forms of rule as social phenomena, nor why they formed an alliance with each other in some regions but not in others. Rather, my concern is to show the way the printing environment favored the interests of these two social forces where they arose. In doing so, I hope to provide an additional reason for why the transformation of world order occurred at this particular historical juncture.

From the Oath to the Contract

Socioeconomic relations during the High to late Middle Ages were characterized by feudalism—that is, a hierarchy of personalized, cross-cutting relationships among vassals and lords.[66] This form of personalized rule evolved out of ancient Germanic practices in which the oath of allegiance played a central role in maintaining trust and discipline among warriors.[67] The oath entailed an act of homage whereby one freeman would submit allegiance to another through the ceremonial placing of joined hands between those of the lord, which resulted in a bond of mutual obligation. The ceremony was highly personal, as evidenced by the bodily gestures of submission often involving a kiss as well as the verbal oath and the joined hands, signaling the vassal's allegiance to the lord "by mouth and hands."[68] Feudalism became the dominant mode of organizing socioeconomic relations following the decline of the Carolingian monarchy in the ninth and tenth centuries, and declined dramatically around the sixteenth century. It was most fully developed in France and Germany, and least developed in Italy, where ancient Roman traditions persisted and city life played a more prominent role in society.[69]

Although the oath of allegiance played an important symbolic role in affirming the social bonds between vassal and lord, it was more than just a symbolic gesture insofar as literacy was indeed rare during the High Middle Ages and social relations were in fact primarily characterized by oral communications.[70] As Le Goff notes, "the feudal system was a world of gesture and not of the written word."[71] The pervasiveness of the spoken word in both a practical and a metaphoric sense over all of feudal society is perhaps best illustrated, as Clanchy suggests, by the evolution of legal procedure.[72] It is evidenced by the fact that prior to the thirteenth century parties were given notice to appear in law courts not by a writ, but by an oral summons which was publicly proclaimed by *criatores* or "criers." Prior to the widespread use of written and printed documents, a great deal of importance was placed on personal, oral testimony as opposed to written documents, which were still considered untrustworthy. Consequently, a person went before the court to have a "hearing." One unfortunate byproduct was that the deaf and dumb appear to have had no legal rights in thirteenth-century England.[73] Wills did not rely on written documents but rather persons witnessing the testator making his bequests "with his own mouth"; they "saw, were present, and heard" the transaction.[74] And of course what prevailed in legal procedures was a mere reflection of society at large. For example, business was conducted, even among nascent commercial entrepreneurs, by word of mouth, if not solely because of tradition and habit, then certainly because "documents were bound to be relatively rare until printing made their automatic reproduction possible."[75] With illiteracy the norm, and written documentation rare, socioeconomic communications in the feudal era were overwhelmingly oral in nature.

The highly personalized oral form of rule that constituted feudal society contributed to the complex web of cross-cutting and overlapping lord-vassal mutual obligations that reached across the territory of Europe. When agreements were reached primarily on a personal basis, it should come as no suprise that the form of those relationships varied enormously from region to region. If we were to assume the perspective of an aspiring capitalist, the feudal environment would appear to be highly constraining. Spruyt describes how:

> The legal climate was unfavourable for trade given the underdevelopment of written codes, the importance of local customary proceedings, the lack of instrumentally rational procedures, and the cross-cutting nature of jurisdictions. Economically, commerce suffered from great variation in coinage and in weights and measures and a lack of clearly defined property rights. Transaction costs were high.[76]

Since money as we know of it today was virtually nonexistent, feudal financial obligations consisted mostly of barter, or in-kind transfers.[77] Legal affairs were characterized by what has been called "banal justice," with each locality assuming its own legal particularities—a situation encouraged by the lack of written laws prior to the thirteenth century in most of Europe with the exception of parts of southern France and Italy.[78] Secular and ecclesiastical lords used their own weights and measures, while many local lords minted their own coins—in France alone there were as many as 300 minters.[79] All of this particularism was closely bound up with the personalized, oral form of rule inherent in feudalism, which encouraged representational, as opposed to abstract, forms of measure, and variation and localism in socioeconomic and legal affairs up until the thirteenth century—a point that will be taken up again in the following section dealing with nascent state bureaucracies.[80]

Of course there were few capitalists in the High Middle Ages who would find any problem with what we now consider to be a high degree of "transaction costs." But beginning in the twelfth century, a profound economic transformation took hold resulting in what Eric Jones calls "the European Miracle."[81] From a multiplicity of causes—improvements in agricultural techniques, changes in climate and demographics, the growth of international trade—economic productivity rose and grew more complex.[82] As Ruggie explains, "economic relations became increasingly monetized, and developments in 'invisibles,' including the great fairs, shipping, insurance, and financial services, further lubricated commerce and helped to create a European-wide market."[83] Out of this dynamic economic interaction re-emerged many towns that had been dormant since Roman times. And within these towns a new group began to coalesce into a coherent social force: the burghers or town dwellers, or what would later be known as the "urban bourgeoisie." Spruyt astutely points out how few interests these new townspeople shared with the clergy and feudal lords who thrived on the old institutions:

> Thus, coupled with the rise of the towns, a new set of interests and ideological perspectives emerged with a new set of demands. The feudal order—based on cross-cutting jurisdictions and on ill-defined property rights and judicial procedures—did not fit the burghers' mercantile pursuits. Market exchange and trade required abstract contractual obligations with money as a medium.[84]

The ideological perspectives and new set of demands to which Spruyt refers flourished as the communications environment began to change, first with the growth of literacy and the use of written records in the urban centers of the thirteenth and fourteenth centuries, and then more dramatically and forcefully with the spread of printing. In fact, one might go so far as to say that the growth of the urban bourgeoisie and the spread of printing worked *symbiotically*, with each spurring on the development of the other. So while Anderson is correct to point out that capitalism set the preconditions for the widespread dissemination of printed material, the relationship between the two is not so easy to disentangle as each, in turn, affected the other.[85] For the rise of capitalism was embedded in, and closely intertwined with, a corresponding transformation in the western European mode of communication. In other words, the shift from an oral to a print culture was also a shift from the *oath* to the *contract*, with all of the consequences for socio-economic organization that ensued. The impersonal bonds of a modern interdependent economy—organic, as opposed to mechanical, solidarity in Durkheim's terms—could not be sustained on such a vast level without a high degree of literacy and the permanency and reproducibility of printed documents.[86] While nascent capitalist entrepreneurs may have found the oral-manuscript culture of the late Middle Ages to be highly constraining, they thrived in the more hospitable printing environment. It should come as no surprise, then, that Rice identifies as one of the key factors in "the astonishingly rapid spread of printing" in early modern Europe, the insatiable demand for printed products among "merchants, substantial artisans, lawyers, government officials, doctors, and teachers who lived and worked in towns."[87]

At the most fundamental level, printing favored the widespread use of what might be called *social abstractions*—bills of sale, deeds, court records, licenses, contracts, constitutions, decrees—that are the essence of modern, contractarian societies. These social abstractions could only emerge, as Stock and Clanchy point out, with a rise in general literacy and a corresponding dependence on written documentation over strictly oral communications—a process that began, as pointed out in the previous chapter, in the High Middle Ages but was accelerated with the mass reproducibility of printing.[88] Printing helped circulate in its many forms a standardized medium of exchange essential for the servicing of a complex division of labor within the newly emerging urban-commercial centers of western Europe. Consider, in this respect, the widespread use of printed paper currency as opposed to metal coins or other tokens in facilitating a standardized medium of economic exchange.[89] Or consider the dependence of the entrepreneur and the financier on the newspaper, which was an invention new to printing. McKusker and Gravesteijn note that "merchants and bankers in the fifteenth and sixteenth centuries, in their continuing quest for better ways to speed the flow of business news, turned for help to the most recent innovation in information technology, the printing press."[90] Thus what might be considered the first forerunner of the newspaper was a published exchange rate printed at the Lyon exchange fairs beginning in the late fifteenth century, in which the "conto" or fixed exchange rate was circulated in print for those attending the fair.[91] The Amsterdam Commodity Price Current (*Cours der Koopmanschappen tot Amsterdam*) was published intermittently as early as 1585, and weekly beginning in 1609.[92] Other commercial and financial newspapers sprouted throughout Europe in the seventeenth century, including in Augsburg (1592), Bologna (1628), Bolzano (1631), Bordeaux (1634), Danzig (1608), Florence (1598), Genoa (1619), Lille (1639), Lisbon (1610), London (1608), Lyons (1627), Naples (1627), Piacenza (1614), and Verona (1631).[93] These newspapers served an essential function in providing a standardized publication for the exchange of commercial information. According to North and Thomas, they have been found in the archives of every important commercial center in Europe.[94] Their presence was both an indication of, and a significant factor in, the rapid growth of urban commercial activity in the seventeenth century.

At a more practical level, both written and printed materials, and the growth of literacy that naturally accompanied them, were indispensable tools in the day-to-day routines of the urban bourgeoisie. Indeed, standard accounting practices and record-keeping, such as double-entry bookkeeping, are practically inconceivable in a purely oral environment. While double-entry bookkeeping emerged in Italy prior to the invention of printing, it was a product of a highly literate urban populace and spread rather quickly throughout European urban centers once printing and literacy took root elsewhere.[95] Nor should it be surprising that more ephemeral qualities associated with the capitalist spirit, such as a meticulous rationalism and an abstract cognitive orientation, flourished in precisely those areas where printing and literacy initially spread the fastest.[96] As a number of theorists have argued, both writing and printing favor and encourage an abstract, rational cognitive orientation by arresting the flow of oral conversation, permitting the comparison and juxtaposition of words and documents, and detaching the content of communications from place, time, and personality.[97] Thus in those areas where we find a high rate of literacy and a penetration of printed material, we also find the flourishing of a highly developed commercial ethos.

Perhaps the best example comes from the United Provinces of the Netherlands, where literacy was high and printing was enthusiastically exploited and encouraged by the Protestant state that was incorporated there in the sixteenth century. North and Thomas note, for example, how the "methods" of the Dutch merchants were more sophisticated, and how the techniques of double-entry bookeeping were widely taught and had become standard accountancy practices.[98] According to Dudley, it is no coincidence that many of these defining features of capitalism—such as the stock exchange and the multinational corporation—were originally developed in the Netherlands, a region that was in many ways at the forefront of the change in the mode of communication. As Dudley explains:

> The result for Dutch society [of exploiting print and literacy to their fullest] was a deeper penetration of market institutions than had existed in previous communities. The examples of the Amsterdam Exchange Bank and the Bourse illustrate this point. The great popularity that these institutions enjoyed from the moment they were founded could be possible only in a literate society familiar with the notion that a written document could be just as valuable as gold or silver coins.[99]

In sum, while the emergence of an urban bourgeois class in early modern Europe was the product of a multiplicity of factors, the social movement flourished in the new communications environment. Printing not only functionally complemented many of the basic routines of the capitalist entrepreneur, but more fundamentally it provided the means by which social abstractions could circulate on a wide scale, leading to a complex division of labor. Without the standardization and mass-reproducibility afforded by printing, it is unlikely that such a complex penetration of contractual socioeconomic relations could have developed as it did. Certainly the oral-manuscript culture of medieval Europe placed significant obstacles in the path of capitalist development. Once that environment changed, however, a complex system of contractarian socioeconomic relations began to thrive.

The consequences of this particular distributional change for world order transformation are twofold: First, the growth of an urban bourgeoisie had what I earlier called a "leveling" effect on patterns of political and economic obligation, at least in urban areas, cutting through the entangled webs of personal loyalties characteristic of the feudal era and opening up the possibility for common rule from a single center.[100] As Axtmann explains, "The disintegration of feudalism at the 'molecular' level of the manor/village resulted in the displacement of political-legal power upwards to the 'national' level."[101] Thus one of the central features of medieval world order—multiple and overlapping layers of personalized authority—dissolved among an increasingly important segment of the population. The *oath* gave way to the *contract* as the basis of early modern urban economic relations.

Second, the rise of a bourgeois class directly contributed to the centralizing drive of state monarchs by providing finances for standing armies in return for standardized, rational administration of legal and commercial procedures within a territorial space. In Mann's words, the newly emerging capitalists "entered and reinforced a world of emergent warring yet diplomatically regulating states. Their need for, and vulnerability to, state regulation both internally and geopolitically, and the state's need for finances, pushed classes and states toward a territorially centralized organization."[102] In this respect, the rise of the urban bourgeoisie can be seen as a *transitional* distributional change insofar as it not only helped to dissolve the architecture of medieval world order (specifically, feudal socioeconomic relations), but it also gave positive impetus to, and was a constitutive force in, the emergence of modern world order (specifically, the centralization/standardization of territorial rule from a single center). The following section takes a look at this process from the perspective of centralizing state bureaucracies.

The Emergence of Modern Centralized State Bureaucracies

As Garrett Mattingly has pointed out, precursors to the modern state can be traced back far into antiquity.[103] The first bureaucracy arose in ancient Sumeria alongside the development of writing, which, as many have noted, is a necessary precondition for its development.[104] However, the roots of the legal and fiscal systems exclusive to *modern* state bureaucracies in Europe date from the eleventh and twelfth centuries and, not surprisingly, were closely bound up with the reestablishment of secular literacy and the lay use of written documents.[105] Of course, secular literacy and the use of written texts were not solely responsible for the rise of the modern state. Technical innovations originating in northern Italian communes—such as administration by an impersonal salaried bureaucracy serving for a limited term and double-entry bookkeeping—provided important precursors to the form that state bureaucracies ultimately took.[106] Certain ideas were also influential in giving birth to state bureaucracies in Europe—especially the rediscovery of Roman law, which helped fix the notion of a distinct "public" realm.[107] And landmark treatises—such as Richard Fitzneal's *Dialogue on the Course of the Exchequer*, written during the reign of Henry II (1154—-1189)—helped to define the impersonal role of the bureaucratic administrator to the state as an abstract entity.[108] However, the preconditions for centralized administrative rule depended not just on ideas, but also, and more crucially, on the technological capacity to carry them out—a distinctly absent feature of political authority for most nascent states in medieval Europe.

Aspiring medieval monarchs found that their moves toward centralization were difficult to sustain because of the constraints of the prevailing social, economic, and political environment which, as outlined earlier, was overwhelmingly constituted by personalized, oral communications. Thus while we find the shells of modern states beginning to develop as early as the twelfth century in countries like England, where written administration was more advanced, the norm for the rest of Europe was a constant tension between the forces of localization and centralization. One reason was that long-range administration based on networks of personal or blood ties was ineffective for sustaining cross-generational rule. It had a tendency to dissolve into petty fiefdoms with local privilege—a pattern that was repeated often throughout the Middle Ages as evidenced, for example, by the dissolution of the Carolingian and Ottonian dynasties.[109] Medieval political rule, in Poggi's words, "possessed an inherent tendency to shift the seat of effective power, the fulcrum of rule, downward toward the lower links in the chain of lord-vassal relations"—a tendency no doubt related to the prevailing personalized-oral communications environment of the time.[110] Consequently, the political map of Europe in the Middle Ages was determined, accordingly to Mattingly, not so much "by geography, or national culture, or historic development" as it was "by the irrelevant accidents of birth and marriage and death."[111]

The complexity by which personalized, cross-cutting lord-vassal entanglements took root in the Middle Ages made any attempts at centralization and rational administration within a territorially defined space extremely difficult for nascent states. Prior to the rediscovery of Roman Law, there was no conception of a distinction between private legal and fiscal prerogatives of local authorities and that of a public realm. In the case of local lords, "On land under his jurisdiction, public economy and the fiscal obligations related to it were identical with the domestic economy of his private household."[112] Raising consistent state revenues—especially from one generation of leaders to the next—was virtually impossible as a typical medieval ruler "knew the total of neither his income nor his outgoings" of his entire domain.[113] One consequence of this entangled particularism was that kings who wanted revenues from the lands under their jurisdiction regularly traveled with a large entourage in order to "consume the produce of their scattered holdings."[114] And since each hommage of lord-vassal obligation was entered into *intuitu personae* (that is, personally) the form of rule varied enormously from relationship to relationship and region to region. According to Poggi:

> the lord's relationship to the ultimate objects of rule, the populace, was mediated differently by each vassal. The size of the fief, the exact terms on which it was granted, the rights of rule over it that remained with the lord or that were vested in the vassal—as these aspects of the basic relationship varied, so did the modalities and content of the exercise of rule.[115]

Nonetheless, by the thirteenth and fourteenth centuries state authority was undergoing, although with occasional setbacks, a gradual process of consolidation and centralization—a kind of "two-steps forward/one-step backward" process. To be sure, the process was not uniform across all of Europe. In Germany and Italy, for example, city-leagues and city-states provided alternative "de-centered" logics of organization. But elsewhere—in England, France, and Holland, for example—centralized forms of rule began to displace the feudal system. Theorists disagree on the primary impetus for this process, or why it finally took hold at this juncture rather than at an earlier time. Some, such as Tilly, place more emphasis on changes in military technologies.[116] Others give as much emphasis to population pressures and an accompanying economic boom.[117] Whatever the ultimate reason, in those areas of Europe a similar pattern can be discerned: In the context of an increasingly dangerous environment, an imperative was placed on the maintenance of a standing army, and where relevant a war fleet, that could be summoned by a central ruler.[118] The new demands of war necessitated that these rulers turn inward to maintain domestic stability and order, and, more importantly, to find a way to raise constant revenues to finance the war machine.[119] Fortunately, the state rulers found willing allies in the urban bourgeoisie, whose interests in order and rational administration converged

with those of the central rulers. And happily for these states, the new towns-
men were able and willing to provide money in the form of taxes in exchange
for the domestic services provided by the state. The specific form that this
relationship took varied from state to state, as Tilly and Mann have documented.[120] But in parts of Europe from the fifteenth to the seventeenth
centuries, the general phenomenon of modern state bureaucracies under
territorially distinct, absolutist rule began to emerge and thrive as the model
form of political authority.

What role did the printing environment play in facilitating the emergence
and success of centralized forms of rule over alternative "de-centered" logics
of organization? Most importantly, the printing environment provided the
tools necessary for standardized, intergenerational rule in the form of rational
bureaucratic administration from a single center. Indeed, as pointed out
above, a necessary precondition for the emergence of bureaucratic administration is some form of writing system. Thus it is not surprising that the
development of modern state bureaucracies in Europe was closely bound
up with the spread of secular literacy in the High Middle Ages. So in those
regions where literacy is relatively high, bureaucratic specialization and development tends to be more advanced. For example, in the case of England,
sixty individuals were employed in its Chancery in the middle of the thirteenth century; by the fifteenth century, more than a hundred were employed at the Court of Common Pleas alone.[121]

Of course, pressures for bureaucratization, in turn, drove secular literacy
and a demand for standardized communications. Early printers were quick
to recognize this market and, as a result, thrived on state commissions for
printed administrative records. As Febvre and Martin point out, state policies
actively encouraged the creation of large, national publishing houses
throughout early modern Europe.[122] And the printed products emanating
from these large publishing centers in turn increased the size of bureaucratic
documentation, which necessitated yet more specialization and personnel.
In Guenee's words, "The proliferation of offices and officials inevitably led
to a proliferation of the documents without which State action would be
impossible and on which its power was based."[123]

The most obvious way the new communications environment favored
the interests of centralized state rulers was by facilitating more effective and
systematic rewards and sanctions in the governance of outlying regions, particularly through the standardization of legal institutions and systems of direct taxation. As Tilly affirms, "Almost all European governments eventually

took steps which homogenized their populations."[124] With means of standardized documentation provided by printing, state rulers could effectively cut through and transcend the vagaries of personalized, feudal obligations that so often produced discrepancies among locales throughout the King's domain. In the printing environment, regularized and impersonal procedures could be more effectively established that did not vary over a territorially defined space or, more importantly, across generations of rule. As an illustration, "between 1665 and 1690 Louis XIV promulgated ordinances and codes that uniformly regulated over all of France such diverse matters as civil and criminal court procedure, the management of forests and rivers, shipping and sailing, and the trade in black slaves."[125] In the printing environment, revenues could be collected efficiently and consistently with the result that the size and power of the state, and the effectiveness of centralized rule, began to grow.

The state's interest in standardization (or *homogenization*, as Tilly aptly calls it), was closely bound up with a desire not only to more efficiently and consistently extract financial revenues, but also to maintain domestic order and security through surveillance of the population and territory—an interest that thrived with the availability of printing. One of the more compelling interpretations of the state's interest in surveillance is Michel Foucault's discussion of the "disciplinary state."[126] Foucault argues that in the transition to the modern state, coercion and overt violence as tools for social order were gradually replaced by a more impersonal "micro-politics" of discipline designed to morally regulate or "normalize" individuals through institutional regulation and bureaucratic administration.[127] Though Foucault is more concerned with the ideas that lay behind this transition, it is easy to see how the material instruments of technology at the disposal of centralized state administrators were crucial in facilitating this reorientation.[128]

Perhaps the best example of the way printing helped to empower the "disciplinary state" is the reproduction of printed maps used for administrative purposes. As Barber notes with respect to England, by the sixteenth century state ministers "came to expect a greater precision in maps than had their predecessors, and several became more sophisticated in their evaluation of, and their awareness of the potential uses of, maps for government." He goes on to say that the government of the time "seems to have shown a growing appetite for printed maps, which were cheaper, increasingly plentiful, and less prone to scribal errors in transmission than their manuscript counterparts."[129] In 1610, a State Paper Office was formally established in

England to house the ever-increasing number of official maps.[130] Likewise, Buisseret notes with respect to France: "At the time of Louis XIV's accession . . . French governing circles possessed a well-developed sense of the usefulness of maps, and there were cartographers capable of responding to their needs. . . . [through] an abundance of presses, mostly concentrated in Paris, capable of printing and diffusing large maps in considerable quantities."[131] For example:

> For economic and financial planning, maps were commissioned to show where the various fiscal divisions, or generalités, ran, and where specific taxes like the gabelle (salt tax) were to be paid. . . . Other maps were ordered when great public works like the canal du Midi were being planned; this canal had a very rich cartography associated with it. Others, again, were commissioned to show the sites of the mines in France, or the nature and extent of its forests.[132]

Another example of the way the printing environment fueled the disciplinary state was in the area of public education, as Luke in particular has shown.[133] Consider in this respect the way the printing environment favored standardized public "examinations" through which each individual was compelled to pass, helping to create a cumulative, individual "archive" of persons under the state. Luke notes how "Printing enabled the 'power of writing' to become universalized and standardized; teachers like wardens examined, evaluated, recorded, and described those in their charge according to standardized (administrative) forms based on underlying classificatory criteria."[134] These standardized, printed examinations helped to instill a sense of rank in the population which, as Foucault describes, defined "the great form of distribution of individuals in the education order. . . . an alignment of age groups, one after another; a succession of subjects taught and questions treated . . ."[135] In this way, standardized public education in the form of printed school textbooks and printed school ordinances served the disciplinary interests of the state, which promoted a uniformity of belief among the population through compulsory schooling of the young.[136]

In sum, the movement toward modern state bureaucracies, which began in the High Middle Ages, was favored by the change in the mode of communication, first with the gradual increase in secular literacy and then, more dramatically, with the introduction of printing. Printing fueled the strategic interests of nascent centralized state bureaucracies by providing the means by which standardized documents—from school textbooks, to public ordinances and fiscal regulations, to maps of the realm—could be mass reproduced and disseminated. In this way, printing provided the tools by which centralizing rulers could promote homogenous policies across territorially defined spaces and thus dissolve the cross-cutting and overlapping jurisdictions characteristic of the medieval world order. As printing provided a means to mass-reproduce documents at little cost, a system of intergenerational rule could be established, thus freezing the tendency that had been repeated throughout the Middle Ages for centralized rule to wither following the death of influential personalities. Moreover, alternative forms of extant political authority that lacked a single, centered form of rule—the Italian city-states and the German city-leagues, for example—could not benefit from the printing environment to the same extent as did centralized state bureaucracies.[137] As a result, the success of the centralized state bureaucratic system of rule became the model of political authority for modern Europe as whole.

In this chapter I have described how the introduction of printing in medieval Europe brought about specific distributional changes that empowered certain actors and social forces at the expense of others. Most immediately affected by the advent of printing was the transnational authority of the Roman Catholic Church, which had come close to establishing a theocratic papal government over much of western Europe in the High Middle Ages based on a monopoly of the reproduction of knowledge. The Church's preeminent position in medieval world order was undercut by forces whose strategic interests coincided with, and were augmented by, the advent of printing—the Protestant Reformation and scientific humanism. The new communications environment favored the interests of these two social forces by permitting the mass reproduction and widespread transmission of ideas outside of the papal-monastic network. The Church's interests, on the other hand, were significantly disadvantaged by the change in the mode of communication, as evidenced by its explicit condemnation of the printing press once its full potential had been unleashed.

The chapter also explored the way in which distributional changes associated with printing helped facilitate constitutive features of modern world order: specifically, contractarian socioeconomic relations among the new urban bourgeoisie, and modern state bureaucracies. The printing environment favored the demands of contractarian socioeconomic relations by permitting the widespread use of social abstractions crucial to modern, interdependent economies. This particular social force was vital to the development of modern political rule insofar as its interests in standardization and order converged with those of centralizing state monarchs, who were willing to provide domestic stability in exchange for the ability to extract revenues through taxes. The capabilities of printing—especially the mass reproduction of standardized documents—also empowered the disciplinary state, which had a vested interest in both the homogenization of the population and the standardization of administration. Although these distributional changes were crucial in the medieval-to-modern transformation of world order, they do not tell the whole story. The next chapter explores the relationship between the change in the mode of communication and the transformation of social epistemology.

4 Print and the Medieval to Modern World Order Transformation: Changes to Social Epistemology

Although distributional changes facilitated by the new mode of communication help explain the transition from the medieval to the modern world order, they do not tell the whole story. Ruggie explains that: "The demise of the medieval system of rule and the rise of the modern resulted in part from a transformation in social epistemology. Put simply, the mental equipment that people drew upon in imagining and symbolizing forms of community itself underwent fundamental change."[1]

In this chapter, I turn to the second of the conceptually distinct effects that arise from a change in the mode of communication: changes to social epistemology. As outlined in the theoretical chapter, social epistemology refers to the web-of-beliefs into which a people are acculturated and through which they perceive the world around them. It encompasses all of the socially constructed ideas, symbolic forms, and cognitive biases that frame meaning and behavior for a population in a particular historical context. According to the ecological holist perspective advanced here, social epistemology is not a mere "superstructure" ultimately reducible to some material "base," but has an independent, constitutive effect on the nature or character of politics and social order. Since these social constructs, symbolic forms, and cognitive biases that comprise the social epistemology of an era obviously blanket a wide spectrum of diverse traits, for analytical purposes we must break them down into some manageable (though not necessarily exhaustive) set. As I outlined in chapter 1, I examine three elements of social epistemology: *individual identity*, *spatial biases*, and *imagined communities*. As will be shown below, changes in all three of these elements of social epistemology were crucial in providing what might be called the "metaphysical" underpinnings of modern world order.

The purpose of this chapter is to trace how changes in these defining symbolic forms and social constructs were in no small part encouraged by the development of the printing environment. This is not to say that they were, in a crude monocausal sense, *generated* by it. To be sure, the emerging modern social epistemology was a product of many different factors having roots that reach back into the late Middle Ages and beyond. Nevertheless, by viewing changes in social epistemology through the lens of the mode of communication we can see how a comfortable "fitness" obtained between certain symbolic forms and printing that may help explain why they resonated so strongly at this particular juncture. Printing favored some of the important latent components of social epistemology that would later be so important in providing the basis upon which political authority was differentiated in modern Europe.

Individual Identity

Probably the most striking and important shift from the medieval to the modern cosmology was in terms of individual identity. As Dumont explains, there are two different notions of individualism: one, the indivisible sample of the human species found in all societies and cultures; and, two, "the independent, autonomous and thus (essentially) nonsocial moral being, as found primarily in our modern . . . ideology of man and society."[2] Only the latter, ideological notion of "individualism" concerns us here. Dumont points out that "some of us have become increasingly aware that modern individualism, when seen against the background of the other great civilizations that the world has known, is an exceptional phenomenon."[3] In other words, the modern notion of individualism is a historically contingent moral idea, one not linked to all human beings in all times and places, despite the intentions of some liberal teleologists or methodological individualists to portray it as such.

Of course, this does not mean that we cannot trace the roots of individualism back before the modern period. Certainly elements of modern individuality can be found in the Christian religion, which upheld the possibility of every person's salvation regardless of status in the temporal realm (though here individuality was subordinate within a strictly hierarchical view of natural order).[4] And traces of what might be considered characteristic features of "modern" individuality can be seen in sporadic flourishes among medieval intellectuals arising as early as the twelfth and thirteenth centuries.[5] Another precursor can be found in the teachings of Franciscan piety, which furthered a religion centered on personal experience and private devotion, and which was popular within the newly emerging towns of the thirteenth century.[6] But it is only in modern Europe that individualism is first exalted as a defining principle of individual identity in marked contrast to the medieval "Chain of Being."[7] In other words, any notion of individualism that can be found in the Middle Ages is certainly the exception within an overarching Christian cosmology.

What was the prevailing notion of the "self" in the Middle Ages? The individual's place in the medieval order followed the Augustinian view of "the arrangement of equal and unequal beings, appointing to each the place fitting for him."[8] Thus inequality and difference were taken-for-granted parts of an organic image of society, one that expressed functional differentiation among constituent parts. The clearest expression of this idea was the division of society into the Three Orders: the *bellatores*, the *oratores*, and the *laboratores* (those who fight, those who pray, and those who labor).[9] As Lyon explains, a person's place in medieval cosmology was the antithesis of modern individualism:

> When time and space have a beginning and an end men are also fixed in status, and the whole message of their culture is to remind them of that place and to warn them that only sorrow can result from any attempt to break the chains that tie them to family, trade, religion, and class. . . . Such a lock-step is consistent with a world in which the final metaphysical solutions had been willed into being, and the person who brooded upon himself was considered ill with melancholy from an excess of black bile in his system.[10]

Most theorists tend to give weight in the emergence of individualism to historical and sociological factors that were outlined in the previous chapter, especially those concerning the rise of towns and commercialism, and the individualist thrust of Protestantism, which helped break through the "natural" order of the Great Chain of Being. C. B. Macpherson, for example, has written of a distinct "possessive individualism" that crystallized among the urban bourgeoisie in early modern Europe—"a conception of the individual as essentially the proprietor of his own person or capacities, owing nothing to society for them."[11] This possessive individualism was not exclusive to moral theorizing or the commercial sector, but was echoed throughout many spheres of society. It was mirrored in the prevailing "atomism" that informed both politics and science, as illustrated in the social contract theorizing of Hobbes and Locke and the radical individualism and inner compulsion expressed by René Descartes.[12] As Charles Taylor explains, atomism echoed "those philosophical traditions . . . which started with the postulation of an extensionless subject, epistemologically a *tabula rasa* and politically a presuppositionless bearer of rights." [13]

That same "atomism" or sense of autonomous individuality that reverberated throughout many spheres of society found its world order counterpart in the notion of state sovereignty, which, like individualism, "betokens a rational identity: a homogenous and continuous presence that is hierarchically ordered, that has a unique center of decision presiding over a coherent 'self', and that is demarcated from, and in opposition to, an external domain of difference and change that resists assimilation to identical being."[14] Indeed, the two (individualism and state sovereignty) are complementary ontological counterparts. Just as politics and society within emerging states gave way to a notion of interactions among atomistic actors, so too did the picture of interactions among political units. Ruggie in particular has shown how this "self-image" of individuals-as-atomistic-actors was gradually transposed onto the world order sphere, with territorial rulers seeing interstate politics as a whole through the same lens—that is, as "atomistic and autonomous bodies-in-motion in a field of forces energized solely by scarcity and ambition."[15] Likewise Dumont explains how "the hierarchical Christian Commonwealth was atomized at two levels: it was replaced by a number of individual States, themselves made of up individual men."[16] This self-image is reflected in Hobbes's view of the state as a "multitude so united in one person."[17] In the words of Otto Gierke:

> The people is made co-extensive with the sum of its constituent units; and yet simultaneously, when the need is felt for a single bearer of the rights of the People, it is treated as essentially a unit in itself. The whole distinction between the unity and the multiplicity of the community is reduced to a mere difference of point of view, according as *omnes* is interpreted as *omnes ut universi* or as *omnes ut singuli*. The eye resolved . . .[18]

What role did printing play in this shift of world views so central to the constitution of modern world order? In *The Invention of the Self,* John Lyon asserts that "the invention and spread of movable type is probably the most important mechanical contributor to the idea of the unique self."[19] Of this contribution, there are many particular aspects. First, printing favored the distinctly modern idea of the sovereign voice, the single, author(itative) individual. Ong explains that "the printed text is supposed to represent the words of an author in definitive or 'final' form. . . . it tends to feel a work as 'closed', set off from other works, a unit in itself."[20] Today, such notions are taken for granted; yet it was not always so. Only with the advent of printing did the idea of a "copyright" begin to take shape. For example, it was not until 1557 that a Stationers' Company was incorporated in London to oversee and ensure printer-publisher rights.[21]

Prior to that time, the medieval "intertextual" practice held sway. According to Chaytor, "to copy and circulate another man's books might be regarded as a meritorious action in the age of manuscript; in the age of print, such action results in law suits and damages."[22] The Middle Ages did not possess the same conception of "authorship" that has prevailed throughout modernity—a conception that may, in fact, be eroding with the emergence of hypermedia today (as will be shown in chapter 7).[23] Indeed, no special Latin word even existed with the exclusive meaning of plagiarist or plagiarism.[24] The lack of a clear conception of the "author" was due in no small measure to the fact that medieval manuscripts were often the product of many authors, or even none to which the work could be attributed, as many were left unsigned.[25] Glosses and marginal comments were habitually worked into subsequent copies of texts. A good example is the *Magna Carta,* which survives today in a number of nonidentical copies, varying because scribes made revisions of their own during the recopying process. Susan Reynolds explains that exact duplication was not the scribe's overriding concern: "The charter mattered, but what mattered to both compilers of statute books and writers of chronicles was its gist, not its exact words."[26] As Ong points out:

> Manuscript culture had taken intertextuality for granted. Still tied to the commonplace tradition of the old oral world, it deliberately created texts out of other texts, borrowing, adapting, sharing the common, originally oral, formulas and themes.[27]

In addition, as the dissemination of popular literature depended mostly on oral transmission, it was impossible for writers to maintain any literary rights, even had they desired to do so in the first place. Assuming medieval writers *did* want selfishly to guard their status as "authors" of particular works, their only option would be to hoard their own material. "But if they did that," Febvre and Martin point out, "it was impossible for them to enjoy the satisfaction every artist seeks by broadcasting his work to as large an audience as possible."[28]

With the introduction of printing, the benefits of authorship, in terms of both personal fame and fortune, became more pronounced. "Contemporary writers who had their names attached to hundreds of thousands of copies of their works became conscious of individual reputation."[29] The "drive-for-fame" became a conscious motivating factor, one that, as Eisenstein suggests, may have been encouraged by the "immortality" afforded by the printed word.[30] In sum, the idea of a single sovereign voice fit the printing environment, where *mechanical* replaced *manual* reproduction, leaving oral transmission and the intertextual practices of generations of scribes behind.

Notions of individual identity exclusive to modernity in Europe were also reinforced by the practice of reading in a print culture. Medieval culture, despite the existence of writing, was still very much an oral culture. The written word was read aloud and was often deliberately constructed for oral performance.[31] Writing was a communal activity. By the twelfth century, however, silent reading began to emerge, first in monasticist scriptoria and then eventually spreading to universities and among lay aristocracy by the fifteenth century.[32] This new interest in solitary, silent reading flourished in the printing environment, which permitted the mass reproduction of smaller, more portable books.[33] In this way printing helped to define the social movement of the time to "create a new private sphere into which the individual could retreat, seeking refuge from the community."[34]

Reading of printed books in a quiet, private place in turn fostered solitary reflection, and private, individual points of view.[35] Intellectual work became "a personal confrontation with an ever-growing number of texts," which encouraged, among other things, a more personal piety "not subject to the discipline and mediation of the Church."[36] Chartier calls this "privatization" of reading "undeniably one of the major cultural developments of the early modern era."[37] This new sense of privacy fostered by print may have encouraged some of the reconfigurations Ruggie describes:

Consider, for example, analogous changes in the linguistic realm, such as the growing use of vernaculars, and the coming to dominance of the "I-form" of speech—which Franz Borkenau described as the 'sharpest contradistinction between I and you, between me and the world.' Consider analogous changes in interpersonal sensibilities, as in new notions of individual subjectivity and new meanings of personal delicacy and shame. These changes, among other effects, led to a spatial reconfiguration of households, from palaces to manor houses to the dwellings of the urban well-to-do, which more rigorously demarcated and separated private from public spheres and functions.[38]

While no doubt the shifts Ruggie describes have their origins in a constellation of factors, we can see how printing encouraged such changes in "interpersonal sensibility" by detaching the individual from the communal performance of a manuscript culture, thus fostering isolation and separation. In print culture, private reading mixed with and encouraged new forms of literary intimacy and explorations of the self, which, in turn, demanded a more clear delineation of private spaces within households.[39] Ong elaborates:

Print was also a major factor in the development of the sense of personal privacy that marks modern society. It produced books smaller and more portable than those common in a manuscript culture, setting the stage psychologically for solo reading in a quiet corner, and eventually for completely silent reading. In manuscript culture and hence in early print culture, reading had tended to be a social activity, one person reading to others in a group. . . . private reading demands a home spacious enough to provide for individual isolation and quiet.[40]

In sum, the gradual rise of individualism as both a prevailing symbolic form and a predominant moral idea flourished in the printing environment. The mass production of printed material favored newly circulating notions of authorship, copyright, and individual subjectivity, while the portability of printed books facilitated the trend toward silent, private reading and intellectual isolation and reflection. The pervasiveness of individualism and atomism as symbolic forms was in turn reflected in the architecture of modern world order, which transposed individual identity to the interstate sphere and thus helped to dissolve the Christian commonwealth of the High Middle Ages into autonomous sovereign state units.

Spatial Biases

As outlined above, political identification at both the individual and state levels came to focus on an autonomous center, "a single fixed viewpoint" in Ruggie's words.[41] Corresponding with this emerging self-image was a more rigid demarcation of political space, a clear separation between insiders and outsiders. In other words, *spatial* representations of political community became more pronounced in contrast to the medieval world order where borders were less fixed, indeed fading into one another at certain points. In Dodgshon's words, "The novelty in the way early states territorialized themselves stemmed from the fresh concepts which they imputed to spatial order."[42] Once again, the movement toward more rigid, linear demarcations of political space was the product of a multiplicity of factors reaching back into trends that originated in the Middle Ages. But one reason why this spatial bias resonated so strongly was that it "fit" the surface form and presentation of printing—especially its visual bias and linear representation.

As historians of the medieval imagination describe, medieval political rule was not conceptualized by the people of the time in spatio-territorial terms. It was Christendom that defined reality, and here the material world crossed over easily into a spiritual world beyond.[43] Indeed, nature was replete with abstract signs of the sacred, and geography was subordinated to a hierarchical conception of the universe. Notions of reality were more intense and fluid, and less exacting than our own.[44] Harvey notes how "external space was weakly grasped and generally conceptualized as a mysterious cosmology populated by some external authority, heavenly hosts, or more sinister figures of myth and imagination."[45] The absence of space as a basis upon which to demarcate political authority no doubt reflected the complex, heterogeneous nature of rights and obligations of the feudal era, but more subtly, it also reflected the prevailing oral-aural bias of communications. "Hearing," much more than "seeing," predominated both metaphorically and in actual practice. Clanchy describes how "medieval letter script was understood to represent sounds needing hearing."[46] Thus John of Salisbury was not out of the ordinary when referring to letters as *vocum indices*, or "indicators of voices."[47] Consider in this respect the way that the scrutiny of accounts was referred to as "auditing"—a label that reflects the fact that individuals primarily had texts read aloud to them even when undertaking commercial accounting.[48] In the predominantly oral environment of the Middle Ages, it is not surprising that the prevailing metaphors and symbolic forms tended to betray a bias toward hearing and speaking.

By contrast to the medieval world order, modern patterns of rule in western Europe came to be *seen* in terms of a rigidly compartmentalized political *space*. This linear spatial bias was most starkly apparent in the transformation of European maps, which by the fifteenth century were "highly linear, incredibly precise . . . partitioned into distinct parcels, and continuous in the sense that, with only a few exceptions . . . [they are] entirely filled."[49] The ideal of political authority gradually crystallized into a sense of spatial exclusion — into mutually-distinct, contiguous territorial spaces. Flat, rigid, and compartmentalized blocks of sovereign territories increasingly defined the legitimate mode of individuation in modern Europe. What accounts for this shift to a concern with rigid spatial representations of political order? The short answer is no one single variable. The "revolution in the European way of 'seeing' the world," as Buisseret explains, "no doubt emerged from a multiplicity of causes."[50]

Certainly the prevailing notions associated with Euclidean geometry and Newtonian physics were crucial components in determining the cultural forms of the period, as were changes in cartography, which accompanied expanding commercial interests around the globe.[51] The rediscovery of Ptolemaic cartography, which imagined how the globe would appear from a vantage outside and looking down on it, coincided with both a commercial and a security interest in the surveillance of territorial space.[52] And the confluence of the new physics with this reinvigorated penchant for map-making was especially important in accustoming Europeans to the idea that the world "might be described under a system of mathematical coordinates."[53] Also decisive were changes in Renaissance painting emphasizing single-point perspective, which "conceives of the world from the standpoint of the 'seeing-eye' of the individual."[54] New forms of realism in artistic expression helped overturn the symbolism of medieval art, which had subordinated accuracy of visual representation to religious hierarchy.[55]

Given less attention than these other factors by some authors, but no less consequential, was the shift in the mode of communication to printing. One way printing favored this new *mentalité* was through the mass reproduction and distribution of printed maps — a topic that was discussed in the previous chapter with respect to state surveillance. The sheer numbers of printed maps circulating (particularly in standardized school texts) gradually accustomed Europeans to visual, grid-like representations of political order, to sharp divisions between "insiders" and "outsiders." Through their standardization and reproduction, they helped infuse a sense of order and fixity to national borders. Generations of students, state administrators, elites, and scholars would be increasingly acculturated into a view of political community derived from these standardized representations of flat, linear spaces.

But more subtly than the dissemination of maps, printing oriented communications away from the prevailing *oral-aural* bias of the Middle Ages to the *visual* bias of the early modern period. The dominant mode of communication shifted from speaking and hearing to silent, visual scanning of standardized printed documents. As this environment deepened and expanded, it crystallized with and reinforced other similar biases and symbolic forms, entrenching linear-ordered space as the predominant *mentalité* of the early Modern period. McLuhan elaborates on the connection:

> Psychically the printed book, an extension of the visual faculty, intensified perspective and the fixed point of view. Associated with the visual stress on point of view and the vanishing point that provides the illusion of perspective there comes another illusion that space is visual, uniform and continuous. The linearity, precision, and uniformity of the arrangement of movable types are inseparable from these great cultural forms and innovations of Renaissance experience.[56]

As McLuhan was fond of noting, printing is a "ditto device" that precisely situates the word in space.[57] It is the mechanical reproduction of "the exactly repeatable visual statement."[58] Initially, early printed books resembled the idiosyncratic surface appearance of medieval manuscripts, varying in style and presentation depending on the printer or the region. But the nomadicism of the early printers, coupled with the expenses of cutting individual type founts and punches, led to a more uniform type-set over time. Once uniform, the surface appearance of the printed page, with its carefully measured margins flush along each border, its ruled lines and standardized roman lettering, conveyed a sense of visual order and linearity that mirrored the spatial bias of the times.[59] A number of innovations new to the printed text, such as alphabetical ordering, sectional divisions, and indexes further complemented an abstract, rational cognitive orientation favoring uniform spatial order and linearity. And the spread of standardized, printed pages, in turn, helped to shift the bias of communications away from speaking and hearing to silent, visual reading. A new "perceptual field" opened up, in Lowe's words, as typography became embedded in western European culture. This perceptual field was characterized by "the primacy of sight" and the corresponding "order of representation-in-space" facilitated by printing and "evident in the town planning, road construction, and landscape gardening of the period." [60]

As with the new physics, geometry, and cartography of the time, a print culture also contributed to the spatial orientation of modern world order: visual, rational, linear thinking translated into a highly rigid and compartmentalized ideal view of political rule—an ideal to which state practice and the map of Europe gradually conformed. Printing helped reorient the bias of communications away from speaking and hearing to silent reading and visual order. Without the standardization of printing and the gradual increase in literacy that accompanied the mass distribution of printed material, the overwhelmingly oral-aural bias of the medieval period might never have been dissolved. The early modern stress on linear, parcelized, territorially discrete units of political authority flourished in the new typographic media environment, where the mode of communication was predominantly through the linear, standardized printed page.

Imagined Communities

One of the most important consequences of the new mode of communication for social epistemology as it relates to world order transformation was the way it fostered the emergence of a new, distinctly modern, imagined community: the nation. The development of printing helped fuse the idea of a distinct national language with a sense of common identity that would gradually become one of the central defining features of the modern European world order. As with other symbolic forms and social constructs discussed in this chapter, printing did not generate nationalism; its roots can be traced back prior to the development of the printing press into the Middle Ages. However, as will be argued below, it is unlikely that nationalism would have developed its essential "linguistic core" if printing had not standardized and fixed vernacular languages in early modern Europe. Furthermore, printing encouraged both directly and indirectly the "homogenization" drive undertaken by centralizing monarchs, which in turn gave rise to an imagined community based on a shared standardized language.

As with most other characteristics of modernity, a form of proto-nation-alism can be traced back into the late Middle Ages.[61] Evidence of a fer-menting national consciousness can be found in country names: by 1000 the word *Polonia* began to appear; in the twelfth century, *Catalonia*; in 1204 Philip Augustus used the description *rex Franciae* for the first time to refer to the *Regnum Francie*, or the Kingdom of France.[62] Although the existence of proper names indicates at least an embryonic sense of national conscious-ness, it was a dim consciousness. Not only was it subordinate to other over-arching senses of group identity, but it also lacked the quasi-mythical at-tachment to a shared language as a "natural" mark of a people and a legitimate basis upon which to differentiate political authority.

To be sure, speakers of various local dialects recognized linguistic differ-ences during the late Middle Ages, especially when diverse groups were brought together during the various Crusades.[63] At times these differences formed an elementary sense of collective identity. For example, when the University of Paris was established in the early thirteenth century, partici-pants from around Europe grouped themselves according to their language, or nation.[64] But vernacular language itself was rarely a defining site of sym-bolic or political contestation as it was to become in the eighteenth and nineteenth centuries. According to Chaytor, "No ruler dreamt of attempting to suppress one language in order to impose another upon a conquered race."[65] Certainly Latin was used and thus established a sense of transnational identity among elites, but the various regional vernaculars and local dialects did not elicit strong emotional bonds among their speakers—at least not enough to form the fundamental basis of political differentiation and legit-imation. As Guenee relates, in the thirteenth century "linguistic boundaries had no relation to political frontiers" and "no one would have thought that a State should correspond to a 'nation.' "[66]

Apart from the hegemonic role of Church-Latin, an important impedi-ment to the fusing of language and nationality prior to printing was the fluidity of language in an oral culture. Written languages never achieved the fixity that was established in print, following closely in their evolution the changes of the spoken word. "For this reason, the French of the *Chansons de Geste*, for example, in the twelfth century differs greatly from that written by Villon in the fifteenth."[67] As Chaytor explains:

The written or printed language professes to represent the standard tongue; from this the spoken language tends continually to diverge, through its readiness to follow individual innovations which become fashionable. The bulwark of resistance to these is the printed language, which is modified only when new forms have become so widespread that they cannot be ignored. When this stage has been reached . . . the basis has been laid for the formation of a national linguistic consciousness, and a language is felt to be the expression of tribal or racial characteristics. For print alone can secure the indispensable conditions of standardisation, the substitution of visual for acoustic word-memory.[68]

In the sixteenth century, with the advent of printing, this type of "linguistic drift" slowed considerably. By the seventeenth century European vernacular languages assumed their current, modern forms.

Ernst Gellner has shown persuasively how this trend toward standardized, uniform national languages was closely bound up with the interests of centralizing state monarchies and the imperatives of industrialization.[69] For Gellner, a high level of competent vernacular literacy, coupled with the standardization of printing (what he calls a "standardized medium"), are critical tools in providing a "common conceptual currency" that is an essential prerequisite for a complex division of labor.[70] As a consequence, "the monopoly of legitimate education" in the early modern era became essential to the state in structuring the national work force, whose impersonal "communications must be in the same shared and standardized linguistic medium and script [sic]."[71] According to Gellner, one result of this deliberate homogenization campaign was that an imagined community based on shared linguistic identity began to emerge—one that was deliberately encouraged by centralizing monarchs through mass public education and the promotion of a literate, educated work-force necessary for the industrialization drive.[72] By the nineteenth century, this sense of community based on shared linguistic identity would gradually evolve into the powerful ideology of modern nationalism.

Gellner's explanation of the rise of nationalism is one that is shared by both Chaytor, and Febvre and Martin. According to Febvre and Martin, the printing press provided the means by which state ministers and cultural elites could encourage "a process of unification and consolidation which established fairly large territories throughout which a single language was written."[73] In all of the major countries in Europe, a process of vernacular standardization was undertaken—a process that was not only vastly encouraged by printing, but would have been virtually impossible without it. Through the means of mass printing, standardized conventions were established with respect to spelling, grammar, and vocabulary.[74] By fixing one dialect as the predominant mode of speech, printing helped reduce other local dialects to the status of regional or local patois, thus undermining more parochial identities while at the same time legitimating a common, standardized language within territorial boundaries.[75] The legitimating of singular "national" languages, in turn, became an important basis of differentiating people from people and state from state, fragmenting the transnational hegemony of Church-Latin with various national vernaculars.[76] It is then but a short step, as Chaytor argues, to regarding "the official language as the national heritage and an expression of national character,"[77] especially if this national character is deliberately cultivated by state officials who have a strategic interest in the homogenization of the populace.[78] In other words, the properties of printing, in conjunction with a conscious unification and homogenization drive, led to the exaltation of language as a quasi-divine mark of shared national identity and a *visible* affirmation of political differentiation.

A slightly different, but no less persuasive, account of the relationship between printing and nationalism is developed by Benedict Anderson in *Imagined Communities*. According to Anderson, the very possibility of imagining the "nation" could arise only after the belief that sacred script-languages offered privileged access to ontological truth began to erode. The Word had to be stripped of its divinity. A further contribution to the emergence of the nation was a shift in temporal horizons from medieval cosmology to "homogenous, empty time." Both of these shifts, according to Anderson, can be attributed to the development of printing and its interaction with capitalism, which assured widespread distribution of the new mode of communication. "The convergence of capitalism and print technology on the fatal diversity of human language created the possibility of a new form of imagined community, which in its basic morphology set the stage for the modern nation."[79]

Unlike Gellner, Chaytor, and Febvre and Martin, Anderson places less emphasis on overt manufacturing of national identity by state elites, and more on the convergence of a number of largely contingent variables. However, the two interpretations do not detract from each other, as a state interest in homogenization would only further the "blind" convergence of other factors to which Anderson points. And Anderson's analysis complements those outlined above by bringing to light other, perhaps less consciously

directed, factors that helped facilitate a sense of national-linguistic identity.
For Anderson, the critical variable in this respect is the newspaper, which
through its simultaneous daily consumption provides an image of "a sociological organism moving calendrically through homogenous, empty
time"—an analog to the nation.[80] The newspaper provides a sense of shared
national experiences, with each communicant aware that the same reading
experience is undertaken simultaneously with thousands, perhaps millions,
of others with whom s/he has had no personal contact.[81] Anderson's emphasis
on the largely indirect role of the newspaper in the development of nationalism is similar to one developed earlier by McLuhan. Like Anderson, Mc-
Luhan argues in *The Gutenberg Galaxy* that through newsprint a people
sees itself for the first time:

> The vernacular in appearing in high visual definition affords a glimpse
> of social unity co-extensive with vernacular boundaries. And more peo-
> ple have experienced this visual unity of their native tongues via the
> newspaper than through the book.[82]

Although the emergence of nationalism as an ideological force did not
reach its peak until the late eighteenth and early nineteenth centuries, its
"incubation" period actually reaches back into the late Middle Ages. However, with the advent of printing a critical barrier to its development was
removed; the linguistic drift of vernaculars that characterized the oral environment of the Middle Ages was arrested and a standardized "national"
language emerged "below" the transnational Church-Latin and "above" the
various local or regional dialects. As a result of the emergence of national
languages, the deliberate cultivation of a homogenous population by state
elites, and the widespread dissemination of printed material, a sense of imagined community arose throughout Europe based on a shared language of a
people. Between the late eighteenth and nineteenth centuries, this sense of
imagined community became the legitimate mode of differentiating political authority, and one of the pillars of modern world order.

Changes in social epistemology are critical elements in the transformation of world orders. Shared symbolic forms and cognitive biases provide the
critical "metaphysical underpinnings" of the architecture of political authority—in particular, the distinct ways in which political communities are
imagined. Although positivists and materialists have for too long slighted the

importance of mentalités collectives in structuring and orienting political behavior, a new theoretical sensitivity is emerging across the social sciences that takes culture and symbolic forms seriously. The historically contingent web-of-beliefs into which a people are acculturated are now widely recognized as a crucial aspect of differentiating culture from culture and epoch from epoch. A critical area of research, then, is the processes by which social epistemology undergoes transformation.

In this chapter, I examined the way the change in the mode of communication to printing contributed to the transformation of social epistemology along three dimensions, each of which was shown to have an important bearing on the character of European world order: First, in generating new forms of authorship and copyright, and by favoring the trend toward silent, private reading and intellectual separation, the printing environment contributed to the distinctly modern sense of atomism or individualism as a prevailing symbolic form and moral idea. The pervasiveness of this symbolic form was, in turn, mirrored at the world-order level by the emergence of autonomous sovereign states. Second, the linear surface appearance of the printed page helped reorient communications from an oral-aural to a visual bias. In doing so, it reinforced the emerging spatial bias of early modern Europe in favor of highly rigid and linear representations of political community. Lastly, the fixity and mass reproducibility of printing helped fuse a sense of group identity around fixed vernacular languages, thus contributing to the modern imagined community of the nation.

Undoubtedly, the medieval-to-modern transformation of European world order was driven by a wide confluence of factors, from broad environmental changes to changes in ideas, thus making it futile to suggest any single "master variable." In part 1 of this study, I have argued that the change in the mode of communication that occurred during this period was critical to altering the distribution of power among social forces and in rethreading the dominant web-of-beliefs of the time. Certainly the transformation would have been much different had there been no change in the communications environment. Centralized forms of political authority, which so often in the past had withered because of the predominantly oral-personalized form of rule characteristic of the feudal system, could not have evolved as fully or as efficiently as they did in parts of western Europe without the availability of mass-reproduced, printed documents. The rise of an urban bourgeoisie, itself a crucial link in the rise of the modern state, could not have developed such a complex commercial culture had their not been available a standardized medium, such as the newspaper, to facilitate commercial exchange. What if the fate of the Protestant Reformation, whose rapid spread and success was so closely tied to the availability of printing, had gone the way of previous heresies? Likewise the flourishing of a scientific humanist spirit? Both of these social forces not only "fit" the printing environment but were also critical in challenging the Church's place in medieval cosmology. Lastly, it would be hard to conceive of the changes to individual subjectivity, the flourishing of linear spatial biases, and the rise of a fixed national-vernacular language as the predominant way of imagining communities all occurring simultaneously without the availability of printing.

While communication technology was obviously an important factor, I would be contradicting my theoretical perspective if I argued that printing was the sole variable or prime mover responsible for this transformation. Nonetheless, because communications are implicated in all spheres of life, from production to security to culture, a focus on the mode of communication did provide a useful *lens* through which to view the transformation of political authority as a whole. Using the same analytical and theoretical lens, then, in part 2 of this study I turn to an examination of the contemporary transformation of world order at a planetary level.

Part 2

Hypermedia and the Modern to
Postmodern World Order Transformation

5 Transformation in the Mode of Communication: The Emergence of the Hypermedia Environment

A web of glass spans the globe. Through it, brief sparks of light incessantly fly, linking machines chip to chip and people face to face.
—Vinton G. Cerf, "Networks," *Scientific American*,
(September 1991), p. 72.

One morning, I awoke at 7:30 A.M. and turned on my personal computer. After issuing a few commands, I had connected myself remotely to the Internet and began reading the fifty-eight electronic mail messages that had collected overnight. The majority of the messages were "postings" from two of the six electronic discussion groups of which I am a member—the International Political Economy-NET and the Mediev-L medieval discussion group. On this particular day the content of the messages on the two discussion groups reflected a variety of ongoing discussion "threads" ranging from the relevance of Aristotle to the early modern state-building process, to Chomsky's views on the media, to the fate of the Chiapas Indians in Mexico. Twelve of the fifty-eight messages were personal: two from a colleague in Tokyo "forwarding" me articles he had recently "downloaded" from the "net" on Japanese studies of electronic communities; one from a colleague based in Taipei offering his reply to my last message on the topic of global consumer culture; three from a professor of psychology at Northwestern University with whom I engage regularly in "on-line" discussions; one from a colleague in Washington, D.C. providing me with details on an upcoming book project; one from a colleague in Pennsylvania outlining his views on the academic job market; two from a colleague in London, Ontario offering critical comments on my interpretation of Richard Rorty and philosophical realism; one from a colleague in San Rafael, California confirming that he had received my last message; and one from a colleague across town asking when I would be next on campus. The day was not unusual.

From the perspective of an average person living fifteen, or even ten, years ago, such a morning routine would likely have been considered the stuff of science fiction. Yet today it is a routine that is carried out by millions of other individuals around the planet. It illustrates the extent to which the mode of communication has undergone dramatic and fundamental change in a very short period of time—a change that is leading to a new communications environment that I refer to as *hypermedia*.

The purpose of this chapter will be to map this emerging communications environment—to trace its sociological and technological roots and to provide an outline of its central properties, or "nature." More so, perhaps, than previous changes in modes of communication, no single technological innovation or instrument of technology signals this transformation. Rather, the emergence of the hypermedia environment reflects a complex melding and converging of distinct technologies into a single integrated *web* of digital-electronic-telecommunications—a process that has roots reaching back to the late nineteenth century, and that encompasses a series of technological innovations that continued through the twentieth century, culminating in the digital convergence that began in the late 1960s.

Perhaps because of this convergence of once-discrete technologies, many observers have tended to focus on various distinct parts of the communications environment rather than the environment itself. The result has been a proliferation of terms and labels that designate a particular component of the environment, none of which satisfactorily captures the new mode of communication as a whole. For example, while "information" is certainly more abundant in the new media environment, it is not unique to it, as all prior modes of communication have distributed information in some particular way—even primitive oral cultures. Likewise, "information superhighway" describes only one small aspect of the new communications environment—the transmission element. Similarly, the term "cyberspace" has taken on meaning as a reference to the artificial "space" one enters on computer networks, but it is not generally associated with television or faxes.[1] While not wishing to add unduly to academic and popular jargon, borrowing from Jean Baudrillard I have chosen the term hypermedia to designate the emerging communications environment.[2] This term not only captures the convergence of discrete technologies, it also suggests the massive penetration and ubiquity of electronic media characteristic of the new communications environment. Furthermore, the prefix "hyper" (meaning "over" or "above") emphasizes two central characteristics of this environment: the speed by which communications currently take place, and the intertextuality or interoperatibility of once-discrete media. As will be described below, the hypermedia environment is not just the television, the computer, the fax machine, the cellular phone, the satellite reconnaissance system, or the hand-held video camera—it is all of the above and more linked *together* into a single seamless web of digital-electronic-telecommunications.

The Pre-history of Hypermedia: Technological and Sociological Roots

As with other innovations in communication technologies, the development of hypermedia did not occur *de novo*, but was contingent on a series of interdependent technological, sociological, and material factors. The "pre-history" of hypermedia thus dates back to the middle of the nineteenth century when social forces drove technological research and development (R&D) into ways to improve long-distance communications. Although smoke and fire signals had been employed by humans for centuries to communicate messages over distances, they were too simple to be employed for anything beyond the most basic of tactical communications. More complex communications, such as that found in spoken, written and printed words, had been constrained by the existing mode of transportation of the time. Thus, prior to 1840 complex communications could move only as fast as the swiftest of technologies—the train—which then had a speed of about 35 miles per hour.[3]

It is entirely conceivable that such constraints would have remained constant had it not been for the development of social forces that focused attention on ways to overcome them. But such was clearly not the case in the latter half of the nineteenth century, during which a person born in 1830 might well have witnessed such communication innovations as photography and telegraphy (1830s), rotary power printing (1840s), the typewriter (1860s), the transatlantic cable (1866), the telephone (1876), motion pictures (1894), wireless telegraphy (1895), and magnetic tape recording (1899). That person might have marveled at the advent of radio (1906), or even television (1923).[4] As Beniger has described in *The Control Revolution*, these innovations can be seen as responses to "control" crises arising out of the Industrial Revolution: that is, attempts to coordinate and manage ever more complex and integrated systems of production, distribution, and consumption of goods and services. In the United States especially, these control crises were particularly acute given the vast spaces opened up by westward territorial expansion, and not surprisingly, it was in North America that most of these innovations originated. Beniger describes how the intensifying industrialization process focused attention on ways to improve communications in the service of managing production, distribution, and consumption:

> Suddenly, in a matter of decades, goods began to move faster than even the winds themselves, reliably and in mounting volume, through factories, across continents and around the world. For the first time in history, by the mid-nineteenth century the social processing of material flows threatened to exceed in both volume and speed the system's capacity to control them. Thus was born the crisis of control, one that would eventually reach, by the end of the century, the most aggregate levels of America's material economy.[5]

Because transportation capabilities were improving at such a great pace and over such large distances, it became an imperative to establish more effective means of communicating information over these large distances. Safety problems were especially acute, particularly the coordination of train traffic.[6] Railroad companies had actually held back the development of planned new lines because of safety problems, a situation that was magnified by a series of spectacular accidents caused by poor communication and coordination. Commerce was being transported so swiftly that firms had difficulty keeping track of inventory and movements of distributed products over large distances, and were unable to track consumer demand effectively.

Samuel Morse focused his energy on the development of the telegraph in the 1830s largely in response to these converging pressures. To be sure, Morse was not alone in his experimentation; in the 1820s and 1830s scientists in France, Russia, Germany, and England worked feverishly to respond to the social needs for more efficient long-distance communication — a reflection of converging social forces in this direction.[7] But it was Morse who constructed the first practical working electromagnetic telegraph in 1838, and demonstrated it to skeptical audiences for years thereafter. In fact, it was not until 1844 that Morse was given a grant by the Congress to construct an experimental line from Washington to Baltimore through which he transmitted the famous line, "What hath God wrought?" One day after Morse's public demonstration, the *Baltimore Patriot* newspaper employed the same Washington-to-Baltimore line to report on a vote in the House of Representatives, concluding that the telegraph represented "the annihilation of space."[8] For the first time, messages could travel faster than messengers. Although communication was no longer strictly tied to transportation, telegraph lines were installed in the right-of-ways of railway lines, and were used initially to coordinate rail traffic.[9] Not long afterward, however, the telegraph came to serve a more broad commercial and administrative function, greasing the wheels of commerce and unifying price and market systems across the continent. By 1862, 150,000 miles of telegraphic cable had been laid around the world, including 15,000 in Great Britain and 48,000 in the United States, spinning the first tentative webs in what would later become the wired world of the hypermedia environment.[10]

The telephone followed soon in the wake of the telegraph, offering the additional advantage of simultaneous transmission of two-way communications. Invented, of course, by Alexander Graham Bell in 1876, the telephone was introduced into a world already fired by the "lightning wires" of the telegraph. As a consequence, legal tussles ensued among the newly founded Bell corporation and the telegraphic monopoly Western Union over the rights and uses of the new device.[11] But the telephone spread rather quickly once the legal entanglements were settled. From 1880 to 1893 the number of telephones in the United States grew from about 60,000 to 260,000, with about two-thirds of those located in businesses.[12] By 1934, 33 million telephones were in operation worldwide.[13] Although initially confined to commercial enterprises and government offices, the telephone eventually provided two-way interactive voice links among individual households, a characteristic that would gradually become one of the central defining features of the hypermedia environment.

Coincidental with these developments in telecommunications, another portentous innovation in communication technology was occurring that provided yet a further seed in the development of hypermedia: the daguerreotype, or the photograph, invented by Louis Daguerre in 1838.[14] In developing an instrument that serves not merely "to draw nature" but "gives her the power to reproduce herself," Daguerre was building on the ancient human practice to reproduce visually worlds of nature and imagination—a practice that is one of the earliest hallmarks of the species itself.[15] Photography, or "writing with light," was initially restricted to idle spectacles, but technological developments in the use of negatives improved the reproductive quality of photographs such that by the 1890s they had become a staple in commercial advertisements, especially in newspapers and magazines.[16] The technology was the first in a series of image spectacles running through the turn of the century, from silent moving pictures in nickelodeons, to the Balaban and Katz movie palaces, to large cinema houses.[17]

From these three initial developments in telecommunications and photography, a spate of innovations in communication technologies followed. Of these, radio, and then later television were the most important. The former was an outgrowth of the wireless telegraph developed by Guglielmo Marconi, and did not really take off until after World War I with the gradual incorporation of hobby radio broadcasts into commercial enterprises.[18] While the television set was invented in 1923, and the first broadcasts were in 1939, it did not emerge as a popular medium until after World War II, a period that will be covered in more detail below. Although the telecommunication technologies built on similar basic scientific principles of electromagnetics, each of the media remained discrete: the television, the photograph, the radio, moving pictures, and the telegraph all clearly entailed separate communications components. One could watch television, or listen to the radio, or look at a photograph, but each involved a physically separate and distinct act.

The sudden sweep of communications innovation in such a short period of time had a significant impact on the prevailing cultural milieu. As many observers have pointed out, these changes reverberated throughout various counter-cultural and avant-garde spheres in the early part of the twentieth century, including art, poetry, and popular music.[19] At a more general level, the "mass" audience that was created with vernacular printing reached its apogee with these innovations, as government-regulated national monopolies were created across the industrialized countries to broadcast television and radio to mass audiences within sovereign-territorial jurisdictions. It was with this single-point/mass broadcast paradigm in mind that critical theorists would later ruminate on the rise of the "One-Dimensional Man" whose life was structured by pervasive mass propaganda—a model deeply informed by the ways in which totalitarian regimes were able to make effective use of mass media leading up to World War II.[20] Somewhat ironically, however, it was the imperatives of that war, and the Cold War that followed, that spurred on the next wave of technological innovations in communications that would lead gradually to the development of hypermedia, and to the eventual dissolution of the "mass" national audience.

The Cold War and Military Research and Development

While the technological innovations of the late nineteenth/early twentieth centuries were closely bound up with commerce and the imperatives of industrial production, it was World War II and the ensuing Cold War that fueled R&D into the next wave of technological change in communications. According to Molina, a complex of capital-government-military-science interests converged during and following World War II to become the dominant social constituency behind the development of microtechnology, particularly in the United States where the pressures of the Cold War were, of course, most acute.[21] While each of these social interests complemented and fed off each other, clearly it was the military interests that played the leading role in shaping and constraining the development of technologies at this time. Later, commercial interests both within and outside the United States would gradually overtake the U.S. military as the dominant social force behind microelectronic development, especially as the Cold War subsided. Out of this confluence of technological innovation, military re-structuring, commercial marketing, and consumer demand came the rapid explosion of the hypermedia environment in the late 1980s/early 1990s.

Military Sources of Technological Innovation

The convergence of interests among the groups forming the Cold War complex can be traced back to the onset of World War II. The harnessing of national energy toward the war effort brought together both private capital and government expenditures behind a common cause, and accelerated R&D of electronic communications within and often between the major industrialized countries. Prior to World War II, military research had primarily exploited civilian-commercial technologies to the needs of war. World War II reversed this relationship, placing military interests at the forefront of R&D—a relationship that was later buttressed by the well-known "spin-offs" argument, whereby military research was seen as useful insofar as civilian applications could be derived from militarily inspired technologies.[22]

World War II research on radars, computers, miniaturization, and guided missiles transformed the electronics industry. The U.S. radar program in particular was a vast undertaking, employing the cooperative efforts of major R&D centers, such as Bell Labs and the Massachusetts Institute of Technology Radio Laboratory, and costing as much as $2.5 billion—more than the entire Manhattan "Atom Bomb" Project.[23] The vast research drive led to a large number of significant developments in electronics in a short period of time, all of which arose out of, and were shaped by, military interests. For example, the first digital computer, the ENIAC, was financed as a military-science project designed to calculate ballistic missile projections.[24] Taken as a whole, the research undertakings of World War II generated not only new technologies and a new complex of interests, but also a "greater understanding of electronic technology, and an army of electronic enthusiasts."[25]

The intense focusing of research interests on military projects that was sustained through the war tailed off sharply immediately following the allied victory. In the United States, government shares of electronic industry sales declined to only about 25 percent of the total.[26] But the decline was short-lived. The onset of the Cold War rebooted the complex of interests that had been moribund since the war, once again focusing R&D on military-related projects. By 1953, government shares of electronic industry sales had risen to more than 60 percent of the total.[27] According to Molina, the influence was far-reaching, affecting all sectors of the electronics industry with the partial exception of telecommunications, which had already established a formidable private monopoly research and development enterprise under the Bell System. Even so, the Bell Labs were often closely intertwined with, and thrived on, military-sponsored contracts for new research and development. "Nowhere was this influence more decisive," writes Molina, "than on the development of the emerging technologies and industries of computers, industrial control systems and, above all, semiconductors."[28] Through the 1950s and 1960s, the Cold War hostility fueled the demand for more efficient, smaller, and speedier communication technologies. One of the more decisive influences on electronic developments was the so-called "space race," unleashed with the successful launch of the Soviet Sputnik satellite in 1957. Not only did the "space race" breed a well-funded civilian program in the National Aeronautics and Space Administration, or NASA, but also a tightly controlled, top-secret complex of space-based intelligence programs, initiating top-secret research into optics, electronics, and computers primarily designed for space-based reconnaissance.[29] The perceived "zero-sum" nature of the Cold War conflict added an urgency to the research into more advanced communication technologies, particularly as the Soviet Union was widely perceived as taking the lead.

During this period, military-funded research brought about such crucial electronic advances as the transistor, the silicon transistor, and the integrated circuit. The latter was an important stepping-stone to the development of the hypermedia environment, allowing the manufacture of multiple electronic functions and components on a single microchip.[30] Closely intertwined with these innovations in components technologies was the evolution of the computer, beginning with the already mentioned ENIAC. Although the designers of the ENIAC, Mauchly and Eckert, had created a commercial enterprise in 1951 to market their own computer, the UNIVAC 1, "there was little commercial recognition of the potential of computers."[31] As Sharpe notes:

> Until 1951, the computer industry was essentially non-commercial: each machine was one of a kind, and support came primarily from universities and government. In fact, it can be plausibly argued that without government (and particularly military) backing, there might be no computer industry today.[32]

During the height of the Cold War, the military remained the primary driving force behind the most significant developments in electronic computing and communications. In 1959—1960, the U.S. space-defense sectors still accounted for more than 70 percent of all computer sales.[33] This dominant social force driving the research and development of electronic communications had an important shaping influence on the nature and direction of technological innovation. Many of today's more consumer-oriented electronic products—such as virtual reality systems or computer games— are direct outgrowths of military technologies (e.g., air force flight simulators).[34] But the secrecy by which such research and development was carried out limited the extent of commercial applications, and the most sophisticated of communication technologies were typically confined to the military because of classification procedures.

Commercial Sources of Technological Innovation

By the late 1960s, however, the influence of the military in this complex began to decline and corporate-commercial interests began to rise. According to Molina, "The relative influence of government-military constituents waned as the emerging technologies and industries matured and corporate capital was able to exploit the vast opportunities offered by the commercial sector."[35] In the United States, the government purchase of semiconductors dropped from 50 percent of the total in 1960 to a low of 6 percent in 1973.[36] Perhaps the best illustration of the shift is in the area of personal computing. The microprocessor, which was probably the single most significant technological innovation in the development of hypermedia, was produced entirely for commercial applications by the U.S. company Intel in the early 1970s.[37] By integrating components needed for the central processing unit of a computer onto a single microchip, the microprocessor dramatically reduced the costs of computer hardware.[38] As a result, a wide variety of small commercial computer enterprises arose to build a market in personal computing—a strategy that initially was smugly dismissed as futile by larger corporate giants, like IBM.[39] Of course, the outstanding example in this respect is the Apple Corporation, founded by college dropouts Stephen Wozniak and Steven Jobs, but many similar fast-rising enterprises capitalized on the burgeoning home computer market beginning in the late 1970s.

At the same time the home computer market was blossoming, companies based in Japan and Europe were tapping into the home electronics market, particularly in the markets for color television and stereo components.[40] U.S. corporations that had traditionally thrived on regular defense outlays began to face stiff competition from these overseas firms at the same time as defense procurements were falling sharply in the 1970s. The result was that a wedge was inserted into the capital-science-government-military complex that had sustained military-oriented R&D into electronic communications through the Cold War.[41] While the so-called "second" Cold War of the early 1980s was able to resurrect the complex partially, through such high-financed military projects as the Strategic Defense Initiative, the momentum had clearly swung to the commercial sector, as private corporations began to engage in transnational joint ventures and strategic alliances to spread the costs of R&D and to gain entry into foreign markets for consumer electronic applications.[42]

The death-knell to the complex has been the abrupt end to the Cold War. Corporations that were once able to rely on military R&D contracts have now been forced into "restructuring" schemes to adapt to new conditions.[43] A new complex has formed as communications-related industries and corporations from around the world, encouraged by national governments, are now focusing on the largely untapped "home" or private market. Corporate-funded research centers, such as the MediaLab at MIT and the

Palo Alto Research Center in California, are beginning to replace military-funded research centers as the drivers and shapers of technological innovation.[44] Their explicit goal, as stated by the directors and top researchers of both companies: *ubiquitous computing*, or an infusion of communication technologies so deeply into everyday life that they become virtually invisible—a new environment.[45] This confluence of seemingly unending dramatic and revolutionary changes in communication technologies, coupled with a desperate search for new markets unleashed by the end of the Cold War, and colored by a pervasive "hype" about a coming communicopia, has led by the 1990s to a virtual stampede of interests focused on developing consumer and business applications of sophisticated electronic technologies. As Grossman aptly put it: "Driving it all is one simple, irresistible money-making idea—the prospect of converting every home and workplace into a computerized box office, shopping mall, video arcade and slot machine, open for business all day long, every day of the week."[46]

Today, the shift in orientation is noticeable in a variety of subtle ways. New products have been tailored to make sophisticated technologies more practical, or "user-friendly." Icons, or images, have replaced text-based controls as computer operating tools—an interface pioneered by the Apple Macintosh computer systems, but one that has been adopted by the extremely popular Microsoft Windows95 operating system. Advertisements for multimedia applications now prominently feature small children, the elderly—even nuns! All of these changes represent a shift in corporate strategies from military to consumer/business applications.

Complementing this corporate drive has been a push "from above" so to speak, as governments around the world have sought to reap the benefits of the "information revolution." Almost every major state has undertaken government-sponsored studies on the impact of new communication technologies, perceiving in an almost quasi-mythical way the economic possibilities inherent in the hypermedia environment. In Singapore, it is the "Vision of an Intelligent Island"; in South Korea, it is the "Initiative for Building the Korea Information Infrastructure"; in the European Community, it is "Europe and the Global Information Society"; in Canada, it is "The Canadian Information Highway."[47] Most prominent in this respect has been the Clinton Administration, and in particular, Vice President Al Gore, who has been a relentless advocate of what has been popularly called "the information superhighway."[48] Out of this fusion of revolutionary technological innovations and a new corporate-government complex of social forces has come the change in the communications environment to *hypermedia*.

The Properties of the Hypermedia Environment

As alluded to above, no single technological innovation or instrument of technology signals the development of the hypermedia environment. Instead, technological developments in three areas have been particularly crucial: digitization; computerization; and improvements in transmission capabilities, particularly fiber optic cables and wireless.

Digitization: Digitization refers to the encoding, transformation, and transmission of all information—whether audio, video, graphics or text—into a series of binary numbers—i.e., 1s and 0s.[49] This revolutionary means of translating information is superior to older (analog) systems primarily because when information is translated into binary numbers, an infinite number of copies can be made without any degradation having occurred. Likewise, unlike analog signals, digital information is more reliable over longer distances since only an on/off configuration requires translation rather than a continuously modulating frequency. Furthermore, digitization allows the integration of previously distinct media in the same system. All information once digitized becomes potentially intertranslatable regardless of whether it is audio, video, or text. As Brand notes, "with digitization the content becomes totally plastic—any message, sound, or image may be edited from anything into anything else."[50] The universal character of the digital signal is thus especially important for transmitting different media along the same communication channels. According to Saxby:

> In the case of analogue channels, the signal varied continuously according to the information in transmission, which meant in practice a different channel for each type of signal—for example telephone or radio broadcast. With digital channels, the only difference to be considered was the binary transmission speed necessary to transmit the information, whether it took the form of data, image or the human voice.[51]

Computerization: The digital "revolution" would not have had such a significant impact, however, had not computing technologies eventually been developed to exploit its potential.[52] Some of the crucial innovations in computing technologies were outlined above, but the critical one was the development of the microprocessor, or what has been called the "computer-on-a-chip," in 1969, and which was marketed in 1971 for US $200.[53] These first silicon-based microprocessors included about 2,300 transistors on each chip, and could perform 60,000 operations per second. The microprocessor revolutionized electronic communications by speeding up computation time with increasing capacity all the while shrinking the size of equipment. As Augarten commented:

> Although Intel did not realize it at first, the company was sitting on the device that would become the universal motor of electronics, a miniature analytical engine that could take the place of gears and axles and other forms of mechanical control. It could be placed inexpensively and unobtrusively in all sorts of devices—a washing machine, a gas pump, a butcher's scale, a juke box, a typewriter, a doorbell, a thermostat, even, if there was a reason, a rock. Almost any machine that manipulated information or controlled a process could benefit from a micro-processor.[54]

Since then, the performance levels and capabilities of computer chips have continued to make dramatic improvements, generally following what has been referred to as Moore's Law (after the former head of Intel, Gordon Moore): the number of transistors stored on a silicon chip will double each year following its inception. To be precise, the number of transistors fabricated on a silicon chip has proceeded through eight orders of magnitude since the transistor was first invented in 1948.[55] Today, the most advanced commercial silicon chips are manufactured with ultraviolet light, further increasing the computing power on ever-more tiny chips. Transistors having dimensions smaller than a micron (a millionth of a meter) are now routinely fabricated in numbers approaching tens of millions on a single semiconductor chip.[56] Although there are physical limits to such trends, researchers believe that the progression will continue into the next century.[57] The resulting expansion of computing capabilities and storage capacities has been enormous. In 1961 the most sophisticated computer could handle 34,000 arithmetic operations per second; in 1981 800,000 arithmetic operations could be handled by a single computer; today, *each microprocessor* (and not an entire computer) can handle up to a billion instructions per second.[58] In

1970, a disk pack the size of a birthday cake was required to store in immediately accessible form a million characters of text; by the 1980s that many data could be stored on a 3.5 inch diskette; today, it can be stored on a semiconductor device no larger than a credit card.[59]

Transmission capabilities: The third area in which technological developments have been crucial to the emergence of the hypermedia environment is innovations in transmission capabilities. In the hypermedia environment, digital information can now move through a variety of physical media, including fiber optic cables, coaxial cables, and copper wires, or through the electromagnetic spectrum in the case of wireless communications.[60] Of these various transmission channels, without a doubt the most significant development is fiber optics cables, which are composed of multiple fine glass wires that vastly augment the relative carrying capacity of cables.[61] In comparison to traditional copper-wire telephone lines, which have a maximum carrying capacity of about one million bits per second, optical fiber carrying lightwaves is now able to handle about a billion bits per second.[62] No practical upper limit on this capacity has yet been determined.[63] Since 1975, the transmission capabilities of optical fiber has increased ten-fold every four years.[64] Today, even though fiber uses less than 1 percent of its theoretical carrying capacity, it can still transmit the contents of the entire *Encyclopedia Britannica* every second.[65] Moreover, fiber optic lines are much smaller than traditional coaxial and copper-wire lines, enabling many more physical transmission channels in the same space.[66]

One limitation to fiber optic lines, however, is the installation expenses associated with replacing existing copper-wire and coaxial cables — especially to individual households and businesses. As a consequence, most of the fiber optic lines that have now been installed in the major industrialized countries act as connections between individual "nodes" or cities, with the final "drop" to homes and some businesses still being copper-wire in the case of telephone and coaxial in the case of cable television. However, further innovations in transmission capabilities, particularly asymmetric digital subscriber loop (ADSL) technologies, are enhancing the bandwidth capacity of existing copper-wire and coaxial cables such that high-speed digital links are available for the so-called "last mile" link.[67] The result is that individual homes can bypass direct fiber optic links while still being able to link into the high-speed digital environment of hypermedia.[68] For example, while 98 percent of Canadian households still have copper-wire telephone connections, the intercity network is entirely digital (including fiber optic cables, satellites, and microwave transmissions) carrying traffic at speeds up to 2.5 Gigabits per second (the equivalent of 32,000 simultaneous voice conversations).[69]

Fiber optics, and traditional copper and cable wires, are not the only means by which information is transmitted today; wireless transmissions, via both microwave towers and satellites, add yet another dense layer of transmission capabilities to the hypermedia environment. The radio portion of the electromagnetic spectrum is used to transmit electronic signals in a frequency spectrum ranging from low-medium frequencies (10–30,000 KHz) to high frequencies (3–30 MHz) to very and ultra-high frequencies (30–100 MHz) to microwave frequencies (3,000–12,000 MHz).[70] Each of the frequency ranges has particular strengths and weaknesses depending on the type of communications being transmitted. Moreover, because the electromagnetic spectrum is a limited natural resource, there are constraints on the amount of information that can be transmitted.[71] However, as with cable and copper wires, compression techniques to enhance bandwidth over the airwaves have been achieved in wireless communications to squeeze more carrying capacity into the electromagnetic spectrum essential for the accommodation of wireless cellular phones, pagers, and other mobile computing devices now flooding the market.[72]

Satellite systems, operating in the microwave band, are placed in a space-based geostationary orbit 22,300 miles above the earth's equator. At this distance, the period of rotation coincides with that of the earth, causing the satellite to appear stationary. The orbiting satellites perform a function similar to that of ground-based microwave relay stations, transmitting electronic information to ground antennas which then relay the information to cable, fiber optic, or copper wires. Because a satellite situated in geostationary orbit is visible to 43 percent of the earth's surface, a satellite situated over, for example, the Indian Ocean, can beam simultaneously to the United Kingdom and Japan.[73] Three communications satellites positioned at appropriate distances from each other can cover the entire globe with the exception of the poles.[74] However, as with the radio spectrum, there are a limited number of "parking spaces" or "slots" for satellites in the geostationary orbit. As a consequence, there has been a considerable battle over the principles upon which such "slots" should be distributed, with richer countries—and in particular the United States—arguing on the basis of "first-come, first serve," while the less developed countries have attempted to achieve a more internationally equitable distribution.[75] More recently, low-earth orbiting (LEO) satellites have been proposed for mobile communications systems, the most famous of which is Motorola's planned Iridium system, which will employ approximately 66 LEO satellites to allow phone communications from point-to-point anywhere on the planet. The Motorola satellites will be launched in the late 1990s, with as many as seven other planned systems following soon thereafter.[76]

The result of these three technological innovations, in conjunction with social forces, has been a *convergence* of both media and industries into a single, integrated planetary web of digital electronic telecommunications. Today, not only are text, video, graphics, and audio intertranslatable, but once-discrete technologies that have been associated traditionally with different communications spheres—particularly computers, telephones, and televisions—are becoming indistinguishable in terms of the information they provide. They are, in the words of an *Economist* survey, "being whirled into an extraordinary whole."[77] The days when one processed text on a computer, watched the television, and spoke into the telephone are drawing to a close. As Gleick aptly put it, "These little boxes will be connected, one way or another, to that vast, entangled, amorphous creature known to those in the business simply as the network."[78]

Indeed, only two obstacles stand in the way of the complete convergence of communication technologies into a single, seamless web of digital electronic telecommunications: industry competition and government regulations.[79] The technological convergence outlined above has suddenly thrust together once self-contained industries in both competition and cooperation as firms traditionally bound within one sector now find themselves under challenge from firms in other sectors, and visa versa. The most acute battle-line is drawn between cable and telephone companies as each is increasingly providing services that are indistinguishable from the other. But other industries—in particular consumer electronics, publishing, and information services—are entering the battle as well.[80] However, existing government regulations that were tailored for the communications of the preconvergence environment still maintain regulatory fences that prevent direct competition. And not only are these regulations a barrier *within* individual national jurisdictions but they also pose problems for *international* interconnectivity as well. As one author commented:

The problem is simple. Although the industrial world is already rich with telecommunications networks and computers, these systems can't always link up with each other because of differing standards and protocols, not to mention old-fashioned telephone monopolies that still control who has access to the wires and switches in many states. So "building" the information superhighway is partly a question of removing barricades on both sides of the Atlantic.[81]

On the one hand, the result has been a concerted push by private corporations and governments around the world for regulatory changes, often in the face of strong political counter-pressures to keep the status quo intact.[82] Debates have been fierce in both the developed and developing worlds regarding the appropriate regulatory framework to facilitate the technological convergence favored by large private capital interests while still ensuring "universal access" and "affordability" for the average consumer. To date, the forces of "liberalization" have clearly gained the momentum, having the support of both big business and large governments — in particular, the United States.[83] It is from these forces that much of the constructed anxieties on "being left behind" about hypermedia emanate.[84] For example, U.S. Vice President Al Gore's push for a single "planetary information network" is interpreted by many as a concerted effort to open national telecommunications industries around the world to private enterprise and competition.[85] One of the more recent and forceful adoptions of liberalization policies has been the planned break-up beginning in 1996 of the German state telephone monopoly Deutsche Telekom, which is expected to be the second largest privatization in the world, the largest being the $70 billion sale of stock in Japan's telephone monopoly in the late 1980s.[86] Throughout the Asia-Pacific region, seemingly all states have moved swiftly to adopt telecommunications liberalization and deregulation.[87] Even China's Ministry of Posts and Telecommunications has made liberalization moves to allow foreign access to their telecommunications infrastructure, as has Vietnam's Post and Telecommunications.[88] Elsewhere in the developing world, the norm is increasingly for a breakup of former state telecommunications monopolies and a massive scramble to attract private investment.[89]

On the other hand, communications firms around the world have entered into a frenzied spate of cross-border, multimedia joint ventures and alliances designed to sidestep existing regulations as well as reduce the costs and risks of operating in what is gradually evolving into a single massive marketplace.[90] The number and scope of these alliances is truly staggering and difficult to track on a day-by-day basis, as firms enter into talks only to have them scuttled by legal entanglements or disagreements.[91] The pace of alliances and deal-making is most furious within the United States. In 1994, some of the largest multimedia mergers were completed in the United States, including AT&T and McCaw Cellular, valued at $11.50 billion; Viacom and Paramount, valued at $9.6 billion; and Viacom and Blockbuster, valued at $7.97 billion.[92] Exemplifying the trend toward tangled cross-border alliances, the Microsoft Corporation of the United States entered into partnership with eight other firms in 1994, including Telstra Corporation of Australia, Deutsche Telecom of Germany, and Rogers Communications of Canada.[93] The cellular telephone company PacTel, based in the United States, has shareholdings in cellular networks in Germany, Portugal, Japan, Sweden, and Belgium.[94] Some of the most furious action is taking place in the Asia-Pacific region, where because of the economic boom and the generally poor state of traditional infrastructures massive investments and developments have been drawn in. In China, for example, where new telephone lines are being laid at the rate of 14.5 million annually, AT&T has signed a $16 million deal with the Ministry of Posts and Telecommunications to construct a massive fiber optic trunk line—one of an expected sixteen to be laid by 2000.[95] Likewise, the demand for handsets has led to joint ventures with Siemens, NEC, AT&T, Northern Telecom, and Alcatel.[96] As privatization of former state communications monopolies proceed, these cross-border, multimedia mergers will only become more dense and complex.

It is too early to predict exactly what type of regulatory arrangements will be reached that will reconcile global standards and interconnectivity with existing national jurisdictions. Nor is it clear exactly what type or types of business enterprises will emerge from the dizzying series of ongoing transnational strategic alliances and mergers in the communications industries once (or if) the dust settles. However, what *presently* exists might best be characterized as a *web of webs* of still separate but increasingly linked communications systems, such as the telephone, movies, television, personal computers, cellular phones, faxes, and more.[97] Each of these systems is gradually becoming interconnected and interoperable as regulatory and technical barriers standing in the way of complete integration are toppled. Some new systems—like the latest generation of multimedia computers—are neither telephones, televisions, nor computers, but a complex amalgam of all three. However, it is doubtful that a single device like the multimedia computer (what Stewart calls "a full-featured information appliance") will emerge as the sole means of communicating in the hypermedia environ-ment.[98] Instead, what appears to be the case is that a number of functional devices—some situated in the home (computers/televisions/telephones/ multi-media systems), some hand-held or portable (cellular phones/personal digital assistants/camcorders/laptop computers), and some that are remote (satellite reconnaissance systems/surveillance cameras)—will coexist in a globally networked web of digital communications.[99] These devices now have the potential to interconnect with each other seamlessly, some at the speed of light, with information moving through the air, bouncing off of satellites, through upgraded existing copper wires and cables, and through fiber optic wires.[100] Rather than a single instrument of technology or means of communication, then, it is this complex, digitally integrated web of com-munications *as a whole* that defines the hypermedia environment.

The Internet and World-Wide Web

The paradigm of the new mode of communication—and clearly the emerging infrastructure for the hypermedia environment—is networked computing, and in particular, the loose conglomeration of worldwide net-worked computers known as the "Internet." As Grossman explains, "the In-ternet serves as a remarkable example of the 'law of unintended conse-quences' run amok."[101] As is well-known by now, the Internet actually began as a U.S. military experiment in the 1970s to design a computer network called ARPANET that would withstand a nuclear attack.[102] The fundamental principle of the network was a distributed form of communications without central control, underpinned by a routing system called "packet switching." Through packet switching technologies, messages would be split up and sent along dispersed routes so that if parts of the network were lost in a military conflagration, they would still arrive at their destination. The ARPANET eventually evolved into a communications tool for public research organi-zations and universities in the United States, to be followed by other similar systems elsewhere. Using what was originally intended to be merely a sidebar feature of the network—electronic mail—discussion groups proliferated on a wide-range of esoteric topics and issues. By the time Internet became the successor to ARPANET in the late 1980s/early 1990s, networked commu-nications had exploded to include private individuals around the world linked through a truly anarchic web of computers, searching and sharing databases and entering into unmediated on-line discussions.[103]

As the editors of a recent special issue of *Scientific American* put it, "the Internet has grown so fast in so many places that no one really knows how big it is or how many people use it."[104] The migration to the Internet in the 1990s has been remarkable as government agencies, research organizations, universities and colleges, businesses, individuals both young and old and of both sexes scramble to get a piece of the action. In 1993 the President, the Vice President, and the First Lady of the United States all acquired Internet addresses (president@whitehouse.gov; vice-president@whitehouse.gov; and root@whitehouse.gov). In 1995 Canadian Prime Minister Jean Chretien was the first head of state to participate in an on-line computer network conference. The result has been an explosion of growth in Internet users according to measurements undertaken by the Internet Society.[105] For example, the number of host computers, or network "nodes," around the world has grown from 1,000 in 1984 to 10,000 in 1987 to 100,000 in 1989, to 1,000,000 in 1992, to 4,851,000 in 1994, to 9,500,000 in January 1996, to 12,881,000 in July 1996.[106] One million new hosts were added in the first six months of 1994 alone, many of which came from outside the United States. In that same first six months of 1994, Germany experienced a 51 percent increase in hosts; France 117 percent; Spain 79 percent; New Zealand 157 percent; Hungary 169 percent; Mexico 45 percent; Chile 170 percent; and Malaysia 204 percent.[107] Although the figures are rapidly made obsolete by exponential growth, there may be as many as 90 million individual Internet users spread unevenly around the world.[108]

For many years the Internet was unwieldy to navigate, with a primarily text-based interface that could often be intimidating to all but experienced computer users. Over the 1990s, however, improvements in software and navigation capabilities gradually made browsing and searching the Internet much more user-friendly. Hoping to cash in on the burgeoning market, a number of private services providers (e.g., Compuserve, America On-Line, Prodigy, and more recently the Microsoft Network and AT&T's Worldnet) emerged as appendages to the Internet, offering a much more accessible gateway.[109] Subscribers to the Internet and these private services could search data bases, exchange text, audio, graphics, and video information, and discuss topics on electronic Bulletin Board Systems (BBS's), USENET newsgroups, and listserves.[110] The number of active USENET newsgroups world-wide now totals around 10,000, with BBS's estimated at around 57,000.[111] Although many are specialized academic discussion groups, others reflect a bewildering variety of ultra-arcane and esoteric topics, like alt.personals. spanking.punishment or alt.barney.die.die.die.

But the truly revolutionary development—the one that has contributed to such exponential growth of the last few years—has been the emergence of the World-Wide Web, which permits the integration of hypertextual links and multimedia in a single platform.[112] Although technically distinct, the World-Wide Web has grown with such rapidity and adaptability that it has practically subsumed the Internet entirely. In conjunction with new browsers, such as Mosaic, Netscape, Spyglass, and Microsoft's Internet Explorer, "surfing" the Internet has suddenly become as easy as switching channels on a TV. Moreover, the ease by which such World-Wide Web "home pages" can be created has contributed even more to the rapid growth of Internet participants. Governments, news services, interest groups, academic institutions, businesses of all sorts, and—perhaps most importantly—individuals seeking to advertise their unique personal hobbies and fetishes, have all rushed to set up World-Wide Web home pages.

As might be expected, the substantive depth of these pages is uneven. But with seemingly every passing month the amount of information deepens and expands. According to measurements done by Matthew Gray of MIT's MediaLab, the number of World-Wide Web home pages has a doubling period of six months, with around 230,000 known home pages at the time of writing.[113] In providing globally-networked, hypertextual, interactive, multimedia digital communications in an anarchic web-of-webs of private and public computer organizations, networked computing in the form of the World-Wide Web is probably the best illustration of the "paradigm" of communications in the hypermedia environment.

What is the geographic distribution of hypermedia? From one perspective, it is truly planetary in its scope considering the extent to which satellite communications ensure that no area of the planet is beyond the reach of hypermedia penetration. Military, commercial, and environmental remote sensing satellites have mapped every square inch of the planet. Communications satellites provide computer and telephone links from even the remotest of regions, and global television networks and direct broadcast satellites beam programs to every continent on earth. There is no doubt that the hypermedia environment now blankets the planet in a dense network of digital-electronic-telecommunications. Indeed, it has for many years. However, it is becoming increasingly dense, spacious, and swift with each passing day.

From a *control* perspective, however, the distribution of hypermedia is clearly concentrated in the Northern hemisphere of the planet, with the wealthiest countries typically accounting for both the highest penetration rates of personal computers, telephones, and televisions, as well as the largest volumes of communications flows.[114] The starkest illustration of the disparities is that 4.7 billion of the world's 5.7 billion people still do not have a telephone.[115] The least telecommunications-developed country—Cambodia—has a teledensity of only 0.06 telephones per 100 people. The 47 least developed countries have an average teledensity of 0.25 per 100 people.[116] In Africa, the communications infrastructure is still so closely tied to colonial legacies that telephone calls made between neighboring countries often leave the continent entirely and are then routed back rather than simply crossing borders.[117] Nonetheless, the most dense penetration rates of hypermedia also happen to correspond to the wealthiest and most powerful segments of the planet. This is certainly not insignificant in terms of world order transformation—especially in light of the planetary reach of hypermedia outlined above.

A Planetary "Central Nervous System"

The central properties of this new communications environment might best be characterized in McLuhan's terms, as a planetary "central nervous system" composed of a web of webs of communications devices—telephones, televisions, computers, camcorders, portable digital assistants, and fax machines—all linked together into a single integrated network of digital-electronic-telecommunications.[118] This network never shuts down, constantly moving information in an instantaneous flow at the speed of light through fiber optic cables, through orbiting satellites, through the air, or through cable and copper. It is increasingly a "ubiquitous" computing and communications environment, deeply saturated by the tools of hypermedia in every facet of life—from the tiny computers that invisibly operate household appliances to the surveillance cameras in the bank and on the street corners, to the automatic teller and "interac" machines that read and process

digital "smart" credit cards, transmitting digital financial information instantaneously to financial institutions, to the 35, 58, or 120 channel television
systems that "narrowcast" programs to specialized audiences around the
world, to the cellular phones, personal digital assistants, and laptop computers that offer mobile telecommunications. It is a communications environment in which all media are intertextual or intertranslatable. Video, audio, text, and graphics are all similarly reduced to binary digits, and thus
can travel through the same channels, and be processed in the same way,
to be displayed on the same screen. It is an interactive environment, in which
communication flows in two directions rather than from a single center.
Everyone has the potential to reach everyone else instantaneously in the
hypermedia environment—"publication" and "broadcasting" are open to all
who are connected.

In sum, the change in the mode of communication was driven by a
complex set of technological, social, and material factors reaching back to
the late nineteenth century. Largely in response to the Industrial Revolution,
and building on newly founded scientific principles of electromagnetics, a
series of innovations in communication technologies occurred rather suddenly in the second half of the nineteenth century. While the telegraph,
and later the telephone, opened up the possibility of complex communications over distances, the photograph, and later the moving picture and the
television, provided the first in a series of image spectacles. The onslaught
of two world wars and the ensuing Cold War significantly altered the urgency
and trajectory of R&D into electronic communications, and formed the basis
for a complex of government-science-military-capital interests centered
mostly in the United States. It was out of this complex of interests that some
of the more important technological precursors to the hypermedia environment arose, including most importantly the computer. However, by the
1970s this complex began to dissolve and was gradually replaced by a more
consumer- and business-oriented push behind the R&D of electronic communications. Corporations outside the United States—in particular those
based in Germany and Japan—began to compete with American firms in
the consumer electronics market at the same time as government expenditures in defense began to erode. The abrupt end to the Cold War added an
urgency to corporate restructuring, and a new science-government-capital
complex began to emerge centered not on military applications of electronic

communications, but the burgeoning entertainment, home-consumer, and business applications market. The conjunction of this new complex with a series of technological innovations brought about, by the late 1980s, the emergence of the hypermedia environment. Using the theoretical and analytical lens employed in part one of this study, the remaining two chapters examine the way the architecture of modern political authority may be undergoing transformation in this new communications environment.

6 Hypermedia and the Modern to Postmodern World Order Transformation: Distributional Changes

In this chapter, I turn to an examination of the distributional changes that may be occurring today as a result of the emerging hypermedia environment. As outlined in the theoretical chapter, distributional changes are those that take place in the relative power of social forces as a result of a "fitness" between the interests of these social forces and the communications environment. In other words, social forces whose interests match the hypermedia environment will tend to flourish, while those whose interests do not will tend to be disadvantaged. The claim being made here is not that the change in the mode of communication to hypermedia *generates* these social forces, but rather that existing social forces will tend to flourish or wither depending on their relative "fitness" with the hypermedia environment. This difference is crucial because it directs analysis to present conditions, rather than to future worlds yet to unfold. Thus my goal here is to identify those social forces in the world today whose interests or "logics of organization" appear to fit the hypermedia environment, and those that do not. On this basis, then, projections about the likely distributional consequences of the hypermedia environment can be made.

As throughout this study, my focus is on the impact of these distributional changes on the architecture of world order—in this case, *modern* world order. The "paradigm" of modern world order is the practice of dividing political authority into territorially distinct, mutually exclusive sovereign nation-states—a mode of differentiation that first arose, as outlined in part

1, in early modern Europe and from there spread gradually through imitation and force to encompass the entire planet. I use the word "paradigm" deliberately in order to underscore that this mode of differentiating political authority has never been absolute, but has accommodated various infringements in practice and in principle throughout modernity. Like many other observers, however, I see developments occurring that indicate this paradigm is being fundamentally transformed—that modern world order, in the words of both Ruggie and Elkins, is "unbundling."[1] My intention in this chapter is to trace those elements of the "unbundling" process that are linked to distributional changes related to the emerging hypermedia environment.

The chapter will proceed in the following way: First, I will explore the distributional changes occurring in international political economy—particularly, the way the hypermedia environment favors the transnationalization of production and the globalization of finance. Second, I will examine the way transnational social movements are flourishing in the nonterritorial spaces of hypermedia, leading to what has been called a "global civil society." Third, I will assess the relative "fitness" of alternative domestic security arrangements in the hypermedia environment, arguing that this environment complements liberal-republican political organizations, or what have been called "negarchies." Finally, I will conclude with some brief observations on the way these distributional changes may be helping to transform the architecture of modern world order.

Hypermedia Markets: The Transnationalization of Production and Finance

Transnational Production

Like other aspects of social organization, production in the modern world order has generally been organized within territorially distinct, mutually exclusive sovereign nation-states. In other words, the production of goods and services, and the organization of economics, has been primarily a "national" affair and has been undertaken in a "national" context. Because of the state survivalist *mentalité* into which state leaders were acculturated, economic production has been shaped and driven primarily by a desire for self-sufficiency and autonomy.[2] As Thomson remarks, "historically, state control of the economy was not meant to be functional to society but to the state's war-making capabilities."[3] If Waltz's notion of functionally undifferentiated "like" units never corresponded exactly to state practice, it was a fair representation of the ideal to which all states strove.[4]

In *practice*, of course, states have varied enormously in the extent to which they have approximated this ideal. And as Marxists have pointed out, "national" economic production has never been completely de-linked from a world economic system characterized by a variety of dependencies between "core" and "peripheral" economies.[5] But, in general, economic production has been organized, planned, measured, and thus overwhelmingly contained within discrete sovereign-territorial boundaries. The most apparent evidence of this is that the vast majority of economic transactions have been internal or domestic as opposed to international.[6] Trade among states— which often reached proportionately high levels relative to Gross National Product (GNP) during times of stability—has been predominantly of the "arms-length" variety, with nationally produced goods and commodities being exchanged across state boundaries.[7] Even if capitalist entrepreneurs had an interest in escaping the self-sufficiency paradigm that bounded production within sovereign-territorial spaces, the existing communications environment placed significant constraints on the degree to which production could become transnationally complex. As Kurtzman notes, "most of the world's economy [during the nineteenth century] remained as separate islands only tangentially linked by slowly moving steam- and sail-powered ships, trains, and (beginning in 1844) the telegraph."[8]

Of course the situation described above refers to general structural characteristics, which in reality have never been static, but have constantly evolved in conjunction with changing technological and social conditions. One discernible evolutionary trend, beginning in the late nineteenth and early twentieth centuries and spurred on by successive developments in transportation and communications, has been a gradual rise in the density of transnational economic ties, including international trade.[9] For example, in the 1835–1968 period (excluding 1920–1945) international trade rose on average by 55 percent each decade.[10] As these ties have grown, so too have questions about the obvious contradiction between transnationalization and the bounded political organization of sovereign-territorial states. In Gilpin's words, a "dominant motif" among observers of international political economy in the latter twentieth century has been "the conflict between the evolving economic and technical interdependence of the globe and the continuing compartmentalization of the world political system composed of sovereign states . . ."[11] Prior to the emergence of hypermedia, these trends were centered predominantly on traditional "arms-length" national transactions, with rising figures composed mostly of changes in the volume of international trade. In the hypermedia environment, however, the transnationalization of trade and production has reached a qualitatively different level and represents not merely a change in the volume of cross-border transactions, but a fundamental change in the nature and organization of production itself. In other words, although the transnationalization process has deep antecedents, it has been qualitatively transformed in the new communications environment with the complex diffusion of production across national boundaries.

The starting point for understanding the "fitness" of transnational production in the hypermedia environment is the way this environment facilitates the strategic interests of businesses and corporations that have an incentive to cross political boundaries. Although "rational-actor" models are often properly criticized for their ahistoricism and cultural parochialism, one area where they approximate the motivations and interests of actors is with respect to capitalist organizations whose overriding motivation is the accumulation of profits and the reduction of costs.[12] Of course, actual decisions of individual firms to "go global" depend on a variety of causal factors which may not be so easily squared with such a model, including institutional path-dependencies, leadership culture, internal power struggles, and national origins.[13] Generally speaking, however, hypermedia create a conducive environment with strong incentives for those firms that operate transnationally. Moreover, as more firms buy into these incentives, the nature of market competition creates strong pressures on other firms to do likewise in order to survive. This creates a "cascading" effect, with the hypermedia environment favoring the success of those firms that decide to operate transnationally, which, in turn, motivates other firms to follow suit. The result, in Morgan's words, is that "telecommunications now constitutes part of the central nervous system of far-flung corporate empires, so much so that it is much more than a mere cost item."[14]

The most obvious and forceful way in which the hypermedia environment favors the transnationalization of production is by providing a way to communicate vast amounts of voice, text, and image data instantaneously throughout the world. McKenzie and Lee note that "Now, by touching a few keys and for the cost of a telephone call, modern managers can, via

satellites, send millions of bits of crucial information on design specifica-
tions, production costs, or schedules to virtually any point on the globe at
almost the speed of light."[15] In other words, hypermedia greatly enhance
what Hepworth has called "multilocational flexibility" by reducing the prior
constraints associated with the risks and costs of operating over large distances for individual firms.[16] Corporations value multilocational flexibility
primarily because it permits the possibility of crossing political boundaries
to evade government regulations, or to search for cheap or specially skilled
labor, low taxes, and other favorable regulatory climates. The reliance of
firms on effective telecommunications for multilocational flexibility has
meant that many have taken to leasing their own private networks—called
"intranets" for secure and reliable communications. One example is the Ford
Motor Company's private telecommunications network called "Fordnet,"
which is designed to secure better synergy among Ford's 20,000 designers
and engineers located around the world.[17] Another example is Rolls Royce's
Tradanet system, developed by General Electric Information Services,
which is used for purchase orders, acknowledgements, and delivery forecasts
with suppliers around the world.[18] This reliance on private-leased lines by
corporations has been one of the primary factors behind the push for "deregulation" and the break-up of national monopoly cartels in telecommunications, described in the previous chapter.[19]

One increasingly popular manifestation of multilocational flexibility is
the segmentation of different components of the production chain of individual firms into multiple national locations, not only to neutralize swings
in currency differentials among national economies, but also to take advantage of "niche" regulatory climates or labor pools around the world that favor
specific processes (e.g., marketing, management, "back-room" data processing, and/or research and development).[20] As Hepworth notes, "These enhanced economies of scale and scope, deriving from the sharing of information and specialized physical assets (computers and telecommunications
facilities), provide the firm with opportunities for reducing the minimum
efficient scale of branch operations (remote plants, sales offices, etc) and
extending their degree of geographical dispersal."[21] For example, United
Technologies operates more than 120 manufacturing plants in 24 countries,
with sales and service offices in 56 countries. Production of its Elevonic 411
elevator exemplifies the segmentation of the production chain: the French
branch built the door systems; the Spanish division handled the small-geared

components; the German subsidiary handled the electronics; the Japanese unit designed the special motor drives; and the United States/Connecticut group coordinated the systems integration.[22] Perhaps the most common example of this transnational disaggregation is data-entry, "back-office" jobs—a phenomenon that has given rise to the term "global office." New York Life Insurance Company, for example, has its claims works done in Ireland, while American Airlines employs more than a thousand data entry employees in Barbados.[23]

The hypermedia environment not only favors the transnationalization of production internal to individual firms, it also facilitates it *among multiple firms*. By making it easier to coordinate strategic alliances, joint ventures, and joint production arrangements among separate firms regardless of the geographical distance that separates them, the hypermedia environment provides a way for individual firms to spread out the risks and costs of research and development, and thus permits an entry into foreign markets that might otherwise be precluded by tariffs or other regulatory restrictions. Although examples of these types of collaborative arrangements existed prior to the hypermedia environment, they have flourished since its development, becoming a much more dominant feature of the global production landscape.[24] According to James and Weidenbaum, "The pace at which cooperative strategic alliances between firms occur is accelerating, particularly in high-tech, high-growth industries, such as computers, semiconductors, telecommunications, electronics, chemicals, and industrial equipment."[25] In the aerospace and automotive industries, "every major company has formed alliances with foreign competitors in an effort to spread the costs and risks of developing new products, as well as to ensure access to overseas markets."[26] Through teleconferencing systems, faxes, and computer networks (in particular, electronic mail), transnational collaborative arrangements can be as closely coordinated as if they were in the same building.[27] Today, it is not uncommon for design teams located thousands of miles from each other to work on the same design in real-time over computer networks.[28]

These types of collaborative ventures have also transformed the nature of subcontracting and traditional supplier-client relationships, with suppliers being drawn more closely into the research and design of their clients' products. Inventories can be adjusted electronically in what has been referred to as "just-in-time" delivery of parts and products.[29] Just-in-time interaction (also known as "zero stock systems") could not take place without the use of Electronic Data Interchange, or EDI, which maintains a constant electronic link between companies like Wal-Mart and one of its major suppliers, Procter & Gamble, or Dominos Pizza, which uses a computer network called "Domilink" to coordinate supplies among its 1,100 workers located at 28 North American sites.[30] Such complex electronic links reduce the constraints of operating supplier-client relationships over large distances, as inventories can be constantly monitored from afar and deliveries adjusted for travel time depending on the product concerned. These electronic connections link companies from all parts of the production chain both domestically and internationally into a rapid-response/mutual adjustment system that often begins the moment the bar-code is scanned at the retail register when the product is purchased.[31]

Examples and illustrations of these new complex transnational collaborative ventures abound. The computer maker Unisys is both a customer of, and supplier to, IBM and Honeywell in the United States, BASF, Philips, and Siemens in the European Community, and Fujitsu and Hitachi in Japan. "Together, these companies engage in joint ventures, coproduce, serve as sources for each other, share output, and compete."[32] More than one-half of Corning Glass's revenues comes from joint ventures—two-thirds of which are with foreign companies, including Siemens in West Germany, Ciba-Geigy in Switzerland, Plessey in the United Kingdom, Samsung in South Korea, and Asahi Glass in Japan.[33] In developing and producing its new 777 commercial jet airliner, Boeing entered into coproduction arrangements with companies from six different countries, including Alenia of Italy (for the outboard wing flaps); Aerospace Technologies of Australia (for the rudder); Mitsubishi, Kawasaki, and Fuji of Japan (for the fuselage panels and doors, and the wing ribs); Korean Air (for the flap covers); Menasco Aerospace of Canada (for the landing gears); and General Electric of Britain (for the primary flight computers).[34]

One of the most complex sectors for these types of coproduction/joint venture relationships is the automobile industry, where alliances among competing automobile manufacturers in different countries have deeply permeated the production of most vehicles. To take just two examples, General Motors owns 40 percent of Isuzu and 5 percent of Suzuki, and has joint ventures with Chrysler, Daewoo, and Toyota. The latter (Toyota) has an equity partnership with Daihatsu, and joint ventures with Chrysler and Volkswagen.[35] Perhaps most significant for long-term world order changes has been the surge in transnational joint ventures and strategic alliances in the global defense industry. As late as 1985 there were no transnational strategic alliances among major national defense firms; by 1993 there were sixteen. Similarly, from 1981 to 1985 there was only one transnational joint venture; from 1991 to 1993 there were sixteen.[36] Bitzinger notes that these trends represent not just a quantitative shift, but also a qualitative one as the process of collaboration is "becoming increasingly less *ad hoc* and more formal, integrative, and permanent."[37] Although hypermedia do not generate these complex transnational processes, which stem from multiple incentives in each case, they do favor them significantly, offering firms a more hospitable communications environment in which to reap the benefits of "going global."

A second way in which the transnationalization of production fits the hypermedia environment is by facilitating more flexible production keyed to the vagaries of local consumer tastes. As hypermedia provide knowledge-intensive/software-based production lines, rapid shifts in production output or major changes in advertisement campaigns are made more feasible than with the traditional mode of labor-intensive, mass-produced finished goods. Bartlett and Ghoshal note that:

> recent developments in computer-aided design and manufacturing, robotics, and other advanced production techniques have made the concept of flexible manufacturing a reality. Companies that previously had to produce tens or hundreds of thousands of standardized products in a single plant to achieve minimum efficient scale now find they can distribute manufacturing among smaller national plants with little cost penalty. In this way they can respond to localized consumer preferences and national political constraints without compromising their economic efficiency.[38]

This particular capability contradicts the widespread belief that globalization of production necessitates homogenization.[39] To the contrary, in order to operate successfully, transnational corporations have to be willing to accommodate local conditions: a strategy captured by the former head of Sony Akio Morito's term "global localization," and a pervasive concept within the multinational business literature today.[40] Ohmae notes how "Coca-Cola's success in Japan was due to the establishment of its route sales force, but also to its rapid introduction of products unique to Japan."[41] Through computer-based, digital-designed and operated manufacturing and advertising systems, hypermedia permit the production of "niche" products that are tailored to suit local conditions. With computer-assisted consumer profiles and other market-surveillance mechanisms, firms can then maintain a constant watch over disparate localities around the globe, enabling diversified responses to local conditions, as well as rapid adjustments in advertising campaigns to influence parochial consumer tastes.[42] Even McDonald's—a symbol of capitalist homogenization if there ever was one—regularly changes many of its product and advertising characteristics to match local consumer profiles. In Japan, for example, it changed the name of its mascot from Ronald McDonald to Donald McDonald and the pronunciation of its name to "Makudonaldo," both of which are easier to pronounce for Japanese speakers.[43]

A third way in which the hypermedia environment favors the transnationalization process is by enabling small, locally based firms to reach a global audience. While globalization is generally associated with massive, multibillion dollar transnational enterprises, hypermedia increasingly allow small firms with niche products to reach a global market, and thus compete with industry giants in select areas. The best example of this phenomenon is the rapid commercialization of the Internet, where individuals or small firms with low initial investment can market products to a rapidly increasing, global Internet audience through the mere posting of web-site advertisements.[44] Everything from floral arrangements to pizzas to computer software to legal consultation is now marketed on the Internet in what has been referred to as a kind of "cyberspace bazaar."[45] Initially, security concerns among credit card companies limited the scope of Internet commercialization. However, innovative credit solutions have been made to sidestep these concerns ("Digicash" and "Cybercash are the two most prominent examples),[46] while credit card companies have entered into research projects with computer security specialists to devise appropriate encryption technologies that will protect on-line use of credit card numbers through anonymity of commercial transactions.[47] What might be called (in an inversion of Morito's phrase) "local globalization" could not take place on such a large scale without the low-cost, planetary reach afforded by hypermedia to the average individual-producer. As the Internet continues its exponential growth around the world, and as more private companies flock to the "net," the connection between a considerable portion of the production, marketing, and sale of goods and services will become detached from "place," existing only in the nonterritorial "space" of globally-linked computer networks.

The result of this functional convergence between the hypermedia environment and the transnationalization of production is a much more complex and crosscutting nonterritorial organization of production. Not only are new corporate structures emerging that are less hierarchical, more "web-like," but also firms all over the planet are now embedded in a global "net-worked" environment, composed of multiple, overlapping, and complex transnational production arrangements ranging from formal equity-sharing or coproduction arrangements to informal alliances and joint ventures.[48] Although it is certainly true that we are nowhere near a completely "borderless" economy, and that there are few truly "placeless" corporations,[49] the changes that have already occurred are significant and growing, suggesting important consequences for the architecture of political authority, as will be explained shortly.

A variety of factors indicate the extent of the changes that are occurring. For example, for advanced economies of the "triad" states—the United States, Japan, and European Community members—from a third to as much as one-half of the trade crossing their borders now consists of internal transfers within the same enterprise.[50] It is estimated that 80–90 percent of all "transborder data flows" are generated by such intra-firm transactions.[51] Another indication of the transnationalization of production is the rise in traded services—a particularly difficult feature to gauge accurately, though one that by most accounts is assuming more importance, especially with the commercialization of Internet. As Ruggie has noted, it is not entirely clear what is meant by "trade in services": "In merchandise trade, factors of production stand still and goods move across borders; in traded services, typically the factors of production do the moving while the good (service) stands still: it is produced for the consumer on the spot."[52] A conservative estimate places service exports at about $700 billion per year worldwide, constituting about 25 to 30 percent of world trade.[53] Another indication is the growth in Foreign Direct Investment (FDI)—a reasonably accurate data source, though one that unfortunately excludes most nonequity relationships and activities, the very ones that are now assuming such great importance.[54] Worldwide outflows of FDI have increased nearly 29 percent a year on average since 1983, three times the growth rate of world exports.[55] A 1995 United Nations Conference on Trade and Development (UNCTAD) study found that the world's

40,000 transnational corporations and their 250,000 foreign affiliates now account for two-thirds of the world trade in goods and services.[56] According to a more recent UNCTAD press release, total FDI flows into developed and developing countries surged by 40 per cent in 1995, to reach US$315 billion.[57] The press release noted that "[t]he tempo of business globalization is accelerating at a dramatic pace. In response to technological and competitive pressures, companies from every developed country, as well as from an increasing number of developing countries, are becoming more active globally."[58] Moreover, trends indicate that the sources of FDI are diversifying geographically to include not only the traditional postindustrialized countries, but also FDI from several of the newly industrializing countries. Within the postindustrialized countries themselves FDI has leveled considerably, with the U.S. ratio of outward/inward FDI moving from 11:1 in 1975 to 1:1 by the end of the 1980s.[59]

To be sure, the geographical distribution of these transnationalization processes is unevenly spread around the world.[60] As some of the figures above suggest, the global pattern of FDI activity is strongly concentrated in the triad regions (and within those countries most of it is still concentrated in the United States and the United Kingdom), with the share going to the developing countries remaining low—some 18 percent of the world total.[61] And despite some exceptions where bargaining agreements feature high technology transfers, the overwhelming majority of the FDI heading to the South is still predominantly tapping into the low-wage, low-skilled labor market.[62] These geographical inequalities are both a reflection and a reinforcement of global power disparities between North and South. But power differentials notwithstanding, there is no region in the world today that is not in some way tied into the globalized economy. With respect to challenges to the modern world order paradigm, these North-South disparities are less significant than the complex diffusion of production across political borders. Before outlining exactly what these changes portend for world order transformation, I will examine similar distributional changes occurring in global financial markets.

The Emergence of Global Finance

According to Stopford and Strange, the international financial structure is "the system by which in a market-based economy, credit is created, bought and sold and by which, therefore, the use of capital is determined."[63] It is different from the international monetary structure—which refers to the "system that governs exchange rate parities"—although the two, of course, are related in important ways. As Stopford and Strange point out, the international financial structure has undergone dramatic changes in the last few decades, proceeding "away from nationally-centered credit systems toward a single system of integrated financial markets. . . . [to] a global system, in which national markets, physically separate, function as if they were all in the same place."[64] In other words, a primarily "state-based" system "with some transnational links" has evolved into a single global financial system—a system that today exerts significant autonomous structural pressure on the macroeconomic behavior of states.[65] As will be shown below, although the emergence of global finance has had multiple causes and antecedents that predate the change in the mode of communication, it has been social forces in favor of global finance working symbiotically with hypermedia that brought about such a fundamental change in the nature of international financial markets: pressures in the direction of financial globalization created a demand for, and spurred on new developments in, communication technologies, while the latter, in turn, fuelled the globalization processes of the former. Without hypermedia, the global financial structure could not exist on so formidable scale as it does today. According to Hepworth, "At the heart of this market transformation are the new information and communication technologies, which have effectively removed the spatial and temporal constraints on twenty-four-hour global securities trading and created pressures for 'deregulation' in all countries across the world."[66]

As many theorists of international political economy have pointed out, the movement of money and finances across borders is not a new phenomenon, but has developed in conjunction with modern industrial capitalism.[67] However, as with production, finance has been predominantly a *national* affair under the modern world order paradigm, first with the development of networks of regional banks channelling local sources of capital into private industry, and later with their absorption into "national" markets, which were more spatially and organizationally centralized, but still territorially discrete.[68] When it occurred, the movement of money across borders was closely associated with the financing of international trade, and was used only sporadically to channel capital into overseas investment.[69] For example, in the latter part of the nineteenth century, massive capital accumulation (mostly in Great Britain) resulted in relatively large overseas investments in railroads, port facilities, and other infrastructural projects in the United States, Canada, and Australia.[70] But these financial flows reduced significantly during and after World War I, and remained subsidiary to trade and government aid for some time thereafter. Right up until the 1950s and 1960s, "international finance served to lubricate trade flows and to finance the operations of transnational firms and governments in a relatively controlled system."[71] The subsidiary role of finance to production throughout this period was a product of both technological constraints that limited the mobility of finance capital, as well as deliberate policy initiatives designed to keep finance the "servant" of production, as outlined, for example, by John Maynard Keynes at Bretton Woods.[72] Generalizing across all states prior to the 1970s, the international financial structure was characterized by "a series of national financial systems linked by a few operators buying and selling credit transnationally, across national frontiers, and across the exchanges (i.e., from one national currency to another) and by a few national asset markets (e.g. stock exchanges) . . ."[73]

The rise of a globally integrated financial sector has had a multiplicity of mutually interacting and reinforcing causes, making it futile to suggest any one "prime mover."[74] Although the hypermedia environment is considered by theorists, almost without exception, to be crucial to this process, it is virtually impossible to disentangle its impact from other factors.[75] It may be useful for analytical purposes, then, to sketch briefly some of the *nontechnological factors* that contributed to the globalization of finance, and then afterward show the way hypermedia reinforced and augmented them.

One reason for the rise in the volume of international financial activity was the transnationalization of production outlined above. As mentioned earlier, the traditional role of international financial movements was to "grease" the wheels of international commerce; as trade increased over the twentieth century, and as production diffused across national boundaries, cross-border financial activities rose in step. Transnational banks in particular became more widespread in the 1960s and 1970s to service the demands of multinational corporations. They offered a substantial transaction-cost advantage over nationally based banks in the international wholesale market by being able to handle smoothly large transactions among banks, governments and large firms with cross-border operations.[76]

Financial innovations were a second big impetus to the globalization of financial activities—especially the creation of the so-called "Eurodollar" market. The Eurodollar market originated in London, where the city's lax regulatory and high rate-of-return financial climate, coupled with its considerable stock of financial expertise and extensive network of banks and financial connections, began to draw investment away from the tight regulations and artificially low-interest rates of the United States.[77] The growth in Eurodollars remained steady until the OPEC crisis of the early 1970s suddenly put billions of so-called "petrodollars" into the hands of oil-producing states, who then reinvested their money not in the United States, where regulatory interference was common and taxes were high, but in the Eurodollar market where they were "untaxed, anonymous, and profitable."[78] The result was a sudden explosion in the volume of financial capital circulating around the globe—"a gigantic pool of quasi-stateless mobile capital, not subject to political authority or accountability."[79]

A third source of the globalization of finance was regulatory changes in the advanced economies, particularly the liberalization of domestic capital controls. The deregulation and liberalization of financial markets can be traced back to the collapse of Bretton Woods in 1971, the closing of the "gold window," and the subsequent removal of controls over the flow of money across borders and a relaxation of interest-rate regulations.[80] The change "redefined money," created "enormous arbitrage possibilities, and set the stage for the invention of a myriad of new financial products."[81] Perhaps more importantly, it began the decoupling process by which speculative capital was divorced from its traditional, subservient role as the "grease" of the "real" economy of trade and production.[82] International finance suddenly had become, in Strange's apt phrase, "casino capitalism."[83] A reduction in regulations governing stockbroker commissions followed, and competition policies among banks and other financial institutions in turn led to more speculation and uncertainty.[84] By the 1980s, under the direction of the Reagan/Thatcher neoliberal movement, deregulation swept through all sectors of the advanced economies, whipping into a frenzy the speculative flows of capital across borders.[85]

None of these changes can be divorced from the development of the hypermedia environment, which was both a product of, and reinforcement to, the nontechnological factors outlined above. In fact, finance capital and communications technologies have had a mutually reinforcing, symbiotic relationship dating back to the telegraph, with each move toward globalization, in turn, spurring on the development of more cost-effective, speedy communications, which in turn has led to more globalization. Daniels, for example, has identified a three-stage process whereby each new innovation leading to the hypermedia environment was gradually incorporated into the routines of foreign exchange dealings, from the first large and expensive computers of the 1970s that handled back-office accounting procedures, to the on-line data services provided by organizations like Reuters and Telerate in the late 1970s, to the complex, digitally integrated hypermedia systems of today.[86] The result is that global financial services have developed the most advanced hypermedia networks in the world, and are today at the forefront of computing and telecommunications innovations—a place traditionally occupied by military research and development. According to Harry Scarbrough:

> Financial services is a highly information-intensive sector, and massive amounts are invested in the processing and manipulation of information. IT [information technology] investments in a major UK bank could easily exceed a billion pounds over a five-year period. The sector also has greater experience of using computer technology than any other industrial sector. Within every major financial services firm, large IT divisions or departments have evolved to guide and control technological development.[87]

The fitness between finances and hypermedia is not difficult to understand when one considers the important relationship between, as the old adage goes, "time and money." Consider that in the United States alone, on an average day, America's 14,000 banks transfer about $2.1 trillion over their local data networks to settle account balances. The cost to a bank of financing a deficit, even if it is only for overnight, translates into strong incentives to develop networks—both national and transnational—that are efficient and quick.[88] The U.S.-based Bank of America, for example, carries out trades in more than 100 foreign currencies for a volume of $60 billion per day.[89] One recent study revealed that a major investment in hypermedia systems gave one major U.S. bank a ten-second advantage over competitors—a powerful advantage that meant gains on the order of *billions* of dollars.[90] The ultimate goal, according to banking technology experts, is "just-in-time" cash, or what has been called a "disappearing float"—a real-time clearance of balances that would be inconceivable without hypermedia.[91]

The consequences of the "time is money" imperative for the financial sector has been an explosion of hypermedia applications, as new innovations in information technology saturate the industry—each new product and

service providing yet more information with more speed, and more computing power than before, *on a global scale*. Stock exchanges now no longer
require a physical trading floor as electronically linked exchanges operate
globally in a 24-hour marketplace. Examples are numerous and increasing,
and include such systems as the Stock Exchange Automated Quotation
(SEAQ) of London; the U.S.-based NASDAQ network; the electronic trading system Globex, developed jointly by Reuters and the Chicago Mercantile
Exchange; the Computer Assisted Trading System (CATS) centered in Toronto, and many more. These larger systems are now joined by smaller,
"private" trading "clubs," like Instinet, Posit, or Was, each of which allow
trading to take place remotely from PCs or terminals located anywhere in
the world at anytime.[92]

Numerous World-Wide Web pages provide niche information on a myriad of financial services and investment information from around the
world.[93] Complex artificial-intelligence software systems are then developed
by securities firms to handle vast, complex stock portfolios that react instantaneously to slight shifts in the market.[94] On-line services, such as Reuters,
Telerate, and Quotron in the United States, and Extel and Datastream in
Europe, plus smaller, hand-held devices like Quotreks, compete with each
other and with global television networks, like the Cable News Network
(CNN)'s Financial Network, or Asian Business News, to provide the most
up-to-date information on international trading activities.[95] Financial institutions now invest heavily in transnational communications infrastructural
projects in order to help facilitate global trading activity as a whole.[96] Hepworth, for example, has documented how leading financial institutions, like
Nomura Securities of Japan or Prudential-Bache Securities of the United
States, are the driving force behind major telecommunications developments around the world, such as teleports and fiber-optic installations.[97]
Leased lines, "virtual private networks," intranets, or specialized electronic
transfer services, like the Society of Worldwide Interbank Financial Telecommunications (or SWIFT), then provide the ever-intensifying, real-time
links among these institutions.[98]

Like the tightening of a knot, each advanced application of hypermedia
in the financial sector furthers and deepens the global integration of capital
markets in a planetary web of complex speculative financial flows. In ways
that are similar to the overlapping layers of transnational production, the
players in the "casino capitalism" market represent a complex montage of
both massive global enterprises and small entrepreneurs with a planetary

reach afforded by hypermedia. The "big" players—financial institutions like Citicorp, Chase Manhattan, Merrill Lynch, Salomon Brothers, Barclays, National Westminster, Warburg, and Nomura—have offices around the world and dominate trading: typically, the top twenty institutions in a market account for between 40 and 60 percent of worldwide transactions.[99] Because of the way the hypermedia environment links the globe into a 24-hour market, companies like Salomon Brothers Inc, which can trade up to $2 trillion U.S. in stocks, bonds, and commodities in a single year, are "always open, everywhere."[100] As Daniels notes, "Telecommunications permits a London-based Eurobond dealer who starts work at 6:00 am to catch the end of trading on the Tokyo exchange, to trade all day in London and to catch four to five hours on the New York exchange. . . ."[101] Stocks, bonds, and other instruments of debt are continuously traded, bounding from exchange to exchange in response to slight shifts in the market—often without human intervention as computer programs handle portfolios for traders. In the words of Thrift and Leyshon, "we might conceive of the international financial system as an electronically networked, constantly circulating, nomadic 'state', operating 24 hours a day around the world."[102]

The entire *volume* of capital speeding through hypermedia currents is thus truly staggering, and at times seems almost incomprehensibly large compared to more readily identifiable figures. Kurtzman offers the following startling comparison:

> Every day, through the "lobe" in the neural network that is New York, more than $1.9 trillion electronically changes hands at nearly the speed of light. These dollars—and the cares, hopes, and fears they represent—appear as momentary flashes on a screen. . . . Every three days a sum of money passes through the fiber-optic network underneath the pitted streets of New York equal to the total output for one year of all of America's companies and all of its workforce. And every two weeks the annual product of the world passes through the network of New York—trillions and trillions of ones and zeros representing all the toil, sweat, and guile from all of humanity's good-faith efforts and all of its terrible follies.[103]

CS First Boston, a leading global bond trader based in New York, trades more money each year than the entire GNP of the United States.[104] To give some indication of the way in which "casino capital" has been decoupled from the so-called "real" economy (which historically it has been assumed to follow), international trade now amounts to about $2 trillion per year. Today foreign exchange transactions alone—carried out over computers linked in near-real time—amount to about $1 trillion *per day*.[105] As will be shown below, these volumes assume a special significance when they are considered in relation to state autonomy over macroeconomic policies.

In response to this massive, global 24-hour marketplace, new spaces and flows are arising, and centers and "hubs" have emerged, that may provide a glimpse of the evolving architecture of the postmodern world order. New York, London, Tokyo, Singapore, and Hong Kong, are among the large cities that are assuming more of an importance as "command centers" in the global "finanscape"—what an *Economist* survey referred to as "Capitals of capital."[106] According to Thrift and Leyshon, these "ordering centers" arise because "the interdependent connectedness of disembedded electronic networks promotes dependence on just a few places like London, New York, and Tokyo, where representations can be mutually constructed, negotiated, accepted and acted upon."[107] They act not so much as *national* cities as they do *world* cites—interfacial nodes in the global hypermedia environment.

Also assuming more importance are the many "offshore" microstates that "have been transformed by exploiting niches in the circuits of fictitious capital."[108] The term "offshore" is especially significant: in Ruggie's words, it signifies the way in which emerging financial practices strain our current stock of concepts and ideas, "as though they existed in some ethereal space waiting to be reconceived by an economic equivalent of relativity theory."[109] Likewise, Roberts notes that "these offshore financial centers are sites that dramatically evince the contrary and complex melding of offshore and onshore, of national and international, and of local and global."[110] For example, because of its strategic location (the same as the New York financial markets) and its lax regulations, the tiny Cayman Islands "houses" 546 banks from all around the world, of which only 69 maintain any kind of physical presence on the islands.[111]

The quintessential "offshore" market is the Eurodollar or Eurocurrency market, the history of which was outlined earlier. Martin calls the Eurocurrency market "stateless" money.[112] The prefix "Euro," as Roberts points out, is a misleading vestige of an earlier time; today, the Eurocurrency market involves a dynamic new geography of flows "stretching from Panama to Switzerland and on to Singapore and beyond."[113] Confusing matters even more is that regulations designed to offer more competitive financial environments have created extraterritorial "offshore" markets onshore, *within* state boundaries, such as those that exist in New York, California, and Japan.[114] Developments such as these, where a "space of flows" seems to dominate and transcend a "space of places" in Castell's terms, strain our traditional ways-of-seeing the world that were constructed and reaffirmed under the modern world order paradigm.[115] They signal not only an "unbundling" of our practices, but of our conceptual baggage as well.[116]

Implications for the Architecture of Modern Political Authority

The distributional changes to global production and finance as outlined above are increasingly well-known among political economists and International Relations theorists. What is less agreed upon, however, is their significance for the modern system of political rule centered on the sovereign state. As many have noted, while flows of finances and commerce across borders have increased, this does not mean that states are no longer important actors. Neither does a loss of control or autonomy necessarily equal a diminution of political authority, as I argued in the introduction to this study. As I see it, however, these distributional changes have three significant implications for the architecture of modern political authority.

The first, alluded to above, is that by creating a much more complex, overlapping, and globally integrated system of production and finance, these changes present fundamental challenges to longstanding *presuppositions* about the nature and character of modern economic organization. Practices that have been taken for granted, such as a "national" economic system, or a "national industry," or "international" trade, are thrown into doubt as production disaggregates and diffuses across territorial boundaries. The distributional changes to production outlined earlier represent not just a quantitative increase in the volume of cross-border transactions, but a qualitative, fundamental change in the nature of production itself—one that cannot easily be reversed given the density and scope of transnational links within and among firms. As these arrangements permeate more and more aspects of economic activity in all sectors, it becomes increasingly difficult for any one state to define, in Robert Reich's words, "who is 'US'?"[117]

Similarly, preconceptions about the "domestic" and the "international," about "inside" and "outside," are strained by the constant flows of capital through cyberspatial currents, by the creation of "offshore" markets, and by the emergence of an electronically linked, 24-hour global trading system. What once seemed the "natural" division of politicoeconomic organization into discrete territorial bundles has given way to a much more fluid and complex global economic system.[118] Of course these ideational changes in and of themselves have no direct impact on the nature of political authority. But their significance should not be too lightly dismissed, particularly when considered in conjunction with the changes to social epistemology that will be outlined in the next chapter. Much like the significance of the medieval trade fairs to which Ruggie alludes, their impact, though largely intangible, may nonetheless be substantial in the way they inculcate new habits of mind and ways-of-seeing the world.

Second, and on a more concrete level, the transnationalization of production and finance is gradually undermining the effective power of state regulatory systems within individual geographical-political jurisdictions.[119] As a number of theorists have observed, the sheer volume and speed of capital mobility creates a "structural" pressure that systematically circumscribes the macroeconomic policy options available to states—a power large enough to warrant, according to Webb, its inclusion as a "third-image" attribute of the international structure.[120] The most compelling evidence is the increasing convergence among state economic policies around the world. Whether referred to as the "transmission belt" state[121] or the "competition" state,[122] states have increasingly defined themselves and their interests according to the pressures and values of global capitalism. Governments at all levels now engage in competitive deregulatory and reregulatory "locational tournaments" designed to attract global investment.[123] Although institutional lags and cultural traditions mean that individual state policies differ to some extent,[124] governments around the world increasingly have molded their policies according to the interests of global market forces.[125] And each deregulatory wave only drives the process further, augmenting transborder capital mobility and creating demands for yet more accommodating policies. Consider the findings of a recent U.N. Conference on Trade and Development study. That study found that of about 375 substantial changes in direct investment laws and regulations between 1991 and 1994 that were undertaken in *developed and developing countries alike,* all but five were in the direction of liberalization.[126] It is important to be clear that what is at stake here is something more than just a loss of *control* over flows; it is a deferment to global market forces on a scale that suggests political authority over macroeconomics may no longer reside solely within sovereign states.

The third implication of these distributional changes also bearing directly on the nature of political authority has been the creation and emergence of multiple and overlapping layers of authority designed to respond to and govern globalizing economic forces. Nearly all states now find themselves enmeshed in an ever-widening network of informal and formal international institutions, regimes, organizations, and regional trading blocs that have arisen in reaction to the transnationalization of production and finance as outlined above.[127] Examples of these layers of global "governance"[128] are numerous and increasing. They range from more informal bodies, like the Trilateral Commission or the "G-7" economic summits;[129] to more formal bodies, such as the recently created World Trade Organization; to regional bodies and agreements, such as the European Commission, the North American Free Trade Agreement, or the Asia-Pacific Economic Council.[130] In addition, there are the more specialized, functional bodies, such as the World Bank, the International Monetary Fund, or the Bank for International Settlements. While it is true that states voluntarily entered into and created such regimes, these webs of global governance establish institutional precedents and routines that cannot easily be reversed.

Transnational Social Movements in the Hypermedia Environment

The second area where distributional changes are occurring that are serving to "unbundle" the modern world order paradigm is the rise of *transnational social movements* with multiple, overlapping, and often competing interests. These new movements represent the emergence of what Lipschutz has called a "global civil society": that is, transnationally organized political networks and interest groups largely autonomous from any one state's control.[131] In ways that are similar to the transnationalization of production and finance outlined above, the rise of a global civil society presents fundamental challenges to the modern world order paradigm by diffusing a dense network of social and interest-group activities across territorial-political boundaries. Although hypermedia do not *generate* these new social movements, they do create a communications environment in which such activities flourish dramatically. As computer networks have grown, transnational social movements have exploded, forming complex nonterritorial based links that defy the organization of political authority in the modern world order.

To some extent, there have always been social movements throughout modernity whose interests transcend political boundaries. A good example, outlined by Nadelmann, is the nineteenth-century anti-slavery campaign initiated by the British and Foreign Anti-Slavery Society.[132] Founded in 1839, the Society lobbied to abolish slavery around the world, calling international conventions and mass meetings and circulating petitions and propaganda to elites in foreign countries. It prompted the creation of similarly dedicated movements in France, the United States, Brazil, and elsewhere, and helped build a global prohibition regime against the slave trade.[133] Religious organizations—like the Quakers, or in more recent decades, Christian and Islamic fundamentalists—also typically have framed their movements' aspirations and interests in universalist terms, beyond the boundaries of modern sovereign states. However, both the constraints of the existing communications environment, coupled with an overriding belief in the legitimacy of sovereign nonintervention, limited the scope of such transnational social movements to a few exceptional cases.[134]

The growth in density of transnational social forces occurred during the twentieth century, arising mostly out of the industrialized Western states where a "pluralization" space was opened up by the expansion of an educated middle class motivated by broad liberal-democratic principles of human rights and social activism, and strategically placed to fill a vacuum left by the "crisis" and retreat of the national-welfare state.[135] These movements continued to grow, and by the 1980s they were becoming a common feature of the world political landscape (though one that was generally overlooked by traditional International Relations theorists). For example, human rights nongovernmental organizations (NGOs) alone increased from 38 in 1950, to 72 in 1960, to 103 in 1970, to 138 in 1980, to 275 by 1990.[136] The Union of International Associations now recognizes some 14,500 international NGOs.[137] Their visibility in a wide variety of international forums and conventions, and their growing influence on both international and domestic policy, make them hard to ignore.[138] As an illustration of the growing importance of some of these groups, NGOs provided $8.3 billion in aid to developing countries in 1992—13 percent of development assistance worldwide.[139]

The movements that together make up this emerging global civil society are not homogenous in their orientation or organization, but rather consist of a multiplicity of "heteronomous" networks of political associations.[140] The causes around which these movements are formed are equally varied. Examples are numerous and include groups in issue-areas such as the environment (e.g. Greenpeace or Earth First!), human rights (e.g. Amnesty International), indigenous peoples' networks, gay and lesbian movements, and women's rights associations. As Spiro notes, "Environmentalists, human rights advocates, women, children, animal rights advocates, consumers, the disabled, gays, and indigenous peoples have all gone international."[141]

The majority of these transnational social movements do not operate through the traditional lobbying procedures and political channels of participation as defined by state structures.[142] Most of them cannot be characterized as political parties campaigning for government office. Indeed, their very importance as a challenge to the modern world order paradigm lies in their willingness to sidestep traditional political structures and sovereign boundaries "to address international problems, and to reflect a global sensitivity."[143] They are "decentered, local actors, that cross the reified boundaries of space as though they were not there,"[144] seeking to organize activities, and educate and motivate populations directly. The rise in the visibility and density of these transnational social movements cannot be divorced from the communications technologies that have empowered them.[145] As Spiro notes, "this explosion in nongovernmental activity reflects the dramatically heightened permeability of national borders and improvements in communications that have allowed territorially dispersed individuals to develop common agendas and objectives at the international level."[146]

Although telephones and faxes have long been staples for international coordination, it has been computer networks—and in particular the Internet—that have vastly transformed the scope and potential of these transnational movements. In fact, transnational environmental groups were among the first to realize the potential of the early computer networks as facilitators of their organization. EcoNet, for example, was formed in 1982—long before the popularity of the Internet—and now spans over 70 countries. Rittner describes the types of activities that take place over EcoNet:

Hundreds of environmentally concerned organizations and individuals use EcoNet in a variety of ways. EcoNet members arrange local, regional, national, and international conferences. Environmental groups regularly post alerts requesting letter-writing campaigns and information. Environmental organizations post electronic newsletters for downloading or reading online. Other organizations download posted articles for their own newsletters. . . . Grant information is available online, and you can read press and news releases. An online version of the National Wildlife Federation's Conservation Directory lists virtually every environmental organization in North America. . . . Frequent news contributors include the Sierra Club, Friends of the Earth, the center for Conservation Biology at Stanford, the International Union for the Conservation of Nature and Greenpeace.[147]

Today, EcoNet is only one part of a vast web of networks operating through the Internet and linked together under the broad umbrella called the Association for Progressive Communications (APC). The APC is a nonprofit consortium of 16 international member networks serving approximately 40,000 individuals and NGOs in 133 countries.[148] According to Sallin, it is "the most extensive global computer networking system dedicated to social and environmental issues."[149] The member networks comprising the APC include Alternex (Brazil); GreenNet (England); Nicaro (Nicaragua); NordNet (Sweden); Pegasus (Australia); Web (Canada); Comlink (Germany); GlasNet (Russia); Equanex (Ecuador); Chasque (Uruguay); SangoNet (South Africa); Wamani (Argentina); GLUK (Ukraine); Histria (Slovenia); and LaNeta (Mexico).[150] One of the larger members of the APC network is the U.S.-based Institute for Global Communications (IGC), which itself is an umbrella organization encompassing a wide variety of social and environmental movements, subdivided into five main specialty networks: EcoNet, PeaceNet, ConflictNet, WomensNet, and LaborNet.[151] Together, these linked networks share enormous databases containing everything from government department phone numbers and addresses to scientific studies to calenders of events to various government regulations and accords, all hyper-linked and searchable by keyword. More than eighty "alternative" news and information services are available through the APC, including the Third World InterPress Service, the UN information service, and Greenpeace News.[152] Members engage in electronic conferences, communicate directly through electronic mail, and distribute information, including urgent human rights or environmental violations. Underlining the increasing importance of these activist networks to global governance, the APC was the primary provider of telecommunications for NGOs and UN delegates to the UN-sponsored 1993 World Conference on Human Rights in Vienna, the 1994 World Conference on Population and Development in Cairo, and the 1995 World Conference on Women in Beijing, among others.[153] Almost every environmental, human rights, or issue-oriented NGO is now either affiliated with, or can be accessed through, the APC network.

Of course, not included in the formal APC network are the many informal transnational social movements linked through Internet bulletin boards, newsgroups, and mailing lists. For example, Asian democracy activists (and any other potential interested party, for that matter) exchange information through computer mailing lists such as BurmaNet (strider@igc.apc.org); China News Digest (cnd-info@cnd.org); Vietnam (viet-net-info@media.mit.edu); or Indonesia-L (apakabar@clark.net). Separate USENET newsgroups typically centered on human rights issues can be found in such areas as soc.culture.burma, soc-culture.saudi-arabia, or soc.culture.china. Countless other "private" exchanges take place through regular electronic mail, and in similar discussion groups on private computer networks like Compuserve, Prodigy, and America On-Line.

Perhaps most significantly, World Wide Web home pages have provided an important mode of global publication and dissemination of information for both formal and informal transnational social movements. Thousands of niche political movements from across the political spectrum and from all points of the planet have built a presence of the web. Through this presence, these movements can distribute alternative sources of news and information, maintain a repository of data related to their particular niche interest, or provide an informal hyperlinked gateway to other complementary movements. For example, one World Wide Web site, called WebActive, lists more than 1200 web pages of "activist" groups, ranging from Abolition 2000 (an anti-nuclear activist group based in Oakland, California) to the British-based League Against Cruel Sports to the Tibet Online Resource Gathering.[154]

Although computer networks form the vital backbone of transnational social movement communications, their day-to-day activities are complemented by other components of the hypermedia environment as well. For example, Greenpeace (which has more than forty offices in thirty countries) has its own satellite communications link, called "Greenlink," which connects its ships and offices.[155] According to one senior official, "Greenlink" is indispensable: "Without it, we could not possibly coordinate the actions we do."[156]

Desktop publishing capabilities provide these movements with more effective (and affective) means of distributing pamphlets and newsletters on a grassroots level. In this way, local nodes in global movements can tailor their strategies and messages to match local conditions. Some elements of global civil society rely on the properties of particular components of the hyper-media environment more than others. Consider the use of fax machines and hand-held video cameras by dissident groups to publicize their activities abroad. While the most often cited example is the Tiananmen Square massacre in Beijing, where radical students were able to reach a global audience through fax machines, these technologies have long been staples in the "Urgent Action" strategies of human rights organizations like Amnesty International, which rely on speedy transmissions to publicize human rights violations to various national and regional centers.[157]

Of course, not all of these transnational social forces are working with the same goals in mind, and not all can be said to be working to the betterment of the human condition: such technologies have also facilitated the rise of transborder criminal activities, including pornographic distribution systems, terrorist activities, and the money-laundering schemes of organized crime.[158] The neo-Nazi movement has been a quite effective exploiter of hypermedia. It has gained a considerable following among younger generations in the United States, Canada, and Europe through the use of computer networks, faxes, video cassettes and other electronic forms of communication. The April 1995 bombing of the federal building in Oklahoma City focused media attention on the use of computer networks by transnational terrorist organizations and militia movements. The commander of the Michigan Militia, Norman Olson, called the Internet "absolutely vital" to his cause.[159] In a search that lasted less than 30 seconds, I was able to acquire from a web-site in Geneva, Switzerland a detailed "Terrorist Handbook" that provides information on the ingredients for and assembling of explosive devices. At the same site, I was also able to acquire a large, detailed document detailing how to go about making an atomic bomb, should I ever wish to do so.

Less important (for the purposes of this study) than the values of these social movements, however, is the extent to which their interests are defined and their actions organized largely without respect to sovereign-territorial boundaries. As Thiele comments, "transnational social movements scramble the distinction between national and international politics that grounds the Westphalian system."[160] By moving around and through political boundaries to influence populations, they not only undermine the connection between sovereignty and a territorially defined populace over which the sovereign authority has ultimate jurisdiction, but also challenge the idea central to the modern world order paradigm that the international *states* system is the legitimate arena where politics across borders takes place.[161] This is especially the case with respect to those movements that lobby to enforce the global institutionalization of norms and principles relating to universal human rights—a direct challenge to sovereignty. As Sikkink argues, "human rights policies and practices are contributing to a gradual, significant, and probably irreversible transformation of sovereignty in the modern world"— a shift that "cannot be explained without taking into account the role of transnational nonstate actors."[162] The monopoly claims of territorial states over legitimate authority, in other words, are increasingly challenged by global civil society networks that buttress their actions on wider, universalist aspirations.[163]

But the question naturally arises: Given the disparate nature of these groups' activities and values, exactly how much political authority and influence can we realistically ascribe to them? Clearly, these movements together do not have the same aggregate structural power as do the global market forces described in the previous section. Most importantly, they lack a common commitment to a shared system of values so important in translating the micro-decisions of individual capitalists into a large-scale structural effect on states. There are likely to be few occasions, for example, when networks of Muslims, gays, neo-Nazis, environmentalists, feminists, and anti-nuclear activists converge in their responses to a single public policy issue.[164] However, while they lack the structural power of global market forces, many of them do increasingly have what might be called (borrowing from Michael Mann) "interstitial" power - that is, legitimate influence on the borders and in the margins, over specific issue-areas.[165] Certainly the work of Sikkink mentioned above suggests this is the case in the human rights arena, as does Wapner's with respect to the influence of transnational environmental activists on mass ecological sensibilities, multinational corporate behavior, and local empowerment.[166] From the perspective of this analysis, we should expect this type of interstitial power among global civil society networks to continue to grow. The aggregate influence of these networks, then, lies not so much in their "structural" effect on individual state policies as in their collective unbundling of authority on the margins, in their "interstitial" influence over disparate public policy issues and mass attitudes.

As with global market forces, however, it is important to be clear that the flourishing of these movements, and the growth of their interstitial power, does not necessarily mean a direct challenge to "the state" *per se.* Such an

"either/or" formulation misses much of the complex inter-relationships between states and transnational social movements. For example, many
(though not all) of these movements work alongside states, with active state
consent and financial support. And given their typically narrow concerns
around particular issue-areas, it is conceptually misguided to judge these
movements in terms of whether or not they can substitute for states altogether. None have such grand ambitions.[167] Rather, it is in their sheer density
and complexity, operating within the "global nonterritorial region" of computer networks, that these movements together present a fundamental challenge to the modern world order paradigm. In other words, the importance
of these movements lies not in their potential substitutability for the state,
but rather in their collective "unbundling" and "de-territorializing" of political authority and processes of political participation.[168]

The Nature of Security in the Hypermedia Environment

The remainder of this chapter examines the nature of security arrangements in the new communications environment. It is important to be clear
about the level of analysis at which this examination is directed. Among
International Relations theorists, "security" issues are traditionally discussed
and examined in an "international" context. Theories of international security generally assume a basic structure—they take for granted the division
of political authority into sovereign states, and they theorize about the security relations among those states. From this perspective, the *nature* of individual domestic security arrangements is an unproblematic "given" that
can be assumed away for the purposes of theorizing. However, when structural changes are occurring in the very architecture of world order, a deeper,
more fundamental level of analysis is required—one that problematizes what
is normally taken for granted.

Consequently, my focus in this section is on the relative "fitness" of alternative "domestic" security arrangements in the new communications environment.[169] For heuristic purposes, I will compare two "ideal-type" security
arrangements, each of which may be treated as alternative "species" in a
changing environment, and each of which represent two fundamentally an-
tithetical modes of organizing security and politics in the world today. Borrowing from Daniel Deudney, I call these two "ideal-type" security arrangements, *real-states* and *negarchies* respectively.[170] The former—real-states—
are characterized by a number of interrelated features, including: a *monopoly*

of violence and coercive capabilities and its *concentration* in the hands of a distinct organization; a *hierarchical* form of political organization, in which authority flows downward from a single center and information is tightly controlled and regulated; and a policy orientation toward economic, political, and cultural *closure* from the outside world—an orientation that arises from the value accorded to self-sufficiency and autonomy. Negarchies, on the other hand, are those security arrangements "in which devices such as balance, separation and mixture serve to limit, check and constrain power, particularly violent and concentrated power."[171] Their central ordering principle is "the rule of the *negative*," in which authority is *dispersed* and *decentralized* among multiple power centers, and the free flow of information is encouraged.[172] Their policy orientation is toward economic, political, and cultural *openness* and *integration* with the outside world.

Of course, actual domestic security arrangements vary in terms of the extent to which they approximate these images or ideal-types. Among existing or recent domestic security arrangements, the states of the former communist bloc and Islamic authoritarian regimes most approximate the realstate. Present-day liberal democracies, on the other hand, most approximate negarchical security arrangements. Of these two ideal-types, real-states are clearly most consistent with the modern world order paradigm. Indeed, to the extent real-states are "favored" in the emerging hypermedia environment (an argument that carries considerable weight with some, as will be shown below), then many of the observations raised earlier in this chapter about fundamental transformation become problematic. Negarchies, on the other hand, while technically not *in*consistent with modern world order, would be more amenable to fundamental transformation given their openness to and accommodation of transnational forces, integration, and multiple layers of authority. The question to be explored in the remainder of this chapter, then, is the following: Between these two types of security arrangements, which will likely be favored in the hypermedia environment? To answer this question, I explore a number of security-related dimensions of the hypermedia environment each of which I contend has a functional bias toward negarchies and away from real-states.

Hypermedia and the Real-state: An Electronic Panopticon?

Upon first consideration, it may seem that the properties of hypermedia functionally complement real-states, enabling *1984*-like "Big Brother" surveillance by centralized authorities of subject populations.[173] Indeed, among a number of theorists studying electronic surveillance, the arguments raised in support of such a thesis appear to be quite strong. This argument often takes as its basis the image of the electronic Panopticon—originally an eighteenth-century architectural plan for a prison devised by Jeremy Bentham, and later employed by Michel Foucault as a general theory of modern surveillance.[174] At the heart of the Panopticon was a system of surveillance whereby through a carefully contrived system of lighting, prisoners would be unable to discern when they were being watched, and control was thus maintained by the constant sense that prisoners were being monitored by unseen eyes.[175] Foucault argued that this model of surveillance was not confined to prisons, but had deep metaphysical roots in modern societies as a whole. Though Foucault himself never raised the issue of an electronic Panopticon, many Foucauldian-inspired theorists have attempted to do so, extending the idea of a Panopticon to contemporary state surveillance. The image that is put forth is of a cyberspatial, Weberian "iron cage" in which hypermedia-empowered state bureaucracies penetrate into the most private corners of citizen life.

The evidence gathered in support of these arguments is considerable, detailing the way the manipulation of information through computer databases and the use of electronic monitoring devices facilitate greater state control in such areas as policing, internal revenue, and other far-reaching facets of bureaucratic administration.[176] For example, Gary Marx has analyzed the way American undercover police surveillance has been boosted by hypermedia technologies to such an extent that the United States is approaching a "maximum security society."[177] Similar observations are made by Stanley Cohen with respect to electronic tagging devices that monitor "freed" criminal offenders.[178] Going further, Diana Gordon argues that state computer databases and computer matching techniques have become so sophisticated and penetrating that, while criminals are more easily tracked, "we are all enclosed in an electronic Panopticon."[179]

Indeed, the extent to which cross-matching and exchange of personal data has become much easier for government bureaucracies of all sorts in the hypermedia environment is hard to deny, as David Flaherty, Oscar Gandy, and others attest.[180] Perhaps the clearest illustration is the Financial Crimes Enforcement Network (FinCEN) of the United States, used primarily to track money laundering activities.[181] FinCEN monitors large financial transactions, and through powerful artificial intelligence computer programs, compares such transactions with government, private, and foreign computer databases, and then with "profiles" of typical financial criminal activities. Through this process, results are obtained that "flag" certain trans-actions as *potentially* criminal. Similar systems have been set up in other countries, who now share data with each other and with Interpol.[182] While there can be little doubt that the hypermedia environment enhances bu-reaucratic surveillance along the lines outlined above, do such trends favor the real-state? Do they signal the rise of an electronic Big Brother?

As a number of critics have pointed out, the most serious flaw in these analyses is their tendency to put forth a distorted image of contemporary surveillance that ignores other countervailing pressures and trends that sug-gest real-states are actually disadvantaged in the hypermedia environment. As Lyon aptly put it, "surveillance theory is dominated by models and met-aphors deriving from the modern era" and "Cartesian obsessions with 'gaze.'[183]" All forms of surveillance are collapsed into a single privileged center. The "state" becomes the equivalent of the guard in the panoptic tower, which according to Foucault, has the power of "permanent, exhaus-tive, omnipresent surveillance, capable of making all visible, as long as it could itself remain invisible."[184] While from one perspective this does indeed appear to be the case insofar as government departments have been able to exploit hypermedia technologies to improve forms of bureaucratic surveil-lance, from other perspectives it appears to be merely a misapplied meta-phor.

First, while governments are able to track and monitor individuals with greater ease in the hypermedia environment, they are less able to *control* the flow of information, or at least prevent individuals from having access to certain types of information. As Neuman explains, "The special character of the new media is that they can as easily be extended horizontally (among individuals and groups) as vertically (in the more traditional connection between the centralized authorities and the mass populace)."[185] The new technologies of hypermedia communications are smaller, more mobile, more amorphous, and thus less easy to track and contain. Consider mobile personal digital assistants—small pocket-sized devices that now allow wire-less two-way communication of digital information through credit-card sized modems.[186] As these devices are linked into LEO satellites, such as those of the planned Iridium system, it will be nearly impossible for authorities to prevent communications from going in and out of their country. Perhaps the best example is portable satellite dishes—now as small as 18 inches in diameter—that provide links to satellite broadcasts for even the remotest of regions. Even though Iran has banned satellite dishes (which sell in the black market for as little as $400) an estimated 200,000 homes still receive television programs by satellite.[187] In Colombia, when the government ordered its 300,000 dish owners to register, only 100 complied.[188] In China, even though private ownership of satellite dishes was banned in 1990, it was reported in early 1994 that about 11 million households owned dishes, with around 30 million people being able to receive Rupert Murdoch's Star TV either through direct satellite reception or by cable relay.[189] Elsewhere in Asia, where states have long maintained strict government controls over national broadcasting and in some cases, like Singapore and Malaysia, have banned satellite dishes altogether, many are now realizing the futility of their policies and reversing course. As Lee and Wang point out, the loss of advertising revenues and audiences from state-run television to illicit satellite broadcasts has forced regulatory changes to allow more competition in Malaysia, Taiwan, Thailand, and South Korea.[190] In India, the state-run Doordashan channel took similar measures, offering five new channels to independent producers after facing competition from Star TV.[191]

These control problems are only further exacerbated by changes in the economic sphere as outlined earlier in the chapter. As structural pressures are put on real-states to conform to liberal *economic* policies and allow the penetration of foreign investment from transnational corporations, it becomes increasingly difficult for these states to keep a "firewall" between information intended purely for economic reasons and other broader forms of social and political communication. This is especially the case as more transnational commerce takes place over the seamless webs of computer networks. Digital information is moved through these networks by a system called "packet-switching," which breaks transmissions down into a series of units and sends them along independent channels to the transmission destination.[192] Even if a state chose to monitor such transmissions it would be an incredibly costly and difficult task, especially as encryption technologies and remailing systems allow virtual anonymity and security of communications.[193] Real-states that hope to attract foreign investment must grapple with the risks of providing a globally networked communications environment on the one hand, while sifting out any politically sensitive information on the other. Such a strategy can be maintained in the short run, but both the technological constraints and economic costs of doing so are high. These contradictory forces are likely to be most pronounced in the coming decades in such states as Singapore, where liberalizing measures have been made in the economic sphere, and where a sophisticated information technology environment has been promoted by the state to attract investment (the "intelligent island"), while centralized control over information is vigorously maintained.[194]

These types of control constraints associated with the properties of the hypermedia environment may help to shed new light on the disintegration of the former Soviet Union.[195] As the central government attempted to break-up or "restructure" the economic command system and adopt modern computing and communication technologies in several advanced industrial sectors, they invariably lost centralized control over other forms of communication as well. The turning point came during the August 1991 coup attempt, when central authorities found they could no longer contain the spread of information both within and beyond their borders. Shane comments that by the time of the coup, "Fax machines and photocopiers, video recorders and personal computers outside the government were no longer exotica but a sprawling, living nervous system that linked the Russian political opposition, the republican independence movement, and the burgeoning private sector."[196] Messages from Boris Yeltsin and others circulated through Compuserve, the "GlasNet" system, and through discussion groups on the Internet.[197] Soviet reporters filed their stories over local lines to a cultural institute in Estonia, which had a computer link with PeaceNet in Sweden; that link forwarded the messages to six other computer networks around the world.[198] Within the Soviet Union, airwaves were saturated with opposition viewpoints, and thousands of Muscovites were able to receive CNN television images intended for the microwave relay that served the Kremlin, the Foreign Ministry, and some hotels. When Yeltsin climbed on the tank to defy the coup, "His image went to thousands of Muscovites via CNN, his words to more thousands via photocopied leaflets and the White House radio station, prompting thousands more to join the protest."[199]

A second reason to be wary of the "panoptic" metaphor is that in focusing only on the enhanced surveillance capacity of the state, it overlooks the way transparency in general has been raised in the hypermedia environment to such an extent that states themselves are caught in a surveillance web. In other words, rather than a single "gaze," the hypermedia environment has *dispersed* and *decentralized* the centers of surveillance to a much wider domain. Evidence of this dispersal can be found in the many forms of private surveillance emerging, ranging all the way from large-scale, commercial data-gathering enterprises, to security cameras in local shops, malls, and banks, to tiny hand-held video cameras. The latter are selling at a rate of 2.5 million per year in what has been referred to as the "democratization of surveillance."[200] The Rodney King beating of March 1991 illustrated the potential power of these private camcorders as they filter into the hands of many more people. The beating was inadvertently captured by George Halliday's Sony minicam. Halliday sent his tape to a local television station, which then forwarded the tape to CNN. Within a day, the tape had been broadcast to a global audience.[201] So prevalent are these mini-sites of surveillance, that news organizations now actually encourage, and sometimes rely on "amateur videos" to capture news items.[202]

This dispersal of centers of surveillance has meant that there are many more "eyes" watching multiple, intersecting sites—many of which converge on states themselves. Today, governments and politicians find themselves under an intense scrutiny by an ever-expanding "pool of watchers" both "internal" and "external" to the state itself. Not only do these include the proliferating global news organizations, like CNN or the BBC, but also local television stations, investigative journalists, and talk television and radio shows, all of which are growing exponentially with the increase in distributional systems. Adding to these dispersed centers of surveillance are the burgeoning transnational social movements described earlier in this chapter, many of which now operate and thrive in the nonterritorial regions of computer networks. In Spiro's words, these nongovernmental organizations monitor "compliance as a sort of new world police force."[203] Alarm bells rung by watchdog groups like Amnesty International now spread rapidly through hypermedia currents, putting into global focus state behavior that deviates from widely accepted norms.[204] Additionally, the two-way, interactive nature of hypermedia has increased the potential not only for direct citizen feedback and participation in political processes, but also for the monitoring of government actions through databases, computer network discussion groups, and World-Wide Web home page modes of dissemination. One glance at some of the USENET groups indicates a wide variety of unmediated discussions on such topics as alt.politics.clinton, talk.politics.medicine, soc.rights.human, or alt.politics.datahighway.[205] The combined effect of all of these dispersed centers of surveillance, as one *Economist* survey put it, is that instead of "Big Brother watching you," "Big Brother is you, watching."[206]

The Emergence of Planetary Surveillance

One component of this dispersed surveillance web likely to have a significant influence on the nature of macro-security in the postmodern world order is the rise of planetary surveillance from space. The first space-based reconnaissance systems were an outgrowth of U.S. and Soviet military research and development in the 1950s.[207] Although reconnaissance has always been an important ingredient of military operations, it was not until after World War II, with developments in optics, electronics, and ballistic missile technology, that serious consideration could be given to the idea of a space-based reconnaissance platform. By 1960, both the United States and the Soviet Union had operational satellite reconnaissance systems taking photographs of military installations on the earth below. The development fundamentally altered the scope of geopolitical strategy: the entire planet itself had now become the focus of constant superpower military surveillance.[208]

The systems were highly guarded secrets—among the most sensitive of all military operations. Beginning in the 1970s, however, other nonmilitary organizations began to emerge that also shared an interest in planetary surveillance. Environmental and commercial satellite reconnaissance systems—such as the American LANDSAT and the French SPOT systems—were launched to provide data for environment researchers, urban planners, and other commercial interests. However, as long as the Cold War persisted, political barriers stood in the way of the dissemination of sophisticated technologies, and as a consequence the use of these systems remained limited.[209] For many years while most of the world's familiarity with satellite reconnaissance was confined to the meteorological images displayed on nightly weather forecasts, the superpowers maintained a monopoly on a vastly superior technology.

Once the Cold War effectively ended, however, these political barriers dissolved. Satellite reconnaissance systems began to proliferate beyond the U.S./Soviet monopoly. Some of this proliferation has been in the form of national and regional military developments, such as the Western European Union's Helios satellite, the Indian IRS-series, or the Israeli Offeq-series of satellites.[210] Other systems have proliferated as a result of a relaxation of superpower secrecy policies. Private companies in the United States, for example, have entered into agreements with the United Arab Emirates, Spain, and South Korea for the development of high-resolution reconnaissance satellites.[211] Also significant has been the sharing of data by the United

FIGURE 3. A commercially available Russian satellite image of the Capitol
Building in Washington, D.C., with a resolution of approxiately 1.5-2 metres.

States and Russia with multilateral arms control organizations. Specifically,
highly sophisticated U.S. imagery has been used by the International Atomic
Energy Agency in its inspections and surveillance of Iraq and North Korea,
while both U-2 aerial and satellite reconnaissance imagery were used during
the United Nations Security Council Observer Mission in Iraq.[212] Proposals
to integrate formally satellite reconnaissance systems into the operations of
multilateral arms control operations have been made in recent years.[213] Even

more significant has been the commercialization of U.S. and Russian imagery. (See figure 3.) Today, anyone with $3000 can purchase high-resolution Russian imagery of virtually any spot on the planet.[214] Citing the Russian competition, U.S. corporations lobbied successfully to undo U.S. national-security restrictions against the dissemination of high-resolution imagery.[215] Over the next few years, several U.S.-based private firms will begin sales of high-resolution images of any point of the earth to anyone who has the money to pay for them.[216]

Perhaps the most important long-term trend, however, is the growth of environmentally dedicated satellite reconnaissance systems.[217] Although there are a variety of national programs (e.g., the Canadian SPAR-satellite, the Indian IRS, and the Japanese JERS), the most significant are the multinational programs currently in development which entail large-scale, globally organized earth-observation activities. By far the most ambitious of these is the planned Earth Observing System (EOS)—a multiyear $8 billion NASA-directed initiative to study the earth's biosphere.[218] EOS will entail two orbiting space platforms plus a series of LEO satellites that will continually monitor the entire surface of the planet in a variety of spectral modes. The imagery and data produced by the EOS, and other similar systems, will be distributed widely to researchers and organizations around the world. What makes these systems so significant is that they likely will remain *permanent* features of global environmental governance well into the future. As one environmental researcher put it, "electronic and optical technologies of every kind will underpin what will ultimately be a vast orbiting and terrestrial infrastructure for monitoring and modelling the global climate and environment."[219]

While each of these systems may be oriented to specific missions, their most important long-term effect may lie in their unintended contribution to world order transformation. Today, the entire planet is under constant surveillance from a wide variety of national, regional, and multilateral organizations. Widely dispersed military, environmental, and commercial satellites now wrap the earth in a continuously orbiting web. Under this increasingly transparent environment, few large-scale activities will escape the notice of others around the world. The preconditions for surprise that in the past often led to security-dilemma situations are thus drastically reduced.[220] Moreover, existing real-states are placed in spotlight from which they cannot hide, as evidenced by the present surveillance grid imposed on Iraq and North Korea.

Such an environment clearly favors those security arrangements, like negarchies, that are open to the outside world while disadvantaging those, like real-states, that are premised on closure. While satellite reconnaissance systems may have originally been deployed by national military organizations, in the long run they may have the unanticipated effect of displacing the focus of security from an *international* to an *intraplanetary* level. In conjunction with the other properties of the hypermedia environment described earlier in this section, planetary surveillance will place considerable technological and political constraints on the viability of real-states.

In this chapter, I sketched out several distributional consequences that are occurring as a result of the hypermedia environment. Of these, the most important are the flourishing of complex transnational production arrangements and global financial markets, which together are creating an increasingly intense web of constraints on the macroeconomic and general public policies available to individual states. It is important to emphasize that these social forces represent more than just an qualitative increase in the amount of flows across borders. They represent an emerging political authority with a right to set the "rules of the game"—a right that is evidenced by the way states around the world have increasingly adopted almost *en masse* policies of deregulation, trade liberalization, and privatization; the way public policy arguments are increasingly framed in terms of the logic of the market; and by the deferment among state elites to credit and bond rating agencies—to "private makers of global public policy."[221]

A third distributional change that I examined in this chapter was the rise of "global civil society networks"—environmental, peace, labor, and feminist activists, among others. Although these heteronomous groups lack a shared set of common values and thus are unable to wield the same type of structural power as global market forces, they are able to influence politics and values "interstitially," through the margins and on the borders, working within and across states. In their sheer density and complexity across a wide spectrum of issue-areas, and in their willingness to bypass traditional state structures to influence and motivate populations directly, they challenge the architecture of political authority in the modern world. Lastly, I argued that the widely dispersed, mutual surveillance properties of the hypermedia environment place considerable constraints on the viability of real-state security arrangements. Combined with the global market forces described above, the properties of the hypermedia environment favor those domestic security arrangements that are premised on decentralization, integration, and openness with the outside world. On this basis, we should expect trends toward the adoption of broadly liberal-republican, or "negarchical," state-security structures to continue.

Taken together, what consequences do these distributional changes have for world order? First, they challenge longstanding preconceptions about the nature of economic, social, and political organization that undergirded the modern world order paradigm. As many of these activities now take place through the nonterritorial regions of computer networks, they undermine taken-for-granted preconceptions about the "natural" order of political authority—the subordination of economics to politics, the principle of sovereign nonintervention, and the spatial boundedness of communities. In many respects, a "space of flows" is coming to dominate and transcend a "space of places" as the defining characteristic of postmodern world order.

A second discernible transformation is the emergence of multiple and overlapping layers of political authority. This is evidenced by both the ever-increasing webs of global governance in the economic sphere, as well as the rise of a global civil society composed of heteronomous networks of transnational social movements. The result is that any one sovereign state now finds itself enmeshed in a vast network of political arrangements, ranging from formal international organizations to informal governing bodies to nongovernmental organizations. These new layers of political authority establish deep institutional precedents both "above" and "below" states that cannot easily be reversed.

Amidst these wider changes, the purpose and forms of states themselves are being transformed. Although it would be conceptually misguided to portray these transformations as the "withering away" of the state (a topic I will discuss at some length in the concluding chapter), the state, as Spiro aptly put it, is "not what it used to be."[222] Perhaps the best way to characterize this transformation is that states are evolving from "container" to "transmission-belt" organizations designed to facilitate flows of information and capital, transnational social movements, and multiple and overlapping layers of authority.[223] While there is enough cultural and historical diversity among states to ensure a variety of separate trajectories within this process, nearly all states have taken similar liberalizing measures in response primarily to the structural pressures of global market forces. These economic pressures are, in turn, complemented by changes in the security sphere, as the general increase in transparency and a dispersal of the centers of surveillance creates a communications environment in which real-states are significantly disadvantaged while negarchies flourish. While these distributional changes are restructuring the architecture of political authority, the changes to social epistemology explored in the next chapter will provide the crucial "metaphysical" underpinnings for an emerging postmodern world order.

7 Hypermedia and the Modern to Postmodern World Order Transformation: Changes to Social Epistemology

In this chapter, I turn to an examination of the changes to social epistemology that are likely to occur as a result of the change in the mode of communication to hypermedia. Social epistemology refers to the web-of-beliefs into which a people are acculturated, and through which they perceive the world around them. It encompasses an interwoven set of symbolic forms, cognitive biases and social constructs that provide the general metaphysical presuppositions and boundaries that frame thinking and practice for a people in time. It is important to reiterate that according to the theoretical perspective advanced here, changes in the mode of communication do not *generate* new symbolic forms, social constructs, or cognitive biases *de novo*, but rather that elements of social epistemology present in society will tend to flourish or wither as a result of a fitness between those elements and the new media environment. This does not mean that each individual person will suddenly shift social epistemological perspectives or abandon long-held philosophical preconceptions as a result of their exposure to a new technology of communication; rather, it means that in a particular communications environment a particular social epistemology will have a better chance of finding a "niche" and thus surviving and flourishing. The process is thus largely intergenerational, rather than intrapsychic.

Also important to reiterate is that the mechanism of selection, as I have envisaged it in this study, is a chance "fitness" between social epistemology and a communications environment. As a consequence, we should expect elements of social epistemology that may once have been marginalized to resonate strongly in the future as a result of this chance fitness—even those that by current standards may seem distasteful, faddish, or downright heretical. In step with this expectation, then, in this chapter I will develop the argument that the symbolic forms, cognitive biases, and social constructs loosely associated with the current of thought known as "postmodernism" will flourish in the new communications environment as a result of a "fitness" between this environment and postmodern social epistemology. In doing so, I realize that I am treading on controversial grounds, for few labels can invoke such polarities of feelings as those that arise from the rather vague appellation "postmodernism." It is important, then, that at the outset of the argument I make clear that I will not be addressing the relative merits of postmodern epistemologies over other competing "modern" epistemologies, nor for the most part will I be engaging in a substantive dissection of the many, often competing theorists who may or may not fall under the umbrella label "postmodern." I am not arguing *for* or *against* postmodernist epistemologies, but merely analyzing postmodern social epistemology as a current of thought—a "species" of social epistemology—and asking whether or not the emerging communications environment has a functional bias in favor of the central characteristics of this current of thought *qua* species—a process that is largely the product of a chance "fitness."

I am not the first to attempt to link the rise of postmodernist thought to broader sociological/material factors. Both David Harvey and Frederic Jameson, for example, see the postmodern movement as a product of a change in the mode of production, or as Jameson calls it, "the cultural logic of late capitalism."[1] Nor am I even the first to draw attention to its connection to communication technologies. For example, Kenneth Gergen offers a rather strong, technological determinist argument linking postmoderism unavoidably to new communication technologies.[2] And some postmodernists, like Baudrillard and Lyotard for example, see a close affinity between changing communication technologies and broader social and cultural transformations.[3] Where this analysis differs, however, is that it does not attempt to *reduce* the entire movement to a single overarching variable—to the mode of production, in Harvey and Jameson's case, or even to the mode of communication, in Gergen's. Contrary to these analyses, it affirms that the rise of postmodern social epistemology reflect a multiplicity of factors. The argument to be made here is rather that postmodern social epistemology will flourish to the extent that it "fits" the properties of the new mode of com-munication—that it will find a more receptive audience among those ac-culturated into the hypermedia environment.

The ultimate purpose of this examination, of course, is to fathom the emerging social epistemology as it relates to world order transformation. Following the analytical division set out in chapter 4, I will assess the relative "fitness" of postmodern social epistemology in the hypermedia environment along three dimensions, each of which has an important bearing on the architecture of world order: *individual identities, spatial biases*, and *imagined communities*. It is anticipated that through this examination a more com-prehensive "blueprint" can be discerned of the emerging architecture of postmodern world order that complements the distributional changes out-lined in the previous chapter. I will outline how I see this "blueprint" taking shape in the conclusion to this chapter, and will return to it in the final, concluding chapter of the study.

The Rise of Postmodernist Thought

Anyone even remotely acquainted with the broad social movement known as "postmodernism" will be aware of the extent to which it defies easy definition. Well-known are the many disputes about the exact nature of the difference between the "modern" and the "postmodern," between "post-modernism" and "poststructuralism," and between both of these and other subsidiary variants, like "deconstruction" or "genealogy."[4] What does seem reasonably clear, however, is that Western societies have been undergoing a broad cultural transformation for the last 20 to 30 years, through which many long-held, fundamental philosophical assumptions have come under attack. Like many others, I feel the label "postmodern" best captures this societal transformation, and that it does indeed highlight a discernible current of thought latent in contemporary (mostly Western) societies.[5] As my purposes are rather broad a great deal of the nuance within this current of thought is sacrificed. However, I am interested only in the broad symbolic forms, social constructs, and cognitive biases that define postmodern social epistemology as a species of thought or *mentalité*, and not in the intricacies that divide it internally.

The historical and sociological roots of postmodernism (or as Huyssen aptly put it, "the pre-history of the post-modern") reflects a multiplicity of factors reaching back into the late nineteenth century.[6] Although space precludes a detailed history of the movement, its intellectual development can be seen along a series of touchstones reaching back to the nihilism of Nietzsche and the historicism of Hegel, to anti-modernist tracts of the early twentieth century, especially those of Heidegger and the existentialists, and the structural linguistics of Saussure.[7] An early resemblance can also be found in early-twentieth-century modernist art and Dadaist poetry.[8] But it was not until the 1960s that a strong disillusionment with modernity as a whole, and a sense of youth rebellion and frustration as evidenced by campus riots in Paris, Mexico City, Berkeley, and elsewhere, that a self-conscious social movement really began to cohere under the broad label "postmodernism."[9] The intellectual "leaders" of the movement since that time have been a group of notorious French theorists, including Derrida, Foucault, Lyotard, and Baudrillard. However, the ideas of these theorists reach well beyond the borders of France, and in North America particularly, the movement has spawned a large academic following.

As Hassen has suggested, the core traits of this *mentalité* are probably best approached as a series of nuances, or oppositions, that distinguish it from modernist style, and which reoccur or resonate similarly in different cultural spheres.[10] In philosophy and the social sciences, for example, it is characterized by a skepticism of metaphysical foundations, or "master narratives," of the search for Absolute Truth, of linear, rational progress, and of universals of any kind.[11] In its stead, it embraces disjuncture and discontinuity, fragmentation, indeterminacy, and at times an unabashed relativism that often reveals itself as a concern for "the other." In linguistics, it is characterized by a "crisis of representation" and a belief in the "indeterminancy" of the sign.[12] In architecture, it reveals itself as a reaction against the functionalist modernism of Mies van der Rohe and Le Corbusier, and a promotion of ornamentation with a montage of historical and cultural forms.[13] In art it is characterized similarly by a pastiche or collage of different styles that often gives the appearance of depthlessness.[14] Much more will be said about these nuances when I turn to the formal examination below. For now it is enough to note that what has been loosely referred to as "postmodernism" does indeed represent a coherent cultural movement centered in Western societies. For heuristic purposes, then, it can be treated as a viable "species" of thought latent in society. The following subsection undertakes a more focused analysis of the relative "fitness" of this species in the hypermedia environment.

Individual Identities

At the heart of postmodern social epistemology is a forceful reaction against modernist views of the "self" and individual subjectivity—the very same attributes that had their origins in transformations described earlier in chapter 4. Modern conceptions of individual identity against which postmodernists react have been anchored on a stable self, unchanging in basic identity, a fixed center possessing certain universal attributes that all members of the human species share. This modern sense of the autonomous individual is perhaps best reflected in Descartes' "cogito" or Kant's mental categories of understanding.[15] Postmodernists reject this view of individual identity, offering in its place a notion of a "decentered" self—a historically constituted identity that is continuously being reconstructed.[16] The postmodern self is an assemblage of its environment, *a multiple self* that changes in response to different social situations. One consequence of this view of the self, according to postmodernists, is that the autonomous individual can no longer provide the philosophical or practical foundations from which to design or achieve human freedom, as Marxists and liberals would have it.[17] As Jameson puts it, for postmodernists "the alienation of the subject is displaced by the fragmentation of the subject."[18] Likewise, Hall comments on how the postmodern self "is experienced as more fragmented and incomplete, composed of multiple 'selves' or identities in relation to the different social worlds we inhabit, something with a history, 'produced,' in process."[19]

For example, Richard Rorty claims that individual selves are "random assemblanges of contingent and idiosyncratic needs" that are "centerless."[20] A self is then nothing more than "a network of beliefs, desires, and emotions with nothing behind it—no substrate behind the attributes."[21] Similarly, for Lyotard each of us lives at the "intersection" of many heterogeneous language games and into which the "social subject itself seems to dissolve."[22] Going further, he writes that "no self is an island; each exists in a fabric of relations that is now more complex and mobile than ever before."[23] For postmodernists, the sovereign rational subject gives way to a belief in "the role of the preconceptual and nonconceptual in the conceptual, the presence of the irrational—the economy of desire, the will to power—at the very core of the rational."[24] What remains is a "subject who is multi-dimensional and without center or hierarchical integration."[25] In short, the postmodern sense of individual identity is characterized by a historically contingent, multiple or "decentered" self.

There are a number of ways the postmodern view of the self "fits" the hypermedia environment—ways that suggest it might resonate strongly as that environment deepens and expands. First, notions of "authorship" and the "sovereign voice" seem to clash in many ways with the digital universe of hypermedia. This is evidenced, for example, by the way copyright and intellectual property rights are currently under threat, and are seen by many as being problematic within the new communications environment.[26] According to communications lawyer Anne W. Branscomb:

> The ease with which electronic impulses can be manipulated, modified and erased is hostile to a deliberate legal system that arose in an era of tangible things and relies on documentary evidence to validate transactions, incriminate miscreants and affirm contractual relations. What have been traditionally known as letters, journals, photographs, conversations, videotapes, audiotapes and books merge into a single stream of undifferentiated electronic impulses.[27]

Within the hypermedia environment, digitization and networked computing provide users with the ability to extract bits of data in different forms and from disparate sources, and then paste them together into an assembled whole. As a consequence, principles of compensation and royalty are being undermined, especially within a distributed network of multiple participants, such as the World-Wide Web, where it is "more complicated to determine who is entitled to claim recompense for value added."[28]

Notions of intellectual property rights that have underpinned authorship since the advent of printing in Europe are thus facing complex challenges as hypermedia disrupts traditional legal presuppositions and boundaries. Under most existing copyright legislation around the world only original expression is copyrighted and not facts or ideas. With hypermedia, "Computers can scan pages of data, and, presumably, as long as they do not copy the exact organization or presentation or the software programs used to sort the information, they may not be infringing the copyright of the 'compilation,' the legal hook on which data bases now hang their protective hats."[29] One practical expression of this "authorless" environment is the prevalence of "samples" in popular music, whereby riffs or lines of standard jazz or rock songs are digitally pasted together to provide a recognizable background — a practice that has itself generated considerable legal controversy.[30] The same holds true for computer-based scanning of images and photographs in computer art, animation, or documentaries.[31] On the World Wide Web, sound and movie clips are shared, modified, and distributed, ending up as the idiosyncratic ornaments of personal home pages.[32] John Perry Barlow's comments provide an interesting glimpse of the way hypermedia are contributing to the dissolution of authorship in this respect:

> all the goods of the Information Age — all of the expressions once contained in books or films strips or newsletters — will exist either as pure thought or something very much like thought: voltage conditions darting around the Net at the speed of light, in conditions that one might behold in effect, as glowing pixels or transmitted sounds, but never touch or claim to "own" in the old sense of the word.[33]

Some, like Barlow, see an inevitable end to modern intellectual property rights. For them, the social and political regulations that have underpinned the commercial protection of ideas since the invention of printing are simply incompatible with a world of networked computers and digital technologies. Others, primarily global entertainment and publishing corporations like Sony, Disney, and Time-Warner, are scrambling to devise new global copyright regulations to prevent "cyberspace piracy." Underscoring the importance of the issues involved, 800 delegates from 160 states gathered in December 1996 at the World Intellectual Property Organization in Geneva, Switzerland to try to reach agreement on Internet copyright laws — a meeting that if nothing else revealed the enormous complexities involved in the task.[34] However these issues are resolved, what is most significant for the purposes of my analysis is the way discussions of the "death" of intellectual property rights mirror postmodernist views of the "death" of the author. In an essay entitled "What is an Author?," Foucault, for example, asks where does an author's work truly begin, and where does it end?[35] Which ideas are an "author's" own and which are borrowed from others, *ad infinitum*. These postmodern views of the disappearance of the "author" in endless reproductions of other "author's" ideas offer a striking resemblance to the perceived threats posed to intellectual property rights in the hypermedia environment.

Both see the idea of fixing a work of expression with a terminal stamp of authorship as something arcane and futile.

A further illustration of the way the hypermedia environment dissolves long-held legal preconceptions of individual autonomy is its challenge to traditional distinctions between the "public" and the "private" spheres. In chapter 4, I provided a description of the way the practice of reading in a print culture contributed to notions of privacy exclusive to modernity through the mass reproduction of smaller, portable books. Today, theorists ranging across disciplines have commented on how the private sphere is being invaded in the transparent hypermedia environment.[36] Although illustrations range from the popularity of more personally invasive "trash" talk television shows to the widespread prevalence of surveillance cameras, perhaps the clearest example of the privacy invasion is the collection of data on consumers through credit card and other electronic transactions. Commercial data-gathering firms, like Equifax Marketing Decision Systems, use the collected data to create a computerized market profile that is purchased by corporations who then "target" individuals with specific advertising.[37] Equifax provides computer-generated demographic maps that sort individuals "as members of segments defined in terms of price sensitivity, coupon use, brand loyalty, television use, and other characteristics of interest to consumer product marketers."[38] As more of peoples' daily lives and transactions are folded into the interconnected, digital webs of the hypermedia environment, the distinction between those aspects of their lives that remain within a "personal" sphere, and those that are widely distributed in the "public," becomes increasingly blurred. In an article aptly titled, "We know you are reading this," *The Economist* offered the following scenario of an "average" American to illustrate the point:

> On a typical day, for example, our hero's driving route may be tracked by an intelligent traffic system. At work, his employer can legally listen in to his business conversations on the telephone, and tap into his computer, e-mail or voice-mail. At the shopping center, the ubiquitous closed-circuit camera may soon be smart enough to seek him out personally. His clothes shop is allowed to put peepholes in the fitting-rooms; some have hidden microphones, too. The grocery stores information about him if he is a member of its "buyers' club." If he uses his credit card, not only does the card company keep tabs on when,

where and what he buys, it may sell that knowledge to eager merchants—hence the junk mail piled on his doorstep.[39]

Although some theorists have expressed concerns that this form of information surveillance is leading to a new Panopticon,[40] the surveillance that
is occurring is more dispersed and decentered as personal information is
collected and shared by a wide variety of firms to be purchased and accessed
by virtually anyone else.

For the purposes of this analysis, what is most interesting is the way this
transparent environment opens up and disperses personal information along
decentered computer networks, much the same as postmodernists conceive
of the self as a networked assemblage without a fixed center. Indeed, what
may have once seemed an intuitively implausible postmodern notion, may
not seem so when one's "electronic identity" is spread across and shared
between global data bases. Where do we locate the human self, asks Mark
Poster, when fragments of personal data are constantly circulating within
computer systems, beyond our immediate control or awareness?[41] Along with
other elements of the transparent hypermedia environment, the circulation
of personal information through computer networks dissolves traditional distinctions between the "private" and the "public" spheres. It was with this
dissolution in mind that Baudrillard commented on how the "most intimate
operation of your life becomes the potential grazing ground of the media."[42]

Another way postmodern notions of individual identity "fit" the hypermedia environment can be found in the practices of those participating in
computer networks. Identities on the "net"—such as age, gender, and oc-
cupation—are malleable because of the concealment that computer networks afford the user. According to Rheingold, the population of online
gender switchers numbers in the hundreds of thousands.[43] These "identity
deceptions" have often been the source of hostilities once the identities of
those IRL (in-real life) are unmasked.[44] But the practice persists, no doubt
as a result of a more experimental attitude toward individual identity that is
encouraged by the Internet. A good example is the many MUDs (Multi-
User Dimensions) that populate the Internet which allow real-time communications among multiple users in an illusionary "virtual world." To join,
MUD participants take on a constructed identity and navigate their way
through the imaginary geographies of the MUD environment, all the while
interacting with other MUD identities.[45]

One directory on the World-Wide Web offers links to more than 676 different MUDs, with titles such as "altered reality," "anarchy," "ancient dreams," "beyond reality," "dreamscape," and many more.[46] Along similar lines are the interactive virtual cities, such as *Minglebrook* or *Dcity*, where dwellers can build their own digital homesteads, or perhaps just pass through as virtual tourists. By encouraging participants to take on constructed characters in different virtual environments, hypermedia favor the idea of a multiple self, one that varies with its social relationships, and is bounded only by the imagination of the individual in different settings.

There are other ways in which the postmodern self may resonate in the hypermedia environment. Kenneth Gergen, for example, suggests that exposure of the average individual to the technologies of social saturation of hypermedia "are central to the contemporary erasure of the individual self."[47] According to Gergen, hypermedia technologies immerse the individual in a dense network of constantly shifting relationships that leads to a populating of the self, or what he calls a condition of "multiphrenia." In Gergen's words:

> Yet we are now bombarded with ever-increasing intensity by the images and actions of others; our range of social participation is expanding exponentially. As we absorb the views, values, and visions of others, and live out the multiple plots in which we are enmeshed, we enter a postmodern consciousness. It is a world in which we no longer experience a secure sense of self, and in which doubt is increasingly placed on the very assumption of a bounded identity with palpable attributes.[48]

While Gergen insights about the bombardment of images may be thought-provoking, his argument is needlessly deterministic. Being immersed in the hypermedia environment does not by necessity induce a sudden individual gestalt-shift to a "postmodern consciousness," as the many participants in ultra-conservative, religious right, neo-Nazi, or Islamic discussion groups on the Internet might attest. What might be said, however, is that the intensifying bombardment of images, alternative identities, and cultures unleashed by hypermedia *opens up a critical space*, or at least creates a conducive environment, in which the *idea* of a postmodern "multiphrenic" self might seem more plausible and thus find a more receptive audience among an increasingly large segment of those acculturated into its environment. When this facet of the hypermedia environment is combined with the dissolution of authorship and copyright, and the breakdown of the private/public distinction, the functional bias of the hypermedia environment toward postmodern notions of fragmented identities, and away from modern conceptions of the autonomous sovereign individual, appears even stronger.

Spatial Biases

In chapter 4, I outlined how the visual uniformity, mass reproducibility, and standardization of printing all helped to foster a rigid, linear demarcation of political space that complemented the spatial bias of early modern Europe. In this section I explore how some of the characteristics of the hypermedia environment may favor the spatial bias of postmodern social epistemology. As many observers have commented, the postmodern *mentalité* consists of a novel approach to space that sets it off rather markedly from modernist style. Two elements in particular stand out: The first, which is perhaps most apparent in postmodern art and architecture, is the use of *pastiche* and *collage*, both of which lend themselves to a nonlinear and overlapping spatial orientation featuring discontinuity and depthlessness. With pastiche, according to Bauman, postmodern art "has transformed history and ethnography of art into a pool of extemporal and exterritorial, permanently usable resources, which can be picked at will and at random." Collage, on the other hand, "denies the traditional principle of stylistic (and often compositional) unity, and practices instead the equivalence and non-contriety of artistic genres, styles, and techniques."[49] The Portland Public Servies Building designed by Michael Graves offers a typical example. The building is an abstraction of different styles from different eras—modernist and Greco-Roman classicist mixed together with wedge-topped columns that evoke the Italian mannerist designs of the fifteenth century.[50]

Contributing to this spatial bias of postmodern social epistemology is its outright rejection of realism and representationalism characteristic of modern philosophies of science and art—the idea of the subject standing over and apart from an independent world of objects that it can more or less accurately represent. Based on antirepresentationalist premises, postmodern social epistemology argues for the plurality of "worlds" and multiple "realities," each of which is contingent on social constructions, or "language-games" that constitute and orient the field of experience.[51] What might be called the "world creationism" of postmodern social epistemology flows out of its dissolution of the theory/fact binary opposition; for postmodernists, no sense can be made of a linguistically naked "given" from which to assess alternative vocabularies. Theory—taken in its broadest sense—constitutes facts and not the other way around. From this theory-laden view of human existence, postmodern social epistemology derives the notion of *intertextuality*—that is, that there can be no reference outside of theory or the "text" apart from other theories and texts.[52] Hence, external reference can only be a matter of intertextuality.

The combined effect of these two traits is a spatial bias that is less exacting and rigid, and more fluid, bypassing the idea of a firm reality that is fixed and immutable and open to a single accurate representation. Instead, the spatial bias of postmodern epistemology embraces discontinuity and juxtaposition, with mutable boundaries superimposed upon one another. This spatial bias is reflected in Foucault's suggestion that we "develop action, thought, and desires by proliferation, juxtaposition, and disjuncture," and "to prefer what is positive and multiple, difference over uniformity, flows over unities, mobile arrangements over systems."[53] Foucault refers to this mind-set as "heterotopia," by which he means the coexistence in "an impossible space" of a "large number of fragmentary possible worlds."[54] Using a quote from Wittgenstein, Lyotard offers perhaps the most compelling picture of postmodern spatial bias: "Our language can be seen as an ancient city: a maze of little streets and squares, of old and new houses, and of houses with additions from different periods; and this surrounded by a multitude of new boroughs with straight regular streets and uniform houses."[55]

The starting point for understanding the relative "fitness" of the postmodern spatial bias in the hypermedia environment is the multimedia convergence faciliated by digital technologies. On a technical level, the hypermedia environment was spawned largely as a result of digitization: the ability to translate all information—video, audio, graphics, and text—into a series of 1s and 0s.[56] As Saxby points out, "digitization brings with it an entirely new environment. . . . All media become immediately translatable into one another, capable of instant recall and transmission to any point within the network."[57] As the hypermedia environment melds graphics, text, and audio in the same mode, communications becomes increasingly "mosaic" or pastiche-like—a characteristic most apparent in the surface appearance of a typical multimedia windows program, where on the screen at any one time might appear in separate windows a renaissance painting, a television feed from CNN, a text on which the author is currently engaged in composition, and a still image of an F-18 fighter plane. The surface similarity between a

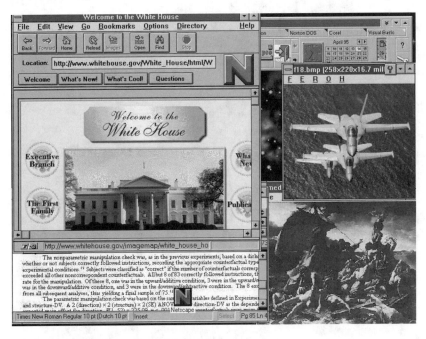

FIGURE 4. A typical multimedia interface

typical hypermedia interface and a typical postmodern work of art is striking in this respect, as depicted in Figure 5.

An even more compelling case for the functional bias of the hypermedia environment toward postmodern spatial biases can be found in the dominant mode of navigation in hypermedia: *hypertext.* As Heim points out, the word "hypertext" refers to an additional or unnoticed dimension.[58] In computer navigation, hypertext is the ability to navigate through databases on a myriad of links between documents that provide that additional or unnoticed dimension. The most common example of hypertext navigation is the keyword search, which allows users to connect disparate documents on the basis of a single word or phrase that ties them together. In words that resound with nuances of postmodern social epistemology, Heim notes how the hypertextual link "indicates the implicit presence of other texts and the ability to reach them instantly. . . . all texts are virtually co-resident."[59] This ability to find "traces" of documents in widely disparate areas complements both the postmodern notion of "intertextuality" as well as a nonlinear cognitive orientation favoring jumps in intuition over the step-by-step logical chain—a

FIGURE 5. Rauschenberg Postmodern Collage, *Lock* (1964).

cognitive trait that mirrors the pastiche and juxtaposition of the postmodern *mentalité*.

Hypertext, more than the dominant mode of navigating through computer searches, has become the *paradigm* of hypermedia participation as a whole. It is, for example, the architectural principle upon which the World-Wide Web itself is organized. Once one enters the "web" and begins surfing from link to link and page to page, one quickly realizes that there is no beginning, middle, end, or indeed any single logical sequence that navigation should follow. It is also found in so-called "personalized newspapers," in interactive television, or CD-ROM based multimedia programs where users click a mouse on a menu of options to enter into layers of audio, text, and video that supplement with more detail or provide tangential routes for various topics within the realm of the program.[60] It is found in the practices of routine television viewing, where audiences—presented with an ever-increasing diversity of channels—engage in "channel surfing" rather than linear, sequential viewing of programs from beginning to end.[61] The same phenomenon is evident in the form of television productions themselves, which increasingly appear as disconnected, nonlinear, pastiche-like montages—a trait most apparent in music videos. Gergen describes how "few of the videos offer a linear narrative; most will jolt the viewer with a rapid succession of images—often less than two seconds long—that have little obvious relation to each other."[62] The pastiche-like orientation is not confined to the radical edge of television either. In television news, discontinuity is produced by hypermedia as "all the divergent spaces of the world are assembled nightly as a collage of images upon the television screen."[63] According to Taylor, television is "the first cultural medium in the whole of history to present the artistic achievements of the past as a stitched-together collage of equi-important and simultaneously existing phenomena, largely divorced from geography and material history and transported to the living rooms and studios of the West in a more or less uninterrupted flow."[64] As distributional systems expand to include competition between cable and telephone delivery, and as communications channels proliferate and diversify, the surface depthlessness and pastiche-like characteristics of hypermedia participation will only intensify.

Other facets of the postmodern spatial bias fit the hypermedia environment—particularly, the blurring of reality and irreality and the embrace of plural "worlds," or what I earlier referred to as "world creationism." One essential characteristic of the hypermedia environment is the way image-based, digital technologies allow the manipulation and creation of so-called "virtual" or "simulated" alternative worlds. Of course, the archetypal example in this respect is the overhyped "virtual reality" systems, in which the user dons a mask and gloves to enter into computer-generated virtual worlds.[65] These systems attempt to convince participants that they are in another "world" by substituting normal sensory input (i.e., sight, touch, and sound) with information produced by a computer. Although such systems have been subject to much hyperbole, and although they are technically limited by their inability to mimic sensory stimulation completely, they are, in fact, only one minor element of the way "world creationism" pervades all aspects of the hypermedia environment.

Consider, for example, the way "world creationism" manifests itself in the escapist alternative and imagined worlds of consumer culture, including movies, videos, television, advertisements, and video games.[66] An MIT Media Lab study reports that more than 70 percent of American homes with children between eight and twelve years of age own a video game system called Nintendo, in which children interact with highly involving, simulated worlds with ever-increasingly sophisticated graphics and audio.[67] Nintendo's main competitor, the Sega Corporation, generated sales in excess of US$3.6 billion worldwide in 1993.[68] Hyper-realistic games, like *Doom* or *Quake*, which feature graphic violence within three-dimensional, multilevel worlds, are distributed freely as "shareware" over the World-Wide Web and can be played on personal computers.[69] What is perhaps most significant is that the video games explicitly cultivate the idea of plural "worlds" and the blurring of reality and irreality as part of their escapist attraction. Take, for example, the following liner-quote on an advertisement for a popular CD ROM video game called "Commanche CD":

> The rotor blades are turning. The fuselage dips. Your chopper is reflected in the river beneath you. Watch out! It's real! Or is it? With Voxel Space from NovaLogic your sense of reality is given the ultimate challenge. With twelve detailed terrains, from arid desert gorges, to lush mountain valleys to frozen wastelands and wide river basins, Commanche is the promise of 3-D simulation action come to life. With Commanche CD you'll take on 100 complete missions. And when the Pentagon calls you, they'll never know you were trained on a personal computer.[70]

Of course, video games like the Commanche CD are only one small element of a communications environment that is deeply saturated by simulations and digital alternative worlds. At a more practical level, advanced computer graphics and architectural software "allow designers and clients to 'walk' through buildings and redesign them long before construction."[71] Military planners employ sophisticated simulations in war games.[72] Neuroscientists and meteorologists regularly employ sophisticated computer simulations to study 3-D images of the brain or complex weather patterns.[73]

Television commercials and advertisements are perhaps the most immediate and, at times, sophisticated employers of created worlds that blur the distinction between reality and irreality as commodities take on a wide range of "free-floating" cultural associations and illusions through the spectacular use of computer graphics.[74] Another example is the computer-generated "special effects" that drive the escapist worlds of movies—now a billion-dollar worldwide industry through first-run theaters and the secondary home-video market. Giant "wrap-around" screens, like those of the IMAX theaters, attract their viewers by offering yet more fantastic simulations, like floating in space above "the Blue Planet," or fighting the "Fires of Kuwait"—"as if you were really there. And, of course, we should not forget the way in which world creationism is now deeply implicated in political campaigns and public-image making—a use of image-based artifact that to many signal the deterioration of public discourse, especially in the United States."[75] Even the long-since "dead" can be created anew as virtual embodiments of the past now pasted seamlessly into the present. Timothy Luke elaborates:

> Now smart movies can cast living-dead digital actors in new supporting roles speaking in sampled voices and moving within morphed bodies alongside real actors. Smart recording studios already stage cyberspatial music jams, allowing us to listen to Hank Williams Sr. and Hank Williams Jr. sing new kinds of digital ballads, hear Nat King Cole do duets with daughter Natalie Cole, and enjoy John Lennon rejoin the still living Beatles to sing on real-time records from cyberspace in hyperreal arrangements.[76]

Given all of this continual bombardment of signs, simulations, images, and "virtual realities" it is easy to see why some, like Baudrillard for example, have concluded that the idea of a "reality" beyond the images—a signified beyond the sign—is irretrievably lost in the swirling maelstrom of the hyper-media environment.[77] For Baudrillard, communication technologies have thrust us onto a stage where there is nothing *but* simulations. Society itself is fashioned into a mirrored, self-reflexive spectacle. In this environment, "false consciousness" or "distortions of reality" or "ideological fetters" no longer make sense, for there is nothing left against which to measure the accuracy of the simulation: "reality" itself is pure simulacra. Following Baudrillard, Vattimo notes that:

If we, in late modernity, have an idea of reality, it cannot be understood as the objective given lying beneath, or beyond, the images we receive of it from the media. How and where could we arrive at such a reality 'in itself'? For us, reality is rather the result of the intersection . . . of a multiplicity of images, interpretations and reconstructions circulated by the media in competition with one another and without any 'central' coordination.[78]

Do these analyses go too far in the direction of technological determinism? Who is the "we" to which Vattimo refers above? As I noted earlier with respect to Gergen, the mere exposure to hypermedia technologies does not *by necessity* force a sudden ontological shift upon those immersed in its environment. No doubt there are many computer scientists personally involved in the design of such sophisticated computer graphics who, if pressed, would hold firm to a scientific realist epistemology. What might be said, however, is that hypermedia create a conducive communications environment where such a spatial bias might find a more receptive audience. It is likely, in other words, that the spatial proclivities of postmodern social epistemology will seem more attractive, more "natural," to the current generation of children acculturated into the irrealism and world creationism of such escapist fare as video games, movies, and advertisements, where the distinction between the "real" and the "virtual" has not only been blurred, but also is *promoted* as a new and interesting *weltenschaung*. Hypermedia do not generate postmodern spatial biases, but they do certainly complement and encourage them so that over time, through an intergenerational "selection" process, their blurring of reality and embrace of plural "worlds" might seem as taken-for-granted as does the idea of a single fixed reality today.

Imagined Communities

The postmodern sense of imagined communities echoes many of the same themes and constructs that were raised with respect to individual identities and spatial biases. As Bauman notes: "Postmodernity is marked by a view of the human world as irreducibly and irrevocably pluralistic, split into a multitude of sovereign units and sites of authority, with no horizontal or vertical order, either in actuality or in potency."[79] Driving this fragmentation and pluralization is a relativistic philosophical position on Truth. According to postmodern epistemologies, no sense can be made of Truth as correspondence to a theory- or language- independent reality because there is no "skyhook" out of our current vocabularies which will afford us, in Rorty's words, "a God's-eye standpoint — one which has somehow broken out of our language and our beliefs and tested them against something known without their aid" — a feat we can no more accomplish than "step outside of our skins."[80] Flowing from this relativistic position, then, is a "multiperspectival" view of the world "composed of an indefinite number of meaning-generating agencies, all relatively self-sustained and autonomous, all subject to their own respective logics and armed with their own facilities of truth validation."[81]

The postmodern imagined community is thus hyperpluralistic and fragmented — the very antithesis of the modern mass community. As shown in chapter 4, the modern imagined community was premised on the fusion of a single "national" identity and sovereign political authority. This singular identity, reinforced in the modern age by printed vernaculars and national mass television and radio, provided a sense of imagined community that corresponded to the division of political authority into territorially distinct, mutually exclusive sovereign states. Although people certainly belonged to many different overlapping communities, there was a pervasive sense that these identities were, or at least should, be ordered hierarchically, beginning most importantly with the nation.[82] The postmodern sense of imagined community disperses this hierarchy to a multiplicity of overlapping "interpretive communities,"[83] and to local identities — a process captured by Lyotard's notion of the " 'atomization' of the social into flexible networks of language games."[84] For Lyotard, and for postmodernists in general, the modern mass audience gives way to a postmodern "diversity of discursive species."[85]

Perhaps no better illustration of the functional bias of the hypermedia environment toward postmodern social epistemology can be found than its promotion of multiple and overlapping transnational "niche" communities. Prior to hypermedia, systems of government-regulated national broadcasting provided the basis to set national agendas and ground public debates within territorially defined political spaces.[86] According to some theorists, they even provided a tool by which central authorities could manufacture consent among the populace and thus shape and constrain the contours of public ideology in the interests of the state.[87] The hypermedia environment increasingly dissolves these shared "public" or "national" information experiences characteristic of the "mass" media age, and replaces them with a bombardment of transnational, decentered, personalized "narrowcasting" and two-way communications in the form of computer networks, video-on-demand, direct satellite broadcasting, and the so-called "500 channel" cable systems.

In the hypermedia environment, individuals have an ever-widening choice among multiple and specialized programs provided by a growing list of private, competing distributional systems that were previously bound within separate regulatory jurisdictions. The recently unleashed competition between telephone and cable is a prime example in this respect. More importantly, perhaps, is the extent to which these competing distributional systems are increasingly *transnational* as states deregulate and allow an interpenetration of broadcasting systems, from global news organizations, to direct broadcasting satellites, to joint-sharing agreements among "national" broadcasting systems.[88] As this interpenetration process is closely bound up with global market forces in favor of the "free flow" of information, even those states and regions that were once adamant about maintaining broadcasting monopolies have reversed their course. In Asia, for example, satellite owners now have a choice of more than forty channels of satellite television, including Star TV, HBO, CNN, ESPN, the Hong Kong-based TVBS, plus a variety of other programs transmitted through domestic satellites from Japan, Russia, Thailand, Australia, and China.[89] Even more satellite systems to service the region are planned for launch in the next several years.[90] In 1980, there were 40 television channels in all of what is now the European Union. By 1994, there were 150, with more than a third delivered by satellite.[91] In Cairo, Samsung sells a package of a fixed dish, receiver, and television set for only $740 through which a choice of three commercial services provide choices like CNN, MTV, ESPN, as well as Arabic programming.[92] With the emergence of the hypermedia environment, the single-point/mass-national broadcasting paradigm is giving way to multi-perspectival/transnational "narrowcasting."

Not only does the hypermedia environment contribute to "de-massification" through an increased diversity of choice among channels, it atomizes it altogether by the increasing "interactivity" of the communication process itself. Perhaps the best example is on-line "personalized" newspapers, which allow users to access sidebar stories or tangentially related news items and video clips at their own discretion. The result is a completely different news experience for each individual user.[93] The same phenomenon is mirrored in multimedia music CD's currently available on the market that allow listeners to alter the composition to suit their mood—to make it possible, as one composer put it, "for you and me to have two different viewpoints on the same piece of music."[94] Similarly, interactive television systems developed in specific test-market regions of North America allow viewers to select camera angles and choose replays while watching sporting events.[95]

This personalized interactivity is taken yet a step further by studies currently being undertaken at the MIT Media Lab with financial support by industry giants like Knight-Ridder, Gannett, Hearst, and Times-Mirror. Here personalized software "agents" are being developed that will electronically scan global networked databases each morning to provide individuals with their own exclusive news package tailored to fit their own unique interests.[96] Indeed, a free World-Wide Web service called CRAYON (Create Your Own Newspaper On the Net) provides subscribers with a large set of global news services from which they can build their own personalized jumping-off points. Through CRAYON, I have a selection of world news sources every morning that include Reuters, *The Times* (London), *The Electronic Telegraph* (London), *The Jerusalem Post*, *This Week in Germany*, *The Irish Times*, *China News Digest*, *The Straits Times* (Singapore), and *The Hindu* (India), among others. Although some of these technologies are still in their embryonic stage of development, they provide further evidence of the "de-massifying" direction in which the hypermedia environment is headed.

The second way the hypermedia environment challenges the national mass-broadcasting paradigm and encourages the rise of multiple and overlapping "niche" communities is by allowing two-way, unmediated, transnational communications among groups of individuals linked through computer networks. On the Internet, and on the many private computer networks, millions of people around the world now participate in these "virtual communities."[97] At last count, there are more than 10,000 specialized USENET newsgroups on the Internet each of which involves largely unmediated communications among people from around the planet on such specialized topics as alt.politics.greens; alt.poli-tics.libertarian; alt.politics.radical-left; alt.fan.dan.quayle; alt.sex.bondage; or alt.tv.simpsons.[98] The prefix "alt" in the various newsgroups listed above refers to "alternative"—a category that permits anyone to start a newsgroup on any topic whatsoever. Here, "publication" is open to anyone merely by the posting of a message on a bulletin board or newsgroup. On the World-Wide Web, users can open up individual "web-sites" which contain any selected pieces of information—audio, video, or text—linked or edited together in any way, open to everyone else on the Internet.[99] This democ-ratization of publication represents a radical inversion of the national mass-broadcasting paradigm. As one *New York Times* article put it in ways that are suggestive of the de-massification of group identities, the Internet offers seemingly "infinite depths of narrowness."[100]

There can be little doubt that the properties of the hypermedia environ-ment outlined above are contributing to the rise of multiple and overlapping transnational "niche" communities observed by commentators across the theoretical spectrum—what Howard Rheingold has aptly described as an "ecosystem of subcultures."[101] The values and goals of these movements are multiple and contradictory and reflect widely varying aspirations, from reli-gious fundamentalist groups, to ethnic diasporas, to functionally defined interest groups, to terrorist organizations, to neo-Nazi movements.[102] What is perhaps the most significant aspect of these communities, however, is the extent to which they are not bound by traditional notions of "territory" or "place" as prerequisites for membership. Geographical propinquity becomes less important as a basis for group identity as communities coalesce around shared interests in the "virtual" spaces of the hypermedia environment. As Appadurai explains, "sentiments whose greatest force is in their ability to ignite intimacy into a political sentiment and turn locality into a staging ground for identity, have become spread over vast and irregular spaces, as groups move, yet stay linked to one another through sophisticated media capabilities."[103] The result is a much more decentered, multiperspectival universe of imagined communities—a "multi-centric" system, in Rosenau's words, comprised of "diverse subnational and supranational sovereignty-free actors."[104] *Nationalism*, the visceral underpinning of modern world order, is giving way to *nichelism*—a polytheistic universe of multiple and overlapping fragmented communities above and below the sovereign nation-state.

Global Village or Planetary Villages?

It should be readily apparent how nichelism complements the fragmented, pluralistic view of imagined communities found in postmodern
social epistemology. But what of the notion of a *global* identity so often
identified with the planetary reach of hypermedia? What of McLuhan's
"global village"? As a variety of observers have pointed out, superimposed
upon all of these fragmented niche communities can be discerned an emerging "global" imagined community.[105] Its identifying features are perhaps
more ephemeral, evidenced not so much by a single cause as by a series of
symbolic forms and discursive representations. Although human history is
replete with ideas concerning the nature and spiritual significance of the
world in the cosmos, it is only in the twentieth century that the idea of a
single global society has been realistically broached, and the problem of its
political and cultural organization examined.[106] To be sure, this intensification of global consciousness is a product of a variety of concerns, foremost
among them the recognition of environmental degradation and the spread
of global consumer culture. However, there can be little doubt that the
development of hypermedia has been one of the primary contributors to this
embryonic sense of global identity, if even in a perceived negative way. In
other words, reflections on the sheer scope of the hypermedia environment
have contributed to a sense of global interconnectedness, beginning somewhat ironically with McLuhan's own aphorism: "the global village." Indeed,
the *perception* of a tightly bound planetary community is hard to deny in a
world that is constantly bombarded with images and reminders of the global
reach of hypermedia. In this respect, the hypermedia environment reinforces
both "the compression of the world and the intensification of consciousness
of the world as a whole."[107]

One immediate and widespread example is the proliferation of images of
the earth. Today, it is hard to escape the "blue earth" image, whether it is
in the form of a floating logo that signals the onset of CNN's Headline News,
as a pamphlet header for an environmental awareness organization, as a
cover-image for an International Relations theory textbook, or as a spinning
ornament on the corner of a World-Wide Web home page.[108] Without a
doubt, it is by far the most saturated corporate logo in the history of commercial advertisement—one that seems to become ever more popular as the

hypermedia environment deepens and expands. Its ubiquity alone is bound to have an impact on peoples' consciousness, as it already has to a considerable extent. As Cosgrove explains, images of the earth, like the Apollo photographs for example, "have been enormously significant . . . in altering the shape of the contemporary geographical imagination."[109] Through computer simulations and space-based sensing technologies, the planet has become for many a kind of virtual abstraction—less an enormous, mysterious biosphere than an object to be manipulated, controlled, and watched.[110]

Does this global imagined community contradict the rise of postmodern "niche" communities? As many critical observers have pointed out, although the spread of global discourse and imagery signifies a sense of imagined community, it is a contested vision, one that is appropriated in different ways by different groups.[111] For example, the one-world image features prominently as a symbol for transnational corporations and high-technology industries for whom it signifies "secular mastery of the world through secular control."[112] For environmental movements, however, the same image represents "a quasi-spiritual interconnectedness and the vulnerability of terrestrial life."[113] Indeed, the very paradoxical way in which the global image is appropriated by different communities *reinforces* the postmodern sense of heterotopia, or the coexistence of a large number of fragmentary worlds in an "impossible space." In other words, the global image itself embodies the very fragmentary and juxtapositional sense of pluralistic imagined communities that marks the postmodern sensibility. Despite the contested nature of the global image, however, the sense of boundedness and integration of the earth will likely prove significant in the long-term primarily as a challenge to modern claims of sovereign jurisdiction, but perhaps also as an imagined basis for an emerging planetary polis.

In this chapter, I have argued that the social constructs, cognitive biases, and symbolic forms of postmodern social epistemology will likely resonate in the future to a considerable extent more than they have to date as a result of a "fitness" between this social epistemology and the emerging hypermedia environment. Given the nature of the analysis, it is difficult to "prove" the argument beyond providing a kind of structured, "thick description" as outlined above. No doubt, other candidates for selection could be broached, though I doubt that any would be as comprehensive in "fitness" with the hypermedia environment as postmodern social epistemology seems to be.

Some might object that since "postmodernism" is largely a Western phenomenon, it is unlikely to have implications for world order as a whole. While it is certainly true that the ideas outlined above have originated in the "West" and are so far largely confined to the West, they may well spread beyond their place of origin. After all, the idea of sovereignty also originated in the "West."[114] Moreover, the fact that the "West" also happens generally to correspond to the richest and most powerful segment of elites in the world today should not be taken too lightly. If I am correct in suggesting that postmodern social epistemology will not be merely a "fad," but will only deepen and expand over time among those acculturated into the hypermedia environment, then it is likely that this social epistemology will have significant consequences, not just for individuals and societies, but also for the evolving architecture of world order as well.

What might these consequences be? Because changes in social epistemology are, by definition, an intergenerational process, any interpretation of their impact on world order transformation is bound to be speculative and somewhat tentative given the time frame involved. However, what is most interesting is the way many of the core features of postmodern social epistemology tend to complement and reinforce changes described in the previous chapter. For example, certainly the postmodern decentered self with multiple identities resonates with the demassification of imagined communities and the enmeshment of sovereign states in multiple layers of authority. And the latter seems especially to "fit" the postmodern sense of juxtaposition and superimposition, and nonlinear, pastiche-like orderings of space, as characterized by Foucault's notion of "heterotopia." The postmodern view of imagined or created worlds is also apropos in a world in which communities and corporations increasingly interact in the nonterritorial spaces of computer networks. And the recognition of "difference" and hyperplurality tends to complement a tightly bounded planet in which once-disparate cultures are thrust into close contact. From the perspective of social epistemology, these observations suggest that the emerging architecture of world order is moving away from territorially distinct, mutually exclusive, linear orderings of space toward nonlinear, multiperspectival, overlapping layers of political authority. Likewise, modern mass identities centered on the "nation" are being dispersed into multiple, nonterritorial "niche" communities and fragmented identities. The next, concluding chapter will attempt to sketch out some of the implications of these transformations.

8   Conclusion

      To understand the larger implications of "epochal" changes as they unfold is notoriously difficult. When bedrock assumptions and the institutions that have reinforced and sustained them dissolve in a maelstrom of change, the very search for a framework or foundation from which to assess such changes becomes inherently problematic. Indeed, if there is one overarching meta-perspective that has informed this analysis it is a view of history as essentially contingent and open-ended, one in which chance rules and unintended consequences loom large. While law-like generalizations that operate beyond the ebb and flow of history run contrary to such a perspective, analytical and theoretical lenses can, and indeed must, be constructed from which to view and interpret current trends. The purpose of this study has been to provide one such analytical and theoretical lens through which to examine the relationship between changes in modes of communication and world order transformation. I have not done so in order to establish that communication technologies are the prime movers of human history—that all other aspects of human existence can be reduced to the unfolding "logic" of successive modes of communication. Rather I hope to fill a remarkable gap in International Relations scholarship at a time when dramatic global changes in communication technologies are occurring, and the only analyses to be found are in popular magazines and the mass media.

      Ironically, it was the theory associated with one of the most widely quoted writers of the "information age" literature—Marshall McLuhan—that provided the material I have used to construct that analytical lens. While both McLuhan and Innis before him may have been somewhat ambiguous in terms of the weight they attributed to modes of communication in human history, I have attempted in this study to articulate an open-ended, nonreductionist medium theory approach, embedding it in a much wider evolutionary perspective on human existence that I refer to as "ecological holism." Apart from explicitly shedding whatever technological determinist accoutrements may be associated with medium theory, the most significant modification is the elaboration of the two conceptually distinct effects that are related to changes in modes of communication: distributional changes and changes to social epistemology. This elaboration allowed me to delineate more clearly the types of effects that arise in conjunction with large-scale changes in modes of communication.

In part 1 of this study, I examined the relationship between the emergence of printing and the medieval to modern transformation of world order in Europe. Distributional changes associated with printing worked in two directions: undercutting the medieval world order while contributing to the constitution of the modern. With respect to the former, the properties of printing favored the strategic interests of the Protestant Reformation and scientific humanism to the detriment of the papal-monastic network. Both of these particular distributional changes were vital in helping to dissolve the cosmological ties that linked Europe into a single Christian Commonwealth. A third distributional change that was facilitated by printing—the rise of the urban bourgeoisie and contractarian socioeconomic relations—was "transitional" insofar as it had a leveling effect on the personalistic ties of feudal social relations and opened up the possibility of common rule from a single center. Finally, the distributional properties of printing favored the strategic interests of centralizing state monarchs who, in alliance with the urban bourgeoisie, set about creating standardized rational policies, and impersonal bureaucracies to administer them over clearly defined territorial spaces.

While it is always difficult to pin down with certainty "what might have been," the absence of printing would have presented some significant constraints in the face of each of these developments. Certainly the rise and decline of previous heresies to the Protestant Reformation gives us some indication of what might have been the fate of Luther's challenge and the Church's containment strategies had there been no printing press available in Europe in the early sixteenth century. To a somewhat lesser extent, the same might be said of the flourishing of the scientific humanist movement, which without printing would surely have been less swift in its spread and success, if not held in check altogether. Likewise, the frequent fragmentation of centralized forms of state rule in the late Middle Ages suggests what might have been in the absence of the printing environment for modern state bureaucracies. While a form of intergenerational rule from a single center could have been sustained with a reliance solely on the written word, it is unlikely that such systems would have developed as swiftly, as comprehensively, and with such characteristic standardization across the wide spectrum of public policy sectors as they did in the parts of Europe where mass-mechanized printing was available. Moreover, such systems of rule might not have proven to be as functionally superior as were other nonterritorial logics of organization, such as city-leagues and city-states, without the availability of printing. Lastly, given the widespread reliance of the urban bourgeoisie on social abstractions—such as contracts, constitutions, and newspapers—it is probably safe to say that such movements would have at least been tempered significantly without the availability of printing technologies.

But distributional changes, which focus only on the relative power of social forces, provide an incomplete picture of world order transformation. The emergence of the printing environment also had important consequences for the social epistemology of the time. Printing provided a communications environment in which modern notions of individual subjectivity and autonomy, and a cognitive bias towards visual, linear, and uniform representations of space, could thrive. Moreover, the standardization of printing provided the means by which both directly and indirectly an imagined community based on shared "national" vernacular languages could take root, forming the embryonic shell of the modern ideology of nationalism. Taken together, these changes in social epistemology formed the "metaphysical underpinnings" for the architecture of modern world order, and thus contributed to the characteristic differentiation of political authority into territorially distinct, sovereign nation states.

Using the same analytical lens as in part 1, I first turned my attention, in part 2, to the distributional changes associated with the emerging hypermedia environment. There I argued that the hypermedia environment favors the complex diffusion of production across territorial/political boundaries by facilitating multilocational flexibility, transnational joint-ventures, and both global localization and "local" globalization—the latter best evidenced by the commercialization of the World Wide Web. I also outlined how global finance "fits" the hypermedia environment, indeed has been qualitatively transformed by it, both in terms of potential velocity and sheer volume of capital flows across borders. I then examined the way the hypermedia environment favors the diffusion of transnational social movements around the globe, leading to what has been referred to as a "global civil society." Finally, I argued that the distributional properties of the hypermedia environment—in particular the high level of transparency in the form of multiple and dispersed centers of surveillance—favor negarchical security arrangements while disadvantaging centralized/hierarchical forms of rule, or real-states.

Turning to social epistemology, I argued that the social constructs, symbolic forms, and cognitive biases loosely orbiting around the current of thought known as "postmodernism" will likely resonate today and in the future as a result of a "fitness" or match between this social epistemology and the hypermedia environment. Postmodern notions of "decentered" selves, pastiche-like, intertextual spatial biases, multiple realities and worlds, and fragmented imagined communities "fit" the hypermedia environment where personal information is dispersed along computer networks and privacy is rapidly dissolving, where disparate media meld together into a digital, intertextual whole, where digital worlds and alternative realities are pervasive, and where narrowcasting and two-way communications are undermining mass "national" audiences and encouraging nonterritorial "niche" communities.

What do these changes portend for the character of political authority at a world level? Do they have implications for the modern system of rule, which has been so resilient in the face of the changes and challenges of the last four centuries? Certainly we must be cautious about making bold projections about the future. But one of the advantages of the theoretical and analytical lens I have put forth in this study is that it does not look to the future, but to the here and now. It examines the existing social forces and ideas that we can identify around us today, and seeks to determine which will likely "fit" the emerging hypermedia environment and which will not. Not only does this help avoid making problematic assertions about futuristic scenarios yet to unfold, but it also gives some indication of the weight of alternative forces and trends. If I am right about the "fitness" of the social forces and ideas I have identified above, then we should expect some significant changes in structures and institutions of political authority at a global level.

Probably the most important characteristic suggested by the trends outlined above is the "decentering" or dispersal of authority to multiple and overlapping sites. One aspect of this dispersal can be traced to the structural power of capital, and to the rise of what Timothy Sinclair has aptly called "private makers of global public policy." While states may have entered into and fully encouraged the transnationalization of production and the freeing up of a variety of controls over flows of capital, the unintended consequence has been that all states—to varying degrees—find themselves subject to the structural power of transnational corporate interests. A corollary of this development—and yet a further dispersal of authority—has emanated from the policy responses to this unleashing of global market forces. As these structural pressures have accumulated, detachment from the global economy has become an increasingly unfeasible and costly option. Instead, in order to coordinate their ever-more integrated economies, states have entered into a complex web of institutional arrangements and regimes at both a regional and a global level. At the same time, the structural power of capital has increased pressures on central state authorities for the devolution of many decisionmaking powers and previously centralized state functions to the local levels and to private authorities. The combined effect of these two processes is a much more complex web of governance structures both "above" and "below" the sovereign state.

Indeed, if there is one clear "winner" in the hypermedia environment, it is the collective interests of transnational capital. The modern subordination of economics to politics has been dramatically reversed by this change such that the core values of most all states are now defined in terms of the interests of capital. As Ohmae put it most starkly, "economic activity is what defines the landscape on which all other institutions, including political institutions, must operate."[1] The spread of capitalist-consumer values on a global scale has been remarkable, and shows little sign of abatement. While it would be wrong (and conceptually misguided, as I will explain shortly) to describe these changes in terms of the "withering away" of the state, they certainly signal an important change in the values that now animate most states. In a virtual stampede, states around the world have engaged in progressive liberalization measures to meet the disciplinary interests of transnational capital. This "hollowing out" of the state, the shifting orientation of states' core values away from self-sufficiency, autonomy, and survival to the accommodation of liberal-capitalist interests, and the integration of states both with each other and with regional and international organizations and regimes, signals yet a further dismantling of the architecture of modern world order toward multiple and overlapping layers of authority.

Adding yet another element to this dispersal of political authority is the density and complexity of transnational social movements, many of whom now operate primarily through the nonterritorial spaces of computer networks. To be sure, these movements vary considerably in the extent to which their actions are both effective and/or considered legitimate. Certainly, the influence of Amnesty International or Greenpeace has more weight in various arenas and jurisdictions than does "The Christian Holocaust" or "STRAIGHT" (the latter being marginalized transnational hate groups). But relative weight notwithstanding, it is surely significant that in the last quarter century tens of thousands of these interest groups have sprouted, in purpose and values united only to the extent that they see politics across borders as no longer the sole domain of the representatives of sovereign states. For these groups, politics is not a process channeled into mutually exclusive, territorially distinct state structures. It is not something that can be tidily boxed and separated into sovereign jurisdictions defined by elites. It is, rather, an open-ended borderless process. Collectively, these social movements add yet more webs of governance into the multiple and overlapping layers of authority and further undermine the organization and differentiation of modern political rule into territorially distinct units.

What makes these trends even more compelling is the way they are complemented by some of the core elements of postmodern social epistemology, in particular the embrace of heterogeneity and pastiche-like, intertextual spaces. It is worth recalling at this point Wittgenstein's remark cited in chapter 7 that, while used by Lyotard as an illustration of postmodern spatial biases, seems especially apropos as a description of postmodern world order: "Our language can be seen as an ancient city: a maze of little streets and squares, of old and new houses, and of houses with additions from various periods; and this surrounded by a multitude of new boroughs with straight regular streets and uniform houses."[2] At a time when "it is becoming increasingly difficult," according to Spiro, "to use the use the word 'we' in the context of international affairs,"[3] what could be more "fitting" than the postmodern sense of multiple identities, decentered selves, and fragmented imagined communities? If I am correct in arguing that postmodern social epistemology will only deepen and expand in the hypermedia environment, then we should expect the trend away from rigid, linear spatial boundaries, and toward multiple and overlapping forms of political authority to continue.

In the much longer term, however, one significant trend suggested by these changes is the way the entire planet has become a focus of constant surveillance. While the participants in the planetary surveillance process range from national and regional military organizations with more narrowly defined security interests, to commercial organizations that sell high-resolution images to anyone on the earth, to environmental organizations monitoring the earth's biosphere, the collective effect of all of these groups taken together is that there are now thousands of "eyes" watching all parts of the planet simultaneously. Of these various "eyes," probably the most significant are the multinational environmental satellite surveillance systems. These long-term cooperative efforts to monitor and model the earth's biosphere will likely remain permanent features of the human-technological interface for the foreseeable future. Although they are designed to address the many interrelated facets of ecological management, their most important effect may lie in the unanticipated consequences of their continuous watch over the planet. With the emergence of the hypermedia environment no matter how the dynamics of world order unfold, they will do so under the total gaze of constantly orbiting surveillance cameras. When coupled with the prevalence of "earth images" and "global symbolism" outlined in chapter 7, these changes suggest the distant possibility of a global imagined community. However, the heterogeneous nature of postmodern social epistemology, and the overlapping layers of political authority, not to mention the dispersed centers of surveillance themselves, would all act as strong constraints against the emergence of a single mass identity. It is more likely that this sense of a global imagined community would coexist in a complex montage of overlapping and fluid multiple identities. For the foreseeable future, pastiche-like "niche" communities will likely dominate the postmodern landscape.

If the trends identified above do indeed become a more prominent feature of the world political landscape, then several general consequences for the practice and theory of world politics follow. We should expect that the faultlines of future conflicts will increasingly be *within* and *across* states, rather than between them. This would appear to hold as much for the states of the post-industrialized North as it would for those of the South. While the lack of state legitimacy and centralized authority in places like Rwanda,

Somalia, and in states of the former Soviet Union and Eastern Europe is obviously more severe than it is in places such as France, Canada, or the United States, similar types of fragmentative forces can be identified among the latter as well. This suggests that the neat divisions between the two worlds of the "post-historical" "strong" states of the "tame" North, and the zones of lawlessness and disorder of the historical "wild" South, may be misplaced.[4] If anything, such divisions between "tame" and "wild" cut across and transcend all geographic regions, applying perhaps more accurately to nonterritorial spheres than to hemispheric or territorially based divisions on a map. In the future, in other words, "quasi-states" may not be a classification pertaining solely to the states of the Third World.[5]

Of course, not all of the forces generating these cross-cutting divisions are fragmentative. Multinational and transnational corporations, global financial interests, and the thousands of Internet-based niche social movements and virtual communities are threading new integrative seams of regional and global authority within and across states. Indeed, one of the more potentially interesting political divisions of postmodern politics will be the interactions between what Robert Cox calls the hegemonic *nebuluese* of global market forces and the counter-hegemonic movements of global civil society.[6] The most significant rivalries will not be between states per se, but between the deepening and expansion of a global capitalist "business civilization" and the increasingly legitimate authority and influence of groups found on such networks as EcoNet, Envirolink, WomensNet, LaborNet, and MuslimsNet; between groups like the Trilateral Commission, the G7, and the Bank for International Settlements on the one hand, and groups such as Greenpeace, Amnesty International, Femmes Libres, and Anjuman Serfroshan-e-Islam, on the other. As it stands, the former have much greater structural power and influence over the shape of world politics than the latter do. And the mesh between postmodern attractions and the escapist worlds of consumer culture, found in video games, virtual realities, large-screen televisions, and giant cathedral-like theaters, greatly favors the continued subsistence and vitality of the global capitalist system. But relative power notwithstanding, the most important dynamic shaping the contours of global governance in years to come will less likely be rival states than it will be the interplay between these two rival hegemonic and counter-hegemonic social forces.

All of the above suggests that the theoretical tools and concepts International Relations theorists have inherited and employed for centuries to study world politics will be in need of revision. Such tools and concepts have rested on assumptions about the unity of authority, fixed territorial rule, and sharp divisions between "inside" and "outside," or "domestic" and "international" spheres.[7] They have formed the presuppositions and assumptions that have gone into such notions as unitary-rational actors, balances and system polarities among states, and the rise and fall of great powers. For theorists and foreign policy practitioners alike, these tools and concepts have provided a kind of conceptual lens or ordering device—a "way-of-seeing" the world—in which boundaries of responsibility are drawn, issues framed, and problems and their solutions visualized. Yet if the characteristics outlined above are accurate, such a paradigm will more likely produce dissonance and confusion, than insight and understanding.

Of course one important caveat is that the transformations described above are all seen from the perspective of changing communication technologies. Throughout this study I have gone to great lengths to argue against monocausal reductionism, and while communication technologies are important insofar as they are implicated in most all spheres of life, they should not be seen as "master variables." In step with this caveat, then, it is instructive to consider briefly some observations made by theorists working in other areas that reinforce the claims made above. For example, in *Beyond Sovereignty* David Elkins has described the "unbundling" of modern territorial politics—a process in which a wide variety of forces are helping to decouple many of the functions and instruments of governance from their territorial roots.[8] Likewise, Philip Cerny has described an emerging "plurilateral" world order, characterized by "cross-cutting ties" and "overlapping memberships"—a system that is neither hierarchic nor anarchic, but "polyarchical."[9] Ken Booth has argued that "Identity patterns are becoming more complex," and "The traditional distinction between 'foreign' and 'domestic' policy is less tenable than ever."[10] Also significant are Ronnie Lipschutz's observations on the "fading away" of anarchy, its replacement by a "global capitalist consumer culture," and the rise of a non-territorially-based "global civil society."[11] Similarly, James Rosenau has written of an emerging "multi-centric world" in which states exist alongside a variety of "sovereignty-free actors" shaping the contours of world politics.[12]

Perhaps most compelling of all, however, are John Ruggie's many observations of contemporary world order transformation. In ways similar to this

study, Ruggie has commented on the emergence of "multiperspectival institutional forms" and "non-territorial regions" driven by changes in production, finances, ecology, and security.[13] What is most significant, however, is
the way in which Ruggie points to a connection between these "multiperspectival" forms and broader changes in *mentalités collectives*. For Ruggie,
there is more than a passing coincidence between postmodern social epistemology and new forms of political authority. Given the affinity between
this study and Ruggie's, it is worth quoting him at some length:

> What is intriguing about this debate are some of the terms used to
> convey the essential features of postmodernity: detotalized, decen-
> tered, and fragmented discourses and practices; multiple and field-
> dependent referents in place of single-point fixed referents; flow-
> defined spaces and the simultaneity of temporal experiences as
> opposed to placed-defined spaces and sequential temporal experi-
> ences; the erosion of sovereign or macro powers over society coupled
> with the diffusion of disciplinary or micro powers within society. . . .
> To the student of international political economy these terms sound a
> great deal like descriptions of certain recently emerged global systems
> of economic transaction: the global markets in currencies, for exam-
> ple, or in credit and even equities; to a somewhat lesser but still con-
> siderable extent global production; and in several of the institutional
> arrangements that have emerged in the global commons . . .[14]

These converging observations made by theorists working along different
lines reinforce the conclusions made in this study from the perspective of
changing communication technologies.

As might be expected, however, universal consensus on the question of
world order transformation has not been reached. Generally speaking, arguments skeptical of the analysis I have set forth are likely to take one of two
forms, each of which can already be found in the existing literature. The
first argument, forcefully presented by Stephen Krasner, is that the very idea
that we could be living through a fundamental transformation of world order
is misguided from the start because there has never been a stable basepoint—
a Westphalian system—from which a transformation could unfold.[15] According to Krasner, "The assertion that the contemporary system represents
a basic transformation because sovereignty seems to be so much at risk is

not well-founded: it ignores the fact that violations of the principles of territoriality and autonomy have been an enduring characteristic of the international system both before and after the Peace of Westphalia."[16] Leaving aside Krasner's anachronistic allusion to there being an "international" system prior to there being "nations" at all, his basic point is an important one that should be addressed. The essence of Krasner's critique is that the changes going on today are nothing extraordinary, but are rather par for the course. To back up his argument, Krasner provides several illustrations of violations of state autonomy and sovereignty over the last three or four centuries.

While Krasner's argument is provoking, I see several reasons why it is not convincing. First, by setting up a very rigid notion of a "Westphalian System" as his counterpoint, Krasner may be overstating the extent to which others (and I suppose he would include myself in this category) see that system as something more than a paradigm or organizing template of political authority. Doing so allows Krasner to point to instances where the system was violated as evidence that this system was not constraining at all. However, simply because a norm was violated in several instances does not mean that the norm itself did not exist at all, that it did not shape and constrain the vast majority of peoples' conceptual horizons of the limits to political authority. Indeed, Krasner comes close to suggesting that the institutions of sovereignty, diplomacy, and public and private property that most everyone agree define the modern period of rule are simple fictions that can be explained away as random interactions among normless, power-seeking actors—a position that contradicts his earlier views on the *institutional depth* of the sovereign state.[17] Second, and relatedly, while Krasner can certainly identify isolated instances where the sovereignty paradigm was violated, he could not identify a period, such as the present, when so many violations are occurring *simultaneously* and at so many different levels from a variety of different directions. It is the cumulative impact of all of these together that suggest not just isolated violations of a norm, but a fundamental challenge to the norm itself.

A second argument, more common than the former, runs along the line that the "state" still exists and performs certain essential functions—that it still enforces regulations and contracts,[18] that it monopolizes coercive powers,[19] and that no viable institutional alternatives to it have emerged as challengers.[20] In short, *the state* has not disappeared or withered away, nor has it been replaced by some alternative institution. These objections certainly clarify an important misconception among liberal interdependence theorists of the 1960s and 1970s, who typically framed the rise of transnational corporations as an explicit challenge to the "state." And no doubt this misconception still animates many popular accounts of flows of information and commerce. But as an objection to the conclusions of this study, they are less convincing, primarily because *political authority* is the focus of my analysis, and not *the state* per se. While political authority was once centered in the hands of sovereign states, and while the arguments I have presented suggest it is now dispersing to multiple domains, I have not argued that as a consequence of this dispersal the state has disappeared or withered away. Quite the contrary. States still perform essential functions. I do not expect them to disappear any time soon. But while a state may still exist and perform crucial functions, it may not necessarily be the locus of political authority. A pen is vital to the signing of a law, but the political authority is wielded by the executive who does the signing, and not by the pen itself.

At the heart of these objections, however, may lie an even deeper set of questions not about transformation *per se* but about the discipline itself and its ability to conceptualize change at all. One gets the sense from these reservations that something is wrong with the way the very problem itself is being posed. Waiting for the state to "disappear" before entertaining the possibility of fundamental transformation is analogous to a seventeenth-century observer pointing to the town cathedral and waiting for it to disappear before accepting the demise of the medieval world order. Under those conditions, we would still be living in the Middle Ages!

Part of the problem may not be empirical at all, but *conceptual*. In other words, the real stumbling block may lie with the discipline's predominant "way-of-seeing" the world. A number of theorists are beginning to recognize the deep pervasiveness of a "state-centric/billiard ball" bias—a kind of ontological blinder that colors our preconceptions about the world around us. Consider in this respect Ruggie's admonition that the two dominant "schools" in the field, realism and liberalism, offer pictures that seem "equally misplaced"—that most theorists "lack even an adequate vocabulary; and what we cannot describe, we cannot explain."[21] Ruggie's critique is mirrored to some extent by Robert Walker's, who believes that our attempts at understanding or questioning transformation "remain caught within the discursive horizons that express the spatiotemporal configurations of another era."[22] Interestingly, this was a point made earlier by Edward Morse, who argued that "the whole terminology of international affairs is still permeated by past ideas and especially by the political and legal concepts of the West-phalia system."[23] In yet more stark terms, Rosenau has described these on-tological blinders as "conceptual jails."[24]

But if the answer is not an empirical one, how do we go about making, in Rosenau's words, a conceptual "jailbreak"? While there are probably many different answers to this question, recent developments in the philosophy and history of science associated with figures such as Thomas Kuhn, Quen-tin Skinner, Mary Hesse, and Richard Rorty suggest that conceptual revo-lutions in the sciences are more appropriately described as "metaphoric re-descriptions" of nature rather than more accurate representations of nature itself.[25] In other words, revolutionary achievements and paradigmatic revo-lutions occur when the old, familiar vocabulary becomes stale, rigid, and dogmatic and is replaced by new metaphors and new ways of looking at the world that dispense with the old vocabulary. The important point is that the creation of a new vocabulary or paradigm cannot be reached by following a set of a priori axioms formulated in the old vocabulary, nor can it be seen as finally hitting upon the one correct representation of "reality." Rather it occurs in a much less "rational," more poetic way, through the creative use of metaphors and analogies that help us see the world around us in a new and interesting light. This preanalytic exercise is what Rorty refers to as "therapeutic redescription"—that is, the use of novel metaphors to re-describe the present in order to shake us free of our current conceptual blinders, which are holding us captive and getting in the way.

How might Rorty's "therapeutic redescription" be applied to International Relations theory? While virtually any theme could suffice, one that seems to be gaining momentum in the field is "neomedievalism." Probably the first to articulate this analogy was Hedley Bull, who considered the possibility that the demise of the Westphalian states system could evolve into something resembling in form the architecture of medieval western Europe:

> All authority in mediaeval Christendom was thought to derive ulti-mately from God and the political system was basically theocratic. It might therefore seem fanciful to imagine that there might develop a modern and secular counterpart of it that embodies its central char-acteristic: a system of overlapping authority and multiple loyalty.[26]

Following Bull's lead, others have latched on to the analogy, typically focusing on the surface similarity between the two eras in terms of crosscutting and overlapping layers of authority.[27] Some have used the analogy to highlight different surface similarities. For example, Ronnie Lipschutz believes that today's liberal-capitalist order "has come to fill a role similar to the systems of rules and rule promulgated by the Church prior to Westphalia."[28] To date, however, most of these analogies have remained parenthetical and tentative. A neomedieval therapeutic redescription, on the other hand, would in effect "run" with these analogies not because there is some fundamental essence, nature, or dynamic underlying the medieval and the postmodern periods that somehow unites them, but rather purely for strategic reasons: that is, to redescribe the present in novel terms in order to shake us free of our current conceptual blinders that are holding us captive and getting in the way, as clearly appears to be the case with the "state-centric" paradigm.

For example, considerable mileage might be gained out of Lipschutz's brief analogy between the global-liberal capitalist paradigm and the transnational authority of the Roman Catholic Church—what Lipschutz refers to as "operating systems." For most people, consumer culture and the liberal-capitalist paradigm are the height of secularity. A redescription of such a system using religious metaphors might help "denaturalize" this paradigm by revealing it as more of a human artifact, one that in its structuring of basic cosmological principles of "natural" behavior—that satisfaction of material well-being through the consumption of goods and services—has significant religious connotations. Such a therapeutic redescription—in drawing attention to the way global-liberal capitalism resembles the transnational authority of the medieval Church—might also help invert the taken-for-granted binary opposition between the so-called "high" politics of military-security affairs and the "low" politics of economics. It might help relieve the problem to which Ruggie refers—the mind-set that sees challenges to the system of states only in terms of entities that are institutionally substitutable for the state—by referring to them as the postmodern equivalents of medieval kings: powerful, yes, but subordinate within the imperatives of the Great Chain of Being. This might help us conceptualize fundamental transformation not in terms of the disppearance of the state and its replacement by a world state or no-state, but in terms of the significance and *purposes* of states today—the way states are increasingly animated by the need to accommodate global market forces rather than to balance the military power of other states, in the same way that medieval kings and princes might have been ultimately animated less with material well-being than with their own salvation.

Examples of this type of therapeutic redescription do exist, but not surprisingly they are found outside of the International Relations field. One illustration is an article written by the editor of *Harper's* magazine, Lewis Lapham, who saw in neomedievalism "a way to think about . . . phenomena as distant from one another as MTV, the Uruguay round of the General Agreement on Tariffs and Trade, the transport of nuclear weapons by oxcart through the Caucasus Mountains, the apparition of H. Ross Perot, and the sales receipts of *Women Who Run with the Wolves*."[29] In a novel redescription, Lapham notes how the "consanguine hierarchies of international capitalism imitate the old feudal arrangements under which an Italian noble might swear fealty to a German prince or a Norman duke declare himself the subject of an English king." Lapham describes how today's "lords and barons of the smaller fiefs" owe their allegiance not to the United States or Britain, but to "Citibank or Bettelsmann or Matsushita." In extending the metaphor of global consumer culture as the New Church, Lapham describes how:

> The hegemony of wealth assumes the ecumenical place once occupied by the medieval church, and within this favoured estate everybody observes the same rituals and pays homage to the same princes. The yachts moored off Cannes or the Costa Brava sail under the flags of the same admiralty that posts squadrons off Miami and Newport Beach, and the American plutocrat travelling between the Ritz Hotel in Paris and Claridge's Hotel in London crosses not into another country but into another province of what has become the latter-day Christendom.[30]

To reiterate, Lapham's therapeutic redescription is not an attempt to uncover a common, fundamental essence of the medieval and the postmodern periods—to get at the "reality" underneath the layers of "false consciousness." It is rather an attempt to "denaturalize" the present, free us of our conceptual blinders by offering a new and interesting "way to think about" the world around us. If such a redescription has its intended effect, if it helps orient us to the world in a different way, then it will have achieved its purpose.

Of course the need for therapeutic redescription is a problem internal to the workings of the discipline, and is only a method to help theorists see the changing world around them in a more productive light. If the conclusions reached in this study are correct, then that world is indeed changing in dramatic and fundamental ways. Whether these changes should be applauded, lamented, or encouraged in certain directions over others are questions that wait another study. Certainly we would expect that not all of the changes will be uniformly "good." The fluidity and increasing porousness of borders will likely bring new forms of instability and tension, while the instantaneous transmission of televised images around the planet will no doubt encourage more acts of random terror. The relativist inclinations of postmodern social epistemology have already fed a rampant hyperlocalism and tribalism that some have described as a kind of "new barbarianism."[31] And the utter banality of the O.J. Simpson spectacle and others like it reveals the depths to which a commercially driven media and a consumer-culture ethos can sink. But not all of the changes will be uniformly "bad" either. With means of two-way communications and the breakdown of mass broadcasting, new forms of democratic participation and acts of creativity become feasible. A growing global civil society concerned with issues of ecology and human rights may eventually meliorate the worst excesses of the global market system. And the postmodern recognition of "difference," coupled with the move away from Cartesian universalism and totalizing metanarratives, may be just the type of *weltenschaung* necessary for the multiple and dispersed authorities of an emerging planetary polity.

Notes

Introduction

1. Throughout this study, I will capitalize "International Relations" when refer-
    ring to theorists or the discipline itself but will leave it lower case when referring
    to actual relations between modern states or nations.
2. John Gerard Ruggie, "Territoriality and Beyond: Problematizing Modernity in
    International Relations," *International Organization* 47 (Winter 1993): 139–
    140.
3. James N. Rosenau, *Turbulence in World Politics: A Theory of Change and Con-
    tinuity* (Princeton: Princeton University Press, 1990).
4. Mark Zacher, "The Decaying Pillars of the Westphalian Temple: Implications
    for International Order and Governance," James N. Rosenau and Ernst-Otto
    Czempiel, eds. *Governance without Government: Order and Change in World
    Politics* (Cambridge: Cambridge University Press, 1992), pp. 58–101.
5. Alvin Toffler and Heidi Toffler, *War and Anti-War: survival at the dawn of the
    21st century* (Boston: Little, Brown, 1993); and Alvin Toffler, *The Third Wave*
    (London: Pan Books, 1983).
6. Daniel Bell, *The Coming of Post-Industrial Society: A Venture in Social Fore-
    casting* (New York: Basic Books, 1973).
7. See David Harvey, *The Condition of Postmodernity* (Oxford: Blackwell, 1989);
    Alain Lipietz, *Mirages and Miracles: The Crisis of Global Capitalism* (London:
    Verso, 1987); and Michael Piore and Charles Sabel, *The Second Industrial
    Divide* (New York: Oxford University Press, 1984).

8. See Jean-François Lyotard, *The Postmodern Condition: A Report on Knowledge* (Minneapolis: University of Minneapolis Press, 1984); and Barry Smart, *Modern Conditions, Postmodern Controversies* (New York: Routledge Press, 1992). For more extensive citations on the topic of postmodernism, see chapter 7.

9. Ruggie, "Territoriality," pp. 143–144.

10. See, for example, Paul Baran, *The Political Economy of Growth* (New York: Modern Reader Paperbacks, 1957); Immanuel Wallerstein, *The Modern World System: Capitalist Agriculture and the Origins of the European World Economy in the Sixteenth Century* (New York: Academic Press, 1974); Robert Gilpin, *War and Change in World Politics* (Cambridge: Cambridge University Press, 1981); William McNeill, *The Pursuit of Power: Technology, Armed Forces and Society Since A.D. 1000* (Chicago: University of Chicago Press, 1984); Charles Tilly, *Coercion, Capital, and European States, A.D. 990–1990* (Cambridge: Basil Blackwell, 1990); and Daniel Deudney, "Dividing Realism: Security Materialism vs. Structural Realism on Nuclear Security and Proliferation," *Security Studies* 2, nos. 3/4 (Spring/Summer 1993).

11. On "ideas" and "knowledge" in the shaping of world politics, see Peter Haas, "Introduction: Epistemic Communities and International Policy Coordination," *International Organization* 46 (Winter 1992): 1–35; and Joshua Goldstein and Robert Keohane, eds., *Ideas and Foreign Policy* (Ithaca: Cornell University Press, 1993), especially the article by John A. Hall, "Ideas and the Social Sciences," pp. 31–54.

12. Paul Heyer, *Communications and History: Theories of Media, Knowledge, and Civilization* (New York: Greenwood Press, 1988), p. xiii.

13. Ibid., p. xiv.

14. Charles Tilly, *Big Structures, Large Processes, Huge Comparisons* (New York: Russell Sage Foundation, 1984), p. 61.

15. See Karl Deutsch, *The Nerves of Government: Models of Political Communication and Control* (New York: Free Press, 1963); and Karl Deutsch, *Nationalism and Social Communication* (Cambridge: MIT Press, 1966). A more detailed overview of Deutsch's work will follow in chapter 1.

16. See the works cited in note 10, above. A more extensive discussion and overview of the treatment of communications in International Relations will follow in chapter 1.

17. Rosenau, *Turbulence in World Politics*.

18. I am thinking in particular of James Der Derian, *Anti-Diplomacy: Spies, Terror, Speed, and War* (Oxford: Blackwell, 1992); and Timothy W. Luke, *Screens of Power: Ideology, Domination, and Resistance in Informational Society* (Urbana: University of Illinois Press, 1989).

19. Edward Comor, ed. *The Global Political Economy of Communication: Hegemony, Telecommunication, and the Information Economy* (New York: St. Martin's Press, 1994).

20. See, for example, Martin Libicki, "The Emerging Primacy of Information," *Orbis* (Spring 1996), pp. 261–276.

21. Two studies that provide insightful overviews of the way past innovations in communication technologies were heralded as either the harbingers of utopia or despair are James Carey, *Communication and Culture: Essays on Media and Society* (New York: Routledge Press, 1989); and Ithiel de Sola Pool, "Foresight and Hindsight: The Case of the Telephone," in *The Social Impact of the Telephone* (Cambridge: MIT Press, 1976).

22. James R. Beniger, *The Control Revolution: Technological and Economic Origins of the Information Society* (Cambridge: Harvard University Press, 1986), pp. 4–5. Despite the title, which suggests yet another prophetic leap into the void, Beniger's analysis is one of the more interesting and balanced approaches to developments in communication technologies.

23. Roderick Seidenberg, *Posthistoric Man: An Inquiry* (Chapel Hill: University of North Carolina Press, 1950); Ralf Dahrendorf, *Class and Class Conflict in an Industrial Society* (Stanford: Stanford University Press, 1959); Daniel Bell, *The End of Ideology: On the Exhaustion of Political Ideas in the Fifties* (New York: Basic Books, 1960); Edmund Berkeley, *The Computer Revolution* (New York: Doubleday, 1962); Kenneth E. Boulding, *The Meaning of the Twentieth Century: The Great Transition* (New York: Harper and Row, 1964); Peter Drucker, *The Age of Discontinuity* (New York: Harper and Row, 1969); Zbigniew Brzezinski, *Between Two Ages: America's Role in the Technetronic Era* (New York: Viking, 1970); Daniel J. Boorstin, *The Republic of Technology: Reflections on Our Future Community* (New York: Harper and Row, 1978); James Martin, *Wired Society* (New Jersey: Prentice-Hall, 1978); and Toffler, *The Third Wave*. In listing these works together I do not want to give the impression that they are all somehow equally insightful or impoverished as the case may be. I am merely illustrating the accumulation of literature addressing some aspect of epochal change in the last few decades. For similar frustrations, see W. Russell Neuman, *The Future of the Mass Audience* (Cambridge: Cambridge University Press, 1991), pp. 5–6.

24. "[P]rophecies tend to take the place of analysis" as Castells puts it. See Manuel Castells, *The Informational City: Information Technology, Economic Restructuring, and the Urban-Regional Process* (Oxford: Basil Blackwell, 1989), p. 1.

25. The "medium" in medium theory refers to the medium through which information is exchanged and not to the size or nature of the theory, as in "medium" versus "grand" theory.

26. Apart from other works by McLuhan cited throughout this study, see especially Marshall McLuhan, *The Gutenberg Galaxy* (Toronto: University of Toronto Press, 1962); and *Understanding Media: The Extensions of Man* (New York: McGraw-Hill, 1964).

27. Neuman, *The Future of the Mass Audience*, p. 48.

28. For Innis, see *Empire and Communications* (Oxford: Oxford University Press, 1950); and *The Bias of Communication* (Toronto: University of Toronto Press, 1951).

29. Robert W. Cox, "Social Forces, States and World Order: Beyond International Relations Theory," in Robert O. Keohane, ed., *Neorealism and its Critics* (New York: Columbia University Press, 1986), p. 210.

30. For various discussions of world order, see Cox, "Social Forces, States and World Orders"; Robert W. Cox, "Towards a Post-Hegemonic Conceptualization of World Order: Reflections on the Relevancy of Ibn Khaldun," in Rosenau and Czempiel, eds., *Governance without Government*; Hedley Bull, *The Anarchical Society: A Study of Order in World Politics* (London: Macmillan, 1977); Hedley Bull and Adam Watson, eds., *The Expansion of International Society* (Oxford: Oxford University Press, 1984); Adam Watson, *The Evolution of International Society* (New York: Routledge Press, 1992); and Daniel Deudney, "Binding Powers, Bound States: The Logic and Geopolitics of Negarchy," (Paper presented at the International Studies Association meeting, Washington D.C. March 28–April 2, 1994).

31. This definition is derived from the works listed in the previous note. It should be apparent that according to this definition "order" is not necessarily synonymous with the absence of conflict. Even anarchic systems in which war is a prominent feature are still "world orders" by this definition. For discussions on this point in particular, see Bull, *The Anarchical Society*, ch. 1; and Cox, "Post-Hegemonic Conceptualization of World Order," pp. 136–137.

32. John Gerard Ruggie, " 'Finding our Feet' in Territoriality: International Transformation in the Making," (Mimeo: 1990), p. 3; See also Ruggie, "Territoriality," p. 148.

33. Cf. Kenneth Waltz, *Theory of International Politics* (New York: Random House, 1979); Robert Jervis and Jack Snyder, eds. *Dominoes and Bandwagons* (New York: Oxford University Press, 1991).

34. For a similar view, see Ruggie, "Territoriality and Beyond"; and Janice E. Thomson, "State Sovereignty in International Relations: Bridging the Gap Between Theory and Empirical Research," *International Studies Quarterly* 30, 2 (June 1995): 213–233.

35. Ruggie, "Territoriality and Beyond."

36. See Thomson, "State Sovereignty in International Relations," p. 216; and Ste-

phen D. Krasner, "Compromising Westphalia," *International Security* 20, no. 3 (Winter 1995/1996): 118.

37. Thomson, "State Sovereignty in International Relations," pp. 216–217.

38. What I am saying is that most political scientists today share a common sense of what is meant by the term "political authority." Hence, it is still useful as an analytic tool to orient thought and discussion around certain social practices. But because it is so today does not mean that it always has been in the past, nor will it by necessity be so in the future.

39. Ruggie, "Finding our Feet," p. 7; See also, John Gerard Ruggie, "International Structure and International Transformation: Space, Time and Method," in Ernst Otto-Czempiel and James N. Rosenau, eds., *Global Changes and Theoretical Challenges: Approaches to World Politics for the 1990s* (Lexington, Mass: D.C. Heath/Lexington Books, 1989), p. 29. For Braudel and the *langue duree* see Fernand Braudel, *On History*, [trans. Sarah Matthews] (Chicago: The University of Chicago Press, 1980); and Stuart Clark, "The *Annales* Historians," in Quentin Skinner, ed., *The Return of Grand Theory in the Human Sciences* (Cambridge: Cambridge University Press, 1985), pp. 177–198.

40. Cox, "Social Forces, States and World Orders," p. 246.

41. For expressions of this trend in medieval studies, see Norman Cantor, *Inventing the Middle Ages: The Lives, Works and Ideas of the Great Medievalists of the Twentieth Century* (New York: Morrow, 1991).

42. Ruggie, "International Structure and International Transformation" in Czempiel and Rosenau, eds., *Global Changes and Theoretical Challenges*, p. 21.

43. Jacques Le Goff, *Medieval Civilization* (Oxford: Oxford University Press, 1988), p. 95.

44. Periodization is tricky business when it comes to the Middle Ages. Although there is a considerable amount of scholarly debate about the proper situating of time-lines and the essential differences between eras, I have chosen to follow the convention of dividing the Middle Ages into three periods: the early Middle Ages, running roughly from the fall of Rome in the fourth century to the tenth or eleventh century; the High Middle Ages, from the eleventh through the thirteenth centuries; and the late Middle Ages, the fourteenth and the fifteenth centuries. For discussion, see Umberto Eco, *Travels in Hyper Reality*, [trans. by William Weaver] (New York: HBJ Books, 1983), pp. 73–75; and Cantor, *Inventing the Middle Ages*, ch. 1.

45. Le Goff, *Medieval Civilization*, p. 95.

46. See Arthur Lovejoy, *The Great Chain of Being* (Cambridge: Harvard University Press, 1957).

47. Marc Bloch, Feudal Society, vol. 1, [trans. by L. A. Manyon] (Chicago: The University of Chicago Press, 1960), p. 81. See also Susan Reynolds, *Kingdoms*

and Communities in Western Europe 900–1300 (Oxford: Clarendon Press, 1984), p. 6; and Jens Bartelson, *A Geneology of Sovereignty* (Cambridge: Cambridge University Press, 1995), pp. 91–95.

48. Ernst H. Kantorowicz, *The King's Two Bodies: A Study in Mediaeval Political Theology* (Princeton: Princeton University Press, 1957), p. 194.

49. Garrett Mattingly, *Renaissance Diplomacy* (London: Cape Publishers, 1955), pp. 19–20.

50. Perry Anderson, *Lineages of the Absolutist State* (London: NLB, 1974), p. 33.

51. Le Goff, *Medieval Civilization*, p. 96.

52. Hendrick Spruyt, *The Sovereign State and Its Competitors* (Princeton: Princeton University Press), p. 55.

53. Mattingly, *Renaissance Diplomacy*, p. 26.

54. Georges Duby, *The Three Orders: Feudal Society Imagined*, [trans. Arthur Goldhammer] (Chicago: University of Chicago Press, 1980), p. 150.

55. John Gerard Ruggie, "Continuity and Transformation in the World Polity: Toward a Neorealist Synthesis," in Robert O. Keohane, ed., *Neorealism and its Critics* (New York: Columbia University Press, 1986), p. 143.

56. Ibid.

57. On the Peace of Westphalia in 1648 as the marking point for the emergence of the modern states system, see Zacher, "The Decaying Pillars of the Westphalian Temple"; Leo Gross, "The Peace of Westphalia, 1648–1948," in Richard A. Falk and Wolfram F. Hanrieder, eds., *International Law and Organization* (Philadelphia: Lippincott, 1968), pp. 45–67; and F. H. Hinsley, *The Pursuit of Peace* (Cambridge: Cambridge University Press, 1963).

58. See on this score, Jacques Le Goff, *The Medieval Imagination*, [trans. Arthur Goldhammer] (Chicago: University of Chicago Press, 1985), especially the section entitled "For an Extended Middle Ages." See also, Krasner, "Compromising Westphalia," p. 141; and Stephen D. Krasner, "Westphalia and All That," in Judith Goldstein and Robert O. Keohane, eds., *Ideas and Foreign Policy: Beliefs, Institutions, and Political Change* (Ithaca: Cornell University Press, 1993).

59. Michael Mann "The Rise of the European State," in James Anderson, ed., *The Rise of the Modern State* (Sussex: Wheatsheaf Books, 1986), p. 16.

60. John Dewey, *Reconstruction in Philosophy* (New York: Mentor Books, 1950), p. 53.

61. On "bundles" as a metaphor for modern world order, see David J. Elkins, *Beyond Sovereignty: Territory and Political Economy in the Twenty-First Century* (Toronto: University of Toronto Press, 1995); and Friedrich Kratochwil, "Of Systems, Boundaries, and Territoriality: An Inquiry into the Formation of the State System," *World Politics* 34 (October 1986): 27–52.

62. Spruyt, *The Sovereign State and Its Competitors*, p. 36.

63. See Gerrit, W. Gong, *The Standard of 'Civilization' in International Society* (Oxford: Clarendon Press, 1984); and Robert H. Jackson, *Quasi-States: Sovereignty, International Relations and the Third World* (Cambridge: Cambridge University Press, 1991). For a useful overview of the changes in the notion of "sovereignty" as a world ordering principle, see J. Samuel Barkin and Bruce Cronin, "The State and Nation: Changing Norms and Rules of Sovereignty in International Relations," *International Organization* 48 (Winter 1994): 107–130.

64. I use the word "paradigm" here to underscore that while the modern world order may be the predominant "way-of-seeing" the world for most people, it may be one that no longer provides a useful mental map of the emerging postmodern practices of world politics. In Kratochwil's words, there is currently a "disjunction between the organizing principles and social reality." Kratochwil, "Of Systems, Boundaries and Territoriality," p. 27. Such "conceptual barriers" to postmodern world order will be the focus of the concluding chapter to this study.

65. Richard Falk, "Sovereignty," in Joel Krieger, ed., *The Oxford Companion to Politics of the World* (New York: Oxford University Press, 1993).

66. For an affirmation of this view, see Robert H. Jackson, "Dialectical Justice in the Gulf War," *Review of International Studies* 18, no. 4 (1992), pp. 335–354.

67. Stephen D. Krasner, "Sovereignty: An Institutional Perspective," *Comparative Political Studies* 21, no. 1 (April 1988): 90.

68. Although space precludes a detailed overview, in the concluding chapter I will outline briefly some of the other studies that point to world order transformation today. For a more comprehensive overview, see Zacher, "The Decaying Pillars of the Westphalian Temple."

69. See, for example, Krasner, "Compromising Westphalia," which will be addressed in more length in the conclusion to this study.

1. Medium Theory, Ecological Holism, and the Study of World Order Transformation

1. I use the word "artificial" quite literally here, meaning produced by human art and effort, to emphasize that disciplinary boundaries are, after all, heuristic conventions and not reflections of any "natural" divisions in the world itself. In Cox's words, "academic conventions divide up the seamless web of the real social world in separate spheres, each with its own theorizing; this is a necessary and practical way of gaining understanding." However, as Cox continues, "It is wise to bear in mind that such a conventional cutting up of reality is at best just a convenience of the mind." Cox, "Social Forces, States and World Orders," p. 204.

2. See, for examples, Thomas C. Sorenson, *The Word War: The Story of American Propaganda* (New York: Harper and Row, 1968); Z. A. B. Zeman, *Nazi Propaganda*, 2nd ed. (New York: Oxford University Press, 1973); J. A. Emerson Vermaat, "Moscow Fronts and the European Peace Movements," *Problems of Communism* (Nov.–Dec. 1982): 43–56; Harold Lasswell, Daniel Lerner, and Hans Speier, eds., *Propaganda and Communication in World History* (Honolulu: University of Hawaii Press, 1980); John Martin, *International Propaganda: Its Legal and Diplomatic Control* (Gloucester: P. Smith, 1969); W. Phillips Davison, "Political Communications as an Instrument of Foreign Policy," *Public Opinion Quarterly* 27 (1963): 28–36.

3. William Dorman and Mansour Farhang, *The US Press and Iran: Foreign Policy and the Journalism of Deference* (Berkeley: University of California Press, 1987); Alan Rachlin, *News as Hegemonic Reality: American Political Culture and the Framing of News Accounts* (New York: Praeger, 1988); Robert M. Entman, "Framing US Coverage of International News: Contrasts in Narratives of the KAL and Iran Air Incident," *Journal of Communication* 41 (Autumn 1991): 6–27. For "frame analysis," see Erving Goffman, *Frame Analysis: An Essay on the Organization of Experience* (Cambridge: Harvard University Press, 1974).

4. Michael Arlen, *Living Room War* (New York: Viking Press, 1969).

5. Karl Deutsch, "Mass Communication and the Loss of Freedom in National Decision-Making: A Possible Research Approach to Interstate Conflict," *Journal of Conflict Resolution* 1 (1957): 200–211; John W. Burton, *Conflict and Communication: The Use of Controlled Communication in International Relations* (London: Macmillan, 1969); Robert Jervis, *Perception and Misperception in International Politics* (Princeton: Princeton University Press, 1976); Jacob Berkovitch, "Third Parties in Conflict Management: The Structure and Conditions of Effective Mediation in International Relations," *International Journal* 40 (Autumn 1985), pp. 736–752.

6. J. M. Mitchell, *International Cultural Relations* (London: Allen and Unwin, 1986).

7. Oran Young, *The Intermediaries: Third Parties in International Conflict* (Princeton: Princeton University Press, 1967); Charles Lockhart, *Bargaining in International Conflicts* (New York: Columbia University Press, 1979); Raymond Cohen, *Negotiating Across Cultures: Communication Obstacles in International Diplomacy* (Washington: United States Institute of Peace, 1991).

8. John R. Wood and Jean Seers, *Diplomatic Ceremonial and Protocol* (New York: Columbia University Press, 1970); Raymond Cohen, *Theatre of Power: The Art of Diplomatic Signalling* (London: Longmans, 1987); James Der Derian, *On Diplomacy: A Genealogy of Western Estrangement* (Oxford: Basil Blackwell, 1987).

9. For a useful overview, see Noam Chomsky, *Necessary Illusions: Thought Control in Democratic Societies* (Toronto: CBC Enterprises, 1989).

10. See Stephen Gill, ed., *Gramsci, Historical Materialism, and International Relations* (Cambridge: Cambridge University Press, 1993). See also, Comor, ed., *The Global Political Economy of Communication*.

11. Hamid Mowlana, *Global Information and World Communication: New Frontiers in International Relations* (New York: Longmans, 1986).

12. Thomas McPhail, *Electronic Colonialism: The Future of International Broadcasting and Communication*, 2nd ed. (Beverly Hills: Sage Publications, 1987).

13. See Kaarle. Nordenstreng and Herbert. I. Schiller, eds., *National Sovereignty and International Communication* (New Jersey: Ablex Publishing, 1979); C. J. Hamelink, *Cultural Autonomy in Global Communications* (New York: Longmans, 1983); and John Tomlinson, *Cultural Imperialism: A Critical Introduction* (Baltimore: The Johns Hopkins University Press, 1991).

14. Deutsch, *The Nerves of Government*; and Deutsch, *Nationalism and Social Communication*.

15. See, for example, Edward Morse, *Modernization and Transformation in International Relations* (London: Collier Macmillan, 1976); Walt Rostow, *Politics and the Stages of Growth* (Cambridge: Cambridge University Press, 1971); Walt Rostow, *The Stages of Economic Growth: A Non-Communist Manifesto* (Cambridge: Cambridge University Press, 1960); and George M. Foster, *Traditional Cultures and the Impact of Technological Change* (New York: Harper, 1962).

16. Walker Connor, "Nation-Building or Nation-Destroying?" *World Politics* 24 (April 1972): 319–355.

17. Donald J. Puchala, "Integration Theory and the Study of International Relations," in Richard L. Merritt and Bruce M. Russett, eds., *From National Development to Global Community: Essays in Honour of Karl W. Deutsch* (London: Allen and Unwin, 1981), pp. 145–164. In pointing to the flaws in Deutsch's treatment of communications, I am not implying that his scholarship as a whole is unworthy of continued study. Quite the contrary. Recent work among epistemic community and social constructivist theorists on cognition and value change demonstrates the utility of going beyond Deutsch. See, in particular, Emanuel Adler and Michael Barnett, "Governing Anarchy: A Research Agenda for the Study of Security Communities," *Ethics and International Affairs.* (Volume 10, 1996).

18. Joshua Meyrowitz, *No Sense of Place: The Impact of Electronic Media on Social Behavior* (New York: Oxford University Press, 1985), p. 15.

19. Ruth Finnegan, *Literacy and Orality: Studies in the Technology of Communication* (Oxford: Basil Blackwell, 1988).

20. Normally, medium theorists are concerned not with the comparative effects of discrete media operating contemporaneously (though this is certainly not excluded) but rather with large-scale changes in modes of communication that signify epochal changes in human history.

21. See Eric Havelock, *Preface to Plato* (Cambridge: Belknap Press of Harvard University Press, 1963); Walter J. Ong, *Orality and Literacy: The Technologizing of the Word* (New York: Methuen, 1982), pp. 79–81; and Ernst Gellner, *Plough, Sword and Book: The Structure of Human History* (Chicago: The University of Chicago Press, 1988). As Gellner says on page 87, "Mankind entered the age of Plato when the authority of concepts became a *theory*, when the Transcendent became manifest as such, and when the paradigmatic incarnation of the concept was no longer, or not exclusively, found in ritual, but rather in writing. Ritual had once underwritten the Word, but the Word itself now became a ritual." [italics in original].

22. "Thou shalt not make unto thee any graven image, any likeness of any thing that is in heaven above, or that is in the earth beneath, or that is in the water beneath the earth." As Postman explains, "It is a strange injunction to include as part of an ethical system *unless its author assumed a connection between forms of human communication and the quality of a culture.*" (Italics in original). See Neal Postman, *Amusing Ourselves to Death* (New York: Penguin Books, 1985), p.9.

23. As cited Heyer, *Communications and History*, p. 44.

24. In addition to other works cited in this study, see especially McLuhan, *The Gutenberg Galaxy*; and McLuhan, *Understanding Media*.

25. Lewis Lapham, "Prime-Time McLuhan," *Saturday Night* (September 1994), p. 51.

26. See Marshall McLuhan and Quentin Fiore, *War and Peace in the Global Village* (New York: Bantam Books, 1968).

27. See McLuhan, *Understanding Media*, pp. 36–44; For a collection of critical responses, see Gerald Emaneul Stearn, ed., *McLuhan: Hot and Cool* (New York: Signet Books, 1969).

28. See *Understanding Media*, pp. 36–45.

29. "The electric light is pure information" is taken from *Understanding Media*, p. 23. "Electric Circuitry Is Orientalizing the West" is from Marshall McLuhan and Quentin Fiore, *The Medium is the Massage* (New York: Simon and Schuster, 1967), p. 145.

30. For a collection of articles that discuss the "Toronto School," see Ian Angus and Brian Shoesmith, eds., "Dependency/Space/Policy: A Dialogue with Harold A. Innis," *Continuum: The Australian Journal of Media & Culture* 7, no. 1 (1993).

31. See especially Innis, *Empire and Communications* ; and *The Bias of Communications*.

32. Harold A. Innis, *The Cod Fisheries: The History of an International Economy* (Toronto: University of Toronto Press, 1954); and Harold A. Innis, *The Fur Trade in Canada: An Introduction to Canadian Economic History* (Toronto: University of Toronto Press, 1956).

33. Heyer attributes the formulating of this distinction to James Carey. See Heyer, *Communications and History*, p. 126.

34. Innis, *Empire and Communications*. The following overview of Innis is indebted to Heyer's informative treatment in *Communications and History*.

35. Heyer, *Communications and History*, p. 115.

36. See Oswald Spengler, *Decline of the West*. [Translated by C. F. Atkinson] (London: Allen and Unwin, 1932); Pitrim Sorokin, *Social and Cultural Dynamics* (Boston: Porter Sargeant, 1957); Arnold Toynbee, A *Study of History* Vol. 1 (Oxford: Oxford University Press, 1934). For an overview, see Stephen K. Sanderson, ed., *Civilizations and World Systems: Studying World-Historical Change* (London: Altimira Press, 1995).

37. Innis, *The Bias of Communications*, p. 33. [emphasis added]

38. On the McLuhanesque renaissance, see Lapham, "Prime-Time McLuhan." A recent Canadian Broadcasting Corporation documentary produced by Toronto's media guru Moses Znaimer on the "TV Revolution" prominently featured interviews with McLuhan. The popular cultural critic Camille Paglia has also drawn significantly from McLuhan. See Camille Paglia, *Vamps and Tramps: New Essays* (New York: Vintage Books, 1994).

39. Havelock, *Preface to Plato*; Eric Havelock, *The Literate Revolution in Greece and its Cultural Consequences* (Princeton: Princeton University Press, 1982).

40. Jack Goody, *Literacy in Traditional Societies* (Cambridge: Cambridge University Press, 1975); Jack Goody, *The Domestication of the Savage Mind* (Cambridge: Cambridge University Press, 1978); Jack Goody, *The Logic of Writing and the Organization of Society* (Cambridge: Cambridge University Press, 1986); Jack Goody, *The Interface Between the Written and the Oral* (Cambridge: Cambridge University Press, 1987); Jack Goody and Ian Watt, "The Consequences of Literacy," *Comparative Studies in Society and History* 5 (1963): 304–345; Walter Ong, *Ramus, Method, and the Decay of Dialogue* (Cambridge: Harvard University Press, 1958); Walter Ong, *Interfaces of the Word* (Ithaca: Cornell University Press, 1977); and Ong, *Orality and Literacy*.

41. Elizabeth Eisenstein, *The Printing Press as an Agent of Change: Communications and Cultural Transformations in Early Modern Europe*, [Volumes 1 and 2] (New York: Cambridge University Press, 1980).

42. Lewis Mumford, *Technics and Civilization* (New York: HBJ Publishers, 1934); and Gellner, *Plough, Sword, and Book*.

43. James W. Carey, "McLuhan and Mumford: The Roots of Modern Media Analysis," *Journal of Communication* 31 (Summer 1981): 168.

44. John Halverson, "Havelock on Greek Orality and Literacy," *Journal of the History of Ideas* 53 no. 1 (1992): 160; 162. [italics in original].

45. Michael Hunter, "The Impact of Print," *The Book Collector* (1980), p. 341.

46. As cited in Paul Levinson, "McLuhan and Rationality," *Journal of Communication* 31 (Summer 1981): 179.

47. Eisenstein, *The Printing Press*.

48. Tilly explains the reasons for this tendency in the social sciences in the following way: "It would be astounding to discover that a single recurrent social process governed all large-scale social change. Perhaps the hope of becoming the Newton of social process tempts social scientists into their repeated, fruitless efforts at discovering that philosopher's stone." Tilly, *Big Structures, Large Processes, Huge Comparisons*, p. 33. Richard Rorty describes this search for master variables or ultimate foundations as attempts to "escape from history." See Richard Rorty, *Philosophy and the Mirror of Nature* (Princeton: Princeton University Press, 1979). More on this search for "ultimate foundations" and attempts to escape history will be said below with regard to the mainstream International Relations field.

49. See Hans Blumenberg, *The Legitimacy of the Modern Age*, [translated by Robert Wallace] (Cambridge: MIT Press, 1982); See also, Le Goff, *The Medieval Imagination*, especially section entitled, "For an Extended Middle Ages."

50. For an overview, see Wiebe Bijker, Thomas Hughes, and Trevor Pinch, *The Social Construction of Technological Systems* (Cambridge: MIT Press, 1989).

51. McLuhan and Fiore, *The Medium Is the Massage*; and Meyrowitz, *No Sense of Place*, pp. 16–23.

52. My views on Darwinian theories of evolution are derived mostly from the following sources: Stephen Jay Gould, *Ever Since Darwin: Reflections in Natural History* (New York: Norton, 1977); Stephen Jay Gould, *Bully for Brontosaurus: Reflections in Natural History* (New York: Norton, 1991); Stephen Jay Gould, *Eight Little Piggies: Reflections in Natural History* (New York: Norton, 1993); and Richard Dawkins, *The Blind Watchmaker* (New York: Penguin Books, 1986).

53. See Robert Carnerio, ed., *The Evolution of Society: Selections from Herbert Spencer's Principles of Sociology* (Chicago: University of Chicago Press, 1974), for the writings of the principal "Social Darwinist," Herbert Spencer.

54. Goody, *The Interface Between the Written and the Oral*, p. 3.

55. Innis, *The Bias of Communications*, p. 4.

56. Neuman, *The Future of the Mass Audience*, p. 40.

57. Gould, *Bully for Brontosaurus*, p. 69.

58. See Spruyt, *The Sovereign state and Its Competitors*, pp. 25, 83, and 179 for elaboration.

59. I put "internal" in quotation marks because what I am talking about here, as will be made clear below, are inherently intersubjective phenomenon.

60. See Havelock, *Preface to Plato*; Ong, *Orality and Literacy*; and Gellner, *Plough, Sword, and Book*.

61. Ruggie, "Territoriality," p. 157.

62. Note that the term "web-of-beliefs" refers not just to specific beliefs that can be held or discarded by individuals, but more importantly the space of possible or probable beliefs that distinguish a population, including unconscious assumptions and cognitive biases. It is also important to note that this notion of a "web-of-beliefs" is not incompatible with a basic "materialist" outlook, and should not be confused with an airy idealism. John Dewey explains in general (and gendered) terms how this process of acculturation into an intersubjective body of meanings bears on the young individual: "The conceptions that are socially current and important become the child's principles of interpretation and estimation long before he attains to personal and deliberate control of conduct. Things come to him clothed in language, not in physical nakedness, and this garb of communication makes him a sharer in the beliefs of those about him. These beliefs coming to him as so many facts form his mind; they furnish the centres about which his own personal expeditions and perceptions are ordered." Dewey, *Reconstruction in Philosophy*, pp. 86–87.

63. See Kenneth Gergen and Mary Gergen, eds., *Historical Social Psychology* (New Jersey, Hillsdale, 1984). "Imagined Communities" is taken from Benedict Anderson *Imagined Communities* (London: Verso, 1991).

64. See Le Goff, *The Medieval Imagination*.

65. See, for examples, Karl Mannheim, *Ideology and Utopia: An Introduction to the Sociology of Knowledge* (New York: Harvest, 1936); Peter Berger and Thomas Luckmann, *The Social Construction of Reality* (New York: Anchor Books, 1967). For an application of social constructivism to international relations, see Alexander Wendt, "Anarchy is what states make of it: the social construction of power politics," *International Organization* 46 (Spring 1992): 391–425.

66. Mumford, *Technics and Civilization*.

67. Ibid., p. 15.

68. Ibid., p. 17.

69. Clifford Geertz, *The Interpretation of Cultures* (New York: Basic Books, 1973), epseically part I, "Thick Description: Toward an Interpretive Theory of Culture."

70. This practice of unearthing unconscious boundaries and biases of thought is, of course, most often associated with the work of Michel Foucault. See especially, Michel Foucault, *The Order of Things: An Archaeology of the Human Sciences* (New York: Vintage Books, 1970); and *The Archaeology of Knowledge and the Discourse on Language*, [Translated by A. M. Sheridan Smith] (New York: Pantheon Books, 1972).

71. See Richard Dawkins, *The Selfish Gene* (Oxford: Oxford University Press, 1976); and Daniel Dennett, *Darwin's Dangerous Idea: Evolution and the Meanings of Life* (New York: Simon and Schuster, 1995), especially chapter 12, "The Crisis of Culture."

72. Dawkins, *The Selfish Gene*, p. 206. Also cited in Dennet, *Darwin's Dangerous Idea*, p. 345.

73. For classical realist speculations on a fixed and determining human nature, see Hans Morgenthau, *Scientific Man vs. Power Politics* (Chicago: The University of Chicago Press, 1946); Reinhold Niebuhr, "Human Nature and the Will to Power," in H. Davis and R. Good, eds., *Reinhold Niebuhr on Politics* (New York: Scribner's, 1960); and Kenneth Waltz, *Man, the State, and War* (New York: Columbia University Press, 1954). On "rational" actor assumptions, see Robert Keohane, *After Hegemony: Cooperation and Discord in the World Political Economy* (Princeton: Princeton University Press, 1984); and Kenneth Oye, ed., *Cooperation Under Anarchy* (Princeton: Princeton University Press, 1986).

74. That said, however, it is important to note that some cognitive traits are presupposed in my theoretical formulation. For example, the mechanism of selection in medium theory for elements of social epistemology assumes that human beings have a tendency to avoid contradictory cognitions about social reality. It is on this basis that I can infer that certain social constructs will flourish or wither depending on their "fitness" with a particular communications environment. People will tend to assimilate social constructs, in other words, that are more consistent with their overall communications experience. That is not to say, however, that such general species-wide traits are responsible for the actual construction of specific social ideas or institutions. As Stephen Gould aptly put it, "the statement that humans are animals does not imply that our specific patterns of behavior and social arrangements are in any way directly determined by our genes. *Potentiality* and *determination* are different concepts." Gould, *Ever Since Darwin*, p. 251.

75. On institutions, see Robert Keohane, "International Institutions: Two Approaches," *International Studies Quarterly* 32 (1988): 379–396; Friedrich Kratochwil, *Norms, Rules and Decisions* (Cambridge: Cambridge University Press, 1989); and John Gerard Ruggie and Friedrich Kratochwil, "International Or-

ganization: The State of the Art on an Art of the State," *International Organization* 40 (1986): 753–76.

76. For discussion, see Lewis Mumford, *Technics and Civilization*; and Daniel Deudney, *Pax Atomica: Planetary Geopolitics and Republicanism* (Princeton: Princeton University Press, 1997).

77. Bruce Mazlish, *The Fourth Discontinuity: The Co-Evolution of Humans and Machines* (New Haven: Yale University Press, 1993), p. 5.

78. See Stephen K. Sanderson, "Evolutionary Materialism: A Theoretical Strategy for the Study of Social Evolution," *Sociological Perspectives* 37, no. 1 (1994): 47–73.

79. See Daniel Deudney, "Bringing Nature Back In," in Daniel Deudney and Richard Matthew, eds., *Contested Grounds: Security and Conflict in the New Environment Politics* (New York: SUNY Press, 1997).

80. One of the starker examples in this respect is the impact of the "Black Plague" on the restructuring of human society in the late Middle Ages. See Ruggie, "Territoriality"; and Barbara W. Tuchman, *A Distant Mirror: The Calamitous 14th Century* (New York: Ballantine Books, 1978).

81. This view closely resembles Robert Cox's "historical-structures" approach, which: "sees human nature and the other structures that define social and political reality—from the structure of language through those of laws, morals, and institutions, and including the state and world-order structures like the balance of power—as being themselves products of history and thus subject to change." Robert Cox, "Production, the State, and Change in World Order," in Czempiel and Rosenau, eds., *Global Changes and Theoretical Challenges*, p. 38.

82. Sanderson, "Evolutionary Materialism," p. 50.

83. On "long-cycles" in world politics, see George Modelski, *Long Cycles in World Politics* (London: Macmillan, 1987); and William R. Thompson, "Ten Centuries of Global Political-Economic Coevolution," (Paper prepared for delivery to the workshop on Evolutionary Paradigms in the Social Sciences, Batelle Seattle Conference Center, University of Washington, Seattle, May 13–14, 1994). On progressive stages of development, see Rostow, *The Stages of Economic Growth*.

84. On an explication of "Darwinist" views of history similar to my own, see Richard Rorty, "Dewey between Hegel and Darwin," in D. Ross, ed., *Modernist Impulses in the Human Sciences: 1870–1930* (Baltimore: Johns Hopkins University Press (1994): 54–68.

85. John Lewis Gaddis, "Tectonics, History and the End of the Cold War," in John Lewis Gaddis, ed., *The United States and the End of the Cold War:*

Implications, Reconsiderations, Provocations (Oxford: Oxford University Press, 1992).

86. Sanderson, "Evolutionary Materialism," p. 53.

87. Keohane, "International Institutions," pp. 379–96.

88. Cox, "Social Forces, States, and World Order," p. 210.

89. Gellner, *Plough, Sword, and Book*, p. 12.

90. For similar views of the ahistorical tendencies of neorealism and neoliberalism see Emanuel Adler, "Cognitive Evolution: A Dynamic Approach for the Study of International Relations and Their Progress," in Emanuel Adler and Beverly Crawford, eds., *Progress in Postwar International Relations* (New York: Columbia University Press, 1993), pp. 43–88; Wendt, "Anarchy," pp. 391–396; and Richard K. Ashley, "Three Modes of Economism," *International Studies Quarterly* 27 (1983). Cf. Waltz, *Theory of International Politics*.

91. Adler, "Cognitive Evolution," p. 43.

92. Ibid., p. 44.

93. See Gilpin, *War and Change in World Politics*.

94. Wendt, "Anarchy," p. 392.

95. For an overview of the "relative vs. absolute gains" debate, see Robert Powell, "Anarchy in International Relations Theory: The Neorealist-Neoliberal Debate," *International Organization* 48 (Spring 1994): 313–344; and David A. Baldwin, ed., *Neorealism and Neoliberalism: The Contemporary Debate* (New York: Columbia University Press, 1993).

96. Adler, "Cognitive Evolution," p. 43.

97. My use of the term "historicism" follows that of Robert Cox, who draws from Giambattista Vico in seeing history as an open-ended evolutionary process. See Cox, "Social Forces, States, and World Order," p. 213. In this sense, it is defined in complete opposition to Karl Popper's use of the term in *The Poverty of Historicism* (Boston: Beacon, 1957) to single out theories that see history in law-like terms.

98. See Cox, "Social Forces, States, and World Order"; Robert Cox, "Multilateralism and World Order," *Review of International Studies* 18 (1992): 161–180; and Cox, "Towards a Post-Hegemonic Conceptualization of World Order."

99. See Deudney, *Pax Atomica*; and Daniel Deudney, *Global Geopolitics: Materialist World Order Theories of the Industrial Era, 1850–1950* (Ph.D. Dissertation, Princeton University, 1989).

100. Wendt, "Anarchy"; Kratochwil, *Rules, Norms, and Decisions*; and Nicholas Onuf, *World of Our Making* (Columbia: University of South Carolina Press, 1989).

101. Carmen Luke, *Pedagogy, Printing, and Protestantism: The Discourse on Childhood* (New York: SUNY Press, 1989), p. 29.

102. Ruggie, "Territoriality," p. 152.

103. Adler, "Cognitive Evolution," p. 47; and Ernst Haas, "Words Can Hurt You: Or Who Said What to Whom about Regimes," in Stephen D. Krasner, ed., *International Regimes* (Ithaca: Cornell University Press, 1983).

104. In a footnote ("Anarchy," p. 398, fn. 27), Wendt concedes that some constructivist approaches may be "oversocialized" when dealing with "presocial but non-determining human needs," but he goes no further in elaborating if and when other "material" factors beyond neurophysiological adaptations, like climate and population for example, would enter into the picture.

105. See, for example, Michael Mann, *The Sources of Social Power.* Vol. 1 (Cambridge: Cambridge University Press, 1986), pp. 500 onwards; Donald E. Polkinghorne, *Narrative Knowing and the Human Sciences* (New York: SUNY Press, 1988); and Janice Thomson, *Mercanaries, Pirates and Sovereigns: State-Building and Extraterritorial Violence in Early Modern Europe* (Princeton: Princeton University Press, 1994), p. 5.

106. Polkinghorne, *Narrative Knowing and the Human Sciences*, p. 20; See also John Gerard Ruggie, "Peace in Our Time? Causality, Social Facts, and Narrative Knowing," *Proceedings of the American Society of International Law* (1995).

107. For discussion, see Philip Tetlock and Aaron Belkin, eds., *Counterfactual Thought Experiments in World Politics: Logical, Methodological, and Psychological Perspectives* (Princeton: Princeton University Press, 1996).

2. From the Parchment Codex to the Printing Press: The Sacred Word and the Rise and Fall of Medieval Theocracy

1. See Cantor, *The Civilization of the Middle Ages*, pp. 422–423.

2. See Ibid., pp. 266–276; See also Gerd Tellenbach, *Church, State, and Christian Society at the Time of the Investiture Controversy* (Oxford: Basil Blackwell, 1959); and Uta-Renate Blumenthal, *The Investiture Controversy: Church and Monarchy from the Ninth to the Twelfth Century* (Philadelphia: University of Philadelphia Press, 1988).

3. On the Crusades, see Jonathan Riley-Smith, *The First Crusade and the Idea of Crusading* (London: Athlone, 1986). For discussion of the Crusades in the context of International Relations theory debates, see Rodney Bruce Hall, "The Medieval 'State' and the Social Construction of Sovereign Identity." (Paper presented at the International Studies Association 36th Annual Convention, Chicago: February 21–25, 1995).

4. James Curran, "Communications, Power and Social Order," in Michael Gurevitch, et al., eds., *Culture, Society and the Media* (London: Routledge Press, 1982), p. 203.

5. Ibid., p. 204.

6. On the connection between physiological changes in the vocal tract that permit the spoken word and the so-called "Great Leap Forward" in human evolution, see Jared Diamond, "The Great Leap Forward," *Discover* (1990), pp. 66–76.

7. Ong, *Orality and Literacy*, p. 84.

8. Goody, *The Interface Between the Written and the Oral*, p. 3.

9. Ibid., p. 18.

10. See Denise Schmandt-Besserat, "The Earliest Precursor of Writing," *Scientific American* 283, no. 6 (1978): 50–59; See also, Bruce Bower, "The Write Stuff: researchers debate the origins and effects of literacy," *Science News* (March 6, 1993): 152–154.

11. See especially, Goody, *The Logic of Writing*.

12. Marc Drogin, *Biblioclasm: The Mythical Origins, Magic Powers, and Perishability of the Written Word* (Maryland: Rowman and Littlefield, 1989), p. 11.

13. See Harold Innis, "Media in Ancient Empires," in David Crowley and Paul Heyer, eds., *Communication in History: Technology, Culture, Society*, 2nd ed. (New York: Longmans, 1995).

14. Gellner, *Plough, Sword, and Book*, p. 71.

15. Goody, *The Logic of Writing*, pp. 16–17.

16. Anderson, *Imagined Communities*, pp. 15–16.

17. Anderson, *Imagined Communities*, p. 14. This belief was more the case during the early Middle Ages, gradually becoming a contested site from the twelfth century onward with the spread of lay literacy, and as evidenced by the debate between nominalists and realists of the time. Nominalists held that only particular physical items constitute reality, while realists believed that universals have a reality which is prior to and apart from the physical. For a more thorough treatment of these issues, see Brian Stock, *Listening for the Text: On the Uses of the Past* (Baltimore: Johns Hopkins University Press, 1990); and Roy Harris and Talbot J. Taylor, eds., *Landmarks in Linguistic Thought: The Western Tradition from Socrates to Saussure* (New York: Routledge Press, 1989), p. xv.

18. "And out of the ground the Lord God formed every beast of the field, and every fowl of the air; and brought them unto Adam to see what he would call them: and whatsoever Adam called evry living creature, that was the name thereof. And Adam gave names to all cattle, and to the fowl of the air, and to every beast of the field. . . . " (Genesis II, 19–20)

    For discussion, see Heyer, *Communications and History*, p. 146–148; See also Cantor, who notes how a common belief that the "road to knowledge lay through the origin of words" can be found in the title of the influential *Etymologies*, written by the early-seventh-century bishop of Seville, Isidore. Cantor, *The Civilization of the Middle Ages*, p. 83.

19. Michel Foucault, *The Order of Things*, p. 33.

20. Drogin, *Biblioclasm*, p. 33.
21. Ibid., p. 38.
22. Ibid.
23. Taken from M. T. Clanchy, *From Memory to Written Record: England 1066–1307*, 2nd Edition (Oxford: Blackwell Publishers, 1993), p. 262.
24. Barraclough, *The Medieval Papacy*, p. 9.
25. See Le Goff, *Medieval Civilization*, pp. 3–36.
26. See Innis, *Empire and Communication*, pp. 83–112; See also, Susan Raven, "The Road to Empire," *Geographical Magazine* (June 1993): 21–24.
27. Le Goff, *Medieval Civilization*, p. 120.
28. Cantor, *The Civilization of the Middle Ages*, p. 64.
29. For discussion, see Rosamond McKitterick, *The Carolingians and the Written Word* Cambridge: Cambridge University Press, 1989, pp. 167–168.
30. For discussions on the difficulties establishing literacy rates in the early Middle Ages, see Ibid.; and Stock, *Listening for the Text*.
31. Cantor, *The Civilization of the Middle Ages*, p. 146.
32. See Innis, *Empire and Communications*, pp. 118–119.
33. Giovanni Miccoli, "Monks," in Jacques Le Goff, ed., *Medieval Callings* [Translated by Lydia G. Cochrane] (Chicago: The University of Chicago Press, 1987), p. 43.
34. Cantor, *The Civilization of the Middle Ages*, p. 153.
35. See Innis, *Empire and Communications*, p. 85–112; and Raven, "Road to Empire."
36. See Leila Avrin, *Scribes, Script and Books: The Book Arts from Antiquity to Renaissance* (Chicago: American Library Association, 1991), pp. 173–175. See also Jack Finegan, *Encountering New Testament Manuscripts: a working introduction to textual criticism*, (Grand Rapids, Michigan: Eerdmans, 1974). On p. 29, Finegan writes: "As to the relative frequency of use of the roll and of the codex, in an enumeration of 476 second-century non-Christian literary papyrus manuscripts from Egypt, 465 or more than 97 percent are in the form of the roll; but eight Christian biblical papyri known from the same century are all in the form of the codex. Likewise in the entire period extending to shortly after the end of the fourth century, out of 111 biblical manuscripts or fragments from Egypt, 99 are codices. That the codex increased in use in comparison with the use of the roll is natural in view of the many obvious advantages of the leaf book, not the least of which is that it is more feasible to write on both sides of a leaf, and hence such a book is cheaper. But the statistics just given indicate a particular and very early preference for the codex form on the part of Christians. This also is natural in view of the advantages of the codex with respect to matters of particular interest to the Christians. For example, the single Gospel according to Luke would probably have filled an average papyrus

roll of approximately thirty feet in length, and Paul's ten collected church letters (including Philemon) would probably have occupied two ordinary rolls, but all Four Gospels or all of the Letters of Paul could readily be brought together in a single codex book. Likewise it is much more difficult to turn quickly to a specific passage in a roll, and much easier to do so in a codex."

I located this quotation at Timothy Seid's "Interpreting Ancient Manuscripts Web," found online at http://www.stg.brown.edu/projects/mss/codex.html.

37. Ibid.
38. Innis, *The Bias of Communication*, p. 49. I have added the italics for emphasis.
39. Avrin, *Scribes, Script and Books*, p. 210.
40. McKitterick, *The Carolingians and the Written Word*, pp. 138–139.
41. See Innis, *Empire and Communications*, p. 117.
42. Innis, *The Bias of Communications*, p. 48.
43. Cantor, *The Civilization of the Middle Ages*, p. 153.
44. Miccoli, "Monks," p. 68.
45. Ibid. See also Le Goff, *Medieval Civilization*, p. 114: "Thus in the library at Cluny a monk who wanted to consult a manuscript by an ancient author had to scratch his ear with a finger in the style of a dog scratching itself with a paw, 'for the pagan is justly compared with this animal.'" And on page 115: "Ancient thought only survived in the middle ages in a fragmented form. It was pushed out of shape and humiliated by Christian thought."
46. Karl Schottenloher, *Books and the Western World: A Cultural History.* [Translated by William D. Boyd and Irmgard H. Wolfe] (London: McFarland & Company, 1968), p. 31.
47. Avrin, *Scribes, Script and Books*, p. 209.
48. Clanchy, *From Memory to Written Record*, p. 125; See also, McKitterick, *The Carolingians and the Written Word*, pp. 136–157.
49. Miccoli, "Monks," p. 39.
50. Cantor, *The Civilization of the Middle Ages*, p. 153.
51. Georges, Duby, "The Diffusion of Cultural Patterns in Feudal Society," *Past and Present* 39 (April 1968): 4.
52. Curran, "Communications, Power and Social Order," p. 202.
53. See especially, Sophia Menache, *The Vox Dei: Communication in the Middle Ages* (New York: Oxford University Press, 1990), pp. 51–78.
54. See Brian Stock, *The Implications of Literacy: Written Languages and Models of Interpretation in the Eleventh and Twelfth Centuries* (Princeton: Princeton University Press, 1983), pp. 35, 60–61.
55. Geoffrey Barraclough, *The Medieval Papacy* (London: Thames and Hudson, 1968), p. 40.
56. Clanchy, *From Memory to Written Record*, p. 318.

57. Bloch, *Feudal Society*, p. 80.
58. Miccoli, "Monks," p. 57.
59. Ibid., p. 58.
60. Cantor, *The Civilization of the Middle Ages*, p. 154.
61. Bloch, *Feudal Society*, p. 80.
62. Barraclough, *The Medieval Papacy*, p. 100.
63. Ibid., p. 103. On the increase in correspondences at this time, see Spruyt, *The Sovereign State and Its Competitors*, p. 50.
64. Jacques Le Goff, "Introduction," in Le Goff, ed., *Medieval Callings*, p. 5.
65. Michael Camille, "Seeing and Reading: Some Visual Implications of Medieval Literacy and Illiteracy," *Art History* 8, no. 1 (March 1985): 26.
66. Camille, "Seeing and Reading," p. 27.
67. Le Goff, *The Medieval Imagination*, p. 6.
68. Le Goff, "Introduction," p. 32.
69. Curran, "Communications, Power and Social Order," p. 207.
70. See especially, Jacques Le Goff, *The Medieval Imagination*. Interestingly, there are affinities between the imagined realm of the medieval mentality and the "virtual realities" of an emerging postmodern consciousness today. See, for discussion, Ronald J. Deibert, "Virtual Realities: neo-medievalism as therapeutic redescription," (Paper presented at the International Studies Association annual conference, Chicago, 1995).
71. See Richard Matthew, "Justice, Order and Change in World Politics" (Paper Prepared for the ISA Annual Convention, March 28-April 1, 1994, Washington, DC).
72. See Cantor, *The Civilization of the Middle Ages*, p. 118.
73. Curran, "Communications, Power and Social Order," p. 206.
74. Ibid.
75. Anderson, *Imagined Communities*, p. 23.
76. Leonard M. Dudley, *The Word and the Sword: How Technologies of Information and Violence Have Shaped our World* (Cambridge: Basil Blackwell, 1991), pp. 146–147.
77. As Menache relates: "The development of the Church in the Central Middle Ages embodies an essential paradox: the ecclesiastical order reached its maximal influence at a time when Western society gradually evolved from corporate frameworks into more developed socioeconomic systems which by their very nature opposed the Church's monopoly." Menache, *The Vox Dei*, p. 78.
78. Barraclough, *The Medieval Papacy*, p. 122.
79. Cantor, *The Civilization of the Middle Ages*, pp. 314–315.
80. Barraclough, *The Medieval Papacy*, p. 128.
81. Ibid.
82. Ibid., p. 154; See also Menache, *The Vox Dei*, pp. 213–273.

83. Cantor, *The Civilization of the Middle Ages*, pp. 376–377; See also Menache, *The Vox Dei*, pp. 216–225.
84. Marcel Thomas, "Manuscripts," in Lucien Febvre and Henri-Jean Martin, *The Coming of the Book: the Impact of Printing 1450–1800*. [Translated by David Gerard, Edited by Geoffrey Nowell-Smith and David Wootten] (London: NLB, 1976), p. 15.
85. Ibid., p. 19; For an overview of the growth of universities, see Alan B. Cobban, *The Medieval Universities, Their Development and Organization* (London: Methuen, 1975).
86. Thomas, "Manuscripts," pp. 19–22.
87. Ibid., p. 22.
88. Cantor, *The Civilization of the Middle Ages*, pp. 308–318, 395, 398–399.
89. See Robert Dodgshon, *The European Past: Social Evolution and Spatial Order* (London: Macmillan), p. 145; and Clanchy, *From Memory to the Written Word*, pp. 42–43.
90. Febvre and Martin, *The Coming of the Book*, p. 29.
91. Febvre and Martin, ibid., p. 26.
92. Avrin, *Scribes, Script and Books*, p. 285.
93. Ibid., p. 287.
94. Eugene Rice Jr., *The Foundations of Early Modern Europe, 1460–1559* (New York: Norton, 1970), p. 3.
95. Avrin, *Scribes, Script and Books*, p. 292.
96. See Febvre and Martin, *The Coming of the Book*, pp. 29–39.
97. Ibid., pp. 39–40.
98. Schottenloher, *Books and the Western World*, p. 50.
99. See Dudley, *The Word and the Sword*, p. 150.
100. Febvre and Martin, *The Coming of the Book*, p. 52.
101. Ibid., pp. 51–53.
102. Dudley, *The Word and the Sword*, p. 150.
103. See Febvre and Martin, *The Coming of the Book*, pp. 71–76.
104. Febvre and Martin, *The Coming of the Book*, p. 77.
105. Ibid., p. 249.
106. Ibid., pp. 248–249.
107. Stephen Saxby, *The Age of Information: The past development and future significance of computing and communications* (London: Macmillan, 1990), p. 45.
108. Febvre and Martin, *The Coming of the Book*, p. 262.
109. This comparison is recounted by Eisenstein in *The Printing Press*, p. 46.
110. Anderson, *Imagined Communities*, pp. 37–38.
111. Ibid., p. 167.
112. Ibid., pp. 167–185.
113. Luke, *Pedagogy, Printing, and Protestantism*, p. 58.

3. Print and the Medieval to Modern World Order Transformation: Distributional Changes

1. For analysis of heresies in the Middle Ages, see Gordon Leff, *Heresy in the Middle Ages: The Relation of Heterodoxy to Dissent* (New York: Barnes and Noble, 1967); R. I. Moore, *The Origins of European Dissent* (London: Allen Lane, 1977); and Edward Peters, *Heresy and Authority in Medieval Europe* (Philadelphia: University of Pennsylvannia Press, 1980).
2. See Barraclough, *The Medieval Papacy*, pp. 164–187.
3. On the "Black Death" plague, see William H. McNeill, *Plagues and Peoples* (New York: Anchor Press, 1976); Robert S. Gottfried, *The Black Death: Nature and Disaster in Medieval Europe* (New York: Free Press, 1983); Tuchman, *A Distant Mirror*, pp. 92–125; and Ruggie, "Territoriality," pp. 153–154.
4. Anderson, *Imagined Communities*, p. 39.
5. See Le Goff, *Medieval Civilization*, p. 148.
6. Febvre and Martin, *The Coming of the Book*, p. 288.
7. On the Inquisition, see Bernard Hamilton, *The Medieval Inquisition* (London: E. Arnold, 1981).
8. Eisenstein, *The Printing Press*, pp. 303–304.
9. Ibid., p. 317.
10. Ibid., p. 375.
11. See Febvre and Martin, *The Coming of the Book*, pp. 170–172.
12. Rice, *The Foundations of Early Modern Europe*.
13. Febvre and Martin, *The Coming of the Book*, p. 172.
14. For a discussion of works that make such strong claims, see Eisenstein, *The Printing Press*, pp. 303–329.
15. See Luke, *Pedagogy, Printing, and Protestantism*, p. 78; This particular argument is one favored by those inclined to a Marxist view of history. See, F. Engels, *The Peasant War in Germany*, [trans. M. J. Olgin] (New York: International Publishers, 1926); and F. Braudel, *The Structures of Everyday Life*, Vol. 1, [trans. S. Reynolds] (New York: Harper and Row, 1979).
16. Luke, *Pedagogy, Printing, and Protestantism*, p. 134.
17. Dudley, *The Word and the Sword*, p. 153.
18. See Febvre and Martin, *The Coming of the Book*, pp. 289–290.
19. See Mark U. Edwards Jr., *Printing, Propaganda, and Martin Luther* (Los Angeles: University of California Press, 1994), p. 1.
20. Ibid., p. 17.
21. Ibid.
22. Anderson, *Imagined Communities*, p. 39.
23. Ibid.
24. Edwards, *Printing, Propaganda, and Martin Luther*, p. 15.

25. Ibid.
26. Ibid.
27. Ibid., p. 16.
28. The study by Hans-Joachim Kohler is cited in Ibid., p. 180. See also, Febvre and Martin, *The Coming of the Book*, pp. 109–115.
29. Edwards, *Printing, Propaganda, and Martin Luther*, pp. 6–7.
30. Luke, *Pedagogy, Printing, and Protestantism*, p. 75.
31. Febvre and Martin, *The Coming of the Book*, p. 295.
32. Edwards, *Printing, Propaganda, and Martin Luther*, p. 7.
33. Quoted in Curran, "Communications, power, and social order," p. 217.
34. Anderson, *Imagined Communities*, p. 40.
35. Eisenstein, *The Printing Press*, p. 68; Febvre and Martin, *The Coming of the Book*, p. 291.
36. Kohler is cited in Edwards, *Printing, Propaganda, and Martin Luther*, pp. 37–39; The original study which Edwards cites is Hans-Joachim Kohler, "The *Flugschriften* and their importance in religious debate: a quantitative approach," in Paola Zambelli, ed., *Astrologi hallucinati: Stars and the End of the World in Luther's Time* (New York: W. de Gruyter, 1986), pp. 153–175.
37. Cf. Gerald Strauss, *Luther's House of Learning: Indoctrination of the Young in the German Reformation* (Baltimore: Johns Hopkins University Press, 1978).
38. See Curran, "Communications, Power, and Social Order," p. 220; See also, Edwards, *Printing, Propaganda, and Martin Luther*, pp. 37–38.
39. Anderson, *Imagined Communities*, p. 40.
40. See Eisenstein, *The Printing Press*, pp. 347–348; See also, Anderson, *Imagined Communities*, p. 40.
41. Ibid., p. 355.
42. Ibid., pp. 415–416.
43. As cited in Luke, *Pedagogy, Printing, and Protestantism*, p. 47.
44. Ibid.
45. As related in Edwards, *Printing, Propaganda, and Martin Luther*, p. 14.
46. Anderson, *Imagined Communities*, p. 40.
47. Curran, "Communications, Power, and Social Order," p. 218.
48. Anderson calls book publishing "one of the earlier forms of capitalist enterprise." See Anderson, *Imagined Communities*, pp. 37–39; See also Febvre and Martin, *The Coming of the Book*, chapter 7; Eisenstein, *The Printing Press*, pp. 310–315.
49. Anderson, *Imagined Communities*, p. 38; and Febvre and Martin, *The Coming of the Book*, pp. 264–265.
50. See Jacques Le Goff, *Intellectuals in the Middle Ages*, [Translated by Teresa Lavender Fagan] (Cambridge: Basil Blackwell, 1993); and Hans Blumenberg, *The Genesis of the Copernican World* (Cambridge: MIT Press, 1987).

51. See Gordon Leff, *Paris and Oxford Universities in the Thirteenth and Fourteenth Centuries: An Institutional and Intellectual History* (New York: Krieger Publishers, 1975); and Le Goff, *Intellectuals in the Middle Ages*.

52. See Carlo M. Cipolla, *Before the Industrial Revolution: European Society and Economy 100–1700* (New York: Norton, 1976); and Mumford, *Technics and Civilization*.

53. See Le Goff, *Intellectuals in the Middle Ages*, pp. 107–119; and Cantor, *The Civilization of the Middle Ages*, pp. 442–448.

54. Eisenstein, *The Printing Press*, pp. 455–456.

55. Eisenstein, *The Printing Press*, p. 517.

56. Febvre and Martin, *The Coming of the Book*, p. 148.

57. Eisenstein, *The Printing Press*, p. 75.

58. Ibid., p. 517.

59. Ibid., pp. 88–113; On the *esprit de système* of the age, see especially Foucault, *The Order of Things*.

60. See Postman, *Amusing Ourselves to Death*, pp. 51–53.

61. See Eisenstein, *The Printing Press*, p. 113.

62. Rice, *The Foundations of Early Modern Europe*, p. 8.

63. On the relationship between the idea of progress and the mode of communication, particularly as it is expressed by thinkers such as Condillac and Condorcet, see Heyer, *Communications and History*, Part 1. The Eighteenth Century.

64. Curran, "Communications, Power and Social Order," p. 218.

65. See Mann, *The Sources of Social Power*; North and Thomas, *The Rise of the West*; and Spruyt, *The Sovereign State and Its Competitors* for overviews.

66. The classic work here is Bloch, *Feudal Society*, Vols. 1 and 2.

67. Ibid., pp. 145–162.

68. Le Goff, *Medieval Civilization*, p. 91.

69. See Le Goff, *Medieval Civilization*, p. 90.

70. See Stock, *The Implications of Literacy*, for a detailed discussion of literacy levels in different regions and periods throughout the Middle Ages.

71. Le Goff, *Medieval Civilization*, p. 92.

72. Clanchy, *From Memory to Written Record*, p. 272.

73. Ibid., p. 275.

74. As cited in Ibid., p. 254.

75. Ibid., p. 263.

76. Hendrick Spruyt, "Institutional Selection in International Relations: State Anarchy as Order," *International Organization* 48 (Autumn 1994): 529.

77. Ibid., p. 537; See also Braudel, *The Structures of Everyday Life*, pp. 436–477 for a lengthy discussion of money and barter from the late Middle Ages through the eighteenth century.

78. See Spruyt, "Institutional Selection," p. 537; See also Clanchy, *From Memory to Written Records*; and Susan Reynolds, *Kingdoms and Communities in Western Europe 900–1300* (Oxford: Clarendon Press, 1984).

79. Spruyt, "Institutional Selection," pp. 537–538.

80. See Spruyt, *The Sovereign State and Its Competitors*, p. 159 for a discussion of the representational, as opposed to abstract, form of measures in the Middle Ages.

81. E. L. Jones, *The European Miracle: Environments, Economies, and Geopolitics in the History of Europe and Asia* (New York: Cambridge University Press, 1981).

82. Ibid.; See also Ruggie, "Territoriality," pp. 152–154.

83. Ruggie, "Territoriality," p. 153.

84. Spruyt, "Institutional Selection," p. 539.

85. Anderson, *Imagined Communities*, p. 144.

86. Emile Durkheim, *The Division of Labor in Society* (New York: The Free Press, 1933).

87. Rice, *The Foundations of Early Modern Europe*, p. 6.

88. Stock, *The Implications of Literacy*; and Clanchy, *From Memory to Written Record*.

89. See Douglass C. North and Robert Paul Thomas, *The Rise of the Western World: A New Economic History* (Cambridge: Cambridge University Press, 1973), p. 55 for an overview of the origins of paper bills of exchange in the Champagne Fairs, and how they were more efficient for commercial purposes.

90. John J. McCusker and Cora Gravesteijn, *The Beginnings of Commercial and Financial Journalism: The Commodity Price Currents, Exchange Rate Currents, and Money Currents of Early Modern Europe* (Amsterdam: NEHA, 1991), p. 21.

91. Ibid., p. 23.

92. Ibid., pp. 43–84.

93. See Ibid.

94. See Douglass C. North and Robert Paul Thomas, *The Rise of the Western World: A New Economic History* (Cambridge: Cambridge University Press, 1973), pp. 136–137 for printed price currents as an important part in the creation of urban markets.

95. See Carolyn Webber and Aaron Wildavsky, *A History of Taxation and Expenditure in the Western World* (New York: Simon and Schuster, 1986), p. 153.

96. Of course the classic work on the capitalist spirit is Max Weber, *The Protestant Ethic and the Spirit of Capitalism*, [Translated by Talcott Parsons] (New York: Scribner's, 1958). However, given Weber's thesis linking the rise of the capitalist ethos to religious impulses, it is not surprising that he pays no attention to the change in the mode of communication at the time—a shortcoming that has

been noted by a number of communications theorists, the most vociferous of which is undoubtedly Eisenstein. See Eisenstein, *The Printing Press*, pp. 378–402.

97. See especially Ong, *Orality and Literacy*; Havelock, *Preface to Plato*; and Goody, *The Logic of Writing*.

98. See North and Thomas, *The Rise of the West*, p. 138.

99. Dudley, *The Word and the Sword*, p. 171.

100. By "leveling" I am referring not to an equality of wealth and opportunity, but rather to the dissolution of personal bondage that characterized the feudal system of rule and its replacement by juridical equality among townspeople. See Spruyt, *The Sovereign State and Its Competitors*, p. 93 for discussion.

101. Roland Axtmann, "The formation of the modern state: the debate in the social sciences," in Mary Fulbrook, ed., *National Histories and European History* (Boulder: Westview Press, 1993), p. 33. For a similar argument, see Anderson, *Lineages of the Absolutist State*; and Charles Tilly, *Coercion, Capital, and European States, A.D. 990–1990* (London: Basil Blackwell, 1990); and Spruyt, *The Sovereign State and Its Competitors*, p. 92.

102. Mann, *Sources of Social Power*, p. 514.

103. Mattingly, *Renaissance Diplomacy*, p. 122.

104. See Goody, *The Logic of Writing*; Gellner, *Plough, Sword, and Book*; Dudley, *The Word and the Sword*; Innis, *Empire and Communications*.

105. This is the thesis of Clanchy's *From Memory to Written Record*; See also Joseph Strayer, *On the Medieval Origins of the Modern State* (Princeton: Princeton University Press, 1970).

106. Webber and Wildavsky, *A History of Taxation*, p. 153.

107. On the rediscovery of Roman Law and its relation to centralizing state bureaucracies, see Anderson, *Lineages of the Absolutist State*, p. 27; Webber and Wildavsky, *A History of Taxation*, p. 182; and Ruggie, "Continuity and Transformation in World Polity," p. 144.

108. See Cantor, *The Civilization of the Middle Ages*, pp. 398–399; See also Clanchy, *From Memory to Written Record*, p. 19.

109. See Spruyt, *The Sovereign State and Its Competitors*, p. 78 for discussion.

110. Gianfranco Poggi, *The Development of the Modern State: A Sociological Introduction* (Stanford: Stanford University Press, 1978), p. 26.

111. Mattingly, *Renaissance Diplomacy*, p. 125.

112. Webber and Wildavsky, *A History of Taxation*, p. 149.

113. Bernard Guenee, *States and Rulers in Late Medieval Europe*, [Translated by Juliet Vale] (London: Basil Blackwell, 1985), p. 92.

114. Ibid., p. 168.

115. Poggi, *The Development of the Modern State*, p. 27;

116. Tilly, *Coercian, Capital, and European States*.

117. See North and Thomas, *The Rise of the West*; and Spruyt, *The Sovereign State and Its Competitors*.

118. For an outstanding (and relatively succinct) narrative of these processes, see Poggi, *The Development of the Modern State*, ch. 4.

119. For a widely accepted account see Anderson, *Lineages of the Absolutist State*; see also James Anderson and Stuart Hall, "Absolutism and Other Ancestors," in Anderson, ed., *The Rise of the Modern State*, p. 31.

120. Tilly, *Coercion, Capital and European States*; and Mann, *Sources of Social Power*.

121. These figures are taken from Guenee, *States and Rulers*, p. 127; See also Clanchy, *From Memory to Written Record*.

122. Febvre and Martin, *The Coming of the Book*, p. 127.

123. Guenee *States and Rulers in Late Medieval Europe*.

124. Charles Tilly, "Reflections on the History of European State-Making," in Charles Tilly, ed., *The Formation of National States in Western Europe* (Princeton: Princeton University Press, 1975), pp. 43–44.

125. Poggi, *The Development of the Modern State*, p. 72.

126. See Michel Foucault, *Discipline and Punish: The Birth of the Prison*, [Trans. Alan Sheridan] (New York: Vintage Books, 1979); For similar interpretations, see Anthony Giddens, *The Nation-State and Violence* (Oxford: Oxford University Press, 1985); Norbert Elias, [Translated by Edmund Jephcott] *The Civilizing Process: The History of Manners and State Formation and Civilization* (Oxford: Basil Blackwell, 1994).

127. For an overview discussion of Foucault's ideas in this respect, see Axtmann, "The Formation of the Modern State," pp. 38–40.

128. Foucault himself briefly alludes to the crucial role played by documentation, or what he calls a "network of writing," as part of the mechanism of discipline, but is remiss in not mentioning print in this regard. See *Discipline and Punish*, p. 189. For discussion which argues that Foucault is remiss in not discussing print, see Luke, *Pedagogy, Printing and Protestantism*, p. 3; and Heyer, *Communications and History*, pp. 141–155.

129. Peter Barber, "England II: Monarchs, Ministers, and Maps, 1550–1625," in David Buisseret, ed., *Monarchs, Ministers, and Maps: The Emergence of Cartography as a Tool of Government in Early Modern Europe* (Chicago: The University of Chicago Press, 1992), pp. 58, 61.

130. Ibid., p. 83.

131. David Buisseret, "Monarchs, Ministers, and Maps in France Before the Accession of Louis XIV," in Buisseret, ed., *Monarchs, Ministers, and Maps*, p. 100.

132. Ibid., p. 99.

133. The following section relies on Luke, *Pedagogy, Printing, and Protestantism*.

134. Ibid.
135. Foucault, *Discipline and Punish*, p. 147; This same passage is cited by Luke, *Pedagogy, Printing and Protestantism*, p. 7.
136. See Luke, *Pedagogy, Printing and Protestantism*, pp. 11–12.
137. See Spruyt, *The Sovereign State and Its Competitors*, pp. 153, and 160 for a discussion of how both the city-leagues and the city-states lacked a single, centralized form of internal rule.

4. Print and the Medieval to Modern World Order Transformation: Changes to Social Epistemology

1. Ruggie, "Territoriality," p. 157
2. Louis Dumont, *Essays in Individualism: Modern Ideology in Anthropological Perspective* (Chicago: The University of Chicago Press, 1986), p. 62.
3. Ibid., p. 23.
4. See Ibid., pp. 23–60; See also, Richard Matthew, "Back to the Dark Age: World Politics in the Late Twentieth Century," (Paper delivered at the ISA Annual Meeting, Chicago, February 1995).
5. See Le Goff, *Intellectuals in the Middle Ages*; See also, Guenee, *States and Rulers*, p. 32, for a link between the nominalism of William of Okham and individualism. Guenee notes how philosophical/epistemological beliefs often translated later into political doctrines in this way: "And so, for example, the great realist-nominalist debate (where for so long the realists, convinced of the reality of general concepts, were set against the nominalists, for whom the individual alone existed) largely determined the poles of political thinking: whilst a realist readily sacrificed a part to the whole, the individual to the State, for a nominalist like William of Okham the individual was all-important and the common good no more than the sum total of individual interests. The 'democratic' trends characteristic of the fourteenth and fifteenth centuries, which set the conciliar movement against the Pope and Estates against the princes, coincided with an upsurge in nominalism."
6. Cantor, *The Civilization of the Middle Ages*, p. 432.
7. Lovejoy, *The Great Chain of Being*.
8. As quoted in Guenee, *States and Rulers*, p. 43.
9. See Duby, *The Three Orders*; Rodney Bruce Hall and Friedrich V. Kratochwil, "Medieval Tales: Neorealist 'Science' and the Abuse of History," *International Organization* 47 (Autumn 1993); and Rodney Bruce Hall, "The Medieval 'State' and the Social Construction of Sovereign Identity," (Paper Delivered at the International Studies Association— 36th Annual Convention, February 21– 25, 1995, Chicago).

10. John Lyon, *The Invention of the Self: The Hinge of Consciousness in the Eigh-teenth Century* (Carbondale: Southern Illinois University Press, 1978), p. 37.

11. C. B. Macpherson, *The Political Theory of Possessive Individualism* (Oxford: Clarendon Press, 1962), p. 3.

12. See Stephen Lukes, "Individualism," in David Miller, ed., *The Blackwell Encyclopedia of Political Thought* (Oxford: Basil Blackwell, 1991), p. 240. Descartes' radical individualism is, of course, well known. See *Discourse on Method and Meditations*, [Translated by Laurence J. Lafleur] (Indianapolis: Bobbs-Merrill, 1960); See also the excellent treatment of the social forces implicated in the Cartesian retreat to individuality in Ernst Gellner, *Reason and Culture: The Historic Role of Rationality and Rationalism* (Oxford: Basil Blackwell, 1992).

13. Charles Taylor, "Atomism," in *Philosophical Papers*, Volume 2 (Cambridge: Cambridge University Press, 1985): 210.

14. Richard K. Ashley, "Untying the Sovereign State: A Double Reading of the Anarchy Problematique," *Millennium: Journal of International Studies* 17 (1988): 230.

15. Ruggie, "Territoriality," p. 158.

16. Dumont, *Essays on Individualism*, p. 73.

17. Thomas Hobbes, *Leviathan*, [Micheal Oakeshott, ed.] (New York: Collier Books, 1962), p. 132.

18. as quoted in Dumont, *Essays on Individualism*, pp. 74–75.

19. Lyon, *The Invention of the Self*, p. 67.

20. Ong, *Orality and Literacy*, p. 133.

21. Ibid., p. 131.

22. Henry John Chaytor, *From Script to Print: An Introduction to Medieval Vernaculars* (London: Folcroft Library Editions, 1945), p. 1.

23. For McLuhan's discussion of the "authorless" Middle Ages, see *Gutenberg Galaxy*, pp. 160–163.

24. Ong, *Orality and Literacy*, p. 131.

25. Febvre and Martin, *The Coming of the Book*, p. 261.

26. Susan Reynolds, "Magna Carta 1297 and the Legal Use of Literacy," *Bulletin of the Institute of Historical Research*, 62 (1989): 241; This passage from Reynolds is cited in Clanchy, *From Memory to Written Record*, p. 265.

27. Ong, *Orality and Literacy*, p. 133.

28. Febvre and Martin, *The Coming of the Book*, p. 23.

29. Ibid., p. 261.

30. Eisenstein, *The Printing Press*, p. 121.

31. Finnegan, *Literacy and Orality*, p. 28.

32. For discussion, see Chartier, "The Practical Impact of Writing," p. 125.

33. Febvre and Martin, *The Coming of the Book*, p. 88.

34. Chartier, "The Practical Impact of Print," p. 111.

35. For an extensive discussion, see Roger Chartier, "The Practical Impact of Print," in Philippe Aries and Georges Duby, eds., *A History of Private Life*. vol. 3 (Cambridge: Belknap Press of Harvard University Press, 1989), pp. 111–159.
36. Ibid., p. 125.
37. Roger Chartier, "The Practical Impact of Writing," p. 125.
38. Ruggie, "Territoriality," p. 158.
39. For discussion, see Orest Ranum, "The Refuges of Intimacy," and Jean Marie Goulemot, "Literary Practices: Publicizing the Private," both of which appear in Aries and Duby, eds., *A History of Private Life*.
40. Ong, *Orality and Literacy*, p. 131.
41. Ruggie, "Territoriality," p. 159.
42. Dodgshon, *The European Past*, p. 164.
43. For a good overview, see Le Goff, *Medieval Civilization*, ch. 6; and Le Goff, *The Medieval Imagination*, Part Two: Space and Time, pp. 47–82.
44. Donald M. Lowe, *History of Bourgeois Perception* (Chicago: University of Chicago Press, 1982), p. 12.
45. Harvey, *The Condition of Postmodernity*, p. 241.
46. Clanchy, *From Memory to Written Record*, p. 285.
47. Ibid.
48. Ibid., p. 267.
49. Edward W. Soja, *The Political Organization of Space* (Washington: Resource Paper no. 8, Association of American Geographers, 1971), p. 9.
50. David Buisseret, "Introduction," in Buisseret, ed., *Monarchs, Ministers, and Maps*, p. 1.
51. R. B. J. Walker, *Inside/outside: International Relations as Political Theory* (Cambridge: Cambridge University Press, 1993), p. 129.
52. See Buisseret, ed., *Monarchs, Ministers, and Maps*, and Harvey, *The Condition of Postmodernity*, pp. 240–253.
53. Buisseret, "Introduction," p. 1.
54. Harvey, *The Condition of Postmodernity*, p. 245.
55. See Samuel Y. Edgerton, Jr., *The Renaissance Rediscovery of Linear Perspective* (New York: Basic Books, 1975).
56. McLuhan, *Understanding Media*, p. 157.
57. McLuhan and Fiore, *The Medium is the Massage*, p. 49.
58. Ong, *Orality and Literacy*, p. 127.
59. Febvre and Martin, *The Coming of the Book*, pp. 77–104 documents the visual appearance of the book.
60. Lowe, *A History of Bourgeois Perception*, p. 26.
61. For a discussion, see Guenee, *States and Rulers*, pp. 50–65.
62. Guenee, *States and Rulers*, pp. 50–51.
63. See Jonathan Riley-Smith, *The Crusades: A Short History* (New Haven: Yale University Press, 1987); and Riley-Smith, *The First Crusade*.

64. See Le Goff, *Intellectuals in the Middle Ages*, pp. 73–74.
65. Chaytor, *From Script to Print*, p. 22.
66. Guenee, *States and Rulers*, p. 53.
67. Febvre and Martin, *The Coming of the Book*, p. 319.
68. Chaytor, *From Script to Print*, p. 34.
69. Ernst Gellner, *Nations and Nationalism* (Oxford: Basil Blackwell, 1983).
70. Ibid., p. 34.
71. Ibid., pp. 34–35. I put [sic] here to indicate that what Gellner calls "script" is more properly termed "print"—a label that Gellner does not use explicitly, though as I point out above, is implicit in his notion of a "standardized medium."
72. Gellner's argument chimes with, among others, that of Charles Tilly, who suggests that state-makers had an "incentive" to "homogenize." First, because a more homogenous population was likely to be more loyal; and second, because "centralized policies of extraction and control were more likely to yield a high return to the government . . . where the population's routine life was organized in relatively uniform ways." See Charles Tilly, "Reflections on the History of European State-Making," p. 79; See also Anderson and Hall, "Absolutism and Other Ancestors," (p. 32) who briefly mention the role of printing in promoting "a more standardized vernacular language from the various dialects in their territory" which gradually undermined Latin.
73. Febvre and Martin, *The Coming of the Book*, p. 319.
74. For an excellent discussion, see Febvre and Martin, *The Coming of the Book*, pp. 319–332; See also Eisenstein, *The Printing Press*, pp. 117–118.
75. Chaytor, *From Script to Print*, p. 45.
76. In the long run, Latin became a "dead langauge," retained only in places, like the Catholic mass, that were bound to the old order through tradition. See Febvre and Martin, *The Coming of the Book*, p. 319. Though the fate of Latin was "sealed" at this time, in the short-run it stubbornly survived as an "international" means of communication, among many European scholars, for example. See pp. 322–323. In Benedict Anderson's words, " . . . the fall of Latin exemplified a larger process in which the sacred communities integrated by old sacred languages were gradually fragmented, pluralized, and territorialized." Anderson, *Imagined Communities*, p. 19.
77. Ibid., p. 46.
78. See also, Luke, *Pedagogy, Printing, and Protestantism*, pp. 61–62.
79. Anderson, *Imagined Communities*, p. 46.
80. Ibid., p. 26.
81. Ibid., p. 35.
82. McLuhan, *The Gutenberg Galaxy*, p. 260.

5. Transformation in the Mode of Communication: The Emergence of the Hypermedia Environment

1.   The term "cyberspace" was coined by science fiction writer William Gibson in *Neuromancer* (New York: Ace Books, 1984). "Information" and "information superhighway" are used widely in popular magazines and newspapers to refer to what I call "hypermedia."

2.   See Jean Baudrillard, *Simulations*, [Translated by Paul Foxx, Paul Patton, and Philip Beitchman] (New York: Semiotext(e), 1983).

3.   See Postman, *Amusing Ourselves to Death*, p. 64.

4.   Beniger, *The Control Revolution*, p. 7.

5.   Ibid., p. 217.

6.   Ibid., pp. 220–226.

7.   Daniel Czitrom, "Lightning Lines," in Crowely and Heyer, eds., *Communication in History*, p. 150.

8.   Postman, *Amusing Ourselves to Death*, p. 66.

9.   Carey, *Communication as Culture*, p. 215.

10. Saxby, *The Age of Information*, p. 65. Saxby provides overviews of parallel developments occurring coincident with Morse's research in Great Britain and Germany.

11. Claude S. Fischer, "The Telephone Takes Command," in Crowley and Heyer, eds., *Communications in History*, pp. 167–172.

12. Ibid., p. 172.

13. Saxby, *The Age of Information*, p. 72.

14. Postman, *Amusing Ourselves to Death*, p. 71.

15. Ibid.; See also, Alexander Marshack, "The Art and Symbols of Ice Age Man," in Crowley and Heyer, eds., *Communications in History*, pp. 10–20.

16. Ulrich Keller, "Early Photojournalism," in Crowley and Heyer, eds., *Communications in History*, pp. 193–200.

17. Douglas Gomery, "Nickelodeons to Movie Palaces," in Crowley and Heyer, eds., *Communications in History*, pp. 201–206.

18. See Susan J. Douglas, *Inventing American Broadcasting: 1912–1922* (Baltimore: Johns Hopkins University Press, 1987).

19. See Stephen Kern, *The Culture of Time and Space: 1880–1918* (Harvard: Harvard University Press, 1983); and Lowe, *History of Bougeois Perception*, especially chapter 6.

20. In particular, I am referring to the work of the early Frankfurt School of Critical Theorists, especially Herbert Marcuse, *One-Dimensional Man: Studies in the Ideology of Advanced Industrial Society* (Boston: Beacon Press, 1964). For a general overview, see David Held, *Introduction to Critical Theory: Horkheimer to Habermas* (Berkeley: University of California Press, 1980).

21. Alfonso Hernan Molina, *The Social Basis of the Microelectronics Revolution* (Edinburgh: Edinburgh University Press, 1989).

22. J-J. Salomon, "Science Policy Studies and the Development of Science Policy," in I. Spiegel-Rosing and Derek de Solla Price, eds., *Science, Technology and Society: A Cross-Disciplinary Perspective* (London: Sage Publications, 1977), p. 48; See also Molina, *The Social Basis*, p. 16..

23. Molina, *The Social Basis*, p. 37.

24. Ibid., p. 38.

25. David Noble, *Forces of Production: A Social History of Industrial Automation* (New York: Alfred Knopf, 1984), p. 47; See also Molina, *The Social Basis*, p. 39.

26. Molina, *The Social Basis*, p. 40.

27. Ibid.

28. Ibid.

29. See Walter McDougall, *The Heavens and the Earth: A Political History of the Space Age* (New York: Basic Books, 1985). The topic of space-based reconnaissance and its relationship to world·order transformation will be taken up in ensuing chapters.

30. Peter Hall and Paschal Preston, *The Carrier Wave: New Information Technology and the Geography of Innovation, 1846–2003* (London: Unwim Hyman, 1988), p. 153; See also, Molina, *The Social Basis*, pp. 49–62.

31. Hall and Preston, *The Carrier Wave*, p. 157.

32. W. Sharpe, *The Economics of Computers* (New York: Columbia University Press, 1969), p. 186; See also, Molina, *The Social Basis*, pp. 44–45.

33. Molina, *The Social Basis*, p. 47.

34. See Thomas B. Sheridan and David Zeltzer, "Virtual Reality Check," *Technology Review* (October 1993), p. 22.

35. Molina, *The Social Basis*, p. 61.

36. Ibid., pp. 54, 61.

37. Ibid., p. 61.

38. Hall and Preston, *The Carrier Wave*, p. 157.

39. See P. Freiberger and M. Swaine, *Fire in the Valley: The Making of the Personal Computer* (Berkeley: Osborne/McGraw Hill, 1984).

40. See Tom Forester, *Silicon Samurai: How Japan Conquered the World's IT Industry* (Cambridge: Blackwell Publishers, 1993), especially chapters three and four.

41. Molina, *The Social Basis*, p. 61.

42. Ibid., p. 132–144. As Molina writes on page 142, "The result is that electronics companies competing in the global and convergent electronics market are not driven by an overriding national interest. Instead, they are pursuing the over-

riding interest of capital, that is, profits and accumulation in a context of global competition."

43. See Trudy Bell, "Jobs at Risk," *IEEE Spectrum* (August 1993).

44. Stewart Brand, *The Media Lab: Inventing the Future at MIT* (New York: Penguin, 1987).

45. For the Media Lab vision, see Nicholas Negroponte, *Being Digital* (New York: Knopf, 1995); Nicholas Negroponte, "Products and Servies for Computer Networks," *Scientific American* (September 1991), pp. 106–113; and the interview with Negroponte in Herb Brody, "Machine Dreams: An Interview with Nicholas Negroponte," *Technology Review* (January 1992), pp. 33–40. For the Palo Alto Research Center, see the interview with Mark Weiser, in Richard Wolkomir, "We're going to have computers coming out of the woodwork," *Smithsonian* (September 1994), pp. 82–90.

46. Lawrence K. Grossman, "Reflections on Life Along the Electronic Superhighway," *Media Studies Journal* 8, no. 1, Winter (1994): 30.

47. Some Asian national communications programs are highlighted in Kris Szaniawski, "As Many Strategies as Countries," *Financial Times Survey* (April 9, 1996): 2. For an overview of different national information and communication programs, see the International Telecommunications Union homepage at http://www.itu.ch/.

48. See Al Gore, "Infrastructure for the Global Village," *Scientific American* (September 1991). This author was present for (but underwhelmed by) Gore's on-line appearance on the private computer network, Compuserve, in the fall of 1993.

49. See Saxby, *The Age of Information*, p. 3; W. T. Stanbury and Ilan B. Vertinsky, "Assessing the Impact of New Information Technologies on Interest Group Behaviour and Policy Making," *Bell Canada Papers III on Economic and Public Policy* (January 1995); Ithiel de Sola Pool, *Technologies Without Boundaries: On Telecommunications in a Global Age* (Cambridge: Harvard University Press, 1990), pp. 20–22.

50. Stewart Brand *The Media Lab: Inventing the Future at MIT* (New York: Penguin Books, 1987) (Cited in Saxby, *The Age of Information*, p. 3.)

51. Saxby, *The Age of Information*, p. 266.

52. This is a point made by Saxby in *The Information Age*, p. 265.

53. See Ken Polsson, "Chronology of Events in the History of Microcomputers," On-Line Document, http://www.islandnet.com/kpolsson/comphist.htm.

54. Stan Augarton, *Bit by Bit—An Illustrated History of Computers* (London: Allen and Unwin, 1986), p. 265. Quoted in Saxby, *The Age of Information*, p. 123.

55. See Robert Keyes, "The Future of the Transistor," *Scientific American* (June 1993).

56. Jack L. Jewell, James P. Harbison, and Axel Scherer, "Microlasers," *Scientific American* (November 1991).

57. Ibid.

58. Richard B. McKenzie and Dwight R. Lee, *Quicksilver Capital: How the Rapid Movement of Wealth Has Changed the World* (New York: The Free Press, 1991), p. 41; See also Gary Stix, "Toward 'Point One'," *Scientific American* (February 1995): 90–95.

59. Lawrence G. Tesler, "Networked Computing in the 1990s," *Scientific American* (September 1991): 89; Experimental computers so small that they can be swallowed have been developed by the U.S. Army. See "Wave of Future: Computers So Small You Can Swallow Them," CNN *Network (On-Line)* (August 22, 1996).

60. Elisabeth Angus and Duncan Mckie, *Canada's Information Highway: Services, Access and Affordability* (Ottawa: Industry Canada, New Media Branch and Information Technologies Industry Branch, 1994), p. 25.

61. See Emmanuel Desuvire, "Lightware Communications: The Fifth Generation," *Scientific American* (January 1992).

62. See Ibid.; and The Editors, "The Computer for the 21st Century," *Scientific American* (Special Issue on the Computer in the 21st Century, 1995), p. 7.

63. Angus and Mckie, *Canada's Information Highway*, p. 25.

64. Desurvire, "Lightwave Communications."

65. Philip Elmer-Dewitt, "Take a Trip into the Future on the Electronic Superhighway," *Time* (April 12, 1993): 50.

66. For a good overview of the capacity of fibre optic telephone lines, see "The Death of Distance," *Economist Survey* (September 30, 1995), available on-line at: http://www.economist.com/surveys/distance/index.html.

67. See Elmer-Dewitt, "Take a Trip," pp. 51–52; Angus and Mckie, *Canada's Information Highway*, p. 26; James Gleick, "The Telephone Transformed—Into Almost Everything," *New York Times Magazine* (May 16, 1993), p. 54.

68. Time-Warner has developed a system called "Road Runner" in the United States which will allow Internet access through television cable connections at speeds of up to 100 times greater than dial-in connections. See "Cable May Speed the Line," CNN *Financial Network on-line* (August 15, 1996) available on-line at: http://cnnfn.com/digitaljam/9608/15/cablemodems_pkg/index.htm.

69. Angus and Mckie, *Canada's Information Highway*, p. 30.

70. Raymond Akwule, *Global Telecommunications: The technology, administration, and policies* (Boston: Focal Press, 1992), pp. 34–35.

71. Ibid., p. 34.

72. See Gleick, "The Telephone Transformed"; "Speak to Me: A Survey of the Computer Industry," *The Economist* (September 17, 1994); and "End of the

Line: A Survey of Telecommunications," *The Economist* (October 23–29, 1993). In late 1993, it was estimated that there were over 30 million cellular telephones in use in some 70 countries around the world, with prices falling at 25% on average per year. See "End of the Line," p. 5.

73. Aharon Kellerman, *Telecommunications and Geography* (London: Belhaven Press, 1993), p. 40.

74. Ibid.

75. Pool, *Technologies Without Boundaries*, pp. 30–31.

76. See Joe Flower, "Iridium," *Wired* (November 1993): 72–77; 118; See also "End of the Line," p. 15; and Stephen K. Black, "A Sobering Look at Cyberspace." *Ridgeway Viewpoints 96–3* (June 1996) On-Line Document, http://www.pitt.edu/rcss/VIEWPOINTS/BLACK2A/black2a.html for a discussion of the way developing countries have tended to pursue satellite and wireless communications because of the poor communication information infrastructures. Bill Gates has made a proposal for a LEO satellite system called Teledesic that would ring the planet with 840 satellites. See "Technology Brief: The Final Frontier," *The Economist* (July 27, 1996), found on-line at http://www.economist.com/issue/27–07–96/st1.html.

77. "Make Way for Multimedia," *The Economist* (October 16, 1993): 15; See also "The tangled webs they weave," *The Economist* (October 16, 1993): 21–24; Elmer-Dewitt, "Take a Trip."

78. Gleick, "The Telephone Transformed," p. 28.

79. As will be explained in more detail below, although the hypermedia environment is "planetary" in scope, this does not mean that every single individual in the world has access. To the contrary, the actual numbers of those "plugged in" to the hypermedia environment represent a very small portion of elites. However, the environment itself—by its very nature—has a planetary reach.

80. See Elmer-Dewitt, "Take a Trip," pp. 50–51.

81. James Pressley, "G-7 Seen Skirting Key Issues at Superhighway Jamboree," *Wall Street Journal Europe* (February 23, 1995).

82. See Andrew Adonis, "Whose Line Is It Anyway?" *Financial Times (London)* (October 11, 1993), for a view of the European moves to deregulate telecommunications; For more general accounts, see William J. Drake, "Territoriality and Intangibility: Transborder Data Flows and National Sovereignty," in Kaarle Nordenstreng and Herbert I. Schiller, eds., *Beyond National Sovereignty: International Communication in the 1990s* (New Jersey: Ablex Publishing Corporation, 1993), pp. 259–313; Stephen D. Krasner, "Global Communications and National Power: Life on the Pareto Frontier," *World Politics*, 43 (April 1991): 336–366; Peter Cowhey, "The International Telecommunications Regime: The Political Roots of International Regimes for High Technology,"

International Organization 44 (Spring 1990): 169–199; and Mark Zacher, *Governing Global Networks: International regimes for transportation and communication* (Cambridge: Cambridge University Press, 1996).

83. On this issue in particular, see Drake, "Territoriality and Intangibility"; and Cowhey, "The International Telecommunications Regime."

84. See Marc Raboy, "Cultural Sovereignty, Public Participation, and Democratization of the Public Sphere: The Canadian Debate on the New Information Infrastructure," (Paper presented to the "National and International Initiatives for Information Infrastructure" Symposium, John F. Kennedy School of Government, Harvard University, January 25–27, 1996) for an excellent discussion in the context of Canada of the way public policy pressures are constructed around not being "left behind" the hypermedia environment.

85. See *New York Times* (March 22, 1994), p. D2; See also, Karen Lynch, "World Net Strategy Laid Out," *CommunicationsWeek International* (March 28, 1994).

86. See Nathanial Nash, "Goldman Wins Big Role in German Sale," *New York Times* (November 26, 1994), p. 139. As Nash notes, "Europe is entering a period of about five to eight years in which vast telecommunications assts, mostly state owned, will be sold to the public."

87. For an overview, see "Asia-Pacific Telecommunications," *Financial Times Survey* (April 9, 1996), which provides detailed articles on liberalization and deregulation measures undertaken in Australia, Japan, South Korea, New Zealand, and elsewhere.

88. Lynne Curry and Andrew Adonis, "China's Telecoms Regimes Under Pressure," *Financial Times (London)* (November 23, 1993); See also, "AT&T China Contract," *New York Times* (November 28, 1994); For India, which is experiencing a similar privatization, see John F. Burns, "AT&T Seeks Stake in India's Phone Market," *New York Times* (January 6, 1995); For Vietnam, see Jeremy Grant, "Red Tape Snags Progress," *Financial Times* (April 9, 1996): 5.

89. See Catherine Arnst, "The Last Frontier: Phone Frenzy in the Developing World is Charging Up the Telecom Industry," *Business Week* (September 18, 1995) for a lengthy special report on the trends towards telecommunications deregulation and liberalization in the developing world.

90. See "Make way for Multimedia"; "The Death of Distance," and "The tangled webs they weave"; John Teresko and William H. Miller, "Tripping Down the information Superhighway," *Industry Week* (August 2, 1993): 32–39.

91. See Andrew Adonis, John Ridding and Arian Genillard, "European Telecoms Lay Down Lines of Defence," *Financial Times (London)* (November 15, 1993); Caroline Monnot, "France Telecom et DBT s'engagement pour le long terme," *Le Monde* (December 7, 1993); Ernest Beck, "US West, France Telecom to Bid for Hungarian Stake," *Wall Street Journal (Europe)* (October 29/30, 1993); Gary Stix, "Domesticating Cyberspace," *Scientific American* (August 1993); and

Anthony DePalma, "AT&T Gets Mexico Partner For Long-Distance Service," *New York Times* (November 10, 1994).

92. Geraldine Fabrikant, "Deal Makers' Phones Could Be Busy," *New York Times* (January 3, 1995).

93. John Markoff, "Microsoft Organizes Its Interactive TV Team," *New York Times* (November 2, 1994).

94. "End of the Line," p. 7.

95. Alan Cane, "Winners in the East Will Inherit the Earth," *Financial Times Survey* (April 9, 1996): 1.

96. Tony Walker, "Subscribers could double by 2000," *Financial Times Survey* (April 9, 1996): 2.

97. Popular media coverage often seems to suggest that the so-called "information superhighway" is something yet to be built. However, this view is mistaken. The infrastructure of the new media environment already exists in the form of the "web of webs" to be described below. Only government regulations and technical barriers, as outlined above, stand in the way of complete integration, and these are fast becoming obsolete. A similar view is expressed by Angus, *Canada's Information Superhighway*, pp. 5, 13.

98. Thomas A. Stewart, "Boom Time on the New Frontier," *Fortune* (Autumn 1993), p. 158.

99. This accords with view of Nicholas Negroponte in "Products and Services for Computer Networks," *Scientific American* (September 1991), pp. 106–113.

100. See Angus, *Canada's Information Superhighway*, pp. 36–37; See also, Negroponte "Products and Services," p. 108 who suggests that a good rule of thumb to define how information is being distributed (or should be distributed) is that things that move will have information sent to them through the broadcast spectrum while things that are fixed, like offices and homes, will be sent through wires.

101. Grossman, "Reflections on Life Along the Electronic Superhighway," p. 32.

102. Kurt Kleiner, "What a Tangled Web They Wove," *New Scientist* (July 30, 1994), p. 36; See also Howard Rheingold, *The Virtual Community: Homesteading on the Electronic Frontier* (New York: Addison-Wesley, 1993), p. 7. See also "The Accidental Superhighway," *Economist Survey* (July 1, 1995) for a good historical overview of the early Internet. Available on-line at http://www.economist.com/surveys/internet/index.html.

103. One of the more useful historical overviews of the Internet's development is provided by Robert H. Zakon's "Hobbes' Internet Timeline v2.2," available at the Internet Society's World-Wide Web site, http://www.isoc.org/.

104. Editors, "The Computer for the 21st Century," p. 6.

105. The Internet Society is the international organization for coordination and cooperation for the Internet. The following statistics were acquired directly

from the Internet Society through the Internet. Their World-Wide Web address is http://www.isoc.org.

106. The January and July 1996 figures were taken from Matrix Information and Directory Services, which is found at: http://www1.mids.org/growth/internet/html/hosts.html, and Network Wizards internet domain survey, found at http://www.nw.com/zone/host-count-history. Along with the Internet Society, the latter two are cross-referenced often on the World-Wide Web, and appear to use reliable survey methods.

107. See the following site for a list of Internet service providers by country, from Andorra to Zambia: http://thelist.iworld.com/country/country.html

108. Estimating with precision the "size" of the Internet is a notoriously difficult exercise. Typically, estimates vary widely depending on the definitions employed. Probably the most reliable and rigorous surveys (and the most widely cited) are those organized by John S. Quarterman in association with Texas Internet Consulting (TIC) and Matrix Information and Directory Services (MIDS) and distributed on-line through the Matrix News (See http://www.mids.org/). The latest survey, conducted in October 1994, made an estimate of 27.5 million who have at least minimal access (i.e, electronic mail), 13.5 million that can use interactive services, such as the World Wide Web, and 7.8 million that can provide interactive services, such as Telnet (remote login), FTP (file transfer) or WWW (hypertext). The same survey estimates that the Internet is approximately doubling each year. Quarterman has argued that a rough estimate of the *total* number of users can be gauged by multiplying the number of hosts by 7.5. According to the most recent survey of hosts found by this author, in July 1996 there were an estimated 12,881,000 hosts, which would equate with approximately 96,607,500 individual users. An important caveat is that not all of these roughly 13 million hosts are reachable by all of these users. Thus Quarterman's more precise definitions of depth of use would come into play. These figures notwithstanding, the Internet as a whole has been growing exponentially around the world and is clearly emerging as a kind of infrastructure for the hypermedia environment. An *Economist* survey of the Internet (July 1, 1995) cited Quarterman's more conservative middle estimate of 13.5 million users in October 1994.

109. For "Prodigy," see Peter H. Lewis, "An Atlas of Information Services," *New York Times* (November 1, 1994); for "Compuserve," see Peter H. Lewis, "The Compuserve Edge: Delicate Data Balance," *New York Times* (November 29, 1994); for "America On-Line," see Peter H. Lewis, "A Cyberspace Atlas: America Online," *New York Times* (November 15, 1994); for "Microsoft" see Peter H. Lewis, "Microsoft's Next Move is On Line," *New York Times* (January 13,

1995). The services offered by these large global and regional commercial providers is becoming increasingly indistinguishable from smaller local service providers, particularly because of the development of the World-Wide Web, which increases the ease of use making the packaged interface of the large providers somewhat redundant.

110. One of the listserves of which I am a member, the International Political Economy-Net, or IPENET, has grown from 64 persons in 1993, to 300 in 1994 to close to 1000 today from over 31 countries. On a *single* peak day in September 1994, 32,000 messages were distributed. These figures are taken from the IPENET E-news #8, distributed on-line on November 13, 1994 from the IPENET manager, Lev Gonick.

111. Negroponte, *Being Digital*, p. 176.

112. See Philip Elmer-Dewitt, "Battle for the Soul of the Internet," *Time* (July 25, 1994), p. 40–46; Steiner, "What a Tangled Web They Wove"; and "The Accidental Superhighway," *Economist Survey*.

113. See Matthew Gray's "Growth of the World-Wide Web," at http://www.mit.edu:8001/people/mkgray/net/web-growth-summary.html.

114. Of the approximately 1 billion television sets in use worldwide in 1992, 35% were in Europe, 32% were in Asia, 20% were in North America and the Caribbean, with Africa, the Middle East, and Latin America accounting for the other 13%. See "Feeling for the Future: A Survey of Television," *The Economist* (February 12–18, 1994).

115. Karen Lynch, "Telecoms funding body set," *CommunicationsWeek International* (February 6, 1995). See also Rex Winsbury, "Who Will Pay for the Global Village? Funding the Buenos Aires Declaration," *Intermedia* (June/July 1994).

116. Winsbury, "Who Will Pay for the Global Village?" See the *World Telecommunications Development Report 1995* (International Telecommunications Union) available on-line at: http://www4.itu.ch/WTDR95/.

117. See Black, "A Sobering Look at Cyberspace." See also Peter Knight, et al., "Increasing Internet Connectivity in Sub-Saharan Africa: Issues, Options, and World Bank Role," (March 29, 1995 On-Line World Bank Draft Report), available on-line at: http://www.worldbank.org/html/emc/documents/africa0395.html. See also Steve Homer, "Still on Hold in the Developing World," *The Independent* (9, 10, 1995) which notes that there are more telephones in Manhattan than in all of sub-Saharan Africa.

118. For a good overview of the properties of the hypermedia environment, see William J. Drake, "Introduction: The Turning Point," in William J. Drake, ed., *The New Information Infrastructure: Strategies for U.S. Policy* (New York: The Twentieth Century Fund Press, 1995), pp. 6–8.

6. Hypermedia and the Modern to Postmodern World Order
Transformation: Distributional Changes

1.   See Ruggie, "Territoriality"; and Elkins, *Beyond Sovereignty*.
2.   See especially Hans Morgenthau, *Politics Among Nations: The Struggle for Power and Peace*, 5th ed. (New York: Knopf, 1973), Part Three: National Power; and Wendt, "Anarchy Is What States Make of It."
3.   Thomson, "State Sovereignty in International Relations," p. 221.
4.   Waltz, *Theory of International Politics*.
5.   See Wallerstein, *The Modern World System*, vols. 1–3; Baran, *The Political Economy of Growth*; and Gunder Frank, *Capitalism and Underdevelopment*.
6.   Part of this is related to the "nature" of capital throughout the modern world order period, which has primarily been fixed and/or concentrated within specific geographic regions making it more "captive" to state regulations and taxes. See chapter 2, "From Captive Capital to Quicksilver Capital," in Richard B. McKenzie and Dwight R. Lee, *Quicksilver Capital: How the Rapid Movement of Wealth Has Changed the World* (New York: The Free Press, 1991), pp. 17–34.
7.   See Michael C. Webb and Stephen D. Krasner, "Hegemonic Stability Theory: An Empirical Assessment," *Review of International Studies* 15 (1989): 183–198.
8.   Joel Kurtzman, *The Death of Money: How the Electronic Economy has Destabilized the World's Markets and Created Financial Chaos* (New York: Simon and Schuster, 1993), p. 207.
9.   For a historical overview of these long-term processes, see Zacher, "The Decaying Pillars of the Westphalian Temple."
10. See Ibid., p. 81.
11. Robert Gilpin, *The Political Economy of International Relations* (Princeton: Princeton University Press, 1987), p. 11.
12. For criticism of "rational-actor" models along these lines, see Ulrich Witt, *Explaining Process and Change: Approaches to Evolutionary Economics* (Ann Arbor: University of Michigan Press, 1992).
13. Peter Dicken, "The Roepke Lecture in Economic Geography—Global-Local Tensions: Firms and States in the Global Space-Economy," *Economic Geography* (1994), p. 111; For a more detailed treatment, see Richard R. Nelson and Sidney G. Winter, *An Evolutionary Theory of Economic Change* (Cambridge: Belknap Press, 1982).
14. Kevin Morgan, "Digital Highways: the New Telecommunications Era," *Geoforum* 23, no. 3 (1992): 319.
15. McKenzie and Lee, *Quicksilver Capital*, p. 11.
16. Mark Hepworth, *Geography of the Information Economy* (London: Belhaven Press, 1989), p. 94.

17. See Morgan, "Digital Highways," p. 326; See also, Paul Taylor, "First the In-
     ternet: Now the Intranet Phenomenon," *Financial Times* (April 3, 1996) for
     many more examples of Intranets in business.
18. See "Rolls Royce Introduces Electronic Commercie Solutions," *Electronic In-
     formation Commerce Resource News* (May 1996), on-line at: http://www.year-
     x.co.uk/ec/zzapr96.htm#rolls.
19. Zacher, *Governing Global Networks*; Krasner, "Global Communications and
     National Power"; and Cowhey, "The International Telecommunications Re-
     gime."
20. Kenichi Ohmae, *The Borderless World: Power and Strategy in the Interlinked
     Economy* (New York: HarperCollins, 1990), p. 8.
21. Hepworth, *Geography of the Information Economy*, p. 94; See also, Peter
     Dicken, *Global Shift: The Internationalization of Economic Activity*, 2nd ed.
     (New York: Paul Chapman, 1992), figure 7.1 for a breakdown of the "produc-
     tion chain."
22. Harvey S. James, Jr. and Murray Weidenbaum, *When Businesses Cross Inter-
     national Boundaries: Strategic Alliances and Their Alternatives* (London: Prae-
     ger, 1993), p. 49; See also, Amy Borrus, "The Stateless Corporations," *Business
     Week* (May 14, 1990): 101.
23. McKenzie and Lee, *Quicksilver Capital*, pp. 51–52; Ruggie, "Territoriality," p.
     141; See also Richard J. Barnet and John Cavanaugh, "Creating a level playing
     field," *Technology Review* (May-June 1994), pp. 46–54, who give a number of
     examples of transnational "back-room" processing centers.
24. For an excellent, comprehensive overview, see James and Weidenbaum, *When
     Businesses Cross International Borders*.
25. Ibid., p. 63.
26. Ibid.
27. See Paul Taylor, "As Costs Fall, Corporate Interest Rises Rapidly, " *Financial
     Times* (April 3, 1996) for an overview of the falling costs and rising popularity
     of videoconferencing among large global multinational corporations.
28. See Lee Sproull and Sara Kiesler, "Computers, Networks, and Work," *Scientific
     American* (September 1991): 116–123.
29. For a discussion of "just-in-time" production, see Harvey, *The Condition of
     Postmodernity*, pp. 147–173; and Richard Meegan, "A Crisis of Mass Produc-
     tion," in John Allen and Doreen Massey, eds., *The Economy in Question* (Lon-
     don: Sage Publications, 1988), pp. 136–183.
30. For discussion, see Thomas A. Stewart, "Boom Time on the New Frontier,"
     Fortune (Autumn 1993); For "Domilink," see Peter H. Lewis, "Trying to Find
     Gold with the Internet," *New York Times* (January 3, 1995); See also Robin
     Mansell, "European Telecommunication, Multinational Enterprises, and the
     Implication of 'Globalization,' " *International Journal of Political Economy*

(Winter 1993–1994): 83–104. As Mansell notes on page 89, "In many cases, the reorganization of the production process involves the exchange of a vast array of information with respect to design, product and process innovations, competitor strategies, component supplier competencies, and consumer profiles. This may be supported by communications services ranging from the simple voice telephone to the high-speed exchange of computer integrated manufacturing design concepts."

31. See Thomas W. Malone and John F. Rockart, "Computers, Networks and the Corporation," *Scientific American* (September 1991): 128–136 for a discussion of supplier-client coordination, especially for the role of scanned bar codes.

32. James and Weidenbaum, *When Businesses Cross Borders*, p. 67.

33. Ibid.

34. Ibid., p. 77.

35. Ibid., p. 85.

36. Richard A. Bitzinger, "The Globalization of the Arms Industry: The Next Proliferation Challenge," *International Security* 19, no. 4, Fall (1994): 182.

37. Ibid., p. 188; See also Molina, *The Social Basis of the Microelectronics Revolution*, pp. 107–132.

38. Christopher Bartlett and Sumantra Ghoshal, *Managing Across Borders: The Transnational Solution* (Boston: Harvard Business School Press, 1989), p. 9.

39. For a representative position, see Benjamin Barber, "Jihad vs. McWorld," *The Atlantic* 269, no. 3 (March 1992).

40. For examples, see Bartlett and Ghoshal, *Managing Across Borders*; C. K. Prahalad, and Y. Doz, *The Multinational Mission: Balancing Local Demands and Global Vision* (New York: The Free Press, 1987); and Samuel Humes, *Managing the Multinational: Confronting the Global-Local Dilemma* (New York: Prentice-Hall, 1993).

41. See Ohmae, *Borderless World*, p. 9.

42. On consumer surveillance in post-industrial societies, see Oscar Gandy, *The Panoptic Sort: A Political Economy of Personal Information* (Boulder: Westview Press, 1993), especially chapter 4.

43. James and Weidenbaum, *When Businesses Cross Borders*, pp. 41–42.

44. See Peter H. Lewis, "Trying to Find Gold with the Internet," *New York Times* (January 3, 1995); and Peter H. Lewis, "Companies Rush to Set up Shop in Cyberspace," *New York Times* (November 2, 1994).

45. See Adam Bryant, "Am I Bid Six? Click to Bid Six," *New York Times* (May 13, 1996) for the reference to the "cyberspace bazaar."

46. See Peter H. Lewis, "Attention Internet Shoppers: E-Cash is Here," *New York Times* (October 19, 1994); "Bank OKs Internet Payment," *Associated Press-Clarinet* (May 8, 1995).

47. Personal Interview, Herbert I. Phillips, Jr., Vice-President, Strategic Solutions, Royal Bank of Canada, January 12, 1995; See also, John Markoff, "A Credit Card for On-Line Sprees," *New York Times* (October 15, 1994); Lawrence M. Fisher, "Microsoft and Visa in Software Deal," *New York Times* (November 9, 1994); Saul Hansell, "Mastercard to Develop On-Line Standard," *New York Times* (January 10, 1995); Kelley Holland and Amy Cortese, "The Future of Money," *Business Week* (June 12, 1995); and Larry Donovan, "Software to Make Signatures Secure Could Prove Boom," *The Globe and Mail* (November 14, 1995).

48. The most exhaustive survey is found in James and Weidenbaum, *When Businesses Cross International Borders.*

49. For criticism along these lines, see Paul Hirst and Grahame Thompson, "The Problem of 'Globalization': International Economic Relations, National Economic Management, and the Formation of Trading Blocs," *Economy and Society* 21, no. 4 (November 1992).

50. James and Weidenbaum, *When Businesses Cross International Borders*, p. 3; See also United Nations, *World Investment Report, 1994*, p. 143.

51. Hepworth, *Geography of the Information Economy*, p. 95.

52. Ruggie, "Territoriality," p. 142; See also, John Gerard Ruggie, "Unraveling Trade: Institutional Change and the World Economy," (Paper Prepared for the Roundtable on Fair Trade, Harmonization, Level Playing Fields and the World Trading System: Economic, Political, and International Legal Questions for the 1990s, Columbia University, January 10, 1992).

53. See William J. Drake and Kalypso Nicolaidis, "Ideas, Interests, and Institutionalization: 'Trade in Services' and the Uruguay Round," *International Organization* 46 (Winter 1992): 37.

54. This is a point Dicken makes in "The Roepke Lecture," p. 109.

55. James and Weidenbaum, *When Businesses Cross International Borders*, p. 52; These flows tailed off slightly in the first two years of the 1990s due to worldwide recession, but have recently begun to pick up pace again. UN, *World Investment Report, 1994*, p. 17.

56. Globalization and Liberalization: Development in the Face of Two Powerful Currents (UNCTAD Report TD/366/Rev.1, December 1995). By extension, then, only one-third of the world trade in goods in services is still accounted for by traditional "arms-length" transactions.

57. UNCTAD Press Release, 13 September 1996.

58. Ibid.

59. Dicken, "The Roepke Lectures," pp. 109–110.

60. On "geographic inequalities" in general, see Andrew Gillespie and Kevin Robbins, "Geographical Inequalities: The Spatial Bias of the New Com-

munications Technologies," *Journal of Communications* 39, no. 3 (Summer 1989): 7–18.

61. Dicken, "The Roepke Lectures," p. 110; See also, Hirst and Thompson, "The Problem of 'Globalization'," pp. 368–369.

62. See Barnet and Cavanaugh, "Creating a Level Playing Field."

63. John M. Stopford and Susan Strange (with John S. Henley), *Rival States, Rival Firms: Competition for World Market Shares* (Cambridge: Cambridge University Press, 1991), p. 40.

64. Ibid., pp. 40–41.

65. Ibid., p. 41.

66. Mark Hepworth, "Information Technology and the Global Restructuring of Capital Markets," in Stanley D. Brunn and Thomas R. Leinbach, eds., *Collapsing Space and Time: Geographic Aspects of Communications and Information* (New York: HarperCollins, 1991), p. 132.

67. See Charles Kindleberger, *International Capital Movements* (Cambridge: Cambridge University Press, 1987); Fred Hirsch, *Money International* (Middlesex: Penguin Books, 1967).

68. This evolutionary trend is adapted from Ron Martin, "Stateless Monies, Global Financial Integration and National Economic Autonomy: the End of Geography?" in Stuart Corbridge, Nigel Thrift, and Ron Martin, eds., *Money, Power and Space* (Oxford: Blackwell, 1994), p. 255.

69. Ibid., p. 255.

70. Gilpin, *The Political Economy of International Relations*, pp. 308–309.

71. Stephen Gill, "Economic Globalization and the Internationalization of Authority: Limits and Contradictions," *Geoforum* 23, no. 3 (1992): 273.

72. Ibid.; See also, Eric Helleiner, "From Bretton Woods to Global Finance: A World Turned Upside Down," in Richard Stubbs and Geoffrey R. D. Underhill, eds., *Political Economy and the Changing Global Order* (Toronto: McClelland and Stewart, 1994), pp. 163–165; and Eric Helleiner, *States and the Reemergence of Global Finance: From Bretton Woods to the 1990s* (New York: Cornell University Press, 1994).

73. Susan Strange, "Finance, Information, and Power," *Review of International Studies* 16 (1990): 260.

74. David M. Andrews, "Capital Mobility and State Autonomy: Towards a Structural Theory of International Monetary Relations," *International Studies Quarterly* 38 (1994): 198.

75. Bryant writes that "The technological nonpolicy factors were so powerful, I believe, that they would have caused a progressive internationalization of financial activity even without changes in government separation fences and the inducement of differing regulatory, tax, and supervisory systems. But I also conjecture that government-policy changes were important enough to have

promoted a significant integration of national financial systems even if there had been no shrinkage in the economic distances between resevoirs due to nonpolicy innovations such as the fall in relative costs of the international communication of information." R. Bryant, *International Financial Integration* (Washington, DC: The Brookings Institution, 1987), p. 69. Bryant is also cited in Andrews, "Capital Mobility and State Autonomy," pp. 198–199.

76. John Langdale, "Electronic Funds Transfer and the Internationalisation of the Banking and Finance Industry," *Geoforum* 16, no. 1 (1985): 2.

77. Geoffrey Ingham, "States and Markets in the Production of World Money: Sterling and the Dollar," in Corbridge et al., *Money, Power, and Space*, p. 45.

78. Susan Strange, "From Bretton Woods to the Casino Economy," in Corbridge et el., *Money, Power, and Space*, p. 58; See also Susan Strange, *Casino Capitalism* (Oxford: Blackwell, 1986).

79. Gill, "Economic Globalization," p. 274.

80. See Richard O'Brien, *Global Financial Integration: The End of Geography* (London: Pinter, 1992), p. 18; See also, Kurtzman, *The Death of Money*, p. 51.

81. Kurtzman, *The Death of Money*, p. 51.

82. Ibid.

83. Strange, *Casino Capitalism*.

84. For a useful, short summary, see Strange, "From Bretton Woods to the Casino Economy," pp. 58–59.

85. For a "Gramscian" view of the hegemony of the neoliberal movement, see especially Stephen Gill and David Law, Global Hegemony and the Structural Power of Capital," *International Studies Quarterly* 33 (1989): 475–499; and Stephen Gill, *American Hegemony and the Trilateral Commission* (Cambridge: Cambridge University Press, 1990).

86. P. W. Daniels, "Internationalization, telecommunications, and metropolitan development: the role of producer services," in Stanley D. Brunn and Thomas R. Leinbach, eds., *Collapsing Space and Time: Geographic Aspects of communications and information* (New York: HarperCollins, 1991), p. 160; See also Kurtzman, *The Death of Money*, pp. 44–46 for an overview of the history of Reuters in the financial sector.

87. Harry Scarbrough, "Introduction," in Harry Scarbrough, ed., *The IT Challenge: IT and Strategy in Financial Services* (New York: Prentice Hall, 1992), pp. 1–2.

88. See Kurtzman, *The Death of Money*, pp. 170–171; Personal interview, Herbert I. Phillipps, Vice-President, Strategic Solutions, Royal Bank of Canada.

89. See Black, "A Sobering Look at Cyberspace." Black cites the following website as the source for this information: http://www.bankamerica.com/batoday/bac-facts.html.

90.   As cited in O'Brien, *Global Financial Integration*, p. 9.
91.   Personal Interview, Herbert I. Phillips, Vice-President, Strategic Solutions, Royal Bank of Canada, January 13, 1995.
92.   Hepworth, *Geography of the Information Economy*, pp. 171–172; On Globex, see "The Screen Is the future, Master," *The Economist* (October 24, 1992): 85–86; See also, Hepworth, "Information Technology and the Global Restructuring of Capital Markets," pp. 138–139; On "private" trading "clubs" and other electronic stock markets, see Kurtzman, *The Death of Money*, pp. 36–37.
93.   See Andrew Allentuck, "Financial Services That Delight, Amaze," *The Globe and Mail* (November 14, 1995).
94.   Nigel Thrift and Andrew Leyshon, "A phantom state? The de-traditionalization of money, the international financial system and international financial centres," *Political Geography* 13, no. 4, July (1994): 309; See also, Maurice Estabrooks, *Programmed Capitalism: A Computer-Mediated Global Society* (London: M. E. Sharpe, Inc., 1988); and Robert X. Cringely, "Fast Money: How Computers Are Used for Trading Securities," *Forbes* (April 11, 1994).
95.   Mark Hepworth, "Information Technology and the Global Restructuring of Capital Markets," in Brunn and Leinbach, *Collapsing Space and Time*, pp. 137–138; On "Quotreks," see Kurtzman, *The Death of Money*, p. 112.
96.   Every year for more than a decade the 300 or so major firms of Wall Street have invested between them about $3.4 billion U.S. in hypermedia—a figure that typically accounts for about 20% of their total outlays. See Kurtzman, *The Death of Money*, p. 26.
97.   Hepworth, *Geography of the Information Economy*, pp. 174–175.
98.   For an overview of SWIFT, see Langdale, "Electronic Funds Transfers"; and Black, "A Sobering Look at Cyberspace," particularly part two.
99.   Martin, "The End of Geography?," p. 261.
100. Kurtzman, *The Death of Money*, p. 109.
101. Daniels, "Internationalization," p. 163.
102. Thrift and Leyshon, "A Phantom State?," p. 311.
103. Kurtzman, *The Death of Money*, p. 17.
104. Ibid., p. 77.
105. Ruggie, "Territoriality," p. 141.
106. See "Financial Centres: A Survey," *The Economist* (June 27, 1992); See also, Nigel Thrift, "On the Social and Cultural Determinants of International Financial Centres: the case of the city of London," in Corbridge, et el., *Money, Power and Space*, pp. 327–355; Ronald L Mitchelson and James O. Wheeler, "The Flow of Information in a Global Economy: The Role of the American Urban System in 1990," *Annals of the American Geographer* 84, no. 1 (1994): 87, 91, 98; and Castells, *The Informational City*. The term "finanscape" is

from Arjun Appadurai, "Disjuncture and Difference in the Global Cultural Economy," *Theory, Culture & Society* 7 (1990): 295–310.

107. Thrift and Leyshon, "A phantom state?," p. 312.

108. Susan Roberts, "Fictitious Capital, Fictitious Spaces: the Geography of Offshore Financial Flows," in Corbridge et al., *Money, Power and Space*, p. 92.

109. Ruggie, "Territoriality," p. 141.

110. Roberts, "Fictitious Capital, Fictitious Spaces," p. 92.

111. Ibid., p. 92.

112. Martin, "The End of Geography?," p. 259.

113. Roberts, "Fictitious Capital, Fictitious Spaces," p. 94.

114. Ibid., p. 100.

115. Castells, *The Informational City*.

116. Elkins, *Beyond Sovereignty*.

117. Robert Reich, *The Work of Nations* (New York: Knopf, 1991).

118. Three outstanding discussions of the way new practices present anomalies to the modern world order paradigm are Elkins, *Beyond Sovereignty*; Ruggie, "Territoriality"; and Walker, *Inside/Outside*.

119. Andrew Leyshon, "The Transformation of Regulatory Order: Regulating the Global Economy and Environment," *Geoforum* 23, no. 3 (1992): 251; Gill and Law, "Global Hegemony and the Structural Power of Capital"; J. Goodman and L. Pauly, "The Obsolescence of Capital Controls? Economic Management in an Age of Global Markets," *World Politics* 46 (1993): 50–82; Michael Webb, "International Economic Structures, Government Interests, and International Coordination of Macroeconomic Adjustment Policies," *International Organization* 45 (1991): 309–342; Richard Cooper, *The Economics of Interdependence: Economic Policy in the Atlantic Community* (New York: McGraw Hill, 1968); and Andrews, "Capital Mobility and State Autonomy."

120. Webb, "International Economic Structures"; See also, Andrews, "Capital Mobility and State Autonomy," for a comprehensive overview.

121. Robert Cox, *Production, Power and World Order: Social Forces in the Making of History* (New York: Columbia University Press, 1987).

122. Philip Cerny, "The Deregulation and Re-regulation of Financial Markets in a More Open World," in Philip Cerny, ed., *Finance and World Politics: Markets, Regimes, and States in the Post-Hegemonic Era* (Aldershot, England: Edward Elgar, 1993).

123. "Locational Tournaments" is a term I borrow from Lynn K. Mytelka's talk at the *Information Technologies and International Relations* symposium, Canadian Department of Foreign Affairs and International Trade, January 13, 1995.

124. See Goodman and Pauly, "The Obsolescence of Capital Controls," for a fairly extensive survey.

125. For an interesting account of the role of credit rating agencies as "private makers of global public policy," see Timothy J. Sinclair, "Economic and Financial Analysis Considered as Knowledge Dynamics of Global Governance," (Paper presented at the annual meeting of the International Studies Association, Chicago, February 1995); and Timothy J. Sinclair, "Between State and Market: Hegemony and Institutions of Collective Action Under Conditions of International Capital Mobility," *Policy Sciences*, 27 (1994): 447–466. For pressures on the developing countries in this respect, see Thomas J. Biersteker, "The 'Triumph' of Neoclassical Economics in the Developing World: Policy Convergence and Bases of Governance in the International Economic Order," in Rosenau and Czempiel, eds., *Governance Without Government*, pp. 102–131.

126. Drew Fagan, "Transnationals fuelling global integration," *Globe and Mail*, (December 15, 1995).

127. See Zacher, "The Decaying Pillars of the Westphalian Temple," pp. 65–67. For "regimes," see Stephen D. Krasner, *International Regimes* (Ithaca: Cornell University Press, 1983). For "institutions," see Keohane, "International Institutions."

128. For an overview of "global governance" as used here, see James N. Rosenau, "Governance, Order, and Change in World Politics," in Rosenau and Czempiel, eds., *Governance Without Government*, pp. 1–29.

129. Gill, *American Hegemony and the Trilateral Commission*; Gill, "Economic Globalization"; and Gill and Law, "Global Hegemony and the Structural Power of Capital."

130. Emphasizing their nonexclusive economic orientation, Dicken aptly calls these regional economic zones, "meso-levels" of regulation. See Peter Dicken, "International Production in a Volatile Regulatory Environment: the Influence of National Regulatory Policies on the Spatial Strategies of Transnational Corporations," *Geoforum* 23, no. 2 (1992): 304.

131. Ronnie Lipschutz, "Reconstructing World Politics: The Emergence of Global Civil Society," *Millennium: Journal of International Studies* 21, no. 3 (1992): 398–420.

132. Ethan A. Nadelmann, "Global prohibition regimes: the evolution of norms in international society," *International Organization*, 44 (Autumn 1990): 495.

133. Ibid.

134. On the principle of sovereign non-intervention, see Jackson, *Quasi-states*.

135. An excellent historical overview is provided by Lipschutz, "Reconstructing World Politics," pp. 400–414.

136. Kathryn Sikkink, "Human Rights, Principled Issue-Networks, and Sovereignty in Latin America," *International Organization*, 47 (Summer 1993): 418.

137. Peter J. Spiro, "New Global Communities: Nongovernmental Organizations in International Decision-Making Institutions," *The Washington Quarterly* 18, no. 1 (1994): 47.

138. See Paul Wapner, "Politics Beyond the State: Environmental Activism and World Civic Politics," *World Politics* 47, no. 3 (April 1995): 311–340 for a good overview of the growing importance of these movements and of the way they have exploited the hypermedia environment to further their interests.

139. Spiro, "New Global Communities," p. 49. See also Leon Gordenker and Thomas G. Weiss, "Pluralizing Global Governance: Analytical Approaches and Dimensions," *Third World Quarterly* (Vol. 16, No. 3, 1995): 365. Gordenker and Weiss note that about 25% of U.S. assistance is channelled through NGOs, and that Vice President Gore committed to increase this figure to 50% by the end of the century.

140. The term "heteronomous" is taken from Lipschutz, which, as he says, "implies that these networks are differentiated from each other in terms of specialisations: there is not a single network, but many, each fulfilling a different function." Lipschutz, "Reconstructing World Politics," p. 391.

141. Spiro, "New Global Communities," p. 45.

142. See Leslie Paul Thiele, "Making Democracy Safe for the World: Social Movements and Global Politics," *Alternatives: Social Transformation and Humane Governance* 18, no. 3 (Summer 1993): 281.

143. Ibid., p. 280.

144. Lipschutz, "Reconstructing World Politics," p. 390.

145. Although Lipschutz is correct in pointing out that information technologies did not "cause" or generate these movements, in going out of his way to point this out he grossly underestimates the extent to which hypermedia is deeply bound up with the rise of global civil society, as any brief glance at the Internet alone will reveal. See Lipschutz, "Reconstructing World Politics," pp. 411–412.

146. Spiro, "New Global Communities," p. 47.

147. Don Rittner, *Ecolinking: Everyone's Guide to Online Environmental Information* (Berkeley: Peachpit Press, 1992), p. 178. I discovered this quotation in W. T. Stanbury and Ilan B. Vertinsky, "Assessing the Impact of New Information Technologies on Interest Group Behaviour and Policy Making," (Revised draft: January 1995. To be published in *Bell Canada Papers III on Economic and Public Policy*), pp. 33–34.

148. Susanne Sallin, *The Association for Progressive Communications: A Cooperative Effort to Meet the Information Needs of Non-Governmental Organizations* (A Case Study Prepared for the Harvard-CIESIN Project on Global Environmental Change Information Policy, February 14, 1994). The APC can be reached via the Internet at http://www.apc.org/

149. Ibid., p. 1.

150. For a detailed overview of each of these member networks, see Ibid.

151. The IGC can be reached via the Internet at http://www.igc.apc.org/

152. Peter White, "The World is Wired," *San Francisco Guardian* (December 1992); and Sallin, *The Association for Progressive Communications.*

153. See http://www.apc.org/un.html for information about the relationship between the APC and the UN. The APC is a NGO with Consultative Status (Category 1) with the Economic and Social Council of the United Nations.

154. WebActive can be found at http://www.webactive.com/.

155. See Stanbury and Vertinsky, "Assessing the Impact of New Information Technologies," p. 34; See also, William T. Stanbury, "New Information Technologies and Transnational Interest Groups," (Paper prepared for delivery at the "Information Technologies and International Relations," symposium, Department of Foreign Affairs and International Trade, January 13, 1995).

156. As cited in Stanbury and Vertinsky, "Assessing the Impact of New Information Technologies," p. 34; See also Wapner, "Politics Beyond the State."

157. A good balanced overview of the role of information technologies in "democratic uprisings" is Adam Jones, "Wired World: Communications Technology, Governance and the Democratic Uprising," in Edward A. Comor, *The Global Political Economy of Communication: Hegemony, Telecommunication and the Information Economy* (New York: St. Martin's Press, 1994), pp. 145–164.

158. Personal Interview with Staff Sergeant Peter German, Vancouver Commercial Crime Division, Royal Canadian Mounted Police, January 13, 1995; For a very detailed overview, see Bruce Zagaris and Scott B. MacDonald, "Money Laundering, Financial Fraud, and Technology: The Perils of an Instantaneous Economy," *George Washington Journal of International Law and Economics* 26 (1992): 61–107.

159. Jared Sandberg, "Militia Groups Meet, Recruit in Cyberspace," *Wall Street Journal* (April 26, 1995).

160. Thiele, "Making Democracy Safe for the World," p. 278.

161. This point is made by Lipschutz in "Reconstructing World Politics," p. 392.

162. Sikkink, "Human Rights, Principled Issue-Networks," p. 411.

163. See Richard Falk, "Challenges of a Changing Global Order," *Peace Research: The Canadian Journal of Peace Studies* 24, no. 4, (November 1992).

164. Although formal alliances and coalitions of NGOs are becoming more common. For discussion, see Gordenker and Weiss, "Pluralizing Global Governance," p. 367.

165. Mann, *Sources of Social Power*, pp. 15–19.

166. Sikkink, "Human Rights, Principled Issue-Networks"; and Wapner, "Politics Beyond the State."

167. This is not to say that such groups might not contribute to the "de-legitimi-zation" of states. Quite the contrary. There are many cases where NGOs fill public service functions traditionally associated with states - functions such as public health and education, for example. In doing so, they might help empower local communities at the expense of national identities and state-building projects. As Wapner puts it, while such groups "may see themselves working outside the domain of the state and focusing on civil society per se, their actions in fact have a broader impact and interfere with state policies." Wapner, "Politics Beyond the State," p. 335. See also Gordenker and Weiss, "Pluralizing Global Governance," p. 370 for examples of NGOs filling tra-ditional state functions, such as the education system in the north of Sri Lanka and the operations of 35,000 schools in Bangladesh.

168. "Global, nonterritorial region" is taken from John Gerard Ruggie, "Inter-national Structure and International Transformation: Space, Time and Method," in Czempiel and Rosenau, eds., *Global Changes and Theoretical Challenges*, p. 31.

169. I deliberately set off the word "domestic" in quotation marks to underscore the extent to which the term may be somewhat anachronistic given that it presupposes a basic division between "domestic" and "international" that is essential to the modern world order paradigm—the very paradigm that I am problematizing. However, as will be shown below, one of the very reasons for the "fitness" of the security arrangement I propose is precisely its accommo-dative capacity to global forces and multiple layers of political authority.

170. See Deudney, *Pax Atomica*; and Deudney, "Binding Powers, Bound States." Real-state is pronounced *re - ahl*.

171. Deudney, " "Binding Powers, Bound States," p. 10.

172. Ibid., p. 11.

173. George Orwell, *1984* (New York: Signet Books, 1949).

174. See Foucault, *Discipline and Punish*.

175. Good overviews can be found in David Lyon, "An Electronic Panopticon? A Sociological Critique of Surveillance Theory," *The Sociological Review* 41 (1993): 655–660; and Gandy, *The Panoptic Sort*; and David Lyon, *The Elec-tronic Eye: The Rise of Surveillance Society* (Minneapolis: University of Min-nesota Press, 1994), especially chapter four.

176. The following section draws on Lyon's informative overview, in "An Elec-tronic Panopticon?" pp. 661–662. See also, Stephen Gill, "The Global Pan-opticon? The Neoliberal State, Economic Life, and Democratic Surveil-lance," *Alternatives* 2 (1995), pp. 1–49 for a similar discussion.

177. Gary Marx, *Undercover Police Surveillance in America* (Berkeley: University of California Press, 1988).

178. Stanley Cohen, *Visions of Social Control* (New York: Basil Blackwell, 1985).

179. Diana Gordon, "The Electronic Panopticon: A Case-Study of the Develop-
      ment of the National Crime Records System," *Politics and Society* 15 (1986):
      387.

180. See David H. Flaherty, *Protecting Privacy in Surveillance Societies: The Fed-
      eral Republic of Germany, Sweden, France, Canada, and the United States*
      (Chapel Hill: University of North Carolina Press, 1989); Gandy, *The Panoptic
      Sort*; Oscar H. Gandy, "The Surveillance Society: Information Technology
      and Bureaucratic Social Control," *Journal of Communication* 39, no. 3 (1989):
      61–76.

181. For a detailed over of FinCEN, see Steven A. Bercu, "Toward Universal Sur-
      veillance in an Information Economy: Can We Handle Treasury's New Police
      Technology?" *Jurimetrics Journal*, 34 (Summer 1994): 383–449.

182. Personal Interview, Staff Sergeant Peter German, Royal Canadian Mounted
      Police, Vancouver Commercial Crime Division, January 13, 1995.

183. Lyon, *The Electronic Eye*, pp. 218–219.

184. Foucault, *Discipline and Punish*, p. 217.

185. Neuman, *The Future of the Mass Audience*, p. 13.

186. See "End of the Line," p. 6.

187. "Iran Prohibits Satellite Dishes To Bar U.S. TV," *New York Times* (December
      27, 1994).

188. "Feeling for the Future," p. 17.

189. Paul S. N. Lee and Georgette Wang, "Satellite TV in Asia: Forming a new
      ecology," *Telecommunications Policy* 19, no. 2 (1995): 140–141; See also Wil-
      liam Shawcross, "Reaching for the Sky," *New Statesman and Society* (March
      24, 1995): 12–14.

190. Lee and Wang, "Satellite TV in Asia," pp. 141–143.

191. Ibid.

192. See Drake, "Territoriality and Intangibility," pp. 270–272.

193. See Peter H. Lewis, "Computer Jokes and Threats Ignite Debate on Anonym-
      ity," *New York Times* (December 31, 1994). Computer systems known as
      "anonymous" remailers receive messages from around the world, strip them
      of their identity, and then send them off to their destination. They are an
      estimated 20 to 25 publicly accessible anonymous remailers around the world.
      As Lewis notes, "The ability to send anonymous and untraceable messages
      can also shield political and religious dissidents, whistle-blowers and human
      rights advocates from possible reprisals." In the United States, attempts have
      been made to counter the spread of encryption technologies through regu-
      lation, in particular through a device known as the "clipper chip," which
      would allow central authorities surveillance access to particular electronic
      technologies that had the clipper chip installed. For an overview, see Steven

Levy, "The Battle of the Clipper Chip," *New York Times Magazine* (June 12, 1994): 44–51.

194. Subscribers to Teleview, Singapore's computer network, must agree not to use it "for sending to any person, any message which is offensive on moral, religious, communal or political grounds." "Feeling for the Future," p. 16; Victor Keegan notes the following with respect to Singapore: "One irony is that the information revolution that Singapore is pioneering may become the Trojan Horse that upsets the political and cultural repression of the regime. How can a society that still bans satellite dishes and many foreign journals continue to do so when the global information highway will give its citizens instantaneous access to multimedia newspapers all over the world, not to speak of pornography?" Victor Keegan, "Who's in Charge Here," *The Guardian* (December 12, 1994).

195. See Gaddis, "Tectonics, History and the End of the Cold War"; Stephen Van Evera, "Primed for Peace: Europe After the Cold War," *International Security* 15, no. 3, 1990/1991): 14–15. For analyses that astutely predicted such a downfall from a communications perspective, see Wilson Dizard, "Mikhail Gorbachev's Computer Challenge," *Washington Quarterly* 9, no. 2, Spring 1986); and Walter R. Roberts and Harold E. Engle, "The Global Information Revolution and the Communist World," *The Washington Quarterly* 9, no. 2, Spring 1986).

196. Scott Shane, *Dismantling Utopia: How information ended the Soviet Union* (Chicago: Ivan R. Dee, 1994), p. 262.

197. Lyon, *The Electronic Eye*, p. 87.

198. White, "The World is Wired."

199. Shane, *Dismantling Utopia*, p. 266.

200. Berko, "Surveying the Surveilled," p. 72.

201. Ibid., p. 73.

202. CNN has set up a hot line to solicit amateur videos, paying $150, a mug and t-shirt for each spot. See Ibid., p. 71. While watching the news coverage of a man firing bullets into the White House earlier this year, I noticed that *three* separate amateur videos captured the melee.

203. Spiro, "New Global Communities," p. 45.

204. Amnesty International, for example, regularly distributes videos of human rights abuse over the World-Wide Web. See, for example, the capture of human rights abuses in the former Yugoslavia at http://www.oneworld.org/amnesty/press_awards/news.html.

205. See Peter H. Lewis, "Exploring New Soapboxes for Political Animals," *New York Times* (January 10, 1995); and Robert Wright, "Hyper Democracy," *Time* (January 23, 1995): 41–46.

206. "Feeling for the Future," p. 17. The *Economist* attributes this quote to Mark Crispin Miller. For a similar critique of the Panoptic metaphor along lines similar to my own, see Martin Hewson, "Surveillance and the Global Political Economy," in Comor, ed., *The Global Political Economy of Communication*, pp. 61–80.

207. For comprehensive historical overviews, see William S. Burrows, *Deep Black: Space Espionage and National Security* (New York: Berkeley Books, 1986); and Jeffrey T. Richelson, *America's Secret Eyes in Space: The U.S. Keyhole Spy Satellite Program* (New York: Harper and Row, 1990).

208. An outstanding and innovative historical analysis of the rise of planetary geopolitics is provided by Daniel Deudney, *Whole Earth Security: A Geopolitics of Peace* (Worldwatch Paper 55, July 1983).

209. I discuss the interplay between environmental and military satellite reconnaissance systems in "Out of Focus: U.S. Military Satellites and Environmental Rescue," in Deudney and Matthew, eds., *Contested Grounds*.

210. For an overview, see Pericles Gasparini Alves, *Access to Outer Space Technologies* (Geneva: UNIDIR Publications, 1992); Jeffrey T. Richelson, "The Future of Space Reconnaissance," *Scientific American* (January 1991); Giovanni de Briganti, "WEU's Satellite System May Fly in 2000," *Defense News* (February 1–7, 1993).

211. William J. Broad, "A U.S. Spy Satellite May be Sold Abroad," *New York Times* (November 17, 1992); Dan Charles, "Governments Queue Up to Buy U.S. Spy Satellite," *New Scientist* (December 1992).

212. A.V. Banner and A.G. McMullen, "Commercial Satellite Imagery for UNSCOM," in Steven Mataija and J. Marshall Beier, eds., *Multilateral Verification and the Post-Gulf War Environment: Learning from the UNSCOM Experience* (Toronto: Centre for International and Strategic Studies, 1992); Joseph S. Bermudez Jr., "North Korea's Nuclear Programme," *Jane's Intelligence Review* (September 1991), p. 408; and Nayan Chanda, "Atomic Shock Waves," *Far Eastern Economic Review* (March 25, 1993).

213. United Nations, "The Implications of Establishing an International Satellite Monitoring Agency," (Report of the Secretary-General, Department of Disarmament Affairs, 1983); Walter Dorn, "Peacekeeping Satelites," *Peace Research Reviews* 10 (1987); Bhupendra Jasani, "ISMA—will it ever happen?" *Space Policy* (February 1992); and F. R. Cleminson, "Paxsat and progress in arms control," *Space Policy* (May 1988).

214. "Russian Spysat Data Creates Buying Spree," *Military Space* (October 19, 1992): 6; and William J. Broad, "Russia is now selling spy photos from space," *New York Times* (October 4, 1992).

215. Tim Weiner, "CIA considers Allowing Sale of Spy Technology," *New York Times* (November 13, 1993); Jeffrey M. Lenorovitz, "Lockheed Wants Austra-

lia to be Satellite Partner," *Aviation Week and Space Technology* (July 5, 1993), p. 70.

216. For an overview of these firms, see Vipin Gupta, "New Satellite Images for Sale," *International Security* 20, no. 1 (Summer 1995): 94-125.

217. For overviews, see Deibert, "Out of Focus"; and Karen T. Litfin, "Watching the Earth: An Inquiry into Global Environmental Monitoring," (Paper delivered at the 1994 Annual Meeting of the American Political Science Association, New York, September 1–4, 1994).

218. Gary Taubes, "Earth Scientists Look NASA's Gift Horse in the Mouth," *Science* (February 1993); and James Asker, "NASA Reveals Scaled Back Plan for Six EOS Spacecraft," *Aviation Week and Space Technology* (March 1992).

219. Glenn Zorpette, "Sensing Climate Change," *IEEE Spectrum* (July 1993), p. 20.

220. John Lewis Gaddis makes this point with reference to the Cold War. See John Lewis Gaddis, "The Long Peace: Elements of Stability in the Postwar International System," *International Security* 10, Spring (1986): 123.

221. Sinclair, "Between State and Market."

222. Spiro, "New Global Communities," p. 46.

223. Peter J. Taylor, "The State as Container: Territoriality in the Modern World-System," *Progress in Human Geography* 18, no. 2 (1994): 151–162.

7. Hypermedia and the Modern to Postmodern World Order Transformation: Changes to Social Epistemology

1. Harvey, *The Condition of Postmodernity*; Frederic Jameson, "Postmodernism, or the Cultural Logic of Late Capitalism," *New Left Review* 146 (1984): 53–92.

2. Kenneth Gergen, *The Saturated Self: Dilemmas of Identity in Contemporary Life* (New York: Basic Books, 1991).

3. Jean Baudrillard, *The Ecstasy of Communication*, [Translated by Bernard & Caroline Schutze] (New York: Semiotext(e), 1987); Baudrillard, *Simulations*; and Lyotard, *The Postmodern Condition*.

4. These definitional questions are taken up in Barry Smart, *Postmodernity* (New York: Routledge, 1993); Smart, *Modern Conditions, Postmodern Controversies*; Mike Featherstone, *Consumer Culture and Postmodernism* (London: Sage Publications, 1991); Bryan Turner, ed., *Theories of Modernity and Postmodernity* (London: Sage Publications, 1990); and Pauline Rosenau, *Post Modernism and the Social Sciences: insights, inroads, and intrusions* (Princeton: Princeton University Press, 1992).

5. As Smart put it, " . . . there appears to be a shared sense that significant cultural

transformations have been taking place in Western societies during the period since the end of the second world war and further that the term 'postmodernism' may be appropriate, for the time being at least, to describe some of the implied shifts in 'sensibility, practices and discourse formations.' " Smart, *Postmodernity*, p. 16. At the end of the sentence Smart quotes Andreas Huyssen, "Mapping the Postmodern," *New German Critique* 33 (1984): 8.

6. Huyssen, "Mapping the Postmodern," p. 24.
7. Friedrich Nietzsche, *The Birth of Tragedy and The Genealogy of Morals*, [Translated by Francis Golffing] (New York: Anchor Books, 1956); Charles Taylor, *Hegel* (Cambridge: Cambridge University Press, 1975); Martin Heidegger, *The Question Concerning Technology and Other Essays*, [Translated by William Lovitt] (New York: Garland Publishers, 1977); Jonathan Culler, *Saussure* (Glasgow: Fontana, 1976). These connections are most explicitly made in the work of Richard Rorty. See Rorty, *Contingency, Irony, and Solidarity*. See also Huyssen, "Mapping the Postmodern"; and Smart, *Postmodernity*, for similar touchstones on the path to the postmodern.
8. Brandon Taylor, *Modernism, Post-Modernism, Realism: A Critical Perspective for Art* (Winchester: Winchester School of Art Press, 1987).
9. Harvey, *The Condition of Postmodernity*, p. 38.
10. I. Hassan, "The culture of postmodernism," *Theory, Culture and Society* 2, no. 3 (1985): 119–132.
11. Without a doubt, the most readable presentation is found in Richard Rorty's various works. Apart from others cited in this study, see especially *Contingency, Irony, and Solidarity*.
12. See Jonathan Culler, *On Deconstruction: Theory and Criticism After Structuralism* (Ithaca: Cornell University Press, 1982).
13. See Charles Jencks, *The Language of Postmodern Architecture* (London: Sage Publications, 1984); and Jameson, "Postmodernism"; and Harvey, *The Condition of Postmodernity*, pp. 66–98.
14. See Taylor, *Modernism, Post-modernism, Realism*; Harvey, *The Condition of Postmodernity*, pp. 54–59; and Arthur Kroker and David Cook, *The Postmodern Scene: Excremental Culture and Hyper-Aesthetics* (Montreal: New World Perspectives, 1987), pp. 20–27.
15. See Gellner, *Reason and Culture* for an overview of Cartesian and Kantian views on individual autonomy and selfhood.
16. As Burkitt notes, "concept of the self has begun to move away from the traditional image of the isolated individual, towards a concept of selfhood which emphasizes the social nature of the person." Ian Burkitt, "The Shifting Concept of the Self," *History of the Human Sciences* 7, no. 2 (1994): 7.
17. This is a point made by Harvey with regard to the postmodernist view of Marxism in *The Condition of Postmodernity*, pp. 53–54.

18. Jameson, "Postmodernism," p. 63.

19. Stuart Hall, "Brave New World," *Socialist Review*, pp. 58–59.

20. Rorty, *Essays on Heidegger and Others*, p. 155.

21. Rorty, *Objectivism, Relativism and Truth*, p. 199.

22. Lyotard, *The Postmodern Condition*, p. 40.

23. Ibid., p. 15.

24. Kenneth Baynes, James Bohman, and Thomas McCarthy, "General Introduction," in Kenneth Baynes, James Bohman, and Thomas McCarthy, eds., *After Philosophy: End or Transformation?* (Cambridge: MIT Press, 1991), p. 4.

25. E. E. Sampson, as quoted in Burkitt, "The Shifting Concept of the Self," p. 11.

26. See Deirdre Carmody, "Writers Fight For Electronic Rights," *New York Times* (November 7, 1994); See also, "The Property of the Mind," *The Economist* (July 27, 1996), available on-line at: http://www.economist.com/issue/27–07–96/wbsf1.html.

27. Anne W. Branscomb, "Common Law for the Electronic Frontier: Networked Computing Challenges the Laws That Govern Information and Ownership," *Scientific American* (September 1991), p. 154.

28. Ibid.

29. Ibid., p. 156.

30. See D. P. Tackaberry, "The Digital Sound Sampler: Weapon of the Technological Pirate or Pallet of the Modern Artist?" *Entertainment Law Review* 87, 1990); and Thomas G. Schumacher, " 'This Is Sampling Sport': Digital Sampling, Rap Music and the Law in Cultural Production," *Media, Culture and Society* 17 (1995): 253–273.

31. See B. R. Seecof, "Scanning into the Future of Copyrightable Images: Computer-based Image Processing Poses Present Threat," *High Technology Law Journal* 5 (1990): 371–400.

32. For example, my own computer turns on to the theme of the popular television show, the X-Files. The "default" key is programmed with the voice of Homer Simpson exclaiming "Doh!" And everytime I close a program, a voice lifted from the movie "Shaft" proclaims "Right On!"

33. John Perry Barlow, "The Economy of Ideas: A Framework for Rethinking Patents and Copyrights in the Digital Age," *Wired* (March 1994), p. 86.

34. See Michel Foucault, "What is an Author?" in Josue V. Harari, (ed.), *Textual Strategies* (Ithaca: Cornell University Press, 1979), p. 35. See Gandy, *The Panoptic Sort*; Branscomb, "Common Law for the Electronic Frontier"; Bruce Phillips [Privacy Commissioner of Canada], "Privacy in the Information Age—An Oxymoron?" (Speech delivered to the University of Toronto XXXI Conference on Law and Contemporary Affairs, January 16, 1995); David Flaherty, *Protecting Privacy in Surveillance Societies: The Federal Republic of Ger-*

many, Sweden, France, Canada, and the United States (Chapel Hill: University of North Carolina Press, 1989); Richard Lipkin, "Making the Calls in a New Era of Communication," *Insight* (July 12, 1993): 6–13.

35. Foucault, "What Is an Author?"

36. Equifax has 15,000 employees in 1,100 locations in the United States, Canada, and Europe. See Anne Wells Branscomb, *Who Owns Information? From Privacy to Public Access* (New York: Basic Books, 1994), p. 189, *fn.* 33. On page 19, Branscomb provides a good overview of the way debit card transactions in grocery stores are used to generate data on consumers. See also Gill, "The Global Panopticon?," pp. 16–17 for a similar discussion.

37. Gandy, *The Panoptic Sort*, p. 92.

38. "We know you're reading this," *The Economist*, (February 10, 1996): 27–28.

39. See especially, *Ibid*; See also Gill, "The Global Panopticon?."

40. Mark Poster, *The Mode of Information: Poststructuralism and Social Context* (Chicago: The University of Chicago Press, 1990), pp. 15–16.

41. Baudrillard, *The Ecstasy of Communication*, pp. 20–21.

42. Rheingold, *The Virtual Community*, p. 164.

43. See Peter H. Lewis, "Computer Jokes and Threats Ignite Debate on Anonymity," *New York Times* (December 31, 1994). For a provoking overview, see Julian Dibbell, "A Rape in Cyberspace," *The Village Voice* (December 21, 1993): 36–42.

44. See Stephen Steinberg, "Travels on the Net," *Technology Review* (July 1994), p. 25; and Josh Quittner, "Johnny Manhattan Meets the FurryMuckers," *Wired* (March 1994), pp. 92–98.

45. "Cyberspace copyright treaties move toward adoption," *CNN Interactive*, (December 20, 1996).

46. The URL of the site is http://www.mudconnect.com/mud.html.

47. Gergen, *The Saturated Self*, p. 49.

48. Ibid., pp. 15–16.

49. Bauman, "Sociology and Postmodernity," p. 792.

50. See S. Kostof, *A History of Architecture: Settings and Rituals* (New York: Oxford University Press, 1995).

51. Once again, the most coherent overview of this position is provided by Richard Rorty in, among other works cited throughout this study, *Contingency, Irony, and Solidarity*; See also Ian Hacking, *Representing and Intervening: Introductory Topics in the Natural Sciences* (Cambridge: Cambridge University Press, 1983); and Nelson Goodman, *Ways of Worldmaking* (Indianapolis: Hackett, 1978).

52. For readable introductions, see Culler, *On Deconstruction*; and David Hoy, "Jacques Derrida," in Quentin Skinner, ed., *The Return of Grand Theory in the Human Sciences* (Cambridge: Cambridge University Press, 1985), pp. 41–64.

53. As cited in Harvey, *The Condition of Postmodernity*, p. 44.

54. As cited in Harvey, *The Condition of Postmodernity*, p. 48.

55. As quoted in Lyotard, *The Postmodern Condition*, p. 40.

56. See "The Tangled webs they weave," *Economist* (October 16, 1993): 21–24.

57. Saxby, *The Age of Information*, p. 299.

58. Michael Heim, *The Metaphysics of Virtual Reality* (New York: Oxford University Press, 1993), p. 30.

59. Ibid., p. 35.

60. For description, see Philip Elmer-Dewit, "Take a Trip into the Future on the Electronic Superhighway," *Time* (April 12, 1993): 50; Nicholas P. Negroponte, "Products and Services for Computer Networks," *Scientific American* (September 1991) also provides a good overview of this "paradigm" of navigation.

61. See Elkins, *Beyond Sovereignty*, p. 54.

62. Gergen, *The Saturated Self*, p. 133 See also Scott Lash and John Urry, *Economies of Sign and Space* (London: Sage Publications, 1994), p. 16.

63. Harvey, *The Condition of Postmodernity*, p. 302.

64. Taylor, *Modernism, Post-Modernism, Realism*, p. 103; see also Bauman, "Sociology and postmodernity," p. 796; and Stuart Ewen, *All Consuming Images: The Politics of Style in Contemporary Culture* (Cambridge: MIT Press, 1984).

65. For overviews of "virtual reality," see Benjamin Woolley, *Virtual Worlds* (Oxford: Basil Blackwell, 1993); Thomas B. Sheridan and David Zeltzer, "Virtual Reality Check," *Technology Review* (October 22, 1993), pp. 20–28; and the special issue on "Virtual Reality," of *IEEE Spectrum* (October 1993).

66. See especially, Featherstone, *Consumer Culture and Postmodernism*; and Ewen, *All Consuming Images*.

67. This study is cited in Nathan Gardels and Leila Conners, "Republic of the Image," *New Perspectives Quarterly* 11 no. 3 (Summer 1994): 2.

68. John Battelle with Bob Johnstone, "Seizing the Next Level: Sega's Plan for World Domination," *Wired* (December 1993): 73.

69. In 1993 — long before the explosion of the World-Wide Web — 15 million people downloaded shareware versions of the game *Doom*. See "A World Gone Soft: A Survey of the Software Industry," *The Economist* (May 28, 1996), available on-line at: http://www.economist.com/surveys/software/index.html.

70. The advertisement appears on page 69 of *Wired* (March 1994).

71. Donald P. Greenberg, "Computers and Architecture," *Scientific American* (February 1991).

72. Der Derian, *Anti-Diplomacy*, chapter 2; and James Der Derian, "Global Swarming, Virtual Security, and Bosnia," *The Washington Quarterly* 19, no. 3, Summer (1996): 45–56.

73. See Stephen Hall, *Mapping the Next Millennium: How Computer-Driven Cartography is Revolutionizing the Face of Science* (New York: Vintage Books, 1992); Timothy Ostler, "Revolution in Reality," *Geographical Magazine* (May 1994): 12–14.

74. See Featherstone, *Consumer Culture and Postmodernism*, p. 14.

75. For an early and still outstanding treatment of this issue in particular, see Daniel J. Boorstin, *The Image: A Guide to Pseudo-Events in America* (1961); and Daniel J. Boorstin, "A History of the Image: From Pseudo-Event to Virtual Reality," *New Perspectives Quarterly* 11, no. 3, Summer (1994): 16–21; Postman, *Amusing Ourselves to Death*; and Kiku Adatto, *Picture Perfect: The Art and Artiface of Public Image Making* (New York: Basic Books, 1993).

76. Timothy Luke, "Simulated Sovereignty, Telematic Territoriality: The Political Economy of Cyberspace," (unpublished draft, 1996), p. 31.

77. Jean Baudrilard, *Simulations*. Translated by Paul Foxx, Paul Patton, and Philip Beitchman (New York: Semiotext(e), 1983). Scott Lash and John Urry make a similar argument in *Economies of Sign and Space*, p. 3.

78. Gianni Vatimmo, *The Transparent Society*, [Translated by David Webb] (Baltimore: The Johns Hopkins University Press, 1992), p. 7.

79. Bauman, "Sociology and Postmodernity," p. 799.

80. Richard Rorty, *Objectivism, relativism and truth: Philosophical Papers*, Volume 1 (Cambridge: Cambridge University Press, 1991), p. 6; and Rorty, *Consequences of Pragmatism*, p. xix.

81. Bauman, "Sociology and postmodernity," p. 799.

82. See Elkins, *Beyond Sovereignty*, especially chapter 6 on "A Community of Communities."

83. "Interpretive communities" is taken from Stanley Fish, *Is There a Text in This Class? The Authority of Interpretive Communities* (Cambridge: MIT Press, 1980).

84. Lyotard, *The Postmodern Condition*, p. 17.

85. Ibid., p. 26.

86. See Edward S. Herman, "The Externalities Effects of Commercial and Public Broadcasting," in Nordenstreng and Schiller, eds., *Beyond National Sovereignty*, pp. 84–115.

87. See Edward S. Herman and Noam Chomsky, *Manufacturing Consent: The Political Economy of the Mass Media* (New York: Pantheon Books, 1988); The classic work in this genre is, of course, Walter Lippmann, *Public Opinion* (New York: The Free Press, 1965) [originally published in 1922].

88. A good discussion of these arrangements in a North American context can be found in Steven Globerman and Aidan Vining, "Trade, Investment and the Culture Industries: Bilateral Issues in the Post-NAFTA Era," (Unpublished draft, 1995).

89. Lee and Wang, "Satellite TV in Asia," p. 135. As Lee and Wang note on page 142, "The debate on banning or restricting the reception of satellite television is clearly alive in nations which have tried to bar its entry into their territory, and the pressure to "liberalize" satellite television is showing no signs of lessening."

90. Ibid., p. 135.

91. "Feeling for the Future," p. 12. As the article goes on to explain, "The explosion of choice has blown gaping holes in Europe's public broadcasters. Italy's RAI, Spain's RTVE and Germany's ARD and ZDF are all facing financial ruin." See Jane Perlez, "Habits Die Hard in Central Europe," *New York Times* (May 13, 1996) for an article on deregulation of state television in Poland, Romania and the Czech Republic.

92. John Tagliabue, "Tapping the Power of Satellite TV," *New York Times* (April 15, 1996).

93. See Gary Stix, "Domesticating Cyberspace," *Scientific American* (August 1993).

94. The composer is Todd Rundgren, whose *No World Order* was released on the compact-disk-interactive format. See Edward C. Baig, "Ready, Set- Go On-Line," *Business Week* (Special 1994 Issue), p. 124.

95. See Elmer-Dewit, "Take a Trip into the Future," p. 50.

96. For discussion see Nicholas Negroponte, "Products and Services for Computer Networks," *Scientific American* (September 1991): 106–113.

97. In Japanese, these "virtual communities" are called "tokumeisei no komyuniti" or communities of anonymity. See Kumiko Aoki, "Virtual Communities in Japan: Their Cultures and Infrastructures," *Asia-Pacific Exchange (Electronic) Journal* 2, no. 1, March 1995).

98. For discussion, see Robert Wright, "Hyper Democracy," *Time* (January 23, 1995): 46; and Stephen Steinberg, "Travels on the Net," *Technology Review* (July 1994): 22.

99. For discussion of "web-sites" see Kurt Kleiner, "What a tangled Web they wove . . . " *New Scientist* (July 30, 1994): 35–39. Academics are increasingly using such personal "web-sites" to "house" unpublished manuscripts and drafts-in-progress for criticism and publicity.

100. See Steve Lohr, "The Great Mystery of Internet Profits," *New York Times* (June 17, 1996).

101. Rheingold, *The Virtual Community*, p. 3.

102. To give just a few examples, a dissident Catholic bishop in France, Jacques Gaillot, set up a World-Wide Web page as a kind of "virtual congregation" that received 250,000 visits in the first six weeks of 1996. See "Virtual Bishop Has Cyberspace Congregation," *CNN On-Line* (September 1, 1996). Using a different part of the hypermedia spectrum, the Christian evangelist preacher Billy Graham preached via satellite to one billion people in 185 countries on a single day. See Hamid Mowlana, "The Communications Paradox," *The Bulletin of the Atomic Scientists* (July/August 1995), p. 40.

103. Arjun Appadurai, "Disjuncture and Difference in the Global Economy," *Theory, Culture, and Society* 7 (1990): 306.

104. Rosenau, *Turbulence in World Politics*.

105. See especially, Mary Catherine Bateson, "Beyond Sovereignty: An Emerging

Global Civilization," in R. B. J. Walker and Saul Mendlovitz, eds., *Contending Sovereignties: Redefining Political Communities* (Boulder: Lynne Reinner, 1990; and Daniel Deudney, "Global Environmental Rescue and the Emergence of World Domestic Politics," in Ronnie Lipschutz and Ken Conca, eds., *The State and Social Power in Global Environmental Politics* (New York: Columbia University Press, 1993).

106. Roland Robertson, "Mapping the Global Condition: Globalization as the Central Concept," *Theory, Culture and Society* 7 (1990): 21.

107. Roland Robertson, *Globalization: Social Theory and Global Culture* (Newbury Park, CA.: Sage Publications, 1992).

108. Consider just the one following anecdotal illustration: in the 1977 third edition of K. J. Holsti's *International Politics* (Englewood Cliffs, NJ: Prentice Hall, 1977) textbook, there is no index entry for the word "global"; in the 5th edition (1988), however, not only is there an entry for "Global system, contemporary" but there are also 10 separate sub-headings, including "rules of," "structure of," and "ideological issues in." Moreover, the 5th edition features a color image of the earth suspended in space.

109. Denis Cosgrove, "Contested Global Visions: One-World, Whole Earth, and the Apollo Space Photographs," *Annals of the Association of American Geographers* 84, no. 2 (1994): 271.

110. See Wolfgang Sachs, ed., *Global Ecology: A New Arena of Political Conflict* (London: Zed Books, 1993).

111. For criticism of the idea of a global imagined community, see Anthony D. Smith, "Towards a Global Culture?" *Theory, Culture and Society* 7 (1991): 171–191.

112. Cosgrove, "Contested Global Visions," p. 287.

113. Ibid.

114. For discussion of this theme, see the articles collected in Bull and Watson, eds., *The Expansion of International Society*.

8. Conclusion

1. Kenichi Ohmae, "Putting Global Logic First," *Harvard Business Review* (January–February 1995): 119. As Robert Cox aptly put it, "States willy-nilly became more effectively accountable to a *nebuleuse* personified as the global economy . . ." Robert W. Cox, "Global Restructuring: Making Sense of the Changing International Political Economy," in Richard Stubbs and Geoffrey R. D. Underhill, eds., *Political Economy and the Changing Global Order* (Toronto: McLelland and Stewart, 1994), p. 46.

2. As cited in Lyotard, *The Postmodern Condition*, p. 40.

3. Spiro, "New Global Communities," p. 45.
4. For suggestions of such divisions, see Fukuyama, *The End of History*, p. 276; Max Singer and Aaron Wildavsky, *The Real World Order—Zones of Peace, Zones of Conflict.* (New Jersey: Chatam House Publishers, 1993); and James M. Goldgeier and Michael McFaul, "A Tale of Two Worlds: Core and Periphery in the Post-Cold War Era," *International Organization* 46 (2), 1992, pp. 467–491.
5. *Cf.*, Jackson, *Quasi-States*.
6. Cox, "Global Restructuring," p. 49.
7. Walker, *Inside/Outside*.
8. See Elkins, *Beyond Sovereignty*.
9. Philip G. Cerny, "Plurilaterialism: Structural Differentiation and Functional Conflict in the Post-Cold War World," *Millennium: Journal of International Studies* 22, no. 1 (1993): 27–51.
10. Ken Booth, "Security in Anarchy: Utopian Realism in Theory and Practice," *International Affairs* 67, no. 3, July (1991): 542.
11. Lipschutz, "Reconstructing World Politics."
12. Rosenau, *Turbulence in World Politics*.
13. See Ruggie, "Territoriality."
14. Ruggie, "International Structure and International Transformation," p. 30.
15. Krasner, "Compromising Westphalia."
16. Ibid., p. 123.
17. Krasner, "Sovereignty: An Institutional Perspective." In that article, Krasner argued (p. 67) that an institutional perspective is necessary to study sovereignty because, "An institutionalist perspective regards enduring institutional structures as the building blocks of social and political life. The preferences, capabilities, and basic self-identities of individuals *are conditioned by these institutional structures*. Historical developments are path dependent; once certain choices are made, *they constrain future possibilities*." [my emphasis added]. Reading the two articles back-to-back can only be described in terms of cognitive dissonance.
18. This is Ethan Kapstein's argument in "We are US: The Myth of the Multinational," *The National Interest* (Winter 1991/1992), pp. 56–62; and *Governing the Global Economy: International Finance and the State* (Cambridge: Harvard University Press, 1994).
19. This is Janice Thomson's argument in the conclusion to *Mercanaries, Pirates, and Sovereigns*; and in "State Sovereignty in International Relations."
20. This is Hendrick Spruyt's argument in the conclusion to "Institutional Selection" and *The Sovereign State and Its Competitors*.
21. Ruggie, "Territoriality," pp. 142–144.
22. Walker, *Inside/Outside*, p. x.

23. Edward Morse, *Modernization and the Transformation of International Relations* (London: Collier Macmillan, 1976), p. 152.
24. Rosenau, *Turbulence in World Politics*, ch. 2.
25. See Thomas Kuhn, "The Natural and the Human Sciences," in David R. Hiely, James F. Bohman, and Richard Shusterman, eds., *The Interpretive Turn: Philosophy, Science, Culture* (Ithaca: Cornell University Press, 1991), pp. 17–24; Thomas Kuhn, *The Structure of Scientific Revolutions*, [2nd ed.] (Chicago: University of Chicago Press, 1970); Quentin Skinner, "Meaning and Understanding in the History of Ideas," *History and Theory* 8 (1969): 3–53; and Mary Hesse, *Revolutions and Reconstructions in the Philosophy of Science* (Sussex: The Harvester Press, 1980).
26. Bull, *The Anarchical Society*, p. 254.
27. See, for example, Cox, "Global Restructuring," p. 53; and Der Derian, *On Diplomacy*. See also Bruce Cronin and Joseph Lepgold, "A New Medievalism? Conflicting International Authorities and Competing Loyalties in the Twenty-First Century." (Prepared for Delivery at the Conference on "The Changing Nature of Sovereignty in the New World Order," Center for International Affairs, Harvard University, April 22–23, 1995).
28. Lipschutz, "Reconstructing World Politics," p. 407.
29. Lewis H. Lapham, "Dungeons and Dragons," *Harper's* (February 1994), pp. 9–11; For another neomedieval therapeutic redescription outside of the International Relations field, see Eco, *Travels in Hyper Reality*.
30. Ibid., p. 11.
31. A pessimistic view along these lines is sketched out in stark terms by Stjepan Mestrovic in *The Balkanization of the West: The Confluence of Postmodernism and Postcommunism* (New York: Routledge, 1994); and *The Barbarian Sentiment: Toward a Postmodern Critical Theory* (New York: Routledge Press, 1993).

Bibliography

Adatto, Kiku. *Picture Perfect: The Art and Artiface of Public Image Making*. New York: Basic Books, 1993.

Adler, Emanuel. "Cognitive Evolution: A Dynamic Approach for the Study of International Relations and Their Progress," in Emanuel Adler and Beverly Crawford, eds. *Progress in Postwar International Relations*. New York: Columbia University Press, 1993: 43–88.

Adler, Emanuel and Michael Barnett, "Governing Anarchy: A Research Agenda for the Study of Security Communities," *Ethics and International Affairs* (Vol. 10, 1996).

Akwule, Raymond. *Global Telecommunications: The Technology, Administration and Policies*. Boston: Focal Press, 1992.

Alves, Pericles Gasparini. *Access to Outer Space Technologies*. Geneva; UNIDIR Publications, 1992.

Anderson, Benedict. *Imagined Communities*. London: Verso, 1991.

Anderson, James and Stuart Hall. "Absolutism and Its Ancestors," in James Anderson, ed. *The Rise of the Modern State*. Sussex: Wheatsheaf Books, 1986.

Anderson, Perry. *Lineages of the Absolutist State*. London: NLB, 1974.

Andrews, David M. "Capital Mobility and State Autonomy: Towards a Structural Theory of International Monetary Relations." *International Studies Quarterly* 38 (1994).

Angus, Elizabeth and Duncan McKie. *Canada's Information Highway: Services, Access and Affordability*. Ottawa: Industry Canada, New Media Branch and Information Technologies Industry Branch, 1994.

Angus, Ian and Brian Shoesmith, eds. "Dependency/Space/Policy: A Dialogue with Harold A.Innis." *Continuum: The Australian Journal of Media and Culture* 7 (No.1, 1993).

Aoki, Kumiko. "Virtual Communities in Japan: Their Cultures and Infrastructures." *Asia-Pacific Exchange (Electronic) Journal* 2 (No. 1, March 1995).

Appadurai, Arjun. "Disjuncture and Difference in the Global Cultural Economy." *Theory, Culture and Society* 7 (1990): 295–310.

Arlen, Michael. *Living Room War*. New York: Viking Press, 1969.

Arnst, Catherine. "The Last Frontier: Phone Frenzy in the Developing World is Charging Up the Telecom Industry," *Business Week* (September 18, 1995)

Ashley, Richard K. "Three Modes of Economism." *International Studies Quarterly* 27 (1983).

———. "Untying the Sovereign State: A Double Reading of the Anarchy Problematique." *Millennium: Journal of International Studies* 17 (1988).

Asker, James. "NASA Reveals Scaled Back Plan for Six EOS Spacecraft." *Aviation Week and Space Technology* (March 1992).

Augarton, Stan. *Bit by Bit—An Illustrated History of Computers*. London: George Allen and Unwin, 1986.

Avrin, Leila. *Scribes, Script and Book: The Book Arts from Antiquity to Renaissance*. Chicago: The American Library Association, 1991.

Axtmann, Robert. "The Formation of the Modern State: The debate in the Social Sciences." In Mary Fulbrook, ed. *National Histories and European History*. Boulder: Westview Press, 1993.

Baig, Edward C. "Ready, Set- Go On Line." *Business Week* (Special Issue, 1994).

Baldwin, David, ed. *Neorealism and Neoliberalism: The Contemporary Debate*. New York: Columbia University Press, 1993.

Banner, A. V. and A. G. McMullen. "Commercial Satellite Imagery for UNSCOM." In Steven Mataija and J. Marshall Beier, eds. *Multilateral Verification and the Post-Gulf War Environment: Learning from the UNSCOM Experience*. Toronto: Centre for International and Strategic Studies, 1992.

Baran, Paul. *The Political Economy of Growth*. New York: Modern Reader Paperbacks, 1957.

Barber, Benjamin. "Jihad vs. McWorld." *Atlantic Monthly* 269 (March 1992).

Barber, Peter. "England II: Monarchs, Ministers and Maps, 1550–1625." In David Buisseret, ed. *Monarchs, Ministers and Maps: The Emergence of Cartography as a Tool of Government in Early Modern Europe*. Chicago: The University of Chicago Press, 1992.

Barkin, J. Samuel and Bruce Cronin. "The state and nation: changing norms and rules of sovereignty in international relations." *International Organization* 48 (Winter 1994):107–130.

Barlow, John Perry. "The Economy of Ideas: A Framework for Rethinking Patents and Copyright in the Digital Age." *Wired* (March 1994).

Barnet, Richard J. and John Cavanaugh. "Creating a Level Playing Field." *Technology Review* (May-June 1994): 46–54.

Barraclough, Geoffrey. *The Medieval Papacy*. London: Thames and Hudson, 1968.

Bartlett, Christopher and Sumantra Ghoshal. *Managing Across Borders: The Transnational Solution*. Boston: Harvard Business School Press, 1989.

Bateson, Mary, C. "Beyond Sovereignty: An Emerging Global Civilization." In R. B. J. Walker and Saul Mendlovitz, eds. *Contending Sovereignties: Redefining Political Communities*. Boulder: Lynne Reinner, 1990.

Baudrillard, Jean. *The Ecstasy of Communication*. Translated by Bernard & Caroline Schutze. New York: Semiotext(e), 1987.

———. *Simulations*. Translated by Paul Foxx, Paul Patton, and Philip Beitchman. New York: Semiotext(e), 1983.

Baynes, Kenneth, James Bohman, and Thomas McCarthy, "General Introduction." In Kenneth Baynes, James Bohman, and Thomas McCarthy, eds. *After Philosophy: End or Transformation?* Cambridge: MIT Press, 1991.

Bell, Daniel. *The Coming of Post-Industrial Society: A Venture in Social Forecasting*. New York: Basic Books, 1973.

———. *The End of Ideology: On the Exhaustion of Political Ideas in the Fifties*. New York: Basic Books, 1960.

Bell, Trudy. "Jobs at Risk." *IEEE Spectrum* (August 1993).

Beniger, James. *The Control Revolution: Technological and Economic Origins of the Information Society*. Cambridge: Harvard University Press, 1986.

Bercu, Steven A. "Toward Universal Surveillance in an Information Economy: Can We Handle the Treasury's New Police Technology?" *Jurimetrics Journal* 34 (Summer 1994): 383–449.

Berger, Peter and Thomas Luckmann. *The Social Construction of Reality*. New York: Anchor Books, 1967.

Berkeley, Edmund. *The Computer Revolution*. New York: Doubleday, 1962.

Berkovitch, Jacob. "Third Parties in Conflict Management: The Structure and Conditions of Effective Mediation in International Relations." *International Journal* 40 (Autumn 1985): 736–752.

Bermudez, Jr., Joseph S. "North Korea's Nuclear Programme." *Jane's Intelligence Review* (September 1991).

Biersteker, Thomas. "The 'Triumph' of Neoclassical Economics in the Developing World: Policy Convergence and Bases of Governance in the International Economic Order." In James N. Rosenau and Ernst-Otto Czempiel, eds. *Governance Without Goverment: Order and Change in World Politics*. Cambridge: Cambridge University Press, 1992: 102–131.

Bijker, Wiebe, Thomas Hughes, and Trevor Pinch. *The Social Construction of Technological Systems*. Cambridge: MIT Press, 1989.

Bitzinger, Richard. "The Globalization of the Arms Industry: The Next Proliferation Challenge." *International Security* 19 (No. 4, Fall 1994).

Black, Stephen K. "A Sobering Look at Cyberspace." *Ridgeway Viewpoints* 96–3 (June 1996) On-Line Document, http://www.pitt.edu/~rcss/VIEWPOINTS/BLACK2A/black2a.html.

Bloch, Marc. *Feudal Society*. Volume 1. Translated by L. A. Manyon. Chicago: The University of Chicago Press, 1961.

Blumemberg, Hans. *The Genesis of the Copernican World*. Cambridge: MIT Press, 1987.

———. *The Legitimacy of the Modern Age*. Translated by Robert Wallace. Cambridge: MIT Press, 1982.

Blumenthal, Uta-Renate. *The Investiture Controversy: Church and Monarchy from the Ninth to the Twelfth Century*. Philadelphia: University of Philadelphia Press, 1988.

Boorstin, Daniel. "A History of the Image: From the Pseudo-Event to Virtual Reality." *New Perspectives Quarterly* 11, no. 3 (Summer 1994): 16–21.

———. *The Image: A Guide to Pseudo-Events in America*. New York: Vintage Books, 1961.

———. *The Republic of Technology: Reflections on the Future of Community*. New York: Harper and Row, 1978.

Booth, Ken. "Security in Anarchy: Utopian Realism in Theory and Practice." *International Affairs* 67, no. 3 (July 1991).

Borrus, Amy. "The Stateless Corporation." *Business Week* (May 14, 1990).

Boulding, Kenneth E. The Meaning of the Twentieth Century: The Great Transition. New York: Harper and Row, 1964.

Bower, Bruce. "The Write Stuff: researchers debate the origins of literacy." *Science News* (March 6, 1993): 152–154.

Brand, Stewart. *The Media Lab: Inventing the Future at MIT*. New York: Penguin, 1987.

Branscomb, Ann. "Common Law for the Electronic Frontier." *Scientific American* (September 1991).

———. *Who Owns Information? From Privacy to Public Access*. New York: Basic-Books, 1994.

Braudel, Fernand. *On History*. Translated by Sarah Matthews. Chicago: The University of Chicago Press, 1980.

———. *The Structures of Everyday Life*. Volume 1. Translated by Sian Reynolds. New York: Harper and Row, 1979.

Brody, Herb. "Machine Dreams: An Interview with Nicholas Negroponte." *Technology Review* (January 1992): 33–40.

Bryant, R. *International Financial Integration*. Washington, D.C.: The Brookings Institution, 1987.

Brzezinski, Zbigniew. *Between Two Ages: America's Role in the Technetronic Era*. New York: Viking Press, 1970.

Buisseret, David. "Monarchs, Ministers, and Maps in France Before the Accession of Louis XIV." In David Buisseret, ed. *Monarchs, Ministers and Maps: The Emergence of Cartography as a Tool of Government in Early Modern Europe*. Chicago: The University of Chicago Press, 1992.

Bull, Hedley. *The Anarchical Society: A Study of Order in World Politics*. London: Macmillan Press, 1977.

Bull, Hedley and Adam Watson, eds. *The Expansion of International Society*. Oxford: Oxford University Press, 1984.

Burkitt, Ian. "The Shifting Concept of the Self." *History of the Human Sciences* 7, no. 2 (1994).

Burrows, William S. *Deep Black: Space Espionage and National Security*. New York: Berkeley Books, 1986.

Burton, John W. *Conflict and Communicaton: The Use of Controlled Communication in International Relations*. London: Macmillan, 1969.

Camille, Michael. "Seeing and Reading: Some Visual Implications of Medieval Literacy and Illiteracy." *Art History* 8, no. 1 (March 1985).

Cantor, Norman. *Inventing the Middle Ages: The Lives, Works, and Ideas of the Great Medievalists of the Twentieth Century*. New York: Morrow, 1991.

Carey, James. *Communication and Culture: Essays on Media and Society*. New York: Routledge Press, 1989.

———. "McLuhan and Mumford: The Roots of Modern Media Analysis." *Journal of Communication* 31 (Summer 1981): 162–170.

Carnerio, Robert, ed. *The Evolution of Society: Selections from Herbert Spencer's Principles of Sociology*. Chicago: The University of Chicago Press, 1974.

Castells, Manuel. *The Informational City: Information Technology, Economic Restructuring, and the Urban-Regional Process*. Oxford: Basil Blackwell, 1989.

Cerf, Vincent. "Networks." *Scientific American* (September 1991): 72–81.

Cerny, Philip. "The Deregulation and Re-regulation of Financial Markets in a More Open World." In Philip Cerny, ed. *Finance and World Politics: Markets, Regimes, and States in the Post-Hegemonic Era*. Aldershot: Edward Elgar, 1993.

———. "Plurilateralism: Structural Differentiation and Functional Conflict in the Post-Cold War World." *Millennium: Journal of International Studies* 22, no. 1 (1993): 27–51.

Chanda, Nayan. "Atomic Shock Waves." *Far Eastern Economic Review* (March 25, 1993).

Charles, Dan. "Governments Queue Up to Buy U.S. Spy Satellite." *New Scientist* (December 1992).

Chartier, Roger. "The Practical Impact of Print." In Philippe Aries and Georges Duby, eds. *A History of Private Life*. Volume III. Cambridge: Belknap Press of Harvard University Press, 1989: 111–159.

Chaytor, Henry John. *From Script to Print: An Introduction to Medieval Vernaculars*. London: Folcroft Library Editions, 1945.

Chomsky, Noam. *Necessary Illusions: Thought Control in Democratic Societies.* Toronton: CBC Enterprises, 1989.

Cipolla, Carlo M. *Before the Industrial Revolution: European Society and Economy 100–1700.* New York: Norton, 1976.

Clanchy, M. T. *From Memory to Written Record: England 1066–1307.* 2nd edition. Oxford: Blackwell, 1991.

Clark, Stuart. "The *Annales* historians." In Quentin Skinner, ed. *The Return of Grand Theory in the Human Sciences.* Cambridge: Cambridge University Press, 1985.

Cleminson, F. R. "Paxsat and progress in arms control." *Space Policy* (May 1988).

Cobban, Alan B. *The Medieval Universities: Their Development and Organization.* London: Methuen Books, 1975.

Cohen, Raymond. *Negotiating Across Cultures: Communication Obstacles in International Diplomacy.* Washington: United States Institute of Peace, 1991.

———. *Theatre of Power: The Art of Diplomatic Signalling.* London: Longmann, 1987.

Cohen, Stanley. *Visions of Social Control.* New York: Basil Blackwell, 1985.

Comor, Edward, ed. *The Global Political Economy of Communication: Hegemony, Telecommunication, and the Information Economy* (New York: St. Martin's Press, 1994).

Connor, Walker. "Nation-Building or Nation-Destroying?" *World Politics* 24 (April 1972): 319–355.

Cooper, Richard. *The Economics of Interdependence: Economic Policy in the Atlantic Community.* New York: McGraw-Hill, 1968.

Cosgrove, Denis. "Contested Global Visions: One-World, Whole Earth and the Apollo Space Photographs." *Annals of the Association of the American Geographers* 84, no. 2 (1994).

Cowhey, Peter. "The International Telecommunications Regime: The Political Roots of International Regimes for High Technology." *International Organization* 44 (Spring 1990): 169–199.

Cox, Robert W. "Global Restructuring: Making Sense of the Changing International Political Economy." In Richard Stubbs and Geoffrey R. D. Underhill, eds. *Political Economy and the Changing Global Order.* Toronto: McLelland and Stewart, 1994.

Cox, Robert. "Multilateralism and World Order." *Review of International Studies* 18 (1992): 161–180.

Cox, Robert. *Production, Power, and World Order: Social Forces in the Making of World History.* New York: Columbia University Press, 1987.

Cox, Robert. "Production, The State, and Change in World Order." In Ernst-Otto Czempiel and James N. Rosenau, eds. *Global Changes and Theoretical Chal-*

lenges: Approaches to World Politics for the 1990s. Lexington, Mass.: Heath/Lexington, 1989.

Cox, Robert. "Social Forces, States and World Order: Beyond International Relations Theory." In Robert O. Keohane, ed. *Neorealism and its Critics.* New York: Columbia University Press, 1986.

Cox, Robert. "Towards a Post-Hegemonic Conceptualization of World Order: Reflections onThe Relevancy of Ibn Khaldun." In James N. Rosenau and Ernst-Otto Czempiel, eds. *Governance without Government: Order and Change in World Politics.* Cambridge: Cambridge University Press, 1992.

Cringely, Robert X. "Fast Money: How Computers Are Used for Trading Securities." *Forbes* (April 11, 1994).

Cronin, Bruce and Joseph Lepgold. "A New Medievalism? Conflicting International Authorities and Competing Loyalties in the Twenty-First Century." (Prepared for Delivery at the Conference on "The Changing Nature of Sovereignty in the New World Order." Center for International Affairs, Harvard University, April 22–23, 1995).

Crowley, David and Paul Heyer, eds. *Communication in History: Technology, Culture, and Society.* 2nd edition. New York: Longmans, 1995.

Culler, Jonathan. *On Deconstruction: Theory and Criticism After Structuralism.* Ithaca: Cornell University Press, 1982.

———. *Saussure.* Glasgow: Fontana, 1976.

Curran, James. "Communications, Power and Social Order." In Michael Gurevitch, Tony Bennett, James Curran,and Janet Woollacott, eds. *Culture, Society and the Media.* London: Routledge Press, 1982.

Czitrom, Daniel. "Lightning Wires." In David Crowely and Paul Heyer, eds. *Communication in History: Technology, Culture, and Society.* 2nd Edition. New York: Longmann, 1995.

Dahrendorf, Ralf. *Class and Class Conflict in an Industrial Society.* Stanford: Stanford University Press, 1959.

Daniels, P. W. "Internationalization, Telecommunications, and Metropolitan Development: The Role of Producer Services." In Stanley D. Brunn and Thomas R. Leinbach, eds. *Collapsing Space and Time: Geogaphic Aspects of Communications and Information.* New York: HarperCollins, 1991.

Davison, W. Phillips. "Political Communications as an Instrument of Foreign Policy." *Public Opinion Quarterly* 27 (1963): 28–36.

Dawkins, Richard. *The Blind Watchmaker.* New York: Penguin Books, 1986.

———. *The Selfish Gene.* Oxford: Oxford University Press, 1976.

de Briganti, Giovanni. "WEU's Satellite System May Fly in 2000." *Defense News* (February 1–7, 1993).

Deibert, Ronald J. "Out of Focus: U.S. Military Satellites and Environmental Rescue." In Daniel Deudney and Richard Matthew, eds. *Contested Grounds: Se-*

curity and Conflict in the New Environmental Politics. New York: SUNY Press, 1997.

———. "Virtual Realities: Neo-Medievalism as Therapeutic Redescription." (Paper Presented at the International Studies Association annual conference, Chicago, February 1995.)

Dennet, Daniel. *Darwin's Dangerous Idea: Evolution and the Meanings of Life* (New York: Simon and Schuster, 1995.

Der Derian, James. *Anti-Diplomacy: Spies, Terror, Speed and War*. London: Blackwell, 1992.

———. "Global Swarming, Virtual Security, and Bosnia." *The Washington Quarterly* 19, no. 3 (Summer 1996): 45–56.

———. *On Diplomacy: A Genealogy of Western Estrangement*. Oxford: Basil Blackwell, 1987.

Descartes, Rene. *Discourse on Method and Meditations*. Translated by Laurence J. Lafleur. Indianapolis: Bobbs-Merrill, 1960.

Desuvire, Emmanuel. "Lightware Communications: The Fifth Generation." *Scientific American* (January 1992).

Deudney, Daniel. "Binding Powers, Bound States: The Logic and Geopolitics of Negarchy." (Paper presented at the International Studies Association annual meeting, Washington, D.C., March 28–April 2, 1994).

———. "Bringing Nature Back In." In Daniel Deudney and Richard Matthew, eds. *Contested Grounds: Security and Conflict in the New Environmental Politics*. New York: SUNY Press, 1997.

———. "Dividing Realism: Security Materialism vs Structural Realism on Nuclear Security and Proliferation." *Security Studies* 2 (Spring/Summer 1993).

———. "Global Environmental Rescue and the Emergence of World Domestic Politics." In Ronnie Lipschutz and Ken Conca, eds. *The State and Social Power in Global Environmental Politics*. New York: Columbia University Press, 1993.

———. *Global Geopolitics: Materialist World Order Theories of the Industrial Era, 1850–1950*. Ph.D. Dissertation. Princeton University, 1989.

———. *Pax Atomica: Planetary Geopolitics and Republicanism*. Princeton: Princeton University Press, forthcoming.

———. *Whole Earth Security: A Geopolitics of Peace*. Worldwatch Paper 55, July 1983.

Deutsch, Karl. "Mass Communication and the Loss of Freedom in National Decision-Making: A Possible Research Approach to Interstate Conflict." *Journal of Conflict Resolution* 1 (1957): 200–211.

———. *Nationalism and Social Communication*. Cambridge: MIT Press, 1966.

———. *The Nerves of Government: Models of Political Communication and Control*. New York: Free Press, 1963.

Dewey, John. *Reconstruction in Philosophy*. New York: Mentor Books, 1950.

Diamond, Jared. "The Great Leap Forward." *Discover* (1990): 66–76.

Dibbell, Julian. "A Rape in Cyberspace." *The Village Voice* (December 21, 1993): 36–42.

Dicken, Peter. *Global Shift: The Internationalization of Economic Activity.* 2nd edition. New York: Paul Chapman, 1992.

———. "International Production in A Volatile Regulatory Environment: The Influence of National Regulatory Policies on the Spatial Strategies of Transnational Corporations." *Geoforum* 23, no. 3 (1992).

———. "The Roepke Lecture in Economic Geography Global-Local Tensions: Firms and States in the Global Space-Economy." *Economic Geography* (1994).

Dizard, Wilson. "Mikhail Gorbachev's Computer Challenge." *The Washington Quarterly* 9, no. 2 (Spring 1986).

Dodgshon, Robert. *The European Past: Social Evolution and Spatial Order.* London: Macmillan Press, 1987.

Dorman, William and Mansour Farhang. *The U.S. Press and Iran: Foreign Policy and the Journalism of Deference.* Berkeley: University of California Press, 1987.

Dorn, Walter. "Peacekeeping Satellites." *Peace Research Reviews* 10 (1987).

Douglas, Susan J. *Inventing American Broadcasting: 1912–1922.* Baltimore: Johns Hopkins University Press, 1987.

Drake, William J. "Territoriality and Intangibility: Transborder Data Flows and National Sovereignty." In Kaarle Nordenstreng and Herbert I. Schiller, eds. *Beyond National Sovereignty: International Communication in the 1990s.* New Jersey: Ablex Publishing, 1993.

———, ed. *The New Information Infrastructure: Strategies for U.S. Policy* (New York: The Twentieth Century Fund Press, 1995)

Drake, William J. and Kalypso Nicolaidis. "Ideas, Interests, and Institutionalization: 'Trade in Services' and the Uruguay Round." *International Organization* 46 (Winter 1992).

Drogin, Marc. *Biblioclasm: The Mythical Origins, Magic Powers, and Perishability of the Written Word.* Maryland: Rowman and Littlefield, 1989.

Drucker, Peter. *The Age of Discontinuity.* New York: Harper and Row, 1969.

Duby, Georges. "The Diffusion of Cultural Patterns in Feudal Society." *Past and Present* 39 (April 1968).

———. *The Three Orders: Feudal Society Imagined.* Translated by Arthur Goldhammer. Chicago: The University of Chicago Press, 1980.

Dudley, Leonard M. *The Word and the Sword: How Technologies of Information and Violence Have Shaped Our World.* Cambridge: Basil Blackwell, 1991.

Durhem, William H., *Coevolution: Genes, Culture, and Human Diversity* (Stanford: Stanford University Press, 1991).

Dumont, Louis. *Essays in Individualism: Modern Ideology in Anthropological Perspective.* Chicago: The University of Chicago Press, 1986.

Durkheim, Emile. *The Division of Labour in Society*. New York: The Free Press, 1933.

Eco, Umberto. *Travels in Hyper Reality*. Translated by William Weaver. New York: HBJ Books, 1983.

Economist, The. "End of the Line: A Survey of Telecommunications." (October 23rd–29th, 1993).

———. "Feeling for the Future: A Survey of Television." (February 12–18, 1994).

———. "Financial Centres: A Survey." (June 27, 1992).

———. "Make Way for Multimedia." (October 16, 1993).

———. "The Death of Distance: A Survey of Telecommunications." (September 30, 1995).

———. "The Internet: The Accidental Superhighway." (July 1st, 1995).

———. "The Screen is the Future, Master." (October 24, 1992).

———. "Speak to Me: A Survey of the Computer Industry." (September 17, 1994).

———. "The Tangled Webs They Weave." (October 16, 1993).

Edgerton, Samuel Y. *The Renaissance Rediscovery of Linear Perspective*. New York: Basic Books, 1975.

Editors, The. "The Computer for the 21st Century." *Scientific American*. Special Issue on the Computer in the 21st Century, 1995.

Edwards, Mark U. *Printing, Propaganda, and Martin Luther*. Los Angeles: University of California Press, 1994.

Eistenstein, Elizabeth. *The Printing Press as an Agent of Change: Communications and Cultural Transformations in Early Modern Europe*. Volumes 1 and 2. New York: Cambridge University Press, 1979.

Elkins, David J. *Beyond Sovereignty: Territory and Political Economy in the Twenty-First Century*. Toronto: University of Toronto Press, 1995.

Elmer-Dewitt, Philip. "Battle for the Soul of the Internet." *Time* (July 25, 1994): 40–46.

———. "Take a Trip into the Future on the Electronic Superhighway." *Time* (April 12, 1993).

Engels, F. *The Peasant War in Germany*. Translated by M. J. Olgin. New York: International Publishers, 1926.

Entmann, Robert. "Framing US Coverage of International News: Contrast in Narratives of the KAL and Iran Air Incident." *Journal of Communication* 41 (Autumn 1991): 6–27.

Estabrooks, Maurice. *Programmed Capitalism: A Computer-Mediated Global Society*. London: M. E. Sharpe, 1988.

Ewen, Stuart. *All Consuming Images: The Politics of Style in Contemporary Culture*. Cambridge: MIT Press, 1984.

Falk, Richard. "Challenges of a Changing Global Order." *Peace Research: The Canadian Journal of Peace Studies* 24, no. 4 (November 1992).

———. "Sovereignty." In Joel Krieger, ed. *The Oxford Companion to Politics of the World*. New York: Oxford University Press, 1993.

Featherstone, Mike. *Consumer Culture and Postmodernism*. London: Sage Publications, 1991.

Febvre, Lucien and Henri-Jean Martin. *The Coming of the Book: The Impact of Printing, 1450–1800*. Translated by David Gerard. London: NLB, 1976.

Finegan, Jack. *Encountering New Testament Manuscripts: A Working Introduction to Textual Criticism*. Grand Rapids, Michigan: Eerdmans, 1974.

Finnegan, Ruth. *Literacy and Orality: Studies in the Technology of Communication*. Oxford: Basil Blackwell, 1988.

Fischer, Claude S. "The Telephone Takes Command." In David Crowley and Paul Heyer, eds. *Communication in History: Technology, Culture and Society*. 2nd edition. New York: Longmans, 1995.

Fish, Stanley. *Is There a Text in This Class? The Authority of Interpretive Communities*. Cambridge: MIT Press, 1980.

Flaherty, David. *Protecting Privacy in Surveillance Societies: The Federal Republic of Germany, Sweden, France, Canada, and the United States*. Chapel Hill: The University of North Carolina Press, 1989.

Flower, Joe. "Iridium." *Wired* (November 1993): 72–77.

Forester, Tom. *Silicon Samurai: How Japan Conquered the World's IT Industry*. Cambridge: Blackwell Publishers, 1993.

Foster, George. M., *Traditional Cultures and the Impact of Technological Change* (New York, Harper 1962).

Foucault, Michel. *The Archaelogy of Knowledge and the Discourse on Language*. Translated by A. M. Sheridan. New York: Pantheon Books, 1972.

———. *Discipline and Punish: The Birth of the Prison*. Translated by Alan Sheridan. New York: Vintage Books, 1979.

———. *The Order of Things: An Archaelogy of the Human Sciences*. New York: Vintage Books, 1970.

Foucault, Michel, "What Is an Author?" in Jose V. Harari, ed., *Textual Strategies*. Ithaca: Cornell University Press, 1979.

Freiberger, P. and M. Swaine. *Fire in the Valley: The Making of the Personal Computer*. Berkeley: Osborne/McGraw Hill, 1984.

Gaddis, John Lewis. "Tectonics, History, and the End of the Cold War." In John Lewis Gaddis, ed. *The United States and the End of the Cold War: Implications, Reconsiderations, Provocations*. Oxford: Oxford University Press, 1992.

———. "The Long Peace: Elements of Stability in the Postwar International System." *International Security* 10 (Spring 1986).

Gandy, Oscar. *The Panoptic Sort: A Political Economy of Personal Information*. Boulder: Westview Press, 1993.

———. "The Surveillance Society: Information Technology and Bureaucratic Social Control." *Journal of Communication* 39, no. 3 (1989): 61–76.

Gardels, Nathan and Leila Conners. "Republic of the Image." *New Perspectives Quarterly* 11, no. 3 (Summer 1994).

Geertz, Clifford. *The Interpretation of Cultures*. New York: Basic Books, 1973.

Gellner, Ernst. *Nations and Nationalism*. Oxford: Basil Blackwell, 1983.

———. *Plough, Sword and Book: The Structure of Human History*. Chicago: The University of Chicago Press, 1988.

———. *Reason and Culture: The Historic Role of Rationality and Rationalism*. Oxford: Basil Blackwell, 1992.

Gergen, Kenneth. *The Saturated Self: Dilemmas of Identity in Contemporary Life*. New York: Basic Books, 1991.

Gergen, Kenneth and Mary Gergen, eds. *Historical Social Psychology*. New Jersey: Hillsdale Press, 1984.

Gibson, William. *Neuromancer*. New York: Ace Books, 1984.

Gillespie, Andrew and Kevin Robbins. "Geographical Inequalities: The Spatial Bias of the New Communications Technologies." *Journal of Communications* 39 (Summer 1989): 7–18.

Gill, Stephen. *American Hegemony and the Trilateral Commission*. Cambridge: Cambridge University Press, 1990.

———. "Economic Globalization and the Internationalization of Authority: Limits and Contradictions." *Geoforum* 23, no. 3 (1992).

———, ed. *Gramsci, Historical Materialism, and International Relations*. Cambridge: Cambridge University Press, 1993.

Gill, Stephen, "The Global Panopticon? The Neoliberal State, Economic Life, and Democratic Surveillance," *Alternatives: Social Transformation and Humane Governance*, 2 (1995):1–49.

Gill, Stephen and David Law. "Global Hegemony and the Structural Power of Capital." *International Studies Quarterly* 33 (1989): 475–499.

Gilpin, Robert. *The Political Economy of International Relations*. Princeton: Princeton University Press, 1987.

———. *War and Change in World Politics*. Cambridge: Cambridge University Press, 1981.

Gleick, James. "The Telephone Transformed—Into Almost Everything." *New York Times Magazine* (May 16, 1993).

Globalization and Liberalization: Development in the Face of Two Powerful Currents. UNCTAD Report TD/366/Rev. 1, December 1995

Globerman, Steven and Aidan Vining. "Trade, Investment and the Culture Industries: Bilateral Issues in the Post-NAFTA Era." (Unpublished Draft: 1995).

Goffman, Erving. *Frame Analysis: An Essay on the Organization of Experience*. Cambridge: Harvard University Press, 1974.

Goldgeier, James M. and Michael McFaul, "A Tale of Two Worlds: Lore and Periphery in the Post-Cold Ware Era," *International Organization* 46, no. 2 (1992):467–491.

Goldstein, Joshua and Robert Keohane, eds. *Ideas and Foreign Policy*. Ithaca: Cornell University Press, 1993.

Gomery, Douglas. "Nickelodeons to Movie Palaces." In David Crowley and Paul Heyer, eds. *Communications in History: Technology, Culture and Society*. 2nd edition. New York: Longmans, 1995.

Gong, Gerrit, W. *The Standard of 'Civilization' in International Society*. Oxford: Oxford University Press, 1984.

Goodman, J. and L. Pauly. "The Obsolescence of Capital Controls? Economic Management in an Age of Global Markets." *World Politics* 46 (1993): 50–82.

Goodman, Nelson. *Ways of Worldmaking*. Indianapolis: Hackett, 1978.

Goody, Jack. *The Domestication of the Savage Mind*. Cambridge: Cambridge University Press, 1978.

———. *The Interface Between the Written and the Oral*. Cambridge: Cambridge University Press, 1987.

———. *Literacy in Traditional Societies*. Cambridge: Cambridge University Press, 1975.

———. *The Logic of Writing and the Organization of Society*. Cambridge: Cambridge University Press, 1986.

Goody, Jack and Ian Watt. "The Consequences of Literacy." *Comparative Studies in Society and History* 5 (1963): 304–345.

Gordenker, Leon and Thomas G. Weiss, "Pluralizing Global Governance: Analytical Approaches and Dimensions," *Third World Quarterly* 16, no. 3 (1995):357–387.

Gore, Al. "Infrastructure for the Global Village." *Scientific American* (September 1991): 150–153.

Gordon, Diana. "The Electronic Panopticon: A Case-Study of the Development of National Crime Records System." *Politics and Society* 15 (1986).

Gottfried, Robert S. *The Black Death: Nature and Disaster in Medieval Europe*. New York: The Free Press, 1983.

Gould, Stephen Jay. *Bully for Brontosaurus: Reflections in Natural History*. New York: Norton, 1991.

———. *Eight Little Piggies: Reflections in Natural History*. New York: Norton, 1993.

———. *Ever Since Darwin: Reflections in Natural History*. New York: Norton, 1977.

Goulemot, Jean Marie. "Literary Practices: Publicizing the Private." In Philippe Aries and Georges Duby, eds. *A History of Private Life*. Volume 3. Cambridge: Belknap Press of Harvard University Press, 1989.

Greenberg, Donald P. "Computers and Architecture." *Scientific American* (February 1991).

Gross, Leo. "The Peace of Westphalia, 1649–1948." In Richard A. Falk and Wolfram F. Hanrieder, eds. *International Law and Organization*. Philadelphia: Lippincott, 1968: 45–67.

Grossman, Lawrence K. "Reflections on Life Along the Electronic Superhighway." *Media Studies Journal* 8, no. 1 (Winter 1994).

Guenee, Bernard. *States and Rulers in Late Medieval Europe*. Translated by Juliet Vale. London: Basil Blackwell, 1985.

Gupta, Vipin, "New Satellite Images for Sale," *International Security* 20, no. 1 (Summer 1995): 94–125.

Haas, Ernst. "Words Can Hurt You: Or Who Said What to Whom about Regimes." In Stephen Krasner, ed. *International Regimes*. Ithaca: Cornell University Press, 1983.

Haas, Peter. "Introduction: Epistemic Communities and International Policy Coordination." *International Organization* 46 (Winter 1992): 1–35.

Hacking, Ian. *Representing and Intervening: Introductory Topics in the Natural Sciences*. Cambridge: Cambridge University Press, 1983.

Hall, John. "Ideas and the Social Sciences." In Joshua Goldstein and Robert Keohane, eds. *Ideas and Foreign Policy*. Ithaca: Cornell University Press, 1993.

Hall, Peter and Paschal Preston. *The Carrier Wave: New Information Technology and the Geography of Innovation, 1846–2003*. London: Unwim Hyman, 1988.

Hall, Rodney Bruce. "The Medieval 'State' and the Social Construction of Sovereign Identity." Paper Presented at the International Studies Association 36th Annual Conference, February 21–25, 1995, Chicago.

Hall, Rodney Bruce and Friedrich Kratochwil. "Medieval Tales: Neorealist 'Science' and the Abuse of History." *International Organization* 47 (Autumn 1993):479–491.

Hall, Stephen. *Mapping the Next Millennium: How Computer-Driven Cartography is Revolutionizing the Face of Science*. New York: Vintage Books, 1992.

Halverson, John. "Havelock on Greek Orality and Literacy." *Journal of the History of Ideas* 53, no. 2 (1992): 148–163.

Hamelink, C. J. *Cultural Autonomy in Global Communications*. New York: Longmans, 1983.

Hamilton, Bernard. *The Medieval Inquisition*. London: E. Arnold, 1981.

Harris, Roy and Talbot J. Taylor, eds. *Landmarks in Linguistic Thought: The Western Tradition from Socrates to Saussure*. New York: Routledge Press, 1989.

Harvey, David. *The Condition of Postmodernity*. Oxford: Blackwell, 1989.

Hassan, I. "The culture of postmodernism." *Theory, Culture, and Socity* 2, no. 3 (1985): 119–132.

Havelock, Eric. *The Literate Revolution in Greece and Its Cultural Consequences*. Princeton: Princeton University Press, 1982.

———. *Preface to Plato*. Cambridge: Belknap Press of Harvard University Press, 1963.

Heidegger, Martin. *The Question Concerning Technology and Other Essays*. Translated by William Lovitt. New York: Garland Publishers, 1977.

Heim, Michael. *The Metaphysics of Virtual Reality*. New York: Oxford University Press, 1993.

Held, David. *Introduction to Critical Theory: Horkheimer to Habermas*. Berkeley: University of California Press, 1980.

Helleiner, Eric. "From Bretton Woods to Global Finance: A World Turned Upside Down." In Richard Stubbs and Geoffrey R. D. Underhill, eds. *Political Economy and The Changing Global Order*. Toronto: McLelland and Stewart, 1994.

————. *States and the Reemergence of Global Finance: From Bretton Woods to the 1990s*. New York: Cornell University Press, 1994.

Hepworth, Mark. *Geography of the Information Economy*. London: Belhaven Press, 1989.

————. "Information Technology and the Global Restructuring of Capital Markets." In Stanley D. Brunn and Thomas R. Leinbach, eds. *Collapsing Space and Time: Geographic Aspects of Communications and Information*. New York: Harper-Collins, 1991.

Herman, Edward S. "The Externalities Effects of Commercial and Public Broadcasting." In Kaarle Nordenstreng and Herbert I. Schiller, eds. *Beyond National Sovereignty: International Communication in the 1990s*. New Jersy: Ablex Publishers, 1993.

————. and Noam Chomsky. *Manufacturing Consent: The Political Economy of the Mass Media*. New York: Pantheon Books, 1988.

Heyer, Paul. *Communication and History: Theories of Media, Knowledge, and Civilization*. New York: Greenwood Press, 1988.

Hesse, Mary. *Revolutions and Reconstructions in the Philosophy of Science* Sussex: The Harvester Press, 1980.

Hewson, Martin, "Surveillance and the Global Political Economy." In Edward Comor, ed. *The Global Political Economy of Communication: Hegemony, Telecommunication and the Information Economy* (New York: St. Martin's Press, 1994), pp. 61–80.

Hinsley, F. H. *The Pursuit of Peace*. Cambridge: Cambridge University Press, 1963.

Hirsch, Fred. *Money International*. Middlesex: Penguin Books, 1967.

Hirst, Paul and Grahame Thompson. "The Problem of 'Globalization': International Economic Relations, National Economic Management, and the Formation of Trading Blocs." *Economy and Society* 21, no. 4 (November 1992).

Hobbes, Thomas. *Leviathon*. Michael Oakeshott, ed. New York: Collier Books, 1962.

Holland, Kelley and Amy Cortese. "The Future of Money." *Business Week* (June 12, 1995).

Holsti, Kalevi J. *International Politics*. 3rd edition. New Jersey: Prentice-Hall, 1977.

————. *International Politics*. 5th edition. New Jersey: Prentice-Hall, 1988.

Hoy, David. "Jacques Derrida." In Quentin Skinner, ed. *The Return of Grand Theory in the Human Sciences*. Cambridge: Cambridge University Press, 1985: 41–64.

Humes, Samuel. *Managing the Multinational: Confronting the Global-Local Dilemma.* New York: Prentice-Hall, 1993.

Huyssen, Andreas. "Mapping the Postmodern." *New German Critique* 33 (1984).

Ingham, Geoffrey. "States and Markets in the Production of World Money: Sterling and the Dollar." In Stuart Corbridge, Nigel Thrift, and Ron Martin, eds. *Money, Power, and Space.* Oxford: Blackwell, 1994.

Innis, Harold Adam. *The Bias of Communications.* Toronto: University of Toronto Press, 1951.

———. *The Cod Fisheries: The History of an International Economy.* Toronto: University of Toronto Press, 1954.

———. *Empire and Communications.* Oxford: Oxford University Press, 1950.

———. *The Fur Trade in Canada: An Introduction to Canadian Economic History.* Toronto: University of Toronto Press, 1956.

International Telecommunications Union, *World Telecommunications Development Report 1995* available on-line at: http://www4.itu.ch/WTDR95/.

Jackson, Robert H. "Dialectical Justice in the Gulf War." *Review of International Studies* 18, no. 4 (1992): 335–354.

———. *Quasi-States: Sovereignty, International Relations and the Third World.* Cambridge: Cambridge University Press, 1991.

James, Harvey S. and Murray Weidenbaum. *When Businesses Cross International Borders: Strategic Alliances and Their Alternatives.* London: Praeger, 1993.

Jameson, Frederic. "Postmodernism, or the Cultural Logic of Late Capitalism." *New Left Review* 146 (1984): 53–92.

Jasani, B. "ISMA Will it Ever Happen?" *Space Policy* (February 1992).

Jencks, Charles. *The Language of Postmodern Architecture.* London: Sage Publications, 1984.

Jervis, Robert. *Perception and Misperception in International Relations.* Princeton: Princeton University Press, 1976.

Jervis, Robert and Jack Snyder, ed. *Dominoes and Bandwagons.* New York: Oxford University Press, 1991.

Jewell, Jack L., James P. Harbison, and Axel Scherer. "Microlasers." *Scientific American* (November 1991).

Jones, Adam. "Wired World: Communications Technology, Governance and the Democratic Uprising." In Edward A. Comor. *The Global Political Economy of Communication: Hegemony, Telecommunications and the Information Economy.* New York: St. Martin's Press, 1994.

Jones, E. L. *The European Miracle: environments, economies, and geopolitics in the history of Europe and Asia.* New York: Cambridge University Press, 1981.

Kantorowicz, Ernst H. *The King's Two Bodies: A Study in Mediaeval Political Theology.* Princeton: Princeton University Press, 1957.

Kaptsein, Ethan. *Governing the Global Economy: International Finance and the State* (Cambridge, Mass: Harvard University Press, 1994).

————. "We Are US: The Myth of the Multinational." *The National Interest* (Winter 1991/1992): 56–62

Keller, Ulrich. "Early Photojournalism." In David Crowley and Paul Heyer, eds. *Communications in History: Technology, Culture and Society*. 2nd edition. New York: Longmans, 1995.

Kellerman, Aharon. *Telecommunications and Geography*. London: Belhaven Press, 1993.

Keohane, Robert. *After Hegemony: Cooperation and Discord in World Political Economy*. Princeton: Princeton University Press, 1984.

————. "International Institutions: Two Approaches." *International Studies Quarterly* 32 (1988): 370–396.

Kern, Stephen J. *The Culture of Time and Space: 1880–1918*. Cambridge: Harvard University Press, 1983.

Keyes, Robert. "The Future of the Transistor." *Scientific American* (June 1993).

Kindleberger, Charles. *International Capital Movements*. Cambridge: Cambridge University Press, 1987.

Kleiner, Kurt. "What a Tangled Web They Wove." *New Scientist* (July 30, 1994).

Knight, Peter, et al., "Increasing Internet Connectivity in Sub-Saharan Africa: Issues, Options, and World Bank Role." (March 29, 1995, On-Line World Bank Draft Report), available on-line at: http://www.worldbank.org/html/emc/documents/africa0395.html.

Kohler, Hans-Joachim. "The *Flugschriften* and their importance in religious debate: a quantitative approach." In Paola Zambelli, ed. *Astrologi hallucinati: Stars and the End of the World in Luther's Time*. New York: W. de Gruyter, 1986.

Krasner, Stephen. "Compromising Westphalia." *International Security* 20, no. 3 (Winter 1995/1996):115–151.

Krasner, Stephen. "Global Communications and National Power: Life on the Pareto Frontier." *World Politics* 43 (April 1991): 336–366.

————, ed. *International Regimes*. Ithaca: Cornell University Press, 1983.

————. "Sovereignty: An Institutional Perspective." *Comparative Political Studies* 21, no. 1 (April 1988): 66–94.

Kratochwil, Friedrich. *Norms, Rules and Decisions*. Cambridge: Cambridge University Press, 1989.

————. "Of Systems, Boundaries, and Territoriality: An Inquiry into the Formation of the State System." *World Politics* 34 (October 1986): 27–52.

Kroker, Arthur and David Cook. *The Postmodern Scene: Excremental Culture and Hyper-Aesthetics*. Montreal: New World Perspectives, 1987.

Kuhn, Thomas S. "The Natural and the Human Sciences." In David R. Hiely, James F. Bohman and Richard Shusterman, eds. *The Interpretive Turn: Philosophy, Science, Culture*. Ithaca: Cornell University Press, 1991: 17–24.

————. *The Structure of Scientific Revolutions*. 2nd edition. Chicago: The University of Chicago Press, 1970.

Kurtzman, Joel. *The Death of Money: How the Electronic Economy has Destabilized the World's Markets and Created Financial Chaos.* New York: Simon and Schuster, 1993.

Langdale, John. "Electronic Funds Transfers and the Internationalization of Banking and Finance Industry." *Geoforum* 16, no. 1 (1985).

Lapham, Lewis H. "Dungeons and Dragons." *Harper's* (February 1994): 9–11.

———. "Prime-Time McLuhan." *Saturday Night* (September 1994).

Lash, Scott and John Urry, *Economies of Sign and Space,* London: Sage Publications, 1994.

Laswell, Harold, Daniel Lerner, and Hans Speier, eds. *Propaganda and Communication in World History.* Honolulu: University of Hawaii Press, 1980.

Lee, Pual S. N. and Georgette Wang. "Satellite TV in Asia: Forming a New Ecology." *Telecommunicatons Policy* 19, no. 2 (1995).

Leff, Gordon. *Heresy in the Middle Ages: The Relation of Heterodoxy to Dissent.* New York: Barnes and Noble, 1967.

———. *Paris and Oxford Universities in the Thirteenth and Fourteenth Centuries: An institutional and Intellectual History.* New York: Krieger Publishers, 1975.

Le Goff, Jacques. *Intellectuals in the Middle Ages.* Translated by Teresa Lavender Fagan. Cambridge: Basil Blackwell, 1993.

———. "Introduction." In Jacques Le Goff, ed. *Medieval Callings.* Translated by Lydia G. Cochrane. Chicago: University of Chicago Press, 1987.

———. *Medieval Civilization.* Oxford: Oxford University Press, 1988.

———. *The Medieval Imagination.* Translated by Arthur Goldhammer. Chicago: The University of Chicago Press, 1985.

Lenorovitz, Jeffrey M. "Lockheed Wants Australia To Be Satellite Partner." *Aviation Week and Space Technology* (July 5, 1993).

Levinson, Paul. "McLuhan and Rationality." *Journal of Communication* 31 (Summer 1981): 179–188.

Leyshon, Andrew. "The Transformation of Regulatory Order: Regulating the Global Economy and Environment." *Geoforum* 23, no. 3 (1992).

Lipietz, Alain. Mirages and Miracles: The Crisis of Global Capitalism. London: Verso, 1987.

Lipkin, Richard. "Making the calls in a new era of communications." *Insight* (July 12, 1993): 6–13.

Lippmann, Walter. *Public Opinion.* New York: The Free Press, 1965.

Lipschutz, Ronnie. "Reconstructing World Politics: The Emergence of Global Civil Society." *Millennium: Journal of International Studies* 21, no. 3 (1992): 398–420.

Litfin, Karen. "Watching the Earth: An Inquiry into Global Environmental Monitoring." Paper Delivered at the 1994 Annual Meeting of the American Political Science Association, New York, September 1–4, 1994.

Lockhart, Charles. *Bargaining in International Conflict.* New York: Columbia University Press, 1979.

Lovejoy, Arthur. *The Great Chain of Being*. Cambridge: Harvard University Press, 1957.

Lowe, Donald M. *History of Bourgeois Perception*. Chicago: University of Chicago Press, 1982.

Luke, Carmen. *Pedagogy, Printing, and Protestantism: The Discourse on Childhood*. New York: SUNY Press, 1989.

Luke, Timothy W. *Screens of Power: Ideology, Domination and Resistance in Informational Society*. Urbana: University of Illinois Press, 1989.

———. "Simulated Sovereignty, Telematic Territoriality: The Political Economy of Cyberspace. Unpublished Draft: 1996.

Lukes, Stephen. "Individualism." In David Miller, ed. *The Blackwell Encyclopedia of Political Thought*. Oxford: Basil Blackwell, 1991: 240.

Lyon, David. "An Electronic Panopticon? A Sociological Critique of Surveillance Theory." *The Sociological Review* 41 (1993).

———. *The Electronic Eye: The Rise of Surveillance Society*. Minneapolis: The University Of Minnesota Press, 1994.

Lyon, John. *The Invention of the Self: The Hinge of Consciousness in the Eighteenth Century*. Carbondale: Southern Illinois University Press, 1978.

Lyotard, Jean-François. *The Postmodern Condition: A Report on Knowledge*. Minneapolis: University of Minnesota Press, 1984.

Macpherson, C. B. *The Political Theory of Possessive Individualism*. Oxford: Clarendon Press, 1962.

Malone, Thomas W. and John F. Rockart. "Computers, Networks, and the Corporation." *Scientific American* (September 1991): 128–136.

Mann, Michael. *Sources of Social Power*. Volume 1. Cambridge: Cambridge University Press, 1986.

Mannheim, Karl. *Ideology and Utopia: An Introduction to the Sociology of Knowledge*. New York: Harvest Books, 1936.

Mansell, Robin. "European Telecommunication, Multinational Enterprises, and the Implications of Globalization." *International Journal of Political Economy* (Winter 1993–1994): 83–104.

Marcuse, Herbert. *One-Dimensional Man: Studies in the Ideology of Advanced Industrial Society*. Boston: Beacon Press, 1964.

Marshack, Alexander. "The Art and Symbols of Ice Age Man." In David Crowley and Paul Heyer, eds. *Communications in History: Technology, Culture and Society*. 2nd edition. New York: Longmans, 1995.

Martin, James. *Wired Society*. Englewood Cliffs, New Jersey: Prentice-Hall, 1978.

Martin, John. *International Propaganda: Its Legal and Diplomatic Control*. Gloucester: P. Smith, 1969.

Martin, Ron. "Stateless Monies, Global Financial Integration and Naional Economic Autonomy: The End of Geography?" in Stuart Corbridge, Nigel Thrift, and Ron Martin, eds. *Money, Power, and Space*. Oxford: Blackwell, 1994.

Marx, Gary. *Undercover Police Surveillance in America*. Berkeley: University of California Press, 1988.

Matthew, Richard. "Back to the Dark Age: World Politics in the Late Twentieth Century." Paper Delivered at the International Studies Association Annual Meeting, Chicago, February 1995.

———. "Justice, Order and Change in World Politics." Paper Prepared for the International Studies Association annual conference, March 28-April 1, 1994, Washington D.C.

Mattingly, Garrett. *Renaissance Diplomacy*. London: Cape Publishers, 1955.

Mazlish, Bruce. *The Fourth Discontinuity: The Co-Evolution of Humans and Machines*. New Haven: Yale University Press, 1993.

McDougall, Walter. *The Heavens and the Earth: A Political History of the Space Age*. New York: Basic Books, 1985.

McKenzie, Richard B. and Dwight R. Lee. *Quicksilver Capital: How the Rapid Movement of Wealth Has Changed the World*. New York: The Free Press, 1991.

McKitterick, Rosamond. *The Carolingians and the Written Word*. Cambridge: Cambridge University Press, 1989.

McKusker, John J. and Cora Gravesteijn. *The Beginnings of Commercial and Financial Journalism: The Commodity Price Currents, Exchange Rate Currents, and Money Currents of Early Modern Europe*. Amsterdam: NEHA, 1991.

McLuhan, Marshall. *The Gutenburg Galaxy*. Toronto: University of Toronto Press, 1962.

———. *Understanding Media: The Extensions of Man*. New York: McGraw-Hill, 1964.

McLuhan, Marshall and Quentin Fiore. *The Medium is the Massage*. New York: Simon and Schuster, 1967.

———. *War and Peace in the Global Village*. New York: Bantam Books, 1968.

McNeill, William. *Plagues and Peoples*. New York: Anchor Press, 1976.

———. *The Pursuit of Power: Technology, Armed Forces and Society Since A.D. 1000*. Chicago: The University of Chicago Press, 1984.

———, "The Rise of the West after Twenty Five Years." In Sanderson, Stephen K., ed. *Civilizations and World Systems: Studying World Historical Change* (London: Altimira Press, 1995), pp. 303–320.

McPhail, Thomas. *Electronic Colonialism: The Future of International Broadcasting and Communication*. 2nd edition. Beverly Hills: Sage Publications, 1987.

Meegan, Richard. "A Crisis in Mass Production." In John Allen and Doreen Massey, eds. *The Economy in Question* London: Sage Publications, 1988: 136–183.

Melko, Matthew, "The Nature of Civilizations." In Sanderson, Stephen K., ed. *Civilizations and World Systems: Studying World Historical Change* (London: Altimira Press, 1995), pp. 25–45.

Menache, Sophia. *The Vox Dei: Communication in the Middle Ages*. New York: Oxford University Press, 1990.

Mestrovic, Stjepan G. *The Balkanization of the West: The Confluence of Postmodernism and Postcommunism* (New York: Routledge, 1994)

———. *The Barbarian Sentiment: Toward a Postmodern Critical Theory* (New York: Routledge, 1993).

Meyrowitz, Joshua. *No Sense of Place: The Impact of Electronic Media on Social Behaviour.* New York: Oxford University Press, 1985.

Miccoli, Giovanni. "Monks." In Jacques Le Goff, ed. *Medieval Callings.* Translated by Lydia G. Cochrane. Chicago: The University of Chicago Press, 1987.

Mitchell, J. M. *International Cultural Relations.* London: Allen and Unwin, 1986.

Mitchelson, Ronald L. and James O. Wheeler. "The Flow of Information in a Global Economy: The Role of the American Urban System in 1990." *Annals of the American Geographer* 84, no. 1 (1994).

Modelski, George. *Long Cycles in World Politics.* London: Macmillan, 1987.

Molina, Alfonso Hernan. *The Social Basis of the Microelectronics Revolution.* Edinburgh: Edinburgh University Press, 1989.

Moore, R. I. *The Origins of European Dissent.* London: Allen Lane, 1977.

Morgan, Kevin. "Digital Highways: The New Telecommunications Era." *Geoforum* 23, no. 3 (1992).

Morgenthau, Hans. *Politics Among Nations: The Struggle for Power and Peace.* 5th edition. New York: Knopf, 1973.

———. *Scientific Man Vs. Power Politics.* Chicago: The University of Chicago Press, 1946.

Morse, Edward. *Modernization and Transformation in International Relations.* London: Macmillan, 1976.

Mowlana, Hamid. "The Communications Paradox." *The Bulletin of the Atomic Scientists* (July/August 1995): 40–46.

———. *Global Information and World Communication: New Frontiers in International Relations.* New York: Longmans, 1986.

Mumford, Lewis. *Technics and Civilization.* New York: HBJ Books, 1934.

Nadelmann, Ethan A. "Global Prohibition Regimes: The Evolution of Norms in International Society." *International Organizaton* 44 (Autumn 1990).

Negroponte, Nicholas. *Being Digital.* New York: Knopf Publishers, 1994.

———. "Products and Services for Computer Networks." *Scientific American* (September 1991): 106–113.

Nelson, Richard R. and Sidney G. Winter. *An Evolutionary Theory of Economic Change.* Cambridge: Belknap Press of Harvard University Press, 1982.

Neuman, W. Russell. *The Future of the Mass Audience.* Cambridge: Cambridge University Press, 1991.

Niebuhr, Reinhold. "Human Nature and the Will to Power." In H. Davis and R. Good, eds. *Reinhold Niebuhr on Politics.* New York: Scribner's, 1960.

Nietzsche, Friedrich. *The Birth of Tragedy and the Genealogy of Morals.* Translated by Francis Golffing. New York: Anchor Books, 1956.

Noble, David. *Forces of Production: A Social History of Industrial Automation.* New York: Knopf, 1984.

Nordenstreng, Kaarle and Herbert I. Schiller, eds. *National Sovereignty and International Communication.* New Jersey: Ablex Publishing, 1979.

O'Brien, Richard. *Global Financial Integration: The End of Geography.* London: Pinter, 1992.

Ohmae, Kenichi. *The Borderless World: Power and Strategy in the Interlinked Economy.* New York: HarperCollins, 1990.

———. "Putting Global Logic First." *Harvard Business Review* (January-February 1995).

Ong, Walter J. *Interfaces of the Word.* Ithaca: Cornell University Press, 1977.

———. *Orality and Literacy: The Technologizing of the World.* New York: Methuen Press, 1982.

———. *Ramus, Method, and the Decay of Dialogue.* Cmabridge: Harvard University Press, 1958.

Orwell, George. *1984.* New York: Signet Books, 1949.

Ostler, Timothy. "Revolution in Reality." *Geographical Magazine* (May 1994): 12–14.

Oye, Kenneth, ed. *Cooperation Under Anarchy.* Princeton: Princeton University Press, 1986.

Paglia, Camille. *Vamps and Tramps: New Essays.* New York: Vintage Books, 1994.

Peters, Edward. *Heresy and Authority in Medieval Europe.* Philadelphia: University of Pennsylvania Press, 1980.

Phillips, Bruce. "Privacy in the Information Age An Oxymoron?" Speech Delivered to the University of Toronto XXXI Conference on Law and Contemporary Affairs, January 16, 1995.

Piore, Michael and Charles Sabel. *The Second Industrial Divide.* New York: Oxford University Press, 1984.

Poggi, Gianfranco. *The Development of the Modern State: A Sociological Introduction.* Stanford: Stanford University Press, 1978.

Polkinghore, Donald E. *Narrative Knowing and the Human Sciences,* New York: SUNY Press, 1988

Pool, Ithiel de Sola. "Foresight and Hindsight: The Case of the Telephone." In Ithiel de Sola Pool, *The Social Impact of the Telephone.* Cambridge: MIT Press, 1976.

———. *Technologies Without Boundaries: On Telecommunications in a Global Age.* Cambridge: Harvard University Press, 1990.

Popper, Karl. *The Poverty of Historicism.* Boston: Beacon Press, 1957.

Poster, Mark. *The Mode of Information: Poststructuralism and Social Context.* Chicago: The University of Chicago Press, 1990.

Postman, Neal. *Amusing Ourselves to Death.* New York: Penguin Books, 1985.

Powell, Robert. "Anarchy in International Relations Theory: The Neorrealist-Neoliberal Debate." *International Organization* 48 (Spring 1994): 313–344.

Prahalad, C. K. and Y. Doz. *The Multinational Mission: Balancing Local Demands and Global Vision*. New York: The Free Press, 1987.

Puchala, Donald J. "Integration Theory and the Study of International Relations." In Richard L. Merritt and Bruce M. Russett, eds. *From National Development to Global Community: Essays in Honour of Karl. W. Deutsch*. London: G. Allen and Unwin, 1981.

Quittner, Josh. "Johnny Manhattan Meets the Furrymuckers." *Wired* (March 1994): 92–98.

Raboy, Marc. "Cultural Sovereignty, Public Participation, and Democratization of the Public Sphere: The Canadian Debate on the New Information Infrastructure." Paper presented to the "National and International Initiatives for Information Infrastructure" Symposium, John F. Kennedy School of Government, Harvard University, January 25–27, 1996.

Rachlin, Alan. *News as Hegemonic Reality: American Political Culture and the Framing of News Accounts*. New York: Praeger, 1988.

Ranum, Orest. "The Refuges of Intimacy." In Philippe Aries and Georges Duby, eds. *A History of Private Life*. Volume III. Cambridge: Belknap Press of Harvard University Press, 1989.

Raven, Susan. "The Road to Empire." *Geographical Magazine* (June 1993): 21–24.

Reich, Robert. *The Work of Nations*. New York: Knopf, 1991.

Reynolds, Susan. *Kingdoms and Communities in Western Europe 900–1300*. Oxford: Clarendon Press, 1984.

———. "Magan Carta 1297 and the Legal Use of Literacy." *Bulletin of the Institute of Historical Research* 62 (1989).

Rheingold, Howard. *Virtual Communities: Homesteading on the Electronic Frontier*. New York: Addison-Wesley, 1993.

Rice, Eugene Jr. *The Foundations of Early Modern Europe, 1460–1559*. New York: Norton, 1970.

Richelson, Jeffrey T. *America's Secret Eyes in Space: The U.S. Keyhole Spy Satellite Program*. New York: Harper, 1990.

———. "The Future of Space Reconnaissance." *Scientific American* (January 1991).

Riley-Smith, Jonathan. *The Crusades: A Short History*. New Haven: Yale University Press, 1987.

———. *The First Crusade and the Idea of Crusading*. London: The Athlone Press, 1986.

Roberts, Susan. "Fictitious Capital, Fictitious Spaces: The Geograpy of Offshore Financial Flows." In Stuart Corbridge, Nigel Thrift, and Ron Martin, eds. *Money, Power, and Space*. Oxford: Blackwell, 1994.

Roberts, Walter R. and Harold E. Engle. "The Global Information Revolution and the Communist World." *The Washington Quarterly* 9, no. 2 (Spring 1986).

Robertson, Roland. *Globalization: Social Theory and Global Culture*. Newbury, Park, Ca.: Sage Publications, 1992.

———. "Mapping the Global Condition: Globalization as the Central Concept." *Theory, Culture, and Society* 7 (1990).

Rorty, Richard. *Contingency, Irony, and Solidarity*. Cambridge: Cambridge University Press, 1989.

———. "Dewey Between Hegel and Darwin." In D. Ross, ed. *Modernist Impulses in the Human Sciences: 1870–1930*. Baltimore, : The Johns Hopkins University Press, 1994: 54–68.

———. *Objectivism, Relativism, and Truth: Philosophical Papers*. Volume 1. Cambridge: Cambridge University Press, 1991.

———. *Philosophy and the Mirror of Nature*. Princeton: Princeton University Press, 1979.

Rosenau, James N. "Governance, Order, and Change in World Politics." In James N. Rosenau and Ernst-Otto Czempiel, eds. *Governance Without Government: Order and Change in World Politics*. Cambridge: Cambridge University Press, 1992: 1–29.

———. *Turbulence in World Politics: A Theory of Change and Continuity*. Princeton: Princeton University Press, 1990.

Rosenau, Pauline. *Post Modernism in the Social Sciences: Insights, Inroads, and Intrusions*. Princeton: Princeton University Press, 1992.

Rostow, W. W. *Politics and the Stages of Growth*, Cambridge: Cambridge University Press, 1971.

———. *The Stages of Economic Growth: A Non-Communist Manifesto*. Cambridge: Cambridge University Press, 1960.

Ruggie, John Gerard. "Continuity and Transformation in the World Polity: Toward a Neorealist Synthesis." In Robert O. Keohane, ed. *Neorealism and its Critics*. New York: Columbia University Press, 1986.

———. " 'Finding our Feet' in Territoriality: International Transformation in the Making." (Unpublished Draft: 1990).

———. "International Structure and International Transformation: Space, Time, and Method." In Ernst-Otto Czempiel and James N. Rosenau, eds. *Global Changes and Theoretical Challenges: Approaches to World Politics for the 1990s*. Lexington, Mass.: D.C. Heath/Lexington Books, 1989).

———. "Territoriality and Beyond: Problematizing Modernity in International Relations." *International Organization* 47 (Winter 1993): 139–174.

———. "Unravelling Trade: Institutional Change and the World Economy." Paper Presented at the Roundtable on Fair Trade, Harmonization, Level Playing Fields and the World Trading System: Economic, Political, and International Legal Questions for the 1990s. Columbia University, January 10, 1992.

Ruggie, John Gerard and Friedrich Kratochwil. "International Organization: The State of the Art on an Art of the State." *International Organization* 40 (1986).

Sachs, Wolfgang, ed. *Global Ecology: A New Arena of Political Conflict* (London: Zed Books, 1993).

Sallin, Susanne. *The Association for Progressive Communications: A Cooperative Effort to Meet the Information Needs of Non-Governmental Organizations*. A Case Study Prepared for the Harvard-CIESIN Project on Global Environmental Change Information Policy, February 14, 1994.

Salomon, J. J. "Science Policy Studies and the Development of Science Policy." In I. Spiegel-Rosing and Derek de Solla Price, eds. *Science, Technology and Society: A Cross-Disciplinary Perspective*. London: Sage Publications, 1977.

Sanderson, Stephen K, "Civilizational Approaches to World-Historical Change." In Sanderson, Stephen K., ed. *Civilizations and World Systems: Studying World Historical Change* (London: Altimira Press, 1995), pp. 15–23.

———, ed. *Civilizations and World Systems: Studying World Historical Change*, London: Altimira Press, 1995.

———. "Evolutionary Materialism: A Theoretical Strategy for the Study of Social Evolution." *Sociological Perspectives* 37, no. 1 (1994): 47–73.

Saxby, Stephen. *The Age of Information: The Past Development and Future Significance of Computing and Communications*. London: Macmillan, 1990.

Scarbrough, Harry. "Introduction." In Harry Scarbrough, ed. *The IT Challenge: IT and Strategy in Financial Services*. New York: Prentice Hall, 1992.

Schmandt-Besserat, Denise. "The Earliest Precursor of Writing." *Scientific American* (1978): 50–59.

Schottenloher, Karl. *Books and the Western World: A Cultural History*. Translated by William D. Boydand Irmgard H. Wolfe. London: McFarland and Company, 1968.

Schumacher, Thomas G. "This Is Sampling Sport: Digital Sampling, Rap Music, and the Law in Cultural Production." *Media, Culture and Society* 17 (1995): 253–273.

Seecof, B. R. "Scanning into the Future of Copyrightable Images: Computer-Based Image Processing Poses Present threat." *High Technology Law Journal* 5 (1990): 371–400.

Seidenberg, Roderick. *Posthistoric Man: An Inquiry*. Chapel Hill: University of North Carolina Press, 1950.

Shane, Scott. *Dismantling Utopia: How Information Ended the Soviet Union*. Chicago: Ivan R. Dee, 1994).

Sharpe, W. *The Economics of Computers*. New York: Columbia University Press, 1969.

Shawcross, William. "Reaching for the Sky." *New Statesman and Society* (March 24, 1995): 12–14.

Sheridan, Thomas B. and David Zeltzer, "Virtual Reality Check." *Technology Review* (October 1993).

Sikkink, Kathryn. "Human Rights, Principled Issue-Networks and Sovereignty in Latin America. *International Organization* 47 (Summer 1993).

Sinclair, Timothy J. "Between State and Market: Hegemony and Institutions of Colletive Action Under Conditions of International Capital Mobility." *Policy Sciences* 27 (1994): 447–466.

———. "Economic and Financial Analysis Considered as Knowledge Dynamics of Global Governance." Paper Presented at the annual meeting of the International Studies Association, Chicago, February 1995.

Singer, Max and Aaron Wildausky. *The Real World Order—Zones of Peace, Zones of Conflict.* New Jersey: Chatam House Publishers, 1993.

Skinner, Quentin. "Meaning and Understanding in the History of Ideas." *History and Theory* 8 (1969): 3–53.

Smart, Barry. *Modern Conditions, Postmodern Controversies.* New York: Routledge Press, 1992.

———. *Postmodernity.* New York: Routledge Press, 1993.

Smith, Anthony D. "Towards a Global Culture?" *Theory, Culture, and Society* 7 (1991): 171–191.

Soja, Edward W. *The Political Organization of Space.* Washington: Resource Paper No. 8. Association of American Geographers, 1971.

Sorenson, Thomas C. *The Word War: The Story of American Propaganda.* New York: Harper and Row, 1968.

Sorokin, Pitrim. *Social and Cultural Dynamics* Boston: Porter Sargeant, 1957.

Spengler, Oswald. *Decline of the West.* [Translated by C.F. Atkinson] London: Allen and Unwin, 1932.

Spiro, Peter. "New Global Communities: Nongovernmental Organizations in International Decision-Making Institutions." *The Washington Quarterly* 18, no. 1 (1994).

Sproull, Lee and Sara Kiesler, "Computers, Networks, and Work." *Scientific American* (September 1991): 116–123.

Spruyt, Hendrick. "Institutional Selection in International Relations: State Anarchy as Order." *International Organization* 48 (Autumn 1994): 527–557.

———. *The Sovereign State and Its Competitors* Princeton: Princeton University Press, 1994.

Stanbury, W. T. "New Information Technologies and Transnational Interest Groups." Paper Prepared for Delivery at the Information Technologies and International Relations symposium, Department of Foreign Affairs and International Trade, Canada, January 13, 1995.

Stanbury, W. T. and Ilan B. Vertinsky. "Assessing the Impact of New Information Technologies on Interest Group Behaviour and Policy Making." *Bell Canada*

Papers III on Economic and Public Policy. Mimeo: January 1995.

Stearn, Gerald Emanuel, ed. *McLuhan: Hot and Cool*. New York: Signet Books, 1969.

Steinberg, Stephen. "Travels on the Net." *Technology Review* (July 1994).

Stewart, Thomas A. "Boom Time on the New Frontier." *Fortune* (Autumn 1993).

Stix, Gary. "Toward 'Point One.' " *Scientific American* (February 1995): 90–95.

Stock, Brian. *The Implications of Literacy: Written Languages and Models of Interpretation in the Eleventh and Twelfth Centuries*. Princeton: Princeton University Press, 1983.

———. *Listening for the Text: On the Uses of the Past*. Baltimore: The Johns Hopkins University Press, 1990.

Stopford, John M. and Susan Strange (with John S. Henley). *Rival Sates, Rival Firms: Competition for World Market Shares*. Cambridge: Cambridge University Press, 1991.

Strange, Susan. *Casino Capitalism*. Oxford: Blackwell, 1986.

———. "Finance, information, and power." *Review of International Studies* 16 (1990).

———. "From Bretton Woods to the Casino Economy." In Stuart Corbridge, Nigel Thrift, and Ron Martin, eds. *Money, Power, and Space*. Oxford: Blackwell, 1994.

Strauss, Gerald. *Luther's House of Learning: Indoctrination of the Young in the German Reformation*. Baltimore: The Johns Hopkins University Press, 1978.

Strayer, Joseph. *On the Medieval Origins of the Modern State*. Princeton: Princeton University Press, 1970.

Tackaberry, D. P. "The Digital Sound Sampler: Weapon of the Technological Pirate or Pallet of the Modern Artist?" *Entertainment Law Review* 87 (1990).

Taubes, Gary. "Earth Scientists Look NASA's Gift Horse in the Mouth." *Science* (February 1993).

Taylor, Brandon. *Modernism, Post-Modernism, Realism: A Critical Perspective on Art*. Winchester: Winchester School of Art Press, 1987.

Taylor, Charles. *Hegel*. Cambridge: Cambridge University Press, 1975.

———. *Philosophical Papers*. Volume 2. Cambridge: Cambridge University Press, 1985.

Taylor, Peter. "The State as Container: Territoriality in the Modern World-System." *Progress in Human Geography* 18, no. 2 (1994): 151–162.

Tellenbach, Gerd. *Church, State, and Christian Society at the Time of the Investiture Controversy*. Oxford: Basil Blackwell, 1959.

Teresko, John and William H. Miller. "Tripping Down the Information Superhighway." *Industry Week* (August 2, 1993): 32–39.

Tesler, Lawrence G. "Networked Computing in the 1990s." *Scientific American* (September 1991): 86–93.

Tetlock, Philip and Aaron Belkin, eds. *Counterfactual Thought Experiments in World*

Politics: Logical, Methodological, and Psychological Perspectives Princeton: Princeton University Press, 1996.

Thiele, Leslie Paul. "Making Democracy Safe for the World: Social Movements and Global Politics." *Alternatives: Social Transformation and Humane Governance* 18, no. 3 (Summer 1993).

Thomas, Marcel. "Manuscripts." In Lucien Febvre and Henri-Jean Martin. *The Coming of the Book: The Impact of Printing, 145–1800.* Translated by David Gerard. London: NLB, 1976.

Thompson, Wiliam R. "Ten Centuries of Global Political-Economic Coevolution." Paper Prepared for Delivery to the Workshop on Evolutionary Paradigms for the Social Sciences, Batelle Conference Center, University of Washington, Seattle, May 13–14, 1994.

Thomson, Janice E. *Mercenaries, Pirates, and Sovereigns: State-Building and Extraterritorial Violence in Early Modern Europe.* Princeton: Princeton University Press, 1994.

———. "State Sovereignty in International Relations: Bridging the Gap Between Theory and Practice." *International Studies Quarterly* 39 (June 1995): 213–233.

Thrift, Nigel. "On the Social and Cultural Determinants of International Financial Centres: The Case of the City of London." In Stuart Corbridge, Nigel Thrift, and Ron Martin, eds. *Money, Power, and Space.* Oxford. Blackwell, 1994.

Thrift, Nigel and Andrew Leyshon. "A Phantom State? The De-traditionalization of Money, the International Financial System and International Financial Centres." *Political Geography* 13, no. 4 (July 1994).

Tilly, Charles. *Big Structures, Large Processes, Huge Comparisons.* New York: Russell Sage Foundation, 1984.

———. *Coercion, Capital, and European States, A.D. 990–1990.* Cambridge: Basil Blackwell, 1990.

———. "Reflections on European State-Making." In Charles Tilly, ed. *The Formation of National States in Western Europe.* Princeton: Princeton University Press, 1975.

Toffler, Alvin. *The Third Wave.* London: Pan Books, 1983.

Toffler, Alvin and Heidi Toffler, *War and Anti-War: Survival at the Dawn of the 21st Century.* Boston: Little, Brown, 1993.

Tomlinson, John. *Cultural Imperialism: A Critical Introduction.* Baltimore: The Johns Hopkins University Press, 1991.

Toynbee, Arnold. *A Study of History* Vol. 1. Oxford: Oxford University Press, 1934.

Tuchman, Barbara W. *A Distant Mirror: The Calamitous 14th Century.* New York: Ballantine Press, 1978.

Turner, Bryan. *Theories of Modernity and Postmodernity.* London: Sage Publications, 1991.

United Nations. *Implications of Establishing an International Satellite Monitoring Agency*. Report of the Secretary-General, Department of Disarmament Affairs, 1983.

———. *World Investment Report 1994*.

Van Evera, Stephen. "Primed for Peace: Europe after the Cold War." *International Security* 15, no. 3 (1990/1991).

Vattimo, Gianni. *The Transparent Society*. Translated by David Webb. Baltimore: The Johns Hopkins University Press, 1992.

Vermaat, J. A. Emerson. "Moscow Fronts and the European Peace Movements." *Problems of Communism* (November–December 1982): 43–56.

Walker, R. B. J. *Inside/Outside: International Relations as Political Theory*. Cambridge: Cambridge University Press, 1993.

Wallerstein, Immanuel. *The Modern World System: Capitalist Agriculture and the Origins of the European World Economy in the Sixteenth Century*. New York: Academic Press, 1974.

Waltz, Kenneth. *Man, the State and War*. New York: Columbia University Press, 1954.

———. *Theory of International Politics*. New York: Random House, 1979.

Wapner, Paul. "Politics Beyond the State: Environmental Activism and World Civic Politics." *World Politics* 47, no. 3 (April 1995): 311–340.

Watson, Adam. *The Evolution of International Society*. New York: Routledge Press, 1992.

Webb, Michael C. "International Economic Structures, Government Interests, and International Coordination of Macroeconomic Adjustment Policies." *International Organization* 45 (1991): 309–342.

Webb, Michael C. and Stephen Krasner. "Hegemonic Stability Theory: An Empirical Assessment." *Review of International Studies* 15 (1989): 183–198.

Webber, Carolyn and Aaron Wildavsky. *A History of Taxation and Expenditure in the Western World*. New York: Simon and Schuster, 1986.

Weber, Max. *The Protestant Ethic and the Spirit of Capitalism*. Translated by Talcott Parsons. New York: Scribner's, 1958.

Wendt, Alexander. "Anarchy Is What States Make of It: The Social Construction of Power Politics." *International Organization* 46 (Spring 1992): 391–425.

Winsbury, Rex. "Who Will pay for the Global Village?" *Intermedia* (June/July 1994).

Witt, Ulrich. *Explaining Process and Change: Approaches to Evolutionary Economics*. Ann Arbor: University of Michigan Press, 1992.

Wolkomir, Richard. "We're Going to Have Computers Coming Out of the Woodwork." *Smithsonian* (September 1994): 82–90.

Wood, John R. and Jean Seers. *Diplomatic Ceremonial and Protocol*. New York: Columbia University Press, 1970.

Woolley, Benjamin. *Virtual Worlds*. Oxford: Basil Blackwell, 1993.

Wright, Robert. "Hyper Democracy." *Time* (January 23, 1995): 41–46.

Young, Oran. *The Intermediaries: Third Parties in International Conflict*. Princeton: Princeton University Press, 1967.

Zacher, Mark. "The Decaying Pillars of the Westphalian Temple: Implications for International Order and Governance." In James N. Rosenau and Ernst-Otto Czempiel, eds. *Governance Without Government: Order and Change in World Politics*. Cambridge: Cambridge University Press, 1992: 58–101.

———. *Governing Global Networks: International Regimes for Transportation and Communication*. Cambridge: Cambridge University Press, 1996.

Zagaris, Bruce and Scott B. MacDonald. "Money Laundering, Financial Fraud, and Technology: the Perils of an Instantaneous Economy." *George Washington Journal of International Law and Economics* 26 (1992): 61–107.

Zeman, Z. A. B. *Nazi Propaganda*. 2nd edition. New York: Oxford University Press, 1973.

Zorpette, Glenn. "Sensing Climate Change." *IEEE Spectrum* (July 1993).

Newspapers and News Sources Consulted

Associated Press-Clarinet

Reuters On-Line

Cable News Network On-Line

CNN's Financial Network On-Line

Communications Week International

Financial Times (London)

Financial Times Survey

The Globe and Mail (Toronto)

Le Monde (Paris)

Military Space

New York Times

San Francisco Guardian (Online)

Wall Street Journal

Wall Street Journal (Europe)

Index

Note: References to figures are designated by an "f" following the page number.

compiled by Fred Leise